THE WESTMINSTER HANDBOOKS
TO CHRISTIAN THEOLOGY

The Westminster Handbook to Thomas Aquinas

Joseph P. Wawrykow

WJK WESTMINSTER
JOHN KNOX PRESS
LOUISVILLE · KENTUCKY

Book design by Sharon Adams
Cover design by Cynthia Dunne
Cover art: Monks Copying Manuscripts
(Corbis/© Archivo Iconografico)

First edition
Published by Westminster John Knox Press
Louisville, Kentucky

This book is printed on acid-free paper that meets the American National Standards Institute Z39.48 standard. ∞

PRINTED IN THE UNITED STATES OF AMERICA

05 06 07 08 09 10 11 12 13 14 — 10 9 8 7 6 5 4 3 2 1

Library of Congress Cataloging-in-Publication Data

Wawrykow, Joseph Peter.
    The Westminster handbook to Thomas Aquinas / Joseph Wawrykow.
       p. cm.
    Includes bibliographical references.
    ISBN 0-664-22469-5 (alk. paper)
    1. Thomas, Aquinas, Saint, 1225?–1274. 2. Theology, Doctrinal—History—Middle Ages, 600–1500. I. Title.

B765.T54W26 2005
230'.2'092—dc22
                                     2005042240

Contents

Series Introduction
v

Introduction
vii

Abbreviations
xv

List of Articles
xvii

Articles
1

List of Latin Terms
171

A Note on the Literature
175

Primary Bibliography
177

Secondary Bibliography
181

Series Introduction

The Westminster Handbooks to Christian Theology series provides a set of resources for the study of historic and contemporary theological movements and Christian theologians. These books are intended to assist scholars and students find concise and accurate treatments of important theological terms. The entries for the handbooks are arranged in alphabetical format to provide easy access to each term. The works are written by scholars with special expertise in these fields.

We hope this series will be of great help as readers explore the riches of Christian theology as it has been expressed in the past and as it will be formulated in the future.

The Publisher

Introduction

Thomas Aquinas was born in either 1224 or 1225 at the family castle at Roccasecca, located about midway between Rome and Naples. At the age of five, he was sent to the Benedictine monastery of Monte Cassino, where he spent the next ten years, receiving his elementary education as well as exposure to the monastic life. In 1239 he was sent to Naples for more advanced education in the liberal arts, likely with the expectation that he would eventually return to Monte Cassino. However, while in Naples he came into contact with the Order of Preachers, more commonly known as the Dominicans (after their founder, St. Dominic), one of the relatively new mendicant (begging) orders, and in 1244 he took the Dominican habit. After overcoming some initial family opposition to this decision, he was sent to Paris in 1245, where he continued his training in philosophy and probably began his theological education. In 1248 he followed Albert the Great to Cologne, where he continued his theological training and perhaps served as an assistant to this great intellectual, who was well versed in theology and philosophy as well as other disciplines. From 1252 to 1256, he was back in Paris as an advanced theology student; at this time he delivered his lectures on the *Sentences* of Peter Lombard, which eventually were made available for copying (see **Scriptum on the Sentences**). In 1256 he assumed one of the Dominican chairs in theology at the University of Paris, the greatest center of scholastic theology in the Middle Ages, a position he held until 1259 (the period from 1256 to 1259 is thus designated the first Parisian regency). In 1259, he was called back to Italy to serve the educational needs of his order by teaching at Orvieto and then Rome. In 1268, he returned to Paris for a second regency, until 1272. After that, he was back in Italy, at Naples, where he continued work on his great *Summa Theologiae* (begun in 1266) and other writings. On December 6, 1273, he had an experience while saying mass that brought his writing career to an end. This has been explained variously by different scholars: Perhaps he suffered a stroke or a breakdown; perhaps he underwent an intense spiritual experience that made academic work seem beside the point. At any rate, he stopped writing, leaving the ST incomplete, in the midst of the discussion, in its Third Part, of the sacrament of penance (the Third Part was also to have contained a discussion of the remaining three sacraments—holy orders, extreme unction, matrimony—and then conclude with a treatment of the final things). Aquinas died in early March 1274, while traveling, at the request of the pope, to the Second Council of Lyons, which the pope had called to bring the Eastern and Western churches back into union. Aquinas was declared a saint of the Catholic Church in 1323; a man of deep humility and holiness, he was celebrated especially for his great, and insightful, literary output.

Aquinas is without question one of the greatest of Christian theologians, and his theology continues to be of interest to Christians both Catholic and Protestant. In his theologizing, he benefited from certain medieval developments. Aquinas was a scholastic theologian, and much of his work was done at the university, itself a medieval innovation. He received his training at the university, first at the *studium generale* at Naples and then at Paris, Cologne, and finally at Paris again. Once he completed his training, he worked as a theologian at the University of Paris (1256–1259; 1268–1272) or in university-like settings in Dominican houses of study back in Italy (1259–1268; 1272–1273). The university as center of learning and education was of relatively recent origin, having taken shape over the course of the twelfth century and having found more or less fixed form early in the thirteenth. That Aquinas's theological achievement owes much to his university setting cannot be doubted. Prior to taking up his own chair in theology, he had to go through the curriculum that had been set by the masters and that provided to all scholars a common educational experience. Thus, in the arts he would have received a solid grounding in the writings of Aristotle, which were more and more available in Latin translation. In the faculty devoted to theology, he would have obtained a closer grasp of Scripture, as well as of the mediating postscriptural Christian theological tradition. As a scholastic *theologian*, Aquinas also would have had a recognizable set of tasks to perform: In the slogan that had been coined at the turn of the thirteenth century, the scholastic master lectured, disputed, and preached (*lectio, disputatio, praedicatio*). Lecturing was always on a set text, and the text of the theological faculty was the Bible. The master of theology at the University of Paris was in fact designated a "master of the sacred page." Preaching too was important, although, unfortunately, only a handful of Aquinas's own sermons have survived. In disputing, the scholastic's dialectical skills came to the fore. Disputations were of two types. One sort, the quodlibetal, was held at Advent and Lent; here, the audience suggested topics, as well as arguments, for discussion, and these disputations could pose a considerable challenge to the master. The other kind of disputation reflected more closely the research agenda of the master. The master would set the topic, and his advanced students would contribute arguments pro and con, with the master eventually determining specific issues of dispute.[1] These disputations could be long-term affairs, extending over a year or more, comprising several questions for dispute that stand in some connection to each other. Even in Italy, when teaching for the Dominicans, Aquinas adhered to the pattern of lecturing, disputing, and preaching. From his final year we have an impressive example of his preaching, in his homilies on the Apostles' Creed, which are available in English translation.[2]

That Aquinas was a member of the Dominican order was also significant for his theological work. The Order of Preachers had been founded early in the thirteenth century to combat heresy. Dominic and his first followers preached against the Cathars in Southern France, dualists who posited a universal conflict between matter and spirit, between evil and good. Dominic recognized that preaching would be more effective the more learned and better informed the preacher was, and so he sent young Domincans to the university towns, to learn from the masters and make use of the new learning in their pastoral work. The Dominicans also quickly developed their own educational system, at both the local and provincial levels, and friars were expected to take advantage of these resources to enhance their pastoral performance.[3] According to the later thirteenth-century work, *The Nine Ways of Prayer of St. Dominic*, study itself could be seen as a form of prayer.[4] In such an environment, the work of Aquinas would have been cherished and promoted, with Aquinas given all conceivable support to engage in his academic work. The fruits of his research would, in turn, be passed on to his fellows, both at the university and in the order, to the benefit of the church. Actually, a handful of Aquinas's writings are distinctively "Dominican." The new mendicant orders could be quite controversial, especially as active at the university. Secular theologians saw these orders as a threat to their monopoly over theological education, and severely attacked them. In defense, Aquinas provided a few writings that countered such attack, while explaining what is involved in this form of discipleship to Christ. It has also been suggested that Aquinas's most famous work, the ST, itself is a distinctively Dominican work, born of Aquinas's desire to improve the education of fellow Dominicans in moral theology, so crucial for pastoral activity (preaching and sacramental activity). Up to this time, Dominicans had learned moral theology through treatises on virtues and vices. In his ST, Aquinas has a hefty section on moral theology (see I-II, II-II), but puts that discussion after an account of God and the procession of creatures from God (Part I). He then places after the ST's Second Part a treatment of Christ (III). Moral theology is thus put in its proper theological and christological context.[5]

Aquinas was a prolific author, and his corpus comprises more than eight million words. A fair number of his writings are due to his professional responsibilities, or to his training to become a master.[6] Hence, his first great foray into systematic theology, the *Scriptum on the Sentences* of Peter Lombard, which originated in his lectures on the *Sentences*, qualified him for elevation to a chair in theology. His biblical commentaries also originated in classroom lectures, whether at Paris or back in Italy in Dominican houses of study. And his numerous collections of disputed questions go back to his magisterial disputations, although he published them in more polished and comprehensive form. The disputed questions nicely complement the presentations in the systematic writings. To take but a few examples: the sixteen questions *de malo* go into considerable detail on sin and vice, topics covered in the First Part of the Second Part of the ST; the ten questions *de potentia*, crafted in the mid-1260s, treat material examined in the ST's First Part, often in much greater detail and complexity;[7] there are briefer disputed questions in Christology[8] and the virtues, including charity.[9]

But not all of Aquinas's writings are to be ascribed to professorial work. Some are extracurricular, reflecting Aquinas's personal interest. This is the case for two of the systematic writings for which he is best known: the **Summa contra Gentiles**, and, the ST itself. In these writings, Aquinas is exploring ways in which the truths of the faith might be best organized, presented, and explored. He is arguably searching in these writings for an improvement over what was available in Lombard's *Sentences*—so too the Aristotelian commentaries[10] and commentaries on select works of Boethius and Pseudo-Dionysius[11] and on the *Liber de Causis*. In none of these cases was Aquinas under professional obligation to write these works. That he engaged these texts closely was due to his perception that a finer grasp of their contents could prove beneficial to his general theological work.

The present volume provides an introduction to the theology of Thomas Aquinas. Individual entries are devoted to important features of his theology. The *Handbook* aims at providing newcomers to Aquinas with a reliable guide to his teaching; it should prove of value as well to more experienced readers of Aquinas. For each entry, I sketch the main points of the teaching on a given topic, indicating the passages in Aquinas on which I have drawn. I would recommend that as one reads the entry one consults these passages, to secure and confirm the teaching. For each entry, I have also provided secondary sources where particular points can be followed up.[12]

These entries are keyed to the ST, on which he worked from 1266 on. At times I cite other writings to shed additional light on a position or to indicate where there has been development in Aquinas's thought on an issue. Each part of the ST is made up of questions, each of which is in turn comprised of articles. The number of articles per question is not set; Aquinas devotes as many, or as few, articles as he needs to explore the question in sufficient depth. An article in the ST is itself composed of four parts; we meet here echoes of the dialectical method associated with the disputation, although the ST itself is not the result of specific disputations. An article looks at an aspect of the topic covered by the question. In the objections that open an article, observations are made that run counter in some way to what Aquinas himself will go on to state on that aspect of his topic. The objections are designed to complicate matters. In the ST, Aquinas seldom has more than three or four objections to an article; by contrast, in the disputed questions, the number of objections per article can run to twenty or thirty. In the next part of the article, the sed contra, Aquinas offers an observation that will make more plausible the teaching that he is about to stake out in the rest of the article. Often in the ST, the sed contra will include a quote from Scripture or some eminent authority; at times, the sed contra offers a brief argument that will anticipate what follows. In the third part of an article in the ST, the body of the article (corpus or solution), Aquinas gives his own statement on the point under investigation. The article then concludes with responses to the opening objections. The objections are helpful in setting things up in a given article. Their observations are plausible, although they do not settle the issue. In his responses to these objections, Aquinas will try to salvage what in them can be applied to his own teaching, while also indicating why the objections are not telling, that is, where they go astray. In reading the article, one should not omit the opening objections and make a beeline for the corpus. Nor should one stop the reading at the corpus. In responding to the objections, Aquinas will add important details to the presentation of his own position in the corpus.

To facilitate the use of the *Handbook*, I include an outline of the ST in Figure A on pages xii–xiii.

As indicated, the very first question of the ST (I.1) stands on its own, providing as it were an introduction and orientation to the theological inquiries that follow. The topic of I.1 is **sacred doctrine**, the truths necessary for salvation that have been revealed by God in Scripture. In this question, we learn that there are two sorts of truth that come under sacred doctrine, the **articles of faith** and the **preambles of faith**. The latter can be demonstrated by argument, but the former cannot. Rather, such truths as the Trinity, the transcendent end of human existence (which is God), and Christ as the way to this end must be revealed and are to be held by faith (a.1). But while the articles cannot be demonstrated, one can think about them, to discern the wisdom of what God has revealed and done; one will also strive to defend them from attack (a.8). In thinking about the faith, the theologian will make use of all of the resources that are at his disposal: Scripture itself, of course; the writings of the church fathers, who have been concerned in their own work with the interpretation and representation of scriptural truth; even the philosophers, whose ideas and terms can be turned, with due caution and needed modification, to Christian ends (I.1.8 ad 2). Since Scripture is the locus of God's revelation, the question includes articles on scriptural language (a.9) and diverse levels of meaning (a.10), rendered possible by the divine authorship. For newcomers to the theology of Aquinas, it would seem most prudent to begin with this opening question, as a way of grasping the context of the theology that Aquinas will attempt in the rest of the writing.

Perhaps the greatest lesson that the opening question provides has to do with the subject matter and focus of sacred doctrine and of the theology that pertains to it. Sacred doctrine and its theology have to do with God. Other things enter into sacred doctrine and its theology only as related to God, as to their beginning and end (I.1.3 ad 1; 7c). This is *theology*, an account of God (and of other things as related to God), in the literal sense. God is the starting point of this theology; the theologian is principally concerned with what God has done and does, in bringing things into existence, in calling them to their end, including the call of rational creatures to God as their end. In bringing rational creatures into being, God intends to share God's own life, of self-knowing and loving, with these creatures, providing for their fulfillment as rational creatures in a way that simply transcends what they are capable of, without the aid of God, by their natural capacities alone.

The organization of the rest of the ST follows this teaching about the proper subject matter of sacred doctrine and its theology. The ST is divided into three main parts; the second part is itself divided into two parts. The First Part (I) has to do with God and the procession of creatures from God. Thus, in I.2–43, Aquinas provides his treatise on God, looking first at what pertains to the unity of the divine essence and then what concerns the distinction of persons. He then completes the First Part by looking at the creation, at what the triune God brings into existence and sustains and governs (I.44–119).

The Second and Third Parts of the ST deal with the movement of the rational creature to God as end. The Second Part is devoted to Aquinas's **moral theology**, looking in turn at the movement to God as end by human acts in general (I-II), and then the movement to God by human acts in particular (II-II). The Third Part (III) treats of **Jesus Christ** who, as the prologue to ST I.2 (where Aquinas gives an overview of the ST) states, is as human (*secundum quod homo*) the way to God as end. The Third Part provides a detailed discussion of Christ; it was also meant to provide a close review of the seven **sacraments** and of the end things, although the experience of December 1274 prevented the full execution of that plan. The Second and Third Parts nicely complement each other; with the Third Part, we are reminded that the moral and affective journey to God is, precisely, through Christ.

For new readers of Aquinas, more familiar perhaps with theological writing from other periods, there will be much that might seem strange in Aquinas's texts. The style, dialectically ordered and employing a myriad of authoritative sources, certainly differs from what we are accustomed to in reading premedieval or postmedieval authors. And yet Aquinas stands in deep continuity with the Christian past, and his use of authority should be seen as an acknowledgment of the multiple debts that he owes to his theological predecessors. It is possible to specify this debt for given areas of theological discourse: For example, his teaching on **grace** and **predestination** from the *ScG* on owes much to the late Augustine; so too the mature Christology offers a restatement of that of Cyril of Alexandria, as endorsed at the ecumenical councils from Ephesus (431) on. But, more generally, what we meet in the theology of Thomas Aquinas is what we meet in such great predecessors as Irenaeus and Augustine and Anselm. In his theological work, he attempts what they had tried: He pursues the understanding of their common Christian faith ("faith seeking understanding"; the *intellectus fidei*), and making full use of both his training and personal genius, in their company reflects on, investigates, proclaims, and defends the Christian faith.

I would be remiss in not thanking the many people whose contributions to this volume have been invaluable. I would like to offer my gratitude in particular to Donald McKim for the invitation to prepare this volume and for his gentle guidance throughout the project, and to David Burrell, CSC, Jean Porter, Thomas Prügl, and John Jenkins, CSC, my colleagues at the University of Notre Dame, for our many conversations over the years about Aquinas. Finally, I am most grateful for the support and encouragement of my family—my wife, Dianne, son, Nicholas, and mother, Anne—as I brought this project to completion.

Joseph Wawrykow
University of Notre Dame

Figure A

OUTLINE OF SUMMA THEOLOGIAE

FIRST PART (I)

On the Nature and Extent of Sacred Doctrine (q.1)
On God (qq.2–119)
    What concerns the divine essence/what pertains to the unity of the divine essence
        (qq.2–26)
      Whether God exists (q.2)
      The manner of God's existence, or, rather, what is *not* the manner of God's
        existence (qq.3–13)
      What concerns God's operations—God's knowledge, will, and power
        (qq.14–26)
    What concerns the distinction of persons (qq.27–43)
      Origin or procession (q.27)
      The relations of origin (q.28)
      The persons (qq.29–43)
        The persons absolutely (qq.29–38)
          In common (qq.29–32)
          Singly (qq.33–38)
            The Father (q.33)
            The Son (qq.34–35)
            The Holy Spirit (qq.36–38)
        The persons comparatively, with regard to the essence, the properties, and
          notional acts, and with regard to each other (qq.39–43)
    What concerns the procession of creatures from God (qq.44–119)
      The production of creatures (qq.44–46)
      The distinction among creatures (qq.47–102)
        In general (qq.47–49)
        In particular (qq.50–102)
          Spiritual creatures: angels (qq.50–64)
          Corporeal creatures (qq.65–74)
          Composed of spiritual and corporeal: human beings (qq.75–102)
      Their preservation and government (qq.103–19)

SECOND PART

On the movement of the rational creature to God

First Part of the Second Part (I-II)

The movement to God by human acts in general
    Happiness, the last end of human life (qq.1–5)
    Human acts in themselves (qq.6–48)
    Their principles (qq.49–114)
      Intrinsic principles: habits (qq.49–89)
        Habits in general (qq.49–54)
        Virtues (qq.55–70)
        Vice and sin (qq.71–89)
      Extrinsic principles (qq.90–114)
        Law (qq.90–108)
        Grace (qq.109–14)

Second Part of the Second Part (II-II)

The movement to God by human acts in particular
  What pertains to humans of all conditions and estates (qq.1–170)
    Theological virtues (with vices and gifts) (qq.1–46)
      Faith (qq.1–16)
      Hope (qq.17–22)
      Charity (qq.23–46)
    Cardinal virtues (with vices and gifts) (qq.47–170)
      Prudence (qq.47–56)
      Justice (qq.57–122)
      Fortitude (qq.123–40)
      Temperance (qq.141–70)
  What pertains to certain humans (qq.171–89)

THIRD PART (III)

On Christ, who as man (*secundum quod homo*) is our way to God/On the Savior of all and the benefits bestowed by him on the human race
  The Savior himself (qq.1–59)
    The mystery of the incarnation itself, whereby God was made human for
      our salvation (qq.1–26)
      The fittingness of the incarnation (q.1)
      The mode of union of the Word incarnate (qq.2–15)
        The union itself (q.2)
        The person assuming (q.3)
        The nature assumed (qq.4–15)
          The human nature and its parts (qq.4–6)
          What was coassumed (qq.7–15)
      What follows on this union (qq.16–26)
    Such things that were done and suffered by the Savior, i.e., God incarnate
      (qq.27–59)
      Those things that relate to his coming into the world (qq.27–39)
      Those things that relate to the course of his life in the world (qq.40–45)
      His departure from the world (qq.46–52)
      Those things that concern his exaltation after this life (qq.53–59)
    The sacraments by which we attain to our salvation (qq.60–)
      In general (qq.60–65)
      In particular (qq.66–)
        Baptism (qq.66–71)
        Confirmation (q.72)
        Eucharist (qq.73–83)
        Penance (qq.84–90)

(Aquinas stopped writing at q.90, in the midst of the treatment of penance. He thus did not complete the plan for the Third Part as announced in the prologue to that part: to discuss all of the sacraments, the end things, and Christ.)

NOTES

1. See Bazan (1985).
2. See Ayo (1988). For some comments on this text, see *articles of faith*.
3. See Mulchahey (1998).
4. See Tugwell (1982), 94ff.; for prayer as study, see the eighth way.
5. See Boyle (1982).
6. For information about the writings, see Emery (1996a). Emery distributes Aquinas's writings into the following categories: theological syntheses; disputed questions; biblical commentaries; commentaries on Aristotle; other commentaries; polemical writings; treatises; letters and requests for expert opinion; liturgical work, sermons, prayers. The Emery catalogue lists the best Latin editions and the translations of certain works into modern European languages.
7. Thus, in *de potentia*, for Trinity, see qq.8–10; and for God's creative activity, see qq.3–5.
8. *De unione verbi incarnati*.
9. *De virtutibus*. For a list of all of the disputed questions, see Emery (1996a), 334–37.
10. For the complete list, see Emery (1996a), 341–45.
11. Aquinas wrote on two works of Boethius (d. 524), *De trinitate* and *De ebdomadibus*. His commentary on Pseudo-Dionysius's *De divinis nominibus* is on a work important for the development of Aquinas's theological epistemology, that is, the account of our knowing and naming God, as found in, e.g., ST I.12–13.
12. I have listed these sources beginning with those of the most importance in my research. In addition, it might prove useful to consult as well one or another of the general introductions to Aquinas's theology that have appeared in recent years, to get some sense of the whole. Of these, Nichols (2003), Kerr (2002), and Van Nieuwenhove and Wawrykow (2005) are all accessible and reliable. For the philosophy of Aquinas, see Wippel (2000) and Kretzmann and Stump (1993). For an orientation to the life and career of Aquinas, Torrell (1996c, 2003) is now the standard work.

Abbreviations

FREQUENTLY CITED WRITINGS OF AQUINAS

ScG   *S. Thomae Aquinatis Doctoris Angelici Liber de veritate Catholicae fidei contra errores infidelium, qui dicitur Summa contra gentiles.* Edited by P. Marc with the help of C. Pera and P. Caramello. 3 vols. Turin, 1961.

Citations of *ScG* give book, chapter, and paragraph number. For example, *ScG* IV.27.1 = book IV, chapter 27, paragraph 1.

Sent.   *Scriptum super libros sententiarum magistri Petri Lombardi Episcopi Parisiensis.* 4 vols. Vols. 1–2 edited by P. Mandonnet, vols. 3–4 edited by M. F. Moos. Paris, 1929–1947.

Citations of *Sent.* are prefaced by the book number, and followed by the distinction, question, article, and part of article numbers. For example, III *Sent.* d.1 q.2 a.5 ad 4 = *Scriptum* on book III, distinction 1, question 2, article 5, response to fourth objection.

ST   *S. Thomae de Aquino Ordinis Praedicatorum Summa Theologiae cura et studio Instituti Studiorum Medievalium Ottaviensis.* 5 vols. Ottawa, 1941.

Citations of ST give Part, question, article, and part of article numbers. For example, ST I.1.10 ad 1 = ST Part One, question 1, article 10, the response to the first objection.

EDITORIAL

a., aa.	articulus, articuli
ad (cum numero)	responsio ad obiecionem (argumentum)
arg.	argumentum
ch., chs.	chapter, chapters
c	corpus (= body of article)
d., dd.	distinctio, distinctiones
lect.	lectio
n., nn.	note, notes
no., nos.	numero, numeros
ob., obj.	obiectio
q., qq.	quaestio, quaestiones
qc.	quaestiuncula
resp.	responsio
sol.	solutio

List of Articles

Adoption (see Grace)	1	Evil	52
Analogy (see Epistemology, Theological)	1	Existence of God (see Preambles of Faith)	53
Angels	1	*Exitus-reditus*	53
Anthropology	4	*Facienti quod in se est*	54
Aristotle (see Philosophy)	8	Faith	56
Articles of Faith	8	Fittingness	57
Authority	13	Gifts of the Holy Spirit	60
Baptism	16	God	61
Beatific Vision	17	Grace	63
Capax gratiae, capax dei, capax gloriae (see Nature and Grace)	19	*Gratia non tollit naturam sed perficit* (see Nature and Grace)	68
Causes	19	Gratuitous Graces	68
Character, Sacramental	20	Holy Orders (see Sacrament; Character, Sacramental)	69
Charity	22	Hope	69
Church	25	Hypostatic Union	71
Coassumed (see Jesus Christ)	28	Image of God	73
Concomitance	28	Instrumental Causality	75
Confirmation (see Sacrament; Character, Sacramental)	29	Jesus Christ	76
Creation	29	Knowledge, Christ's	80
Creed (see Articles of Faith; [Pseudo-]Athanasian Creed)	32	Knowledge, God's	82
Cross	32	Law	85
Death	35	Mary	90
Devil	37	Matrimony (see Sacrament)	92
Doctors of the Church	38	Merit	92
Epistemology, Theological	41	Miracle (see Transfiguration)	95
Eschatology	44	Missions	95
Esse	49	Moral Theology	96
Eternity of the World (see Philosophy)	52	Natural, Supernatural (see Grace)	97
Eucharist (see Concomitance; Real Presence; Sacrifice, Eucharistic; Transubstantiation)	52	Nature (see Person)	97
		Nature and Grace	97
		Negative Theology	99

Omnis Christi actio nostra est
   instructio   99
Original Justice   100
Original Sin   102
Penance   104
Person   106
Philosophy   108
Pope   112
Prayer   113
Preambles of Faith   115
Predestination   118
Prophecy   120
Providence (see Predestination)   123
(Pseudo-)Athanasian Creed   123
Real Presence   124
Resurrection of Christ   126
Revelation (see Scripture;
   Sacred Doctrine; Prophecy)   128
Sacrament   128
Sacred Doctrine   132
Sacrifice, Eucharistic   133

Salvation (see Cross; Sacred
   Doctrine; Prophecy; Beatific
   Vision; Eschatology; Grace)   135
Scriptum on the Sentences   135
Scripture   137
Sin   142
Subalternation   145
Summa contra Gentiles   145
Supernatural (see Grace;
   Nature and Grace)   147
Temptation   147
Theologian   149
Theological Virtues   154
Theology   156
Transfiguration   157
Transubstantiation   159
Trinity   161
Viator   165
Vice (see Sin)   167
Virtue   167

Articles

Adoption *see* **Grace**

Analogy *see* **Epistemology, Theological**

Angels Angels make numerous appearances in the ST, in the course of Aquinas's meditations on the subject of *theology*, God, and creatures as they are related to God as to their beginning and end. The angels are especially prominent in the First Part of the ST, devoted to God and the procession of creatures from God as from their creator. The treatise on the angels is extensive (I.50–64), offering in turn introductory comments on these nonmaterial subsistent forms (q.50); the ways in which angels, themselves noncorporeal, might make use of bodies and relate to bodies (qq.51–53); their natural constitution and activity as fully rational beings, possessed of intellect (qq.54–58) and will (qq.59–60) and so able to know and love; their initial creation, and God's bestowal of grace and call to glory (qq.61–62); and, finally, the fall of some angels into sin and resultant punishment (qq.63–64). Aquinas picks up the thread again at the end of the First Part, in the consideration of divine government and the execution of divine providence (see *predestination*). God brings things to the end set for them by God through intermediaries; and so in I.103–19 Aquinas discusses how angels, both good and bad, might help or hinder the realization by human beings of the end set for them by God. That theme is pursued in turn in the next part of the ST (I-II, II-II) on the movement of the human creature through moral activity to God as end, with regard to the fallen angels. The *devil* is an external principle of sin (see, e.g., I-II.80), and so Aquinas will ask how the fallen angels figure in sinning, both in the human fall and subsequent sin. Here, the work of the fallen angels in *temptation* comes to the fore. Since Jesus encountered demons, was tempted by them, confronted them in his passion and death, and overcame them through the *cross*, the fallen angels also are discussed in the ST's Third Part, devoted to *Jesus Christ* and his saving work and its application to others. In meeting and overcoming temptation, Christ himself provides a model for emulation (see *Omnis Christi actio nostra est instructio*). In all of his reflections on the angels, good and bad, Aquinas is governed by the scriptural witness. On the basis of *Scripture*, he acknowledges that there are different kinds of angels, distributed according to a hierarchy of greater to lesser. He knows that the good angels are in the service of God in the aiding of human beings, to give them the opportunity for growth in character and in the virtues needed to reach God, and that, with God's permission, the bad angels will encourage humans to fail, to succumb to temptation, at the prompting of the demons, and so qualify for damnation. But Aquinas was also the beneficiary of a rich, non-Christian tradition of reflection on spiritual substances, and he employed extra-Christian analysis to enrich his own reading of the scriptural witness, all the while observing the hierarchy of *authority* that he limns in his reflections on *sacred doctrine* and its theology. The interest of Aquinas in the angels is suggested not only by the sheer number of questions that he devotes to them but also by the acuity of his analysis. They were interesting theologically in themselves; they were also good to contemplate because of the added light they could shed on God and on humans.

Angels are ontologically and so intellectually superior to humans. The human person is a composite substance, a union of soul and body. Both are essential to the human; the soul, the form of the body, employs the body as its instrument, and needs the body for its characteristic intellective work. Through the body the soul senses, obtaining the sense information that provides the basis of human intellection (see *anthropology*). *Death* means the separation of soul from body, but this is not final. The soul perdures, and at the end of history—at the general resurrection of the dead (see *eschatology*)—soul and body will be reunited, to enjoy or suffer the end for which the body-soul composite has qualified by its activity in the present life. Angels, for their part, are spiritual substances, as are souls, but spiritual substances that do not require union with body for their characteristic activities of willing and knowing. Rather, angels are wholly incorporeal; whatever contact they have with bodies—as in helping or hindering human beings—is incidental, not essential to the angel as angel. Without body, these spiritual substances know what they know by an intuitive grasp that is directly of the intelligible, and perfectly so. Angels know perfectly what they know, and by a simple act of intuition.

The contrast, again, is with humans, whose knowledge is discursive, beginning with sense, and involving a movement over time from not knowing to coming to know something about the world, by grasping the intelligible species abstracted from the phantasms that emerge from sensation through the activity of the active intellect.

While angels constitute a higher form of being, they nonetheless fall short of God and the divine being and activity. They are creatures, as are humans. They need not have existed. That they do exist, and with the nature that they possess, is due to God's creative act. As is true generally of *creation*, angels receive all that they have—their essence and *esse*—from God. In their form of life, they proclaim God in the way determined by God, in God's wisdom. Thus, their intellection mimics, outside of God, the divine knowing by which God knows God perfectly. Their intellection, however, is not that knowledge that God has (see *knowledge, God's*); superior to humans, the angels are inferior to God.

Following the biblical witness, Aquinas limns a parallel between the story of the angels and the story of humans. In both stories, the difference, as well as connection, between the natural and the supernatural is acknowledged without being reified or made absolute. For, as is the case for the first humans (see *original justice*), the angels were created in grace. As first made, and so endowed with their natural capacities, the angels were called to the special end that is God. They were invited to enter into God's own life and so were made like God. In attaining that end (see *beatific vision*), they would have been raised to the knowing and loving of God that is proper to God. Such is a gift; it far transcends the natural capacities of any creature, angelic or human. God has willed to share God's own life, to elevate certain creatures to this special end. To make the attainment of this end possible, God granted to the angels grace. Grace provides a participation in the divine, such that the one who has grace is oriented to God as end and elevated, in the present life, to the supernatural level, capable of action that would please God and bring one to the end set by God for those to whom God wills eternal life.

In Aquinas's telling, most angels accepted the offer of eternal life, willing God as God wills to be willed, as made possible by grace. These angels willed God perfectly, and so have received the good that they willed. They were confirmed in the good that is God, and enjoy the beatific vision. Other angels, however, rejected the offer. They did not will out of the grace in which they had been created, but willed otherwise than God intended. They have sinned, testifying to their pride. They did aspire to likeness to God, but not as God intended. Rather than come to that end by grace, they wanted that end through their own natural powers. They tried to save themselves, rather than be saved through God's grace. Consequently, they fell from God and from grace, and into sin. Aquinas speaks of the *devil* and the other fallen angels then lapsing into the sin of envy, as they try subsequently to prevent other rational creatures—that is, humans—from reaching the same end, the end to which God has also called human beings.

While trading on the parallel between the angelic and the human fall, Aquinas is careful to observe the differences. First, each fallen angel fell for itself by a malicious act: the wrong exercise of will. Each tried to put itself in God's place. Humans, on the other hand, fell in Adam. The whole nature was found in the first human, and Adam is the active principle of human generation. Thus, all who come after him in the same nature sin in their active principle (see *original sin*), the Adam who stands at the head of the human race. The other crucial difference is that the human fall is not irrevocable. Humans have the chance for repentance. Their life is construed along the lines of a journey (see *viator*) that is made up of many steps. Steps away from the end

that is God can be retraced, and the person, with God's aid (see *Facienti quod in se est*), can get back on the right track to God and through morally and supernaturally good acts come closer to the end that is God. Only when life in the present world comes to its term is a fall from God irrevocable and final. If one dies in grace, one will attain to God in the next life; if one dies in sin, one will go to hell, as just recompense for sin. Until physical death, there is still a chance for repentance to God. With angels, to the extent that there is talk of a "journey," it is a journey of a single step, the decision made by the angels as created in grace for or against God, for or against the grace, with its ordering, in which they were made. Again, those who choose God receive the supernatural end to which they have been called, as a result of that proper use of grace. Those who choose against God forfeit grace forever. Their decision against God is full and therefore final. There is no chance for repentance; they will live eternally with the consequence of their decision, namely, separation from God. Those who have decided for God too have taken the only step that they will. Their communion with God as the result of choosing God, by grace, is final and eternal.

In his discussion of the human nature taken up by the Word in becoming incarnate, Aquinas will point to this difference to explain why it was fitting for human nature, not angelic, to be assumed to the Word. In III.4.1, Aquinas observes the dignity of both human and angelic natures. Both are rational and so resemble the divine nature, on which they are patterned, in a way that transcends nonrational creatures. To continue the point, salvation of rational creatures, the vision of God, surely is beyond the natural capacities of such creatures, but it is not completely at odds with it. Neither grace nor glory destroys the nature, but they perfect it as the gift of God (*Gratia non tollit naturam sed perficit*). Coming to the beatific vision would require the destruction and total reconfiguration of a nonrational being (e.g., a tree, a squirrel). In this light, then, both the angelic and the human versions of creaturely rational nature would be worthy of being assumed by the Word. Yet there is a second feature, proper to the human, that eliminates an assumption of angelic nature in the act of incarnation: need. The fall of the angels was complete, and they are confirmed in the end that they chose. The fall of humans, while grievous, was not final. Humans are discursive beings, able to change their ways, to intend properly, and to act in ways conducive with the will of God. The Word took up human nature, then, in order to make available the grace that can call these rational creatures back to correct relationship to God and fruitful movement toward the end to which God has called them.

Angels, in turn, play a role in human history, as God's agents. As Aquinas argues in the discussion of divine government at the end of the First Part of the ST, there is a hierarchy among the good angels, with the seraphim and cherubim at the upper end, angels at the lower end, and other levels of angels in between (I.108). All good angels will be employed by God to help people come to God as end, by illuminating them, passing on saving truth, and offering them opportunities to grow in grace and so in conformity with God's will. It is a basic tenet of this presentation of the instrumental role of angels in helping humans come to God that higher levels of angels help humans indirectly, through lower angels. Thus, at God's instigation, the seraph might commission a lower angel to enter history to help in the prosecution of God's will. In talking about the angels as instruments of God, there is no great problem. God intends good, and can use what is not God in the communication of the good, in the execution of God's predestining will. The good angels are apt instruments of God.

As for the fallen angels, God does not work through them directly. God causes only good, but the fallen angels are intent on disrupting the divine plan by tempting humans to the sin that will qualify them for hell. God does not predestine anyone to hell, which is *evil* in itself, nor does God cause sin, also evil in itself, a privation of the good that God does cause. However, the tempting in which the devils engage can be turned to God's end, by providing a person the opportunity to reject temptation and so grow in the good that brings one closer to God as end. Or one can fall to temptation and sin; God will then retrieve good from that sin by rendering to it what it deserves, thus showing the good of God's justice. In terms of the activity of the fallen angels, God does not cause it but permits it, and uses it for God's own purposes, thus showing God's sovereignty over history.

Aquinas's conviction that higher beings act on lower beings through intermediaries causes him, with the tradition, to question one scriptural presentation of the angels. Isaiah is said to have been purified by a seraph. From Pseudo-Dionysius on (Pseudo-Dionysius passed himself off as a disciple of the apostle Paul, although in reality he was a sixth-century author), the tradition had debated what this means. For a seraph would not, according to this principle, come into direct contact with a human. The consensus that emerged is that Isaiah writes loosely here. It was an angel, a lower form of angelic being who purified him, doing so at the command of a higher angel, a seraph, who worked through this agent; the entire process was at the behest, of course, of God (I.112.2 ad 2). Aquinas is known for his sensitivity to the literal sense of Scripture; this is one of the very few times that his reading will be at odds with what appears to be the plain teaching of a text.

Foster (1967); Hankey (1997); Goris (2003); Nichols (2003), ch. 6.

Anthropology   Aquinas gives in the ST considerable attention to the human being, and to what it means to be human.

Each of the ST's parts examines the human in its distinct way. In the First Part, Aquinas discusses the constitution of the human as a creature of God, looking at the human as a body-soul composite (ST I.76), enumerating the various powers of soul (I.77–83), and, in a basic way, describing the exercise of the intellective powers in knowing (I.84–89). In this part, Aquinas also considers the state of human beings as originally made by God; the discussion in qq.90ff. underscores the intentionality of creating (see *creation*), including God's plan to share God's own life with certain rational creatures (see *predestination*; *original justice*).

In the Second Part of the ST, Aquinas turns to the human person as a moral agent, considering all that will fall under a *moral theology*, viewed in terms of the movement of the rational creature to God as end. The link between the two parts is provided by the teaching on the human person as the *image of God*. First introduced in I.93, the human as image of God is invoked in the prologue to the First Part of the Second Part (I-II), to introduce the moral theology. Actually, the First Part of the Second Part is dependent on the First Part in another way. Among the things that are treated in moral theology are the principles of action, both interior and exterior. The latter have to do with God instructing by *law* and assisting by *grace*. The former have to do with powers and habits. In the First Part of the Second Part, Aquinas will have to discuss habits (see *virtue*), but there is no need to look at human powers at that point, for he has already discussed the topic in the First Part (see the prologue to ST I-II.49; the reference is to I.77ff.).

Finally, Aquinas's basic convictions about the human are given fine expression and nuancing in the Third Part, in the extended discussion of *Jesus Christ*. Aquinas's is a thoroughly incarnational Christology; in Christ, the Word has been made flesh, has taken up all that is required to be human and expressed that, so that the Word is the subject of Jesus' sufferings and doings. In Christ, the human nature as taken up by the Word according to whom all have been made is elevated, ennobled, in the sense that in him it is shown in its perfection and so in its full possibilities and correct orientation. Jesus is "true man," in the double sense of being fully human and of showing other humans how we are meant to be in order to stand right before God (see *Omnis Christi actio nostra est instructio*).

As in other areas of Thomistic discourse, there is a tendency in treating the anthropology to segregate, or to fixate on what is stated in a given set of questions to the exclusion of what is stated elsewhere on the topic in the ST. In the present case, there has been a tendency to so privilege the teaching of I.75–102, or even just qq.75–89, as if the full anthropology were to be found only there. When that happens, it is possible to imagine that Aquinas's anthropology is at bottom "philosophical," dependent in particular on what Aristotle had to say about body and soul and human operation. This is a mistake. The anthropology, as becomes clear in treating it in its entirety and as developed over the entire ST, is thoroughly theological. The human person is understood to be God's creation, to have been made by God for God, to be able to come to God as end by its proper operations, and to do so through Christ, who, as the prologue to I.2 insists in explaining the overall organization of the ST, as human is our way to God. As Aquinas explains in the ST's first question (7c; 3 ad 1), sacred doctrine and its theology consider things *sub ratione Dei*, with reference to God as beginning and end. In whatever part of the ST that is in play, Aquinas sticks resolutely to this criterion, considering the human as proceeding from God (as in the First Part) or as proceeding to God (as in the ST's Second and Third Parts).

In his first foray into anthropology in the ST, in ST I.75ff., Aquinas stresses the following: A human being is a mixed substance. As body, the human is corruptible, susceptible to change and to passing out of existence. The soul, on the other hand, is spiritual and incorruptible. It does not pass out of existence; when the human composite ceases to be, the soul continues to exist.

Both body and soul are essential to being human, and each requires the other. In putting the relation between the soul and the body that is constitutive of the human, Aquinas can speak of the soul as the form of the body (I.76.1). This means that it is by soul that body is actualized as human. Without a human soul, then, a body would not be, and would not be human.

Aquinas acknowledges various powers in soul; he definitely does not acknowledge in the one human many souls (I.76.4). In this latter point, he is engaging in a debate with fellow scholastics, many of whom thought of many souls, many different substantial forms, that go to make up any human. As will become clear in his Christology, Aquinas's denial of multiple substantial forms will have a significant impact on his account of the *Triduum Sacrum* and why it is that the body in the tomb can be said to be identical with that of the living Jesus (III.50.5).

The various powers contained in the one human soul can be enumerated as follows, from bottom up: the vegetative, sensitive, and intellective powers (I.77). The vegetative have to do with nutrition, growth, and generation (I.78.2). The next kind provides for sensation, so important for the human coming to know things in accordance with her nature, as well as for appetites that follow on sensation. In this regard, Aquinas distinguishes between concupiscible and irascible appetite, the first having to do with inclining the soul to seek what is suitable, according to the senses, and to fly from what is hurtful, the second being that by which the human resists those attacks that hinder what is suitable and that inflict harm (I.81.2). The intellective powers cover the capacity for reasoning and understanding, as well

as the rational appetite that is will (I.79, 82–83). There is in each human both a passive and active intellect. The active is responsible for abstracting intelligible species from the phantasms that arise from sense knowledge; these intelligible species are imprinted on the passive intellect, which retains these species (I.79).

In addition to talking about the soul as form of the body, Aquinas can also speak of the body as the instrument of the soul, that through which the soul acts. In nutrition and sensation, this is clear enough, and so the soul in such activities is dependent on the body. It is the human (the body-soul composite) that grows and feels and sees and the like. The case for discursive thinking, the characteristic intellectual activity of a human, is a bit more complicated. In thinking, there is not a physical organ; it is the intellective soul that abstracts, links ideas, forms judgments. Yet to abstract and the like presupposes sensation, which is an activity of the body-soul unity; the intellect can be active only on the basis of what the senses gather and can present to it. In this sense, then, even the intellective part of the soul is dependent on the body.

Given this stress on the person as a psychosomatic unity, it makes sense for Aquinas to gesture at the yearning of soul for body. At the end of a person's physical life (see *death*), body and soul are separated; the body corrupts, but the soul continues to exist. Indeed, the separated soul receives what is due to the human for the life pursued, whether hell, if a sinful life was led, or heaven or at least purgatory, if one lived correctly, as God wills (see *eschatology*). Yet while the soul does come to its appropriate place, its beatitude (or damnation) is not complete, for an essential part of the human is missing: its body. Only with the resurrection of the body, and the attendant reunion of the soul with its body, will full enjoyment be possible for the blessed. Body too now receives what is due to the person.

As will be evident from this brief sketch, in this part of his anthropology Aquinas has learned much from Aristotle, especially but not exclusively from *De anima*. In his openness to Aristotle, in the recognition that Aristotle could contribute well to a Christian theological project, Aquinas was distinctive. Many of his contemporaries were more suspicious of Aristotle, and in anthropology they showed a preference, when it came to the Greeks, for Plato. For Aquinas, there is a one-sidedness to anthropologies inspired by Plato. The point is nicely made by a question that Aquinas raises in the course of ST I.75.4: Is the soul the man? That is, is it the soul alone that is essential to being human, so that whatever else is found in a human is but accidental or incidental? For Aquinas, both body and soul matter and are essential to being human. Aristotle provides him with the resources to make and secure this point. In Aristotle—with his insistence on both body and soul, depiction of the soul in the full range of its powers, and his accounting of the ways in which soul uses body, including in knowing—Aquinas found a most congenial conversation partner. The lessons of Aristotle fit well in a theology that is so serious about *creation*, about ascribing the establishment of the material as well as the spiritual to God, about delineating God's intentionality in creating, an intentionality that includes bringing the whole human, (resurrected) body and soul, to eternal life.

Yet for some at least, a first reading of ST I.75–89, especially if read on its own, may prove puzzling. Is such material—as on powers of the soul, or on the human way of knowing—really needed in a Christian theology? Despite his best intentions, as articulated in the opening of the ST and elsewhere (see *sacred doctrine*; *Authority*), might Aquinas have at least here lapsed into *philosophy*, let his enthusiasm for Aristotle get the better of him, and so digressed from properly theological work? That the decision to include this material was theologically sound can be suggested in a variety of ways. For one thing, it fits in well in the First Part, where Aquinas considers God and the procession of creatures from God. Different sorts of creatures proceed from God, are made by God. And each sort of creature proclaims God outside of God in the way intended by God (see *creation*). Thus, in order to make clearer what God has done in creating humans, and how humans—in their nature and characteristic activities—proclaim God, it is crucial to describe in detail this composite substance, with its range of powers, and how it knows.

The wisdom of including this set of questions can be seen from another angle, by considering what this detailed presentation makes possible elsewhere in the ST. Because he has been so thorough here, Aquinas can proceed with relative dispatch to make additional theological points, by assuming and building on what is presented in ST I.75ff. To offer here but three quick examples: First, the discussion in detail of the powers of the soul facilitates in I-II.49 the discussion of the other intrinsic principle of the movement to God as end; the habits (see *virtue*) are, after all, perfections of the powers of the soul. Second the discussion of knowing in accordance with the natural capacities of the human also provides a convenient reference point in the consideration of the supernatural knowing that is found in the movement of the person to God as end (see *viator*). To do something presupposes the capacity for doing that. Knowing God as God is transcends our natural capacities; such will require an elevation through the granting of a higher light, the light of glory, in order to see God face to face in the next life (see *beatific vision*). And, in related fashion, to get to an end one has to know of that end and how to suitably reach that end. For that, there is need of an added light now, in the present life, which is provided by *faith*, supernaturally perfective of the intellect that belongs to every human as human. Third, the present discussion of the human greatly facilitates the account of

Jesus Christ, the Word of God become human. The opening foray in anthropology in the ST's First Part makes it easier to show what it means for the Word to take up a full human nature (body and soul, with the full range of powers of the soul). It also helps Aquinas to distinguish that nature from what he terms (ST III.7ff.) the coassumed, the perfections (including knowledge; see *knowledge, Christ's*) and defects assumed by the Word in becoming human in order to further his salvific work on our behalf.

Pegis (1934); Passau (2002); Merriell (1990); Schneider (1972); Bernath (1969); Heintzmann (1986); Borresen (1968).

Aristotle   *see* **Philosophy**

Articles of Faith   The articles enjoy a preeminent status in Aquinas's theological project. Articles of faith are propositions about the material object of faith—that is, God—and what has to do with God's operation in bringing rational creatures to God as end. In doing the work of the theologian, it is with the articles of faith that Aquinas is principally concerned.

The articles are themselves the focus of detailed reflection at two principal places in the systematic writings; what Aquinas states about the articles in these places should shape our conception of what he is doing in the rest of the theology. First, the articles come in for considerable comment in terms of sacred doctrine, God's teaching of the truths necessary for salvation (see, e.g., ST I.1). There are two categories of truth that fall under sacred teaching. Both the preambles and the articles are revealed by God. But while the preamble can in principle be demonstrated by rational argument (and so by some will be known, not held by faith), the articles lie beyond the power of reason to demonstrate. They cannot be demonstrated; they must be held by faith for as long as one is in this world. Yet, as Aquinas will also insist,

this does not mean there is no place for argument in dealing with the articles. Rather, as he states at ST I.1.8, one can defend the articles from allegedly rational attack, that is, against those who claim that it can be proven that given claims of the faith are opposed to reason. Since the articles lie beyond reason but are in themselves not contrary to reason, such allegedly rational argument can be rebutted. This, of course, is not to suggest that the attacker will thereby be transformed into one who holds the previously contested article of faith (that is, has been argued to the act of faith or some other epistemic act). Faith is a gift and not the result of rational argument, but such negative apologetic will succeed in removing an impediment to faith, namely, the imagined conflict of the article with rational standards.

Argument, however, can do more with the articles of faith. Aquinas in fact has a full-blooded version of the by-then traditional "faith seeking understanding," a phrase that nicely describes much of his own theological work (see *Theology*; *Theologian*). One can think about the faith, drawing upon all of the resources at one's disposal: Scripture, principally, and the writings of attested church doctors and theologians, but also, as appropriated to Christian ends, the writings of the philosophers, whose terms and insights, developed in reflection on the things of this world, can be adapted to Christian theological ends (see *authority*). Thus, one will think about each of the articles and try to get a better sense of what is involved in such a specific claim. One will also strive to grasp the coherence of the faith, of the ways in which discrete articles mesh with other articles and how the articles mutually inform each other. Aquinas's conviction is that beliefs about God, for example, will inform beliefs about humans and about Christ, and so too what the Christian holds about Christ will shape beliefs about God and humans. A goal of the theologian will be to illumine these connections, and thus to show the overall wisdom and plausibility of the faith. The aim of such inquiry into the articles, individually and in their mutual conditioning, will not be knowledge; faith does not here give way to knowledge, at least this side of the eschaton (see *beatific vision*). The starting point of the inquiry is faith, and one remains in faith at the end of discrete inquiries and at the end of the entire theological investigation; the gain is that one will understand better what one believes and how it is that God has acted wisely in doing and revealing what are summarized as the articles of the faith (see also *fittingness*).

The other principal locus for the treatment of the articles in themselves is the treatise on faith, where in examining the object of faith (as at ST II-II.1) Aquinas will add to this depiction of the articles. The articles hold center stage in aa.6–10. But what Aquinas teaches in the earlier articles of II-II.1 prepares well for that later exposition of the articles of faith. Is God, the First Truth, the object of faith (a.1)? "Object" should be taken in two senses, in terms of formal and material object. The First Truth is the only formal object of faith; people believe because it is God who teaches, who reveals the truths needed for salvation. Materially, however, there is more than one object of faith; many things are affirmed in faith. Yet, Aquinas quickly adds, all the things that are believed either are God or stand in relation to God, inasmuch as through certain effects of the divine operation human beings are helped on the journey toward the enjoyment of God. This discussion of the object of faith, in other words, picks up nicely the soteriological thrust of the ST's first question, on sacred doctrine, as well as echoes the teaching there (e.g., I.1.3 ad 1; a.7c) that sacred doctrine treats matters *sub ratione Dei* and that everything that comes under this doctrine is either God or stands in relation to God as to its beginning and end.

In the next article (II-II.1.2), Aquinas asks whether the (material) object of faith is something complex, by way of a proposition. If one considers that in which the act of faith terminates, this is a reality and not a proposition (the point is underscored in II-II.1.2 ad 2). The principal reality in which the act of faith terminates is God, who is eminently simple and undivided (see *negative theology*). But Aquinas points out at the head of the body of this article that what is simple in itself is not simple to us. The thing known is in the knower according to the mode of the knower. The mode proper to the human intellect is to know the truth by synthesis and analysis. Hence, things that are simple in themselves are known by the intellect with a certain amount of complexity; the object of faith is something complex by way of proposition.

The fourth article adds a final point that will figure in the presentation of the articles of faith in this question. Faith is not a matter of vision, which is deferred until the next life. Rather, echoing Hebrews, Aquinas states that faith has to do with something unseen, about God and about the bringing of rational creatures through divine operation to God as end.

In the second half of the question (II-II.1.6–10), Aquinas builds on these insights in presenting the articles of faith. The teaching in these later articles is rich and wide ranging, treating such topics as the meaning of "article" in this context; the number of articles of the Christian faith and the way in which it may be said that their number has increased over time; the summarizing of the articles into the creeds of the Christian religion; the responsibility for the articulation of the faith and the collection of articles into creed; and the relation between creed and Scripture. Drawing on the etymology of the Greek word rendered as "article" in his Latin, Aquinas observes that an article is a part that is related to other articles and parts; articles are said to be parts that fit together. The object of faith is something unseen in connection with God. Thus, any matter that for a special reason is unseen is a special article of the faith; whereas when several matters are known or not known, under the same aspect, we are not to distinguish several articles. In effect, what Aquinas is gesturing to here (II-II.1.6c) is that there is, at least from our perspective, a second formal object of faith (6 ad 2) in addition to the God who reveals. In terms of what is believed, God is the formal object of faith and so the reason for affirming in faith the material objects of faith. That there are discrete articles is due to the fact that different parts of the faith are from our perspective unseen in different ways. As examples of different articles of faith, Aquinas cites in 6c God suffering and God rising again from the dead; these are known or unknown under different aspects, and so are different articles of faith. But that God suffered, died, and was buried present the same difficulty, so that if one is accepted, it is not difficult to accept the others; wherefore all these belong to one article.

Has the number of the articles increased over time (a.7)? While the substance of the faith is always the same, the number of articles explicitly believed has in fact increased. All of the articles were virtually contained in what Aquinas here calls certain primary matters of faith; eventually, what was implicit was made explicit, was articulated in the faith. Taking his cue from Hebrews 11:6 ("Whoever would approach [God] must believe that he exists and that he rewards those who seek him"), Aquinas states in 7c that these primary matters of faith are God's existence and God's providence over the salvation of people. As he immediately makes clear in the same passage, "God's existence" is taken in a rich and pregnant sense and certainly is not to be confused with what can be proven (as in ST I.2) by arguments from creaturely effects (that is, that God exists; see *preambles of faith*). The existence of God in the present context includes all that we believe to exist in God eternally, in whom we believe human happiness to consist. As for belief in providence, this includes all

those things that God dispenses in time, for human salvation, and that are the way to that happiness. As history proceeded, what was implicit in the certain primary matters of faith was teased out. In 7 ad 2, Aquinas makes a nice point in this regard about God's skill as a teacher. In this gradual unfolding or articulation of the object of faith, God has taken into account human capacity, condescending to that capacity, and so introducing only gradually the fully articulated faith. Here he cites Galatians 3, where the apostle Paul compares the state of the Old Testament to childhood, to underscore that the full actualization of the faith as object comes only with Christ.

This in turn allows Aquinas in the next article (II-II.1.8) to restate the certain primary matters of faith in more explicitly christological terms. In this article, he is explaining why the articles are suitably formulated. He knows of two ways of counting up the articles. By one way of reckoning, there are two groups of seven articles of faith; others say that there are two groups of six. But in either way of counting, the principal headings remain the same. In 8c, he notes that to faith two sorts of things belong: those the sight of which we will enjoy in eternal life and those by which we are brought to eternal life. In eternal life, the secret of the Godhead will be seen, which will bring happiness; so too will be seen the mystery of Christ's incarnation, by whom people have access to the glory of the sons of God (Rom. 5). On this basis, then, Aquinas states that the two principal distinctions in matters of faith are the majesty of the Godhead and the mystery of Christ's human nature. Accordingly, half of the articles (seven or six, depending on the reckoning) will deal with the Godhead, the other half with Christ's human nature. When a total of fourteen articles is posited, covered in the first group are: the unity of the Godhead; three articles corresponding to the three persons of the Trinity; and three articles on the works proper to the Godhead (one of which, that on creation, deals with the order of nature; another of which refers to the order of grace and covers human sanctification; and the third of which refers to the order of glory and deals with the resurrection of the dead and life everlasting). When a total of twelve articles is posited, the three articles that according to the first way of reckoning are thought to pertain to the three divine persons are counted as one, and the article in that other reckoning dealing with the work of glorification is divided into two. As for those articles that fall under Christ's human nature, when a total of seven is posited, these refer to: Christ's incarnation or conception; his virginal birth; his passion, death, and burial; his descent into hell; his resurrection; his ascension; and his coming for judgment. In the other way of counting (where there are a total of six articles under this heading), claims about conception and nativity are thought to form a single article.

In the final two articles of II-II.1, Aquinas turns to the creed. Granted that the articles of faith are gathered into creeds—whether the Apostles' Creed, which Aquinas believes goes back to the apostles, or the Nicene Creed, which he terms an "explanation" of the Apostles' Creed (II-II.1.9 ad 6)—is such gathering suitable (a.9)? The answer provided in the corpus is somewhat obvious: Of course it is suitable, for this gathering of the truths—or, as he puts it here, "maxims"—of the faith into creed greatly facilitates the proclamation of the faith to all. More interesting is what Aquinas states in ad 1. The objection had claimed unsuitability because of an imagined competition that creed formulation would create between creed and Scripture. It is Scripture, this objection states, that is the rule of faith, and there can be no addition or subtraction from this rule. In response, Aquinas clarifies the relation between creed and Scripture. The same faith is proclaimed in both. Yet creed is not redundant, nor should it be seen in competition with Scripture. The truth of faith as contained in Scripture is stated diffusely, under various modes of expression, and sometimes

obscurely, so that in order to gather the truth of faith from Scripture one needs long study and practice, which are unattainable by all those who require to know the truth of faith, many of whom have no time for study. Thus, Aquinas continues, it was necessary to gather together a clear summary from the sayings of Scripture, to be proposed to the belief of all. Hence, the creed is not an addition to Scripture; its articles are taken from Scripture, nicely summarizing the scriptural message on the key points of the faith. The creed with its articles thus keeps the focus on what is essential in Scripture, namely, the truths revealed by God that are necessary for salvation. Here Aquinas is content to say that the articles and the creed are rooted in Scripture. It is not too much to add that as astute summary of the essential points of scriptural teaching, the creed can in turn serve as the hermeneutical guide to the subsequent reading and study of God's Word in the Bible.

In a.10, Aquinas assigns the work of drawing up the symbol of faith to *pope* and council working in concert. It belongs to the pope to call the council, which will as circumstance requires further articulate the faith and issue a new edition of the creed. Here the threat of heresy is at the fore. While the truth of faith is sufficiently explicit in the teaching of Christ and the apostles, some people are so evil minded as to pervert the apostolic teaching and other doctrines and Scripture to their own destruction. Thus, as time went on it was necessary to express the faith more explicitly against errors that arose (ad 1); this is what the council summoned by the pope is to do. The pope is to confirm the decisions of the council (ad 2). In ascribing this responsibility to the pope, Aquinas refers to scriptural passages affirming Petrine primacy (e.g., Luke 22; as in 10c). From the quote from the Council of Ephesus in ob.2, it is also clear that the pope and council are guided in their work by the Holy Spirit.

Granted that the pope and council play important roles in maintaining the one faith by making it more explicit as occasion demands, is it possible for the pope to bypass a council and act on his own? Aquinas does not raise the matter in ST II-II.1, but it does come up in the disputed question *de potentia* (10.4 ad 13). There Aquinas refers to the seventh ecumenical council, which was called while the church was under attack. Only a few bishops could attend, and so in order to address the heresy in question, the pope had to act on his own. From this passage, it would appear that that action was extraordinary and exceptional; the rule would be for the pope to call the council, which under the guidance of the Holy Spirit would further articulate the faith, and then have the pope confirm the decisions of the council.

While the articles have great importance for the Thomistic theological enterprise—providing the grist, as it were, for Aquinas's theologizing—they take on added importance in select writings. In these writings, they provide the structure for the writing, in whole or in part. Thus, in the *Compendium Theologiae*, a work of uncertain dating that was left unfinished in the middle of its second part, Aquinas proposed to follow the example of Augustine in his *Enchiridion* and so discuss the truths of the religion according to the three theological virtues. Under *faith* he would treat what has to be believed; under *hope* he would discuss the end to which humans aspire; under *charity* he would discuss how one should live in order to reach God. It is with regard to the first part that the articles are prominent. Aquinas recalls the principal division of the articles as dealing with either the divine majesty or the humanity of Christ as the means to the end that is God; accordingly, he uses the articles on God and on Christ to structure what in effect is a bipartite treatise on faith. In the first part of the treatise, he recalls at the outset how the articles on God themselves fall into three sections—on the divine unity; the Trinity of persons; and the divine effects, from creation, through sanctification, through glory—and dis-

tributes the many chapters of the discussion of faith appropriately.

In the *De articulis fidei et ecclesiae sacramentis ad Archiespicopum Panormitanum*, an occasional piece that he composed at the request of an acquaintance, the articles provide the structure of the first part of the work (the greater part) as well as the subject matter. This work, which enjoyed a great distribution in the later Middle Ages, especially in German lands as a de facto catechism, acknowledges the two ways of counting the articles (fourteen or twelve), favoring in the actual presentation the latter, distributing these articles under the principal headings of the Godhead and the humanity of Christ. For each article, Aquinas follows the same basic procedure: He names the article, looks at errors opposed to it and that may therefore account for its articulation, comments on the scriptural passages that give rise to the article, and finally cites the appropriate phrase in the creed. In terms of the internal composition, with attention to heresy and the scriptural basis for an article, the procedure is somewhat reminiscent of what we meet in *ScG* IV, which is roughly contemporary with this writing, although the *ScG* does not make the articles a principle of organization. In the second part of the treatise, Aquinas looks at the seven sacraments of the New Law, in order. He discusses the sacraments separately because of the request of his acquaintance for a work on both the articles and the sacraments, but he notes (in the short prologue to the second part of the treatise) that he could have discussed the sacraments among the articles, under the sanctification covered under the Godhead.

The final work in which the articles of faith provide the organizational and substantive cue is the homilies on the Apostles' Creed, which Aquinas delivered in his native Neapolitan dialect, in Naples, during Lent in his final year of activity. These conferences (*Collationes super Credo in Deum*) were subsequently translated by his secretary into Latin, which is the form in which we have received them. The sermons bespeak Aquinas's typical preoccupation with the doctrinal, as he explores the key maxims of the faith. Again, they are thoroughly scriptural, as he shows how specific claims in the creed summarize the scriptural witness. He also shows how the creed counters various heresies about the faith that have emerged and that thus have occasioned the finer articulation of the faith. The Nicene Creed can also figure here, as in some of the homilies (e.g., V) he notes where the later creed is more precise than the earlier, a nice illustration of the comments in ST II-II.1: that a later creed is to stand in continuity with an earlier, maintaining the substance of that earlier-expressed faith while meeting the challenge of later heresy through closer articulation, and that the Nicene Creed in particular is a commentary on the Apostles' Creed, a claim that is understandable given his acceptance of the dating of the Apostles' Creed to the time of the apostles. Yet the homilies are notable for their concern for the spiritual implications of correct belief. Along with the rooting of creed in Scripture and explanation of the ways in which specific phrases in the creed meet heresy, Aquinas also points to the effects of correct belief. As is quite appropriate in homilies delivered during Lent to an audience of brothers and perhaps laypeople, Aquinas interposes in the sermons reflections on the benefits that God has granted to those whom God calls to God. For example, in an early homily (I), he talks about the many benefits of faith. Through faith, the soul is wedded to God and eternal life is begun. Faith guides the present life, for by faith one knows where one should go, and how; through faith, people can conquer temptation. So too he comments (in III) with great enthusiasm about the proper attitude that may be engendered by reflection on the doctrine of creation. From consideration of God's creating, we come to know the divine majesty, are led

to give thanks and to have patience in adversity, are drawn to the right use of created goods, and are able to come to a knowledge of human dignity. To give a final example, he offers what in effect is a reading of the spiritual impact of the ascension (IX). The ascension is to be taken literally; it is something that has occurred to Christ and is of significance for an assessment of his importance. But it is helpful for us as well. Christ ascended so that he might lead us, showing the way of ascent. His ascension also provides us with security, for Christ ascended that he might intercede for us. And he ascended so that he might draw us to himself; if we rise in Christ, we will, after Christ, seek the things that are above (Col. 3:1).

Ayo (1988); Emery (1999).

Authority In the construction of his theology, Aquinas was much concerned with authority. *Authority* has two related meanings. First, it refers to a teacher whose words are worthy of respect and have credibility. Second, it refers to a saying, of whatever length, that is worthy of respect and has credibility. Aquinas's theology is an "authoritative" one. In his pursuit of understanding of the truths of the faith, he has learned much from those who have gone before him. Through their writings, they have, in their respective ways, shaped his sensibilities and made possible his own achievement in theology. In the articulation of his theology, he invokes them and their words; through his quoting and paraphrasing, Aquinas thus makes patent his own participation in a larger tradition of proclamation, investigation, and defense of Christian truth.

Aquinas acknowledges different kinds of authority and ascribes to each its proper force. An especially good discussion of what might be termed the "hierarchy of authorities" comes in ST I.1.8 ad 2. The topic of this article is whether there is a place for argument in *sacred doctrine*. On the face of it, it would seem not. Sacred doctrine is the body of truths necessary for salvation that is revealed by God. It contains two sorts of truth: the *articles of faith* and the *preambles of faith*. At least with regard to the articles, it would seem difficult to find a place for argument, for by definition these truths, constituting the major part of sacred doctrine, cannot be demonstrated. Rather, they are revealed and must be held by faith. In ST I.1.8 ob 2, Aquinas makes a more detailed case against argument in sacred doctrine and by extension in the *theology* that pertains to sacred doctrine. There are two sorts of argument. One proceeds by reason. But such seems inappropriate in sacred doctrine, for the use of reason in argument would work against the merit of faith; one should simply accept by faith what is revealed, and so impress God by one's trust. The other kind of argument involves authority; here one quotes another to make or secure a point. But, the objection continues, this is definitely out of keeping with the great dignity of sacred doctrine, which as earlier articles in ST I.1 have insisted, is much superior to any of the philosophical or human disciplines that we know. It is, in the words of ST I.1.5, the most noble discipline, when compared with the human disciplines. But advancing an argument on the say-so of someone else (rather than making the case for oneself, through one's own reasoning) is something we find in the lower human disciplines, dependent as they are on principles received from higher disciplines.

In his response to the objection, Aquinas addresses the "elimination of merit" concern. There is no suggestion that one can argue to the truths of the faith, that one can demonstrate them; to try to do so would be presumptuous (cf. ST I.1.1 ad 10). But once these truths are held, one can try to uncover the plausibility, the wisdom, of what God has done and revealed for human salvation. On the basis of faith, one can think about the

faith; at the end of the process, one may well have a better understanding of what one holds by faith. But the brunt of Aquinas's comments in ST I.1.8 ad 2 have to do with the alleged inappropriateness in sacred doctrine of argument from authority. What is true of the lower human disciplines is definitely not true in sacred doctrine. Consider the difference: The lower human disciplines borrow from the higher human disciplines principles that can be discerned by reason. In sacred doctrine, however, the articles are above reason and cannot be derived through the use of reason. Rather, to have them, they must be revealed by God, who is the principal teacher of sacred doctrine. Hence, the argument from authority is necessary and completely in keeping with the tremendous dignity of this doctrine, revealed by God for human salvation.

Aquinas continues in this same passage by identifying three types of authority that can figure in sacred doctrine. The first and chief authority is God, along with the human authors of Scripture. God teaches the saving truths that are found in Scripture, revealing these truths to the human authors of Scripture. The authority of the human authors of Scripture when it comes to the truths of sacred doctrine is certain and intrinsic—intrinsic or proper, because what they teach in their writings is at the center of sacred doctrine; certain, because these authors come to share in the authority of God, who has revealed these truths to them. God is most certain; God does not lie. Hence, what God reveals to them, which they convey in their writings, is most certain. Next come the doctors of the church. Their authority is also proper or intrinsic. With the authors of Scripture, they are principally concerned with God's saving truth. But their authority is less; it is not certain—for God has not revealed the truth to them as God has done for the human authors of Scripture—but only probable. Here Aquinas acknowledges that their authority comes as interpreters of Scripture. That they are successful more often than not in identifying and conveying God's saving Word through their own encounter with scriptural revelation has been recognized by the church. But they are not infallible; they can be wrong, or they can state their interpretation in infelicitous ways, and so their authority is only probable. The other authority mentioned in this particular passage may come as a surprise: philosophy. Yet Aquinas's explanation for including the philosophers here has a certain plausibility. The authority of the philosophers is only probable, and it is exterior or extrinsic. In the latter point, Aquinas acknowledges that in their work the philosophers are not concerned with Christian revelation. They have other topics and ambitions. But what they have written can at times be useful to Christians, as Christians pursue the understanding of the faith. Thus, they can be brought, as it were, from the outside to the inside of sacred doctrine; their ideas, that is, can be put to Christian service, to explicate and defend Christian truth. Their authority is not only extrinsic; it is also only probable, for they can, as can the church doctors, be wrong.

ST I.1.8 ad 2 is an extremely useful guide to Aquinas's use of authority in his discrete theological discussions. In effect he is telling us that Scripture is the fount of all theological work: Here God has revealed saving truth, the proper subject matter of the theologian. In working out a theology, it is Scripture, whose authority is proper and certain when it comes to the truths of the faith, that will stand to the fore (see *Scripture*). In his approach to Scripture and his pursuit of the understanding of the faith, the work of those in the faith who have gone before him and who have been deemed largely successful in their reading of Scripture will be of great benefit, and Aquinas will make considerable use of the writings of such doctors as Augustine, Ambrose, Cyril, and John of Damascus in the presentation of his own theology (see *doctors of the church*). In his struggle to interpret the truths of

the faith and to show their cogency and meaningfulness for his own time, Aquinas will, as Paul advocates (2 Cor. 10:5), "take every thought captive to obey Christ" (quoted in ST I.1.8 ad 2) and so will draw on the philosophers to explicate Christian truth (see *philosophy*). He is also keenly aware that these different authorities have different importance. By contrasting the authority that is certain and intrinsic with that which is intrinsic and probable and that which is extrinsic and only probable, he is making clear the distinctive and supreme authority of Scripture.

However, the passage is not comprehensive, and leaves out of account others who figure in the theological process. What about the ecumenical councils, which are charged with the articulation of the faith (see *articles of faith*)? Their authority is to be assimilated to that of the human authors of Scripture. In its work, a council is much concerned with the correct interpretation of Scripture, the closer fixing of what it is that God in Scripture is proclaiming, as necessitated by heretical challenge to the faith. In its work of articulation, the council will be guided by the Holy Spirit, the same Spirit involved in the scriptural revelation. Thus, the authority of the Fathers in council will differ from that of individual Fathers (for no revelation or special inspiration is given to a church doctor). And what about other theologians, that is, contemporaries of Aquinas whose work he might have drawn on? For that matter, what about the theological work of Aquinas himself? In practice, the working theologian is pursuing the same set of tasks as the church doctor (see *theologian*). But his work has not been tested by the church over time, and so the nature of its authority, if any, has not been identified. While he is working, he lacks "authority"; what he produces of his own is but "opinion." Yet it may be that the church will come to recognize the power of what a theologian has written and that in that case, as in fact happened with Aquinas himself, his theological writings will come to be recognized for their authority.

_____

Valkenberg (2000); Jordan (1986a, 1994).

Baptism A *sacrament* of the New Law, baptism was instituted by Christ to bring those who wish to follow him into conformity with him. Baptism is understood in terms of Christ's death on the *cross* and his *resurrection*: The believer dies with Christ (to sin) and rises with Christ, to new life. This conformity to Christ can be put in terms of formal causality (see *causes*); Christ's dying and rising are the pattern of the dying and rising of those who have decided to follow Christ. But as a sacrament of the New Law, baptism also causes, efficiently, what it signifies. Thus, those who are put into conformity with Christ in being baptized receive from Christ the spiritual benefits promised through this sacrament, made available through the death and resurrection of Christ. Baptism conveys grace and so new life, centered in Christ.

As with other sacraments, in discussing baptism in the ST (III.66–71) Aquinas employs a threefold sacramental formula in order to do justice to the complexity of this sacrament: *sacramentum tantum* (sign only), *res et sacramentum* (thing and sign), and *res tantum* (thing only). In baptism, the washing with water as the priest states the baptismal formula is the "sign only"; this washing signifies the spiritual washing that comes in baptism. By the "thing only" is designated the spiritual effects of baptism. In baptism, one is cleansed of sin—of *original sin* in the first place, but also of actual *sin* and of all the effects of sin. Baptism brings forgiveness and the removal of the guilt before God for sin; by baptism one is no longer liable to the punishment imposed by God for sin. Through baptism *grace* is given, the grace that heals the sinful, fallen self and orients the person to God as end. By the "thing and sign," Aquinas means the

sacramental character that is imprinted on the soul in baptism (III.66.1c). This character is indelible and cannot be lost through subsequent sin; hence, baptism is not repeatable (66.1 ad 1; a.9c). By this character, the recipient is ordered to full participation in the sacramental life, by which the person can come to God as the end of the spiritual journey. In baptism, through which one is conformed to Christ and set on the path to God that is through Christ (see *viator*), one has begun the spiritual journey to God.

Aquinas acknowledges the scriptural order to "believe and be baptized" (III.68.8). Baptism is the "sacrament of faith." In terms of the adult, the one who is to be baptized must personally believe, have already come to the act of *faith* that is part of conversion and marks correct relationship to God. Thus, in baptism, there will be the conveying of the spiritual benefits, of character and of baptismal grace. But baptism at the same time offers the opportunity for the public protestation of faith. Being baptized is thus also an exterior act of worship by which the baptized person acknowledges God as source and end, through Christ. However, it may be that an adult approaches baptism fictively—that is, not as a believer—and so the reception of baptism will be a lie about how one really stands before God and Christ. In this case, the person will be physically washed and will receive the baptismal character; that is infallibly given through baptism. But the person will not receive the *res tantum*, the grace that baptism offers. The offer is made but, in effect, is rejected, due to the recipient's lack of faith. That person remains in sin and remains liable to God's punishment.

By Aquinas's time, infant baptism was undoubtedly the norm. Here too faith is needed ("believe and be baptized"). The infant herself is incapable of the act of faith. In the case of the infant, what Aquinas calls the "faith of the church" suffices, and the proclamation of this faith is made on the infant's behalf by the godparents, who present the infant for baptism (III.68.9 ad 1 and 3).

The priest will be the normal minister of this sacrament (III.67.2). By ordination, the priest has received a separate character that designates the priest to act in Christ's stead. As with the other sacraments, in baptism the minister acts as an *instrumental cause*. The priest is not the source of grace and does not act on his own behalf. Rather, Christ works through him, to convey the grace of the Holy Spirit. Hence, the physical performance and word, enacted by the priest in the baptismal rite, is the medium through which Christ and the Holy Spirit work to convey grace. Aquinas also refers to others who might baptize in case of emergency. Baptism is a sacrament of necessity, and one must be baptized in order to reach God. When a priest is not available and there is an emergency—that is, there is an unbaptized person who wants to be baptized and is in danger of dying—then any person can serve as the minister of this sacrament. The lay believer may baptize in case of emergency (III.67.3), but even a nonbeliever can baptize (III.67.5). In baptizing, the nonbeliever is not expected to give up her nonbelief. But the nonbeliever will have to intend by her words and actions what the church intends in baptizing in order for the baptism to be valid: to convey God's healing grace and to inaugurate the person's new relationship to God in Christ.

On the basis of Christian history and the tradition, Aquinas can speak of different sorts of baptism. The principal focus in any of his discussions of baptism is on the sacrament of baptism, the baptizing with water by which one receives sacramental character and baptismal grace. Aquinas knows as well of baptism by repentance and desire (*ex voto*), and baptism by blood (III.66.11). In the former, he is thinking of the adult who is unbaptized, wishes to be baptized, but is prevented from receiving the baptism of water. That person as moved by the Holy Spirit intensely desires to be right before God and to be joined to Christ; by this intense desire, which includes justifying faith—the faith formed by charity that orients one correctly to God as end—that person does receive the spiritual benefits normally conveyed through baptism. Of course, if opportunity eventually does present itself, that person will proceed to the fount to proclaim the faith and to fulfill Christ's will; a desire is in vain if it is not fulfilled when it can be. The other baptism, of blood, is that of the martyrs; they too, by the witness of their faith, receive what they lacked the opportunity to receive through baptismal water.

———

Walsh (1993, 2005); Torrell (2003).

Beatific Vision   Salvation consists of entering into God's own life by coming face to face with God and knowing and loving God as God is. In the direct vision of God, the deepest desire for knowing and loving of the human is realized, but the human who reaches beatitude is fulfilled in a way that utterly transcends his natural capacities (see *nature and grace*). Such knowledge and knowing is proper to God and is offered to the elect as, radically, gift. Aquinas affirms that the truth that the end is God in God's self must be revealed (see the very first article of the ST, I.1.1c) and cannot be demonstrated by human reason (see *articles of faith*). He cites in this regard such biblical texts as Romans 6:23 ("The free gift of God is eternal life") and John 17:3 ("This is eternal life, that they may know you, the only true God"), both quoted at I.12.4 sed contra, and 1 John 3:2 ("We will see him as he is"), quoted at I.12.1 sed contra. The affirmation of blessedness as a transcendent gift that must be revealed by God comes, as is already apparent, at different points in the ST—in the treatment of *sacred doctrine* and in the account of our knowing of God in the next life and in this (ST I.12)—as part of Aquinas's *theological epistemology*. Aquinas also treats the topic as part of the consideration, at the head of I-II, devoted to the movement through moral activity of the rational creature to God as end, of happiness (qq.1–5), stating there, as he had in I.1.1c, that the end of the human journey is God, the triune God who has freely and lovingly established God's self as the end of rational creatures, in whom alone true and full happiness can be found (I-II.3.8; I-II.5.8).

Reaching beatitude marks the end of the journey of the human and comes, with the few exceptions noted below, only in the next life, when the *viator* is ushered into the immediate presence of God. Once reached, beatitude is permanent; the journey is over, and the human is now a *beatus* (lit., "blessed"), one who has attained God and lives with God.

The knowledge of the vision is quidditative: What God is in God's nature will then be known by the human. What renders the vision possible is the light of glory. Seeing God directly lies beyond the natural capacities of the person. To see God, a new perfection is required; this is a gracious intelligible light that God provides to allow the person to know God as God is. Yet while the vision provides a knowledge of God in God's essence, Aquinas is insistent that the knowledge granted the human is not total, in the sense of utterly comprehensive. The light of glory is a created light, and the human remains human even in this rising to God; the finite is unable to totally grasp God as God is. Such total knowing of the divine essence remains the preserve of God; beatific vision is but a sharing, a participation in the manner set by God for the creature in God's own life.

In the present life, there is no quidditative knowledge of God. One does not know God as God is, nor is one able to render a definition of God that would be adequate to the divine reality. Rather, one can attain in the present life at best to a knowledge of the truths that must be affirmed about God, without knowing these various perfections so affirmed as they exist in God. In denying quiddita-

tive knowledge to the human in this life, Aquinas can advance two distinct reasons. The first has to do with how people know: The knowledge of the human originates in the information provided by the senses, and one can proceed in knowing only as far as the senses can take us. But God is not sensible, and even though God is the cause of all that is—and so things are patterned on God in accordance with the divine intention in making them and so can point beyond themselves to God—effects fall short of their cause and so cannot render God as God is. While in explaining why there cannot be quidditative knowledge of God in this life Aquinas will often advert to the human way of knowing, he can also come at the matter from, as it were, the other angle—by stressing the utter plenitude of the divine reality, which cannot be grasped by the human. God remains in God's transcendence and mystery. When he is thinking of this other reason for denying quidditative knowledge of God in this life, Aquinas can make use of his teaching about essence and *esse*. In everything other than God, *what* something is and *that* it is (its "to be") are different. But to articulate the divine transcendence, Aquinas insists that in God what God is (the divine essence) and God's act of being are identical. The affirmation of identity would seem to be especially apt in putting God beyond the grasp of our intellect this side of the eschaton.

In beatitude, God's role is double. God is the direct object of contemplation. But God also plays the key role in making the vision by the human of God a reality. God provides the intelligible light by which the divine essence is seen. God provides the means for the move in self-transcendence and perfection into God's own presence and activity.

In discussing the beatific vision in the first ten articles of ST I.12, Aquinas insists that the vision comes in the next life. This is the general rule. But on the basis of Scripture, Aquinas acknowledges some exceptions, for the most part momentary. Thus, he will allow that Moses and Paul were granted the vision, for a time, in the present life, as a special gift and as an encouragement on their path to God (I.12.11 ad 2). In II-II.175, Aquinas returns to the topic in greater detail, here discussing closely what is reported of Paul in 2 Corinthians 12:2. Yet as part of his account of *Jesus Christ*, Aquinas insists on the great exception to the rule. In the discussion of the **knowledge** that was **Christ's**, Aquinas posits four knowings of Christ, one pertinent to him as God and three having to do with his real humanity. Among the three human knowings is the beatific vision, which, Aquinas says, was the prerogative of the one who is Savior from the first moment of his conception. It was appropriate that Jesus enjoy the beatific vision throughout his life, for as human he is the way to God as end. Hence, in himself, he shows the end to which humans are called and that they will attain when they take this path.

Rocca (2004), part 1, ch. 2; Torrell (1997); Gradl (2004); Hoye (1975); Staley (1989); Wieland (2002).

Capax gratiae, capax dei, capax gloriae   see **Nature and Grace**

Causes   Aquinas refers for Christian purposes to the Aristotelian causes throughout his theology. He cites four causes in order to explicate Christian truth. A final cause is the end of the act, the purpose for which it is done. An exemplary cause is the model on which something is based. An efficient cause is responsible for doing, identifying the one who performs the act. A material cause is that out of which something is made. In employing the Aristotelian causes in his theology, Aquinas is trading on his own philosophical training as well as that of his target audience. Prior to his entry into theological study, the aspiring scholastic theologian would have gone through a rigorous philo-

sophical training, working through the Aristotelian corpus, as this was now available in Latin translation. This training provided a certain cast of mind that proved helpful in the doing of theology—although in Aquinas philosophy and theology are not the same (see *theology; philosophy; sacred doctrine*)—and the philosophical gestures through the invocation of the causes would have been readily appreciated by his readers. Aquinas was keenly aware, however, that in speaking of Christian things in terms of these causes, certain modification was required. These causes express well the things of this world that can be observed and analyzed. But the Christian theologian is concerned with a *God* who is utterly transcendent, not to be reduced to the things of this world. Hence, in employing such conceptuality, the theologian must be attentive to the ways that God nonetheless escapes our categories. The causes can help to organize reflection on God and on God's dealings with the world but will not, in Aquinas's usage, presume that they grasp or explode the mystery of God.

A few examples will help to clarify what is involved in the use of these causes in formulating this theology. For Aquinas, sacred doctrine and its theology have to do with God and with other things as they are related to God as their beginning and end (see ST I.1.3 ad 1; 7c). Implicit in this account of theology are two of the Aristotelian causes: efficient and final. Things other than God are treated in this science as proceeding from God, their maker, as their efficient cause, and as proceeding from God to show the divine goodness and to come to God as their final end. In his *ex professo* treatment of **creation**, Aquinas will bring in a third cause, the formal or exemplar cause: God is the efficient cause of the being of creatures, and does so in wisdom, in accordance with the plan for the wise communication of being to what is not God. All things, in their natures, activities, and specific ends, are patterned on God in the way established by God in creating. Only the material cause does not figure in the account of creation. God in creating does not work on some preexisting stuff that is then formed by God, nor does God make things out of God's own substance. Only then would there be room here for a material cause. Rather, creation is *ex nihilo*, and "nothing" is not a thing.

In bringing rational creatures into existence, God intends for them God's own life, to share God's goodness in a special way. God intends for human beings to attain to eternal life through their characteristic actions of knowing and willing, in a supernatural key, as aided by God's grace (see *theological virtues; viator*). In terms of the human person as called to God as end, for that person God as end is the final cause, and whatever proximate ends that the person intends to achieve through discrete actions will be ordered to the final end that is God. Such proximate ends are in fact good to the extent that they are so ordered and their attaining brings the person closer to God as final end. The person is also a doer, is herself an efficient cause. Thus, the person deserves praise for the good that she does, blame for the sin that she performs. In doing the good that really does bring one closer to God as end, there are in fact two efficient causes, the one ordered to the other. Without *grace*, the person would not be able to do what is perfective of the person and brings her closer to God as end. But grace does not act in spite of the person's God-given rational and other capacities, but through them. Hence, Aquinas can refer to the person as the *instrumental cause* through whom God acts, by grace in the furthering of God's will of salvation for that person. The person as instrument is not a mere puppet in the hands of God. The person is animate and has, by virtue of the person's establishment as human and so endowed with will, control over the person's action. But without grace, correct use of those capacities will be lacking,

due to sin and its effects, and the graced use of the capacity will be in accordance with God's predestining will. And so in assessing the good that a person does, both the person as agent and the God who acts through this agent as principal efficient cause must be given their due. The distinction and coordination of God as principal efficient cause and instrumental causes through which God works threads its way through the theology, including in the discussion of *sacrament, Jesus Christ* as divine and human, and God's revelation to the human authors of *Scripture*.

———

Fabro (1961); Te Velde (1995), part 2.

Character, Sacramental   Among the effects of some of the Christian *sacraments* is character (ST III.63). A character is an invisible mark on the soul. The character provides a spiritual power, perfective of the soul, that has to do with the worship of God. Once character is received through a sacrament, it cannot be effaced; hence, the sacraments that convey character are not repeatable. Through the sacramental character, one is marked in a special way and has a special spiritual power that renders possible divine worship. Through the character that is conveyed in *baptism*, one is marked as a member of Christ's body (see *church*), and by this character one becomes qualified to receive the other sacraments, to participate in the divine worship in that way. Through the character that is conveyed in holy orders, the recipient is marked as a representative of Christ who can administer the sacraments. The spiritual power in this instance is an active power. By the priestly character, one is designated as qualified to act *in persona Christi*, in the person of Christ, as the duly designated agent of Christ in dispensing the sacraments. The sacramental characters that Aquinas enumerates thus help to provide order among the sacraments. Through baptism, the recipient is ordered to the other sacraments, including the chief of the sacraments, the Eucharist. Holy orders prepares its recipient for the performance of the other sacraments, to the benefit of all members of Christ's body.

Through the affirmation of the priestly character conferred in holy orders, Aquinas makes clear what is required, and what is not required, of the minister through his acting in the person of Christ in administering the sacraments. There will be a difference in this regard between what is required of a person in order to reach eternal life and what is required of the priest in acting *in persona Christi*. To reach the end of the human journey to God in heaven, one must be conformed to Christ, a conformation that occurs through theological virtues and their acts, and the graced, morally good acts by which the person lives out the Christian life (see *grace*). But in a post-Donatist world, the requirements of the sacramental minister are recognized to be of a different sort. Here personal approximation to the virtues of Christ is not a prerequisite of successful sacramental administration. Rather, what is required is that the one who dispenses the sacraments be duly designated to act for Christ in this way—and such occurs through the character granted in holy orders. As long as the one who serves as minister has the priestly character—and in sacramental performance observes the rite of the church and intends what the church intends in saying the sacramental formula and performing the proper sacramental action—the sacrament will be valid and will offer what Christ has promised to offer through that particular sacrament. The personal moral or theological qualities of the priest make no difference in this regard.

In his discussions of the sacraments, Aquinas attempts to find the appropriate balance between important claims. He recognizes and insists that there is an objective efficacy in the sacraments. When the due representative of Christ performs the sacramental rite, the grace associated with that sacrament is infallibly offered. That is not the same thing, however, as saying that that grace is infallibly received. The offer may be rejected, in the sense that the recipient of the sacrament is incorrectly disposed and so does not receive the grace therein conveyed. For example, in the sacrament of the Eucharist, not all will benefit from their encounter with the Christ truly present as the term of the sacramental conversion. To employ the sacramental formula that Aquinas favors in treating all of the sacraments (see *sacrament*), not all recipients receive the *res tantum*, the grace and spiritual benefits that are the end of the sacrament. Some will reject the offer of grace. Yet the offer will be made, and the performance of the sacrament does have an effect. Here the middle part of the formula will come into play, the *res et sacramentum*. In the Eucharist, that is the true presence of Christ. That occurs when the sacrament is correctly performed, regardless of the personal disposition of any of the recipients. It is Christ who offers the *res tantum*. In some cases, where the recipient is ill disposed, Christ's offer is rejected; the person therefore stops at the level of the *res et sacramentum*. In baptism and in holy orders, character stands at the level of the *res et sacramentum* and so is to be reckoned in terms of objective sacramental efficacy. When baptism is correctly performed, a character is imprinted, which occurs regardless of the personal disposition of the recipient. For example, an adult may approach baptism in a fictive mode, not really believing as is required for fruitful reception. Hence, that person will not receive the baptismal grace that is offered in that sacrament; she will not receive the *res tantum*. But all recipients of baptism receive the character that is the *res et sacramentum* and in principle are ordered to the sacraments for which they qualify by this character. If they are in fact in the correct relationship with God, the reception of the other sacraments will be fruitful; they will attain to the *res tantum*. The same is true in holy orders. A person who is being ordained may lack the personal spiritual dispositions needed to accept the offer of grace at the level of the *res tantum*; in that regard, personal disposition does matter. But regardless of personal disposition, that person nonetheless receives the priestly character, the *res et sacramentum*, that makes him suited to work in Christ's stead.

In discussing sacramental character, Aquinas's focus is primarily on baptism and holy orders. The spiritual power that is character may be passive, as in baptism, qualifying one for reception of the other sacraments; it may be active, as in holy orders, qualifying the one who is ordained to dispense the sacraments. Aquinas also notes that a third sacrament, confirmation, conveys character as well, a character that too is indelible; hence, confirmation too is not to be repeated. The character that is given in confirmation presupposes that given in baptism and builds on it. Confirmational character marks a more mature stage of the person in the faith (ST III.72.5–6). Baptism is appropriate to those who are new in the spiritual life. Thus, it gives power that is concerned with the salvation of that individual. As the person grows in the faith, the person is ready for more. Thus, just as the apostles proceeded to preach the faith and to defend it from attack only after they had received of the fullness of the Holy Spirit, the person who receives confirmation is ready to engage in spiritual combat and defend the faith against the attacks of its enemies. Only one who is mature can engage in such activity, and the confirmational character readies the mature Christian for work of that sort.

Walsh (2005).

Charity   The third of the *theological virtues*, charity is in Aquinas's reckoning the greatest of all of the virtues, here following Paul's judgment in 1 Corinthians 13. Charity is friendship (*amicitia*) with God (ST II-II.23.1). This simple characterization covers much. Not every love is friendship. The love that is friendship involves *benevolentia*, willing the good for the friend; the contrast is with the *amor concupiscentiae*, which wills a good for oneself (as in loving wine or a horse, as an object of desire; see II-II.23.1c). The *amor amicitiae* is, as well, mutual: Friends love each other. Finally, the love that friends express for each other is based on something that they share in common, a communication in some good.

In terms of the theological virtue of charity, the good that grounds this friendship is the divine nature. God wills the salvation of the individual, which means that God has called people to the end that is God. In reaching God, in the next life, people will come to enjoy God as God is; they will enter into the life of self-knowing and loving that is proper to the triune God. God wills to share this life with people. And with regard to the present life, God orders people to this end through habitual *grace*, the theological virtues, and, in a particular way, through the gift of charity. Charity orders the person to God as end, and in the acts of charity the person is united, now, to God in the way that the beloved is in the lover (II-II.23.6c and ad 3). The good that is the foundation of this love is due to the divine initiative and shows the creative power of God's love: God's love causes good (see ST I.20). From that infused good which perfects the rational will (the habit of charity), people are capable of love in response to God, and so there is the mutual loving (God's loving; the human's in response, out of the virtue of charity) that is essential to the *amor amicitiae*.

While infused and, radically, gift of God, charity is susceptible to growth, just as the acquired *virtues* are. One grows in the virtue of charity by acts of charity, just as one who has the habit becomes more courageous by acting courageously as circumstances require. Through these acts of charity, one at the same time gets closer to the end of the human journey to God as established by God (see *viator; merit*). Aquinas also recognizes degrees of charity. In the spiritual journey to God as end, there is spiritual growth, a progression, that runs from a beginning stage through a greater proficiency to perfection in charity in this life (see ST II-II.24.9c). There is a nice parallel here with the growth of the human body. The growth of the body has certain fixed divisions according to those particular actions or pursuits to which a human is brought by the growth of the body. Hence, a human is an infant until he has the use of reason, and after that there is another state of the human wherein he begins to speak and to use his reason, while in turn there is a third state, that of puberty, when he begins to acquire the power of generation, and so on until he arrives at perfection (that is, the full possession and use of his natural powers). So too the diverse degrees of charity are to be distinguished according to the different pursuits to which a human is brought by the increase of charity. For at first it is incumbent on the possessor of charity to occupy himself chiefly with avoiding sin and resisting his concupiscences (see *original sin*), which move him in opposition to charity. This concerns beginners, in whom charity has to be fostered lest it be extinguished. Secondly, the human's chief pursuit is to aim at progress in the good, which is the pursuit of the proficient, whose main aim is to strengthen their charity by adding to it. Thirdly, the human eventually aims chiefly at union with and enjoyment of God, which belongs to the perfect who desire to be dissolved and to be with Christ. The charting of the possible progress is itself a nice reminder of the transformative power of grace and the theological virtues, as well as the limits of that transformation. Grace does bring new being; one in principle is healed of sin and raised to the supernatural level and so ordered to God as one's end. There is a change between the person as prior to and as after the infusion of grace and the virtues. But the transformation may never be completed in this life and certainly is not at the first infusion of grace and the virtues; the new person at that point is very much at the beginning of a process and is herself a work in progress. The change is real; the change continues as the person grows in grace and the virtues by acting in conformity with them.

One who receives charity does not necessarily maintain charity; charity can be lost through sin. To be precise, charity is lost through mortal sin (ST II-II.24.12c). By charity, one is in a loving relationship with God, made possible by the divine initiative. One is in community with God, and one's actions should be appropriate to the friendship that is charity. A sin is mortal when it destroys community, when it takes one out of correct relationship with God and sets one at odds with God. By mortal sin, charity is destroyed. Charity is maintained when it is exercised, when the person wills God as end and acts in a way that brings the person to God as end. Yet as the discussion of the topic in the treatise on grace makes evident (I-II.109–14; see 109.9–10)—a discussion that finds an echo in the treatise on charity (see ST II-II.24.11c)—staying in grace and the theological virtues, including charity, is itself a grace of God, due to the grace of perseverance that is granted to the individual not as reward for merit but as a gift, in accordance with God's predestinating will. The grace of perseverance is the presupposition of the correct use of charity by the person—who wills and so loves correctly—that keeps the person in charity and on the path to God.

God as end is the object of charity. There are other objects—the self, other humans, the body—but these are put by Aquinas, following Augustine, in a structured relation to God as the principal object of charity. We love these others as standing in relation to the One who beatifies and who is our end through charity. We love ourselves as made by God for God, as called to the end that is God. We love other humans for the same reason, as made by God for God. And we love our bodies, as called to the end of the whole human person that is God and as participating in the movement in this life that prepares one for that end and as eventually coming to share in the fulfillment that is heaven (see *eschatology*). All that is loved in charity is loved with reference to God (ST II-II.25.1, 4, 5, 6, 8).

Charity is the "form of all of the virtues" (ST II-II.23.8; I-II.62.4c). Charity can be the form of the virtues because it perfects the will, which commands or elicits all of the acts of the human person. By charity, the will directs the acts of the other virtues, whether perfective of the powers of the sensitive soul or of the intellective soul, to God as the end. The "forming" here is by efficient causality, not formal or final (II-II.24.8 ad 1). In the same vein, Aquinas can also call charity the "mother" or "root" of all of the virtues (II-II.23.8 ad 2; I-II.62.4c). Such a designation is the equivalent of "form" of the virtues in the sense here specified; it does not mean that the other virtues arise or take their origin from charity as from their matter or ultimately are simply different names for charity. There are many virtues, which perfect different powers of soul and orient the person to the ends associated with those powers. What charity does is provide an overarching orientation of the discrete virtues, so that in their actualization the human person does will God as end and so comes closer to God through these acts.

As is the case for the other virtues, charity is perfected by a *gift of the Holy Spirit*, which makes the possessor of charity more pliable to the promptings of the Holy Spirit in reducing the virtue to act. Wisdom is the gift associated with the virtue of charity, a gift that perfects the intellect (II-II.45.2). Whenever he talks about "wisdom"—whether in discussing sacred doctrine (I.1.6) or the wisdom that is a *gratuitous grace*—Aquinas calls on Aristotle to provide the formal definition. It pertains to wisdom to contemplate the highest cause and to order other things in that light (II-II.45.1c). Hence, by the gift of wisdom, there is a

contemplation of God and ordering of things in that light such that in the expression of charity, God will be the end of the act and the person will be correctly related to what is not God and will order those things to God as end. There is, then, a double aspect to the gift of wisdom. It is speculative; it is also practical, inasmuch as it judges of human acts according to the standard that is God and directs human acts according to divine rules (II-II.45.3c). This invocation of wisdom provides, not incidentally, a nice reminder of the importance of both intellect and will for Aquinas's account of the human person as agent. In acting, the will is important, for it is will that commands or elicits acts. This is, as has been stated, the basis for calling charity, perfective of the will, the form of the virtues. Yet one can will only what one knows. On the supernatural level, Aquinas makes the point that in the order of generation, faith has the precedence (I-II.62.4c). Faith assents to truths about God; only as known through faith can one love God. That this particular gift perfects charity continues the point: The act of charity is facilitated by a perfection of the intellect; one loves what one knows, God and how things stand as ordered to God.

In constructing this teaching on charity, Aquinas is indebted to a variety of sources. The contribution of Aristotle is not insignificant. Aquinas has benefitted from his reading of the *Nichomachean Ethics* and in particular from the account of friendship there, so crucial to the portrayal of Christian charity. Yet Aquinas has bent Aristotle to Christian purposes, to account for a virtue unknown to the pagans and to present a friendship between the human and the triune *God*, who is so utterly transcendent and yet so utterly immanent. In proclaiming charity, the starting point and touchstone is the scriptural proclamation, as this has been mediated through such interpreters as Augustine. In discussing charity, as elsewhere, Aquinas has in fact observed in his practice the hierarchy of authorities (see *authority*) sketched at the outset of the ST.

Aumann (1978); Falanga (1948); Hughes (1975); Kühn (1965); Mansini (1995a, b); Schockenhoff (2002); Sherwin (2004); Wadell (1992).

Church Aquinas's systematic writings lack a discrete "treatise on the church." There is no such treatise that might stand alongside those on, say, the Trinity (e.g., ST I.27–43) or Christ (e.g., ST III.1–59); a tractate on the church is an innovation of later Catholic theology. But this is not to imply that Aquinas lacks a well-developed notion of the church. His in fact is a rich ecclesiology, one that is profoundly theological and stresses the role of the church in God's salvific plan. He calls upon and gives expression to this ecclesiology in the course of his examination of such central theological topics as sacrament and Christ. In this teaching about the church, the stress is put on the spiritual and the soteriological, on the ways in which the church functions in bringing God's saving grace to people and in the bringing of people to God. While the emphasis is on the spiritual, on the role of the church in God's bringing of people to God as end, the hierarchical and institutional component of the church is not lacking. Aquinas discusses this in a manner fully in keeping with the soteriological thrust of his most fundamental insights about the church.

Nourished by biblical and patristic teaching, Aquinas knows of a wide variety of ways of designating church. In close conformity with Paul's teaching in Romans 12 and 1 Corinthians 12, Aquinas's favorite designation is church as "mystical body of Christ" (*corpus mysticum Christi*), followed in terms of frequency by another cherished designation, namely, church as "congregation of the faithful." By calling the church the mysti-

cal body of Christ, Aquinas has in mind as his point of comparison the natural body (ST III.8.1c), not, as some scholars have imagined, the political or social body (where notions of hierarchy and institution would inevitably be at the fore). There are three aspects of "body" that figure in Aquinas's account of the church: A body is one; it has diverse members with diverse functions; and the head of a body holds the primacy, as the source of the distinctive powers of the person and as director of the whole. In the mystical body, Christ is the head. It is in Christ that God issues the call to eternal life. It is in Christ, the Son of God become human in order for people to be able to come to God and by whose *death* and *resurrection* human salvation has been rendered possible, that the fullness of grace resides. Those who respond to this call to God in Christ come to be in Christ; they come to belong to Christ, who is their head, and to his people, Christ conveys his *grace*. The response to the call is itself a gift, presupposing the infusion of the grace and of the *faith*, *hope*, and *charity* (see *theological virtues*) by which people move from their sin to Christ and so to the correct path to God as their end. Justifying faith is itself a grace and manifests the gift of the Holy Spirit, given by Christ the head to those who come to belong to Christ and who find their correct orientation to God through Christ; to such, the Holy Spirit thus becomes their vital life force, the energy, as it were, that issues in the life for God that brings one to eternal life. To put this even more explicitly in the language of "body": Christ is head as the source of new, spiritual being, who gives his Spirit to individuals now made one body to make possible their movement to God. In this connection, Aquinas refers to the Holy Spirit as the "soul" or the "heart" (ST III.8.1 ad 3) of the mystical body. There is one body, for the many human beings have been called together and remade into one—those who belong to Christ as their head and who receive from Christ the Holy Spirit, who now moves them and directs them and leads them to God as end. There is oneness here because of the oneness of grace. There is oneness as well because of the oneness of the faith that all in this body share, about God and about God's acts in making the attainment of God in heaven possible (see *articles of faith*). There is also oneness in hope, for all now agree on what it is for which they are striving, and oneness in love, for all are one in their love of God and of all else in relation to God. Talk of the "mystical body of Christ," as well as of the "congregration of the faithful [in Christ]," nicely captures the Thomistic sequence in discussing church and indeed everything having to do with human-God relations. God reaches out (in identifying God's self as the end of human beings; in providing Christ as the way to this end; in conveying God's word and power in Christ); on the basis of that reaching out, people in responding correctly (by the gift of God) are remade, refashioned, into God's people, a people united by their faith and love and hope in God through Christ.

There is a fundamental equality among the members of the body of Christ: All have received the same call to salvation; full members of the church have responded in the same way and have received the same virtues, which incline them and facilitate their movement to their end in God. Yet there is diversity in the church, just as there are diverse members of the natural body. Different Christians will live out their calling in different ways, as aided by gifts of God in addition to justifying grace and the theological virtues, but all to the benefit of other members and of the church as a whole. There are different states in the church (see II-II.179ff.), with their different obligations and duties; some are called to the contemplative life, others to the active life, others to a mixed form (as is the case with Aquinas's own Dominican order). Some are called to the ordained ministry in one form or another, others to the lay life. All are needed, and all people in the church

are equally valued by God. To explain the diversity, Aquinas (as at ST II-II.183.2c) implies a parallel with creation itself. What is not God cannot proclaim God as God is; rather, in God's plan different things proclaim the goodness of God in the way set for them by God, and the totality of creatures proclaim as best as possible God outside of God (see *creation*). So too the diversity within the church reflects a certain beauty and order, and each member testifies to God and God's plan in the way set for it by God, and together all show the goodness of God. But, at bottom, the diversity is functional; different members, each with a role to play, are needed for the thriving and growth of the body as a whole. There is in this respect a nice connection drawn with the teaching about the acts of the theological virtues as the correct response to God, both initially (as at first entry into the church) and subsequently, as people continue in the movement to God. The diverse members are in fact members of the *one* body, and what diverse members do is not for their own sake but for God and for those with whom they are joined as a spiritual corporate entity moving together to God as their end. Mutual service (ST II-II.183.2 ad 1, where Eph. 4 is aptly cited) in love, and not, say, the quest for power and dominance, is the hallmark of this notion of church in oneness and diversity.

While the natural body is helpful in expressing the basic features of this Christ-centered and Spirit-infused body, Aquinas is aware of its descriptive limits. Hence, as he progresses through ST III.8, whose topic is the grace of Christ as he is the head of the church, Aquinas discusses (in a.3) the sense in which Christ is said to be the head of all human beings. An important difference between the mystical and the natural body is that while the members of the natural body are all together, the members of the mystical body are not all together, neither as regards their natural being, since the body of Christ is made up of the people who have been from the beginning of the world until its end, nor as regards their supernatural being since, of those who are at any one time, there are some who are without grace but will have it, and some have it already. In light of this difference between the two bodies, Aquinas can then parse membership in the church, and so Christ's headship, as follows: We must consider the members of the mystical body not only as they are in act but also as they are in potentiality. And with regard to the latter, there are some who are in potentiality who will never be reduced to act, and some who at some time will be reduced to act. Of those who are reduced to act (that is, actually come to be in reality in Christ's body), there are three classes: reduction to act by faith, by charity in this life, and by the fruition of the life to come. Thus, it is that if we take the whole of the world in general, Christ is the head of all humans, but diversely. First and principally, Christ is the head of such as are united to him by glory. Secondly, he is head of those who are actually united to him by charity and, thirdly, of those who are actually united to him by faith (see *faith*, in particular on the faith that justifies and how, as faith informed by charity, that faith differs from mere or unformed faith; that distinction lies behind the distinction here between charity, as more actual membership, and faith). Fourthly, Christ is head of those who are united to him merely in potentiality but who will be reduced to act according to predestination. Finally, he is head of those who are united to him in potentiality but who will never be reduced to act. With regard to these last, when they depart from this world, they will cease to be potentially Christ's. What is clear from this statement of church in terms borrowed from Aristotle (potential-actualization), the church at bottom is a transhistorical entity centered in Christ, an entity that potentially contains all people but actually involves only those who have entered, or will enter, the body through the correct response to God in Christ.

In ST III.8, Aquinas continues the ruminations on Christ as head by asking whether Christ alone is head of the church (a.6). Might others be called "head"? And if so, in what sense? Again, the analogue of the natural body comes into play. A head of a body influences the other members in two ways: by an intrinsic influence, inasmuch as motive and sensitive force flow from the head to the other members, and by a certain exterior guidance, inasmuch as by sight and the other senses rooted in the head, a human is guided in his exterior acts. With respect to the first, the intrinsic influence, there can be no question of another head in addition to Christ. To be head is proper to Christ: The interior influx of grace is from no one other than Christ, whose humanity, through its union with the Godhead, has the power of justifying. But with regard to exterior guidance, Aquinas allows that others may, and do, provide this and so may also be called "heads." Yet, even in this regard, Aquinas is at pains to stress the difference between Christ as head and these others, and does so in such a way that their subordination and subjection to Christ the head is palpable. For one thing, Christ is the head of all who belong to the church in every place and time and state, but all other people are called "heads" with reference to certain places (as bishops in their dioceses), or with reference to a determined time, as the *pope* is the head of the whole church during his pontificate, and with reference to a determined state, the wayfaring state. Perhaps even more tellingly, Christ is the head of the church by his own power and authority; others are "heads" only in the sense of taking Christ's place, or as 2 Corinthians 2:10 nicely puts it, as working "in the person of Christ" (KJV), as Christ's ambassadors.

As ST III.8.6 also suggests, Aquinas is not inattentive to the historical and visible and institutional aspects of the church. While the church at its core has to do with Christ giving grace and people accepting and living out of this grace in faith, hope, and charity, the church exists in history and has a visible expression. Although Aquinas hardly puts the stress on it, there is an institutional dimension to the church that he acknowledges and appreciates, and he insists that the hierarchy that governs the church has received its mandate from Christ through the apostles. Thus, the pope is Christ's main representative on earth in terms of governance and jurisdiction, as established by Christ in his promise to Peter, in whose line the pope follows. Bishops too fill offices established by Christ, inasmuch as they are the legitimate, designated successors of the apostles, who at the level of the diocese exercise jurisdiction over the members of the historical church. There is, similarly, a concrete, visible, and historical dimension to the granting of grace. While grace can be conveyed extrasacramentally, more typically grace is conveyed through the sacraments, which are visible signs of the sacred reality that is Christ (see *sacraments*). In the performance of the sacraments, it is the ordained ministry that as a rule takes the lead; while exceptions are permitted in case of necessity (see, e.g., *baptism*), it belongs to the priest, viewed as the representative of Christ acting *in persona Christi* and serving as the instrumental cause of the conveying of grace, to perform the sacrament. While mapping the hierarchical and the institutional aspects of the church, in the course of the discussion, for example, of the sacraments or of jurisdiction and the maintenance of order in the church, Aquinas nicely and consistently expresses his main insights about the church. The church has importance because of what God and Christ do in and through it. This is true when Aquinas is reflecting on the mystical body; it holds as well for his ruminations on the visible church in the world. What governs all of his reflections is the call of God to eternal life and his conviction that it is through Christ that people can reach God. By pope and bishops, and through the determinations of the councils, order is kept in the church; this

order is to be evaluated and appreciated in terms of the fundamental ordering of people to God as end. Through this governance, the body of those united to Christ in faith and love is sustained in its movement to God; so too, in their proper way, is the contribution of the sacraments. The church thus has great value in terms of service, to God and Christ, in the working out of God's saving plan, and to the members of the church who thrive through this Christ-centered activity of the church.

Sabra (1987); Congar (1939, 1974a, b); Prügl (2004); Rikhof (1976); Bonino (2002); O'Neill (1963).

Coassumed   *see* **Jesus Christ**

Concomitance   Aquinas employs this notion in exploring Christ's eucharistic presence (see *real presence*; *transubstantiation*). In the eucharistic conversion, the substance of the bread is changed by the power of God into the substance of Christ's body, which as modified by its accidents remains in heaven; the substance of the wine is changed into the substance of Christ's blood. Yet Christ is more than body and blood. The whole Christ consists of the full human nature (body and soul) and the full divine nature united in the person of the Word (see *Jesus Christ*). For Aquinas, the whole Christ indeed becomes present in the Eucharist. The substances of Christ's body and blood are present as the direct term of the conversion. The "rest" of Christ becomes present concomitantly, along with these substances. That the divine person, the bearer of the humanity (including the soul of Christ), becomes present concomitantly would not seem to be especially challenging. More difficult is the assertion that the accidents of Christ's body and blood also become present concomitantly—not in their proper mode, but in the manner of substance (ST III.76.4 ad 1).

The assertion allows Aquinas to guard against a gross physicalism and to provide a ready answer to questions that might be raised to put the teaching on Eucharist into doubt. For example, does Christ in becoming present leave heaven? No, because he remains located in heaven via the mediation of his bodily accidents, which while "present" after the consecration, are not, however, present in their proper manner in the Eucharist. In like fashion, the concomitant, not proper, presence of the bodily accidents figures in Aquinas's treatment of eucharistic apparition miracles (III.76.7–8), reports of which had a certain currency in the Middle Ages. When Christ is seen by some in the consecrated host, why is this? Aquinas insists that it is not due to the mode of Christ's eucharistic presence. Only if the bodily accidents were present in their proper mode would Christ be visible (or touchable or chewable, for that matter). But these accidents are present in the mode of substance, and so if and when there is such an apparition, that is due to a miracle separate from the transubstantiation that accounts for real presence.

The affirmation of the concomitant presence of the bodily accidents in the mode of substance also figures in Aquinas's handling (III.77.7 ad 1) of the oath that Berengar had been forced to affirm in 1059. In the oath, Berengar states that "the bread and wine which are placed on the altar are the true body and blood of Christ after the consecration, and are truly handled and broken by the priest's hands, broken and crushed by the teeth of believers." The oath was something of an embarrassment to later scholastics. Although it countered the merely symbolic interpretation of the Eucharist that Berengar had championed, it also seemed to make the Eucharist more of a dental than a mental matter. And so, while insisting on the reality of the presence (the body and blood of Christ are substantially present, as the direct term of the conversion), Aquinas simply notes that Christ's bodily accidents are not present in such a way that they can be felt or torn or tasted.

That the whole Christ is present in the Eucharist (see *real presence*) is of tremendous import for Aquinas. It provides the possibility of a sacramental encounter with the one who makes salvation possible, as a foretaste of the direct encounter with God and Christ that will characterize heaven. Christ as really present in this sacrament is a *viaticum*, offering the nourishment that sustains the Christian on the road to God as end.

———

Megivern (1963).

Confirmation   see **Sacrament; Character, Sacramental**

Creation

The doctrine of creation stands at the heart of Aquinas's theology, informing his approach to a wide array of topics—from his account of how we know and name *God* (see *epistemology, theological*), through the depiction of providence and **predestination** and human freedom. Through this doctrine, Aquinas asserts the dependence of creatures on God and even their resemblance to God, while underscoring the divine transcendence and otherness of God from what God creates. In his *ex professo* accounts of creation (e.g., ST I.44–49; *ScG* II; *De potentia* qq.3–5), Aquinas is especially concerned to stress the following.

Creating is to be ascribed to God alone. Against various Neoplatonists, he rejects an emanationist schema that would have the Ultimate Being bring lower beings into existence only through intermediaries. Rather, God's creative action is direct; God brings all things, whatever their ontological status, into being.

Creating is a free act of God. God is under no compulsion to create. While creating is compatible with God's nature as good—Aquinas can here cite the Dionysian slogan, "Good is diffusive of itself"—creating adds nothing to God, and God would be as much God as God is without creating. That God creates is wholly volitional; God freely wills to communicate God's goodness to what is not God. Again, Aquinas's assertion is directed against any necessitarian, emanationist schema.

Creating involves God's love. Aquinas consistently differentiates human loving from God's. Both kinds of loving involve the good. For human loving, this is a good that already exists, or is imagined to exist (i.e., something is perceived to be good but in fact is not). Such real or apparent good elicits the human act of love. God's loving, however, is causal. Good comes to be as the result or term of God's love (see ST I.20). Aquinas secures the point by asking whether God loves the "better" more, that is, what has more good. The answer is yes, but this is not because God perceives a greater good in one sort of being than in another. The human has more good than the squirrel (the example is mine), for the human is capable of what the squirrel can do, but of much more as well. The human can move about locally and can sense, as can the squirrel, but the human is capable as well of willing and discursive thought. God has willed good to both the squirrel and the human; that they exist and exist with their respective natures is due to God's love. But to complete the point, God loves the human more, has willed to the human the greater good of the rational soul.

Creating thus imputes to what is created a high value, although definitely not the ultimate value reserved to God alone. What God makes is good, as God proclaims, and so is to be appreciated for its intrinsic worth. The point is, of course, not surprising in a theologian who belonged to a religious order founded in the first place to combat, through its preaching, Cathar dualists. Yet even some orthodox Christians have had a tendency to play up the spiritual at the expense of the material. Given its intrinsic worth, the material can enter in significant ways into the movement of people to God as end, as is apparent in Aquinas's teaching about the **sacraments** as means of grace, employing as they do material things, and in his insistent incarnational Christology (see *Jesus Christ*), in which he stresses the full reality of Christ's humanity, body as well as soul.

Creation bespeaks the radical dependence of creatures on God. Everything that a creature has and is, is due to God's creative activity. Aquinas conceptualizes the point in terms of the distinction in creatures between essence (what something is) and *esse* (that something is, the act of being of a thing). Both essence and *esse* are granted by God. Aquinas holds firmly as well to a creation *ex nihilo*. There is nothing preexisting on which God might work in creating, giving shape, as it were, to a putative "unformed matter." And so, creation is not a change, as if there were a subject to which something happens. Rather, simply due to God's creative initiative and willing, things come to be.

Creation is an ongoing act. That is, Aquinas does not imagine that creation is a once-for-all event that has occurred in the past, as if God made things, and granted creatures their natures, and then receded from the scene. That things exist and continue to exist is due to God's will, to keep beings in existence.

Creation is purposeful, and the communication of goodness in love is structured by God's wisdom. There are in fact two important points that Aquinas wishes to make in this regard. First, each creature is designed by God to proclaim the goodness of God outside of God, and the whole universe of creatures, each endowed with its God-given nature, proper activity, and natural end, is meant to proclaim what it means to be God outside of God. The creation is not, of course, God, and what is true of God as God—thematized by Aquinas in terms of the denial to God of a real distinction between essence and *esse*—cannot be reproduced outside of God as God is. Yet creatures do resemble God, as intended by God, in their nature, act(s), and end, and so do proclaim this God in their being and activity. Aquinas is sensitive in his theological epistemology to how creatures represent God while falling short of their cause. Second, and even more fundamental, that God creates wisely figures into Aquinas's account of human salvation. There is in fact a profound continuity between creating and saving. God brings rational creatures into existence with the purpose of sharing with them God's own life. In God's wisdom, God intends for rational creatures the special end of life with God in heaven, to which they will come, in God's plan, through their correct response (of affection and action; see *grace*; *theological virtues*; *merit*; *predestination*) to God's call in Christ. Again, Aquinas also invokes God's loving in underscoring the roots of God's saving activity in God's creating. That something exists is due to God's causal love; that something exists as human is due to God's causal love; that a human is called, as to his supernatural end, to God's own life in heaven is due to God's causal love. The expression of this love is sapiential.

Creating can be put in terms of three of Aristotle's four *causes*: God is the efficient, formal, and final cause of the creation. God is the efficient cause, for here God acts, and only God acts; it is God who calls things into being and gives each being its nature, act, and end. God is the final cause of creating, for God creates in order to communicate God's goodness and to share that goodness with what is not God in the measure and mode appropriate to different sorts of creatures. God is the formal cause as well—not as if God were the form of things (God is not, but is always other than what God brings into existence) but as endowing each thing with the form that actualizes it and makes it the sort of thing that it is and as capable of its peculiar activity. Only material causality fails to figure in this account. God is not the material out of which things are made; God creates out of nothing, by God's

causal will purposefully and lovingly expressed.

Finally, but definitely not incidentally, creating according to Aquinas is the action of the triune God, and each of the divine persons exercises its proper causality in the bringing of creatures into being (see *Trinity*). God is the cause of things by God's intellect and will, just as the craftsman is the cause of the things made by his craft. The craftsman works through the word conceived in his mind, and through the love of his will regarding some object. Hence, Aquinas notes, also God the Father makes the creature through his Word, which is his Son, and through his love, which is the Holy Spirit. And so the processions of the persons are the type of the productions of creatures inasmuch as they include the essential attributes, knowledge, and will (ST I.45.6). Thus, as Aquinas says elsewhere, the creation is to be read in light of the Trinity and the activity of the divine persons in bringing things other than God into existence. An especially fine comment to this effect comes at ST I.32.1 ad 3. In response to an objection that had imagined that the Trinity can be established by demonstrative argument (it cannot; see *articles of faith*), Aquinas offers two reasons why the revelation of the Trinity by God was necessary for us. It is the first that concerns us here:

> It was necessary for the right idea of creation. The fact of saying that God made all things by His Word excludes the error of those who say that God produced things by necessity. When we say that in Him there is a procession of love, we show that God produced creatures not because He needed them, nor because of any other extrinsic reason, but on account of the love of His own goodness. So Moses, when he had said, "In the beginning God created heaven and earth," subjoined, "God said, Let there be light," to manifest the divine Word; and then said, "God saw the light that it was good" (Genesis 1:4), to show the proof of the divine love. The same is also found in the other works of creation.

The reference to Genesis serves as a nice reminder of the fundamental inspiration of Aquinas's commitment to and teaching about creation. That Aquinas thinks that some pre-Christian Greek philosophers had a fairly good knowledge of creation seems evident. He ascribes to Aristotle a doctrine of creation that would make God the efficient as well as the final cause of all things, and explicitly notes that when it comes to creation, only by insisting on an eternal creation and supposing that he can demonstrate that (not a creation with a temporal beginning; see *philosophy*) has Aristotle fallen short of Christian teaching. Likewise, Aquinas came to see in Plato a doctrine of creation fairly close to the Christian. Yet neither Aristotle nor Plato could in Aquinas's estimation know the Trinity of persons involved in the bringing into being and sustaining of all that is not God; that knowledge is due to God's revelation in Scripture (see *articles of faith*), as is God's ordering of rational creatures to God's own life, to participation in the beatific vision by which rational creatures enter into the inner life of the triune God. In affirming creation and thinking it out in the kind of detail that he has and seeing its broader implications for God-human relations (as covered elsewhere in the theology), Aquinas would seem to be consistent with what he says about *sacred doctrine* and the hierarchy of *authorities* called upon in explicating and exploring this doctrine. Aristotle can be called upon to help clarify and interpret Christian truth, and he may well have anticipated this doctrine in significant respects. But the starting point and governing insight in Aquinas's account of creation is the revelation in Scripture of the triune God, who creates purposefully and in love.

_____

Te Velde (1995); Burrell (1993); Aertsen (1988); Blankenhorn (2002); Dewan (1991); Emery (1995); Sokolowski (1982); Tanner (1988); Wright (1957); Blanchette (1992); Johnson (1989, 1992).

Creed   *see* **Articles of Faith; (Pseudo-)Athanasian Creed**

Cross   Aquinas's account of *Jesus Christ* is thoroughly incarnational, taking incarnation in two related senses. It is incarnational in that it involves an act of the second person of God. The Word has become human, has taken up everything required for being human (the human body, the human soul). The Word has assumed human nature to itself without loss to itself. Hence, what is true of the Word from eternity—the Word is God, one and the same God as the Father and the Holy Spirit; the Word is a distinct person in the Godhead—remains true in the act of incarnation. Something else comes to be true of the Word as incarnate: The Word is truly human. It is incarnational in a second sense, for the story of Jesus as rendered in the Gospels is the story of the Word as incarnate. The Word is the subject of that story; the person of Jesus is the Word. In retelling the story of Jesus, one must attend to the full reality of Jesus, the Word incarnate. Some things that are said of Jesus have to do with the humanity of the Word as incarnate. Others have to do with the divine personhood, or with the divine nature that is fully and eternally possessed by the Word. The two natures are united in the person of the Word; they are united in a way that they are truly affirmed of the Word, but without confusion. The natures remain in their integrity.

In turning to the passion and death of Jesus (see especially III.48–49), Aquinas is fully attentive to the grammar of the incarnation. For Aquinas, with the *Resurrection*, the *Cross* stands at the core of the story of the Word incarnate, providing the key to the salvific importance of Jesus (see, e.g., *sacrament*). The Word is the subject of the suffering and death, and eventually resurrection, of Jesus. The Word is the subject as fully incarnate, as the bearer of the humanity. Both natures are in fact crucial to the account of Christ's salvific work. In the union of the two natures in the Word that is the person of Jesus, the God who alone can save and those who need the saving are in effect united. The Word is God; the Word incarnate is human, and as human works on our behalf to bring people to God, their end. The divinity of the Word supplies the efficacy of what Jesus does. God is the principal cause of salvation; what God does is of infinite value and effect. But God does not save apart from humans. Rather, in taking up human nature and making that humanity the Word's own, the Word of God has taken up what is the instrument for the working out of salvation (see *instrumental causality*). The Word of God employs the humanity of the Word as the instrument of salvation (III.48.6 ad 3); as the prologue to ST I.2 has made clear, it is Christ as human—that is, the Word as truly human through the incarnation—who is the way for humans to God as end. It is what the fully divine Word does in the flesh that matters for human salvation.

Throughout Christian history, theologians have proposed various ways of accounting for Christ's saving significance. In ST III.48, Aquinas shows himself the beneficiary of earlier Christian reflection on Christ's saving work. Aquinas does not select a single way to depict that work. Rather, in this question he enumerates four ways in which Christ makes human salvation—the reaching of God in heaven, where God will be known face to face (see *beatific vision*)—possible: merit, satisfaction, sacrifice, redemption. By listing four ways rather than one, Aquinas is likely insinuating that no single way is adequate to the mystery of human salvation wrought through Christ, and that a multitude of ways can better render the centrality of Christ in God's plan for humans.

The context of the discussion of Christ's salvific importance is the view of human existence as a journey to God (see *viator*), as that is initiated and sustained by God. God has called human beings into existence and has ordered them to God as their transcendent end. To reach God, one must act, as determined by God, in a morally and supernaturally good way. However, the successful completion of the journey to God requires overcoming great obstacles. Human beings are not God, but are creatures who ontologically fall short of God. If they are to reach that end, they must be elevated, as it were, to God's own level, to the supernatural plane. And, even more tellingly, reaching God as end requires a moral likeness to God, by which one is readied to enter in the next life into the vision of God. But by sin, people have gone off track, insulted God, made themselves prone to more sinning, and made themselves even more unlike God morally. Thus, to reach God as end, both an ontological and a moral gap must be bridged. This is done through *grace*, the grace that both elevates and heals, the grace that is given by God through the death and resurrection of Christ.

Of the four ways discussed in III.48, two have to do directly and exclusively with the overcoming of sin and its effects. Sin establishes a debt before God, for by sinning one withholds from God the goodness and the honor that is attached to morally good action. In acting voluntarily as one should, one renders an acknowledgment to God that God is one's creator and end for whom one should voluntarily act in everything that one does. In sinning, the acknowledgment that should be given by the good act is withheld. Repeated sinning increases the debt, and since the God whom one is offending by sin is of infinite value, the debt that is piled up is infinite. To get right with God, the debt must be paid. But humans cannot pay the debt; they have put themselves in a bind. Every morally good act is meant to give honor to God. Stopping from sinning and doing what is right is a good step, but what about the debt owed for past sins? The problem is that every morally good action is owed to God and its honor is owed to God; by doing the good, one is offering to God the good that is owed for that particular act. People owe the debt but cannot come up with a way, in acts, that might make up the lost honor. God, however, will have God's honor and good restored one way or another. If people will not voluntarily make up the stolen honor—that is, if they will not satisfy—then God will take from them, against their will, honor, and so restore the stolen good in that way. Here, the idea of **death** as the punishment imposed on people for sin is prominent. If there had been no sin, there would have been no death. Sin introduces death, which is imposed to obtain the honor lost through sin. Christ, however, is not in the bind that people have put themselves in through sinning. As Scripture reminds us, Christ was without sin. Moreover, he had the fullness of grace (see ST III.7), and in his human acting and suffering always did what was good, morally and supernaturally. As sinless, he need not have died. That he did die was a voluntary action, a free and loving action, aided by grace, by which he took up the sentence against sinners—death—and underwent that. But since he need not have died, he has in fact done something that is not required, and so his act can be satisfying, not penal (as dying is for sinners). And since he possesses the fullness of grace and the complete charity that goes with that grace, when he voluntarily died, he did so lovingly, and for the sake of God, to fulfill God's will for humans, whom God wants to attain heaven. He did something that could pay a debt. And since he is God, what he does has infinite value. Hence, his action as human was able to pay the full debt owed to God by our sin.

In related fashion, by sin people have sold themselves into bondage to the **devil**. The devil had induced (but not compelled) the fall (see **original sin**) and continues to tempt people to sin (see **temptation**). By giving in to the devil, people have sold themselves short (see **fittingness**, with reference to ST III.1.2c) and have been put, in a sense, in bondage to the devil. As had Anselm before him, Aquinas denies that redemption, which

is also aimed at overcoming sin, means paying a debt to the devil, as a ransom. The devil's rights are secondary, only there, such as they are, because people have acted against God, have fallen into the trap of sin, which inclines them to more sin and makes them prone to accede to the devil's prompting. God, to whom alone people belong, even when people do not acknowledge this subjection by sinning against God's will, permits the devil to tempt and so to exercise some "right" over the sinner. But when Christ, the God become human, dies for sin, he both pays the debt owed to God (satisfaction) and redeems fallen people from bondage to sin and therefore the devil by giving to God what God seeks: the morally good act that in his case is of infinite significance. Whatever claim on the human that the devil may have is thereby ended, because, more importantly, the guilt of sin is removed and the human is put right before God (ST III.48.4–5).

The first of the ways mentioned in ST III.48 (a.1) for figuring Christ's salvific importance, merit, is not directly aimed at sin and its effects. **Merit** is the establishment of a right to a reward from God. One does something, and in return a reward is owed in justice. As Aquinas makes clear in his *ex professo* treatment of merit (in ST I-II.114), there can strictly speaking be no justice between humans and God. Justice presupposes an equality, and between humans and God there is the ontological gap. But God has ordained that the acts done by the person in grace will be treated by God as deserving of a reward from God. In terms of Christ, then, in affirming his merit, Aquinas insists that Christ's good actions as human, including his dying on the cross, are meritorious because they are done in grace, thus fulfilling this requirement for merit. By grace, and by the charity that follows on grace, what Christ as human does is done freely and voluntarily and in full love of God; hence, on the basis of the divine ordination, Christ's actions deserve reward from God, a reward that Christ can pass on to those who need it. And again, since Christ is God, what the Word incarnate does is of infinite value; by his loving death on our behalf, Christ has established the right to heaven, to the great reward that God seeks to give to those called to God as end.

The final way of figuring Christ's work, sacrifice, would seem to work both ways, that is, as overcoming the gulf caused by sin and, in the more positive way, as in meriting. Sacrifice involves an offering up of something holy to one who is worthy of such offering. In the sacrifice of the cross, Christ, our priest (see ST III.22), has voluntarily offered up the sacrifice of greatest value, himself, and has done so in order to please God. In terms of sin and its overcoming, this sacrifice can be said to appease God by offering, instead of our sins and as a remedy for them, the pure and good and valued life that Christ possesses. And as offered in the fullness of grace and charity, this sacrifice, this good act, also is pleasing to God.

"Every action of Christ is for our instruction" (*Omnis Christi actio nostra est instructio*). What Christ does, so should his followers. Christ shows us how to live, in loving obedience to the will of the Father. This idea is inserted into the heart of Aquinas's ecclesiology (see *church*), which is construed as the mystical body of Christ. Christ is the head of this body, and those who come to Christ and take up his cross are his members. They are alive, joined to Christ by their faith and charity and by the grace of the Holy Spirit given to them by their head. The head shows his members how they should live if they are to come to God through Christ. Thus, just as he did, so should they merit and satisfy and offer sacrifice. There is, of course, much that separates his acting and that of his members. He is God, become human, become innocent human full of grace and charity, and so what he does is of the greatest value. And the sequence, for Aquinas, must be observed. It makes no

sense to talk of other humans meriting or truly sacrificing or satisfying apart from, or prior to, Christ. His work must precede, and his work in fact settles the issue; by his work, and his alone, things are set right for people before God and the gates of heaven are opened (see, e.g., ST III.49.5). But to benefit from Christ's work, one must be joined to him, become his disciple, and strive to emulate him. Christ's grace makes possible new action, action that as good can bring one into greater conformity with Christ. Or, to put it from another angle, talk of merit or satisfaction for the Christian will always be derivative. It is Christ's whose merits and satisfaction make salvation possible. Any merit or satisfying or sacrifice that the Christian does, as part of the movement through Christ to God as end, will always be secondary and dependent, rendered possible by Christ's great acts on our behalf and showing that one in fact is striving to grow through Christ into God.

Catao (1965); Lynn (1962); de Margerie (1983); Patfoort (1993); Bracken (1985); Hoogland (2003); Cessario (1982).

Death   The human being is a composite substance, made up of soul and body (see *anthropology*). For Aquinas, following Aristotle, the soul is the form of the body. There is a single soul for a human being, with many powers, from the nutritive through the sensitive to the rational. It is the one soul that actualizes body and makes this being alive and human, a point that Aquinas makes against theologians of a Platonist persuasion, who imagine many psychic forms in the human, including one that makes the human, human (ST I.76.3–4). For a human being, death involves the separation of soul from the body of which it is the form. In terms of a question that was much discussed in the thirteenth century, this means that strictly speaking there is not for Aquinas a numerical identity between the body of the living human and the dead; a body that ceases to be living is not the same as the living body. At the end of time, however, body and soul will be reunited, and the body, raised to its perfection, will come to share in the beatitude of the entire human person (see *eschatology*).

Moderns have a tendency to think of mortality as part of being human, a notion that they share with pre-Christian philosophers. To be human in this view means to be mortal, which in this telling is an essential aspect of human nature. Aquinas's position, in continuity with the Christian theological tradition, is more nuanced. Physical dying is not entirely unnatural, although it is not to be placed in the definition of the human; dying is primarily penal, a punishment imposed for sin. This becomes clear in Aquinas's discussion of the original state, that is, the state in which human beings were first created, and prior to the fall (see *original justice*). The first human was also a composite substance. The soul, created by God and infused by God, is immortal; the body is corruptible, and so can dissolve, as can the union of the two. But the first people were made in grace, and among other things, this grace stayed the tendency to corruption that is natural to a material thing (the body). If the first people had not sinned, the human person would have been confirmed in this grace. The body would not corrupt; the body-soul composite would not dissolve. In short, if there had been no sin, there would have been no physical death. Rather, people, confirmed in grace, would have been elevated to the state that is now promised to the blessed: a raising to God's own life, in which the human composite, body and soul, will share. But people did sin, and so people die, as the just punishment for the refusal to keep God's will (ST I-II.85.5).

This teaching about death as primarily penal, and as not essential to being human, has profound christological implications. In the first place, Jesus was fully human. But that does not require that he die; only if dying were essential to being human, which it is not, would Jesus have had to die, as the rest of us do. Jesus was sinless, as Scripture informs us, and so he was not subject to the punishment of dying. That he does die marks his free, voluntary acceptance of what pertains to the rest of us, as sinners (III.14.1). And so his death, purely voluntary, can come to have an importance for the rest of us (see *cross*).

Aquinas's teaching about the unicity of substantial form—that is, that there is only one soul in the human, not a multiplicity of souls, including one that is the form of the human—was highly controversial during his life and after. The teaching was attacked on many fronts, including in the discussion of the *Triduum Sacrum*. Was the body in the tomb numerically the same as that of Jesus while alive? For a theologian of Platonist leanings, the answer would be easy, for while life has ceased, the form that makes a human human has remained; thus, there is the desired identity. But doesn't Aquinas's teaching mean that there is no numerical identity of Jesus' body, as alive and then as dead? Aquinas returns repeatedly to the topic in his writings, including in *Quodlibet* IV, q.5 (1271) and ST III.50.5. In his response to the criticism, he makes a fundamental distinction between what is the case "in a certain respect" and what is the case "absolutely." In terms of the former, there is not a numerical identity between Jesus' body dead and alive; what holds for all people after the separation of the one soul from the body of which it is the form also holds for Jesus. But with regard to what is the case absolutely, there is an identity that is proper to Jesus. Here Aquinas calls on his teaching about *hypostatic union*. In the act of incarnation, there has been a union of two natures in one person. The Word of God, who from eternity is a distinct person in God and one and the same God as the Father and the Holy Spirit (and so fully possessed of the divine nature), has in the act of incarnation taken up human nature and come to express that as well, without loss to itself as fully divine Word. The human nature in the case of Jesus is the human nature of the Word; the Word has become human, has taken up what is essential to being human—the human body and the human soul—and made these its own. As with other humans, dying does mean the separation of soul from body. But in the case of Jesus, the hypostatic union remains in effect. The body from which the soul has been separated remains the body of the Word, who continues in union with the separated body; the soul that has been separated from the body continues to be the soul of the Word. Hence, simply and absolutely, the body in the tomb continues to be the body of Jesus when alive; the identity is provided by the Word.

_____

De Margerie (1983); Zimmermann (1992).

Devil   The devil and other fallen angels appear at different points in Aquinas's theology. They are discussed first at the end of the treatise on angels (ST I.50–64, at qq.63–64). Aquinas returns to them and the other (good) angels in his account of divine government, which is the execution of divine providence (I.103–19, especially at qq.109, 114). He then refers to them in the treatment of *temptation* and *original sin*, in the Second Part of the ST (I-II and II-II), when talking of people in general. Finally, the devil will figure in the reflection on Jesus Christ in the ST's Third Part: in III.41, when focusing on Christ and his temptation; in III.48–49, when discussing the effects of the *cross* and the complicity of different agents in putting Christ to death (see, e.g., q.49.2; 48.4–5); and in III.8, as a counterpoint to the presentation of Christ as head of the *church*. As is the case with the reflections on the *angels* in general, in his approach to the devil and the fallen angels Aquinas is governed by the scriptural witness, which proclaims the existence and activ-

ity of angels, good and bad, although he draws as well on non-Christian reasoning about spiritual substances in his presentation. Aquinas is convinced that the fallen angels do exist—they are not, in other words, mere projections of human anxiety and self-incrimination, or mere symbols of evil—and that they are forces to be dealt with as people endeavor to attain to God as their end.

The story of the devil begins with the creation of the angels and their call to eternal life, to enter directly into God's presence and to become like God, by knowing and loving God as God knows and loves God. Such an end transcends the natural capacities of the angels, impressive as these are; only by grace could they attain to this transcendent end. All angels were made in grace, and so all angels had the possibility of attaining to this end. In Aquinas's reckoning, most angels used this grace and so willed properly; they willed God as their end, to be attained as God willed them to attain God, by grace. Such angels were confirmed in grace and their end; that confirmation is irrevocable and final, for in willing, the angels willed God fully. Other angels, however, did not will out of grace. They misused their will and so lost their grace. For Aquinas, the fall of the angels anticipates that of humans; in both cases, there is the sin of pride (I.63.2; II-II.163.1). These angels wanted to be like God but wanted to attain this by their natural powers, not by grace. They rejected the grace in which they had been made, in the effort to make themselves, by themselves, like God. This use of will is final and irrevocable; these angels have rejected God, and they have done so decisively. They are forever apart from God, confirmed in their malice.

In this fall, one of the angels, of the highest stature, led the way. In his example of pride, he induced (but did not compel) other angels to similarly overreach (I.63.8). This is the fallen angel that can be designated "the devil."

The sin of pride leads, in turn, to the sin of envy. The fallen angels are jealous of God and do not want God to be acknowledged as the God who is the end of those whom God has called into existence. And these angels are envious of human beings, who have been called, as they were, to God as end. Thus, the fallen angels do all that they can to disrupt and prevent the movement of humans to God. No angel can work inwardly on a human; the inward moving of the person is reserved to God, as in *grace*. But the fallen angels are clever and zealous in their envy, and draw on their considerable resources to tempt people away from God and to sin. Aquinas insists on the ingenuity of the devil in his detailed accounts of the temptation of Adam (II-II.165) and then of Jesus (III.41). In both cases, the devil started out slowly in the temptation and then worked up to more serious temptation that addressed these spiritual men at their strengths. In the case of Adam, the series of temptations was successful: Adam succumbed to the temptation to move away from God by rejecting the grace in which he had been created in favor of lesser goods suggested to him by the devil. In the case of the second Adam, the temptations were just as clever, but were rebuffed by the Jesus who is the moral exemplar (see *Omnis Christi actio nostra est instructio*) and who shows all people what they should do when tempted, namely, reject the devil, by acting out of the grace that perfects their nature. The tempting by the fallen angels continues after the human fall; in a fallen world, human beings, born into original sin, are bombarded by temptation. In addition to those that come from the fallen angels, other temptations come from within the person, the fruit as it were of the successful tempting at the head of human history that cast the race into misery. In this tempting, the fallen angels need not be successful. They cannot compel sin; they can only suggest sin. Succumbing to sin is a human achievement. Sinning in a fallen world is that much more likely, once sin has entered the scene through the human

fall. Temptation can be overcome through the correct use of the will, itself made possible by grace. As for God, God does not tempt. God permits temptation, permits such testing of human beings. Those who fail the test will receive what they deserve. Those who overcome the devil by resisting temptation and doing the good, with God's grace, that God seeks, will make it to eternal life.

In III.8, Aquinas presents the heart of his ecclesiology. The church is the body of Christ, comprised of all those who are joined to Christ their head by their faith and charity. To those who would follow him, Christ gives his Spirit, who renders the members capable of faith and charity and of growing in conformity to their head. At the end of the question (aa.7–8), Aquinas ponders whether there is a like congregation that would have another head. What about the wicked, that is, those who reject God in favor of themselves? Do they form a body? The head of that body is the devil, who has succeeded in directing those who belong to this head away from God as end and to their eternal damnation. The parallel between the two heads is only partial, however; while the fallen angels can only suggest sin but not make people act against their will, by the giving of his Spirit, Christ not only leads his members to eternal life but works inwardly in them, moving them to the acts that bring the people of God to God as their end.

Foster (1967), appendix 2.

Doctors of the Church

Aquinas's theology is highly learned. He read extensively and in a wide range of genres, and he brought his prodigious learning to bear in the construction of a distinctive theology. Chief among his sources is *Scripture*, which he encountered in private reading and in liturgical practice throughout his life, but also in his professional work as a scholastic *theologian*. The scholastic theologian, after all, was technically a master of the sacred page, and the textbook for scholastic lecturing was the Bible. In his reading of Scripture and his own attempt to plumb the riches and interconnections of the different aspects of the scriptural message, Aquinas was much aided by the writings of the church fathers, themselves concerned with the faithful interpretation of God's word in Scripture. As in ST I.1.8 ad 2, Aquinas was aware that different sorts of writing had different status and different authority in theological work (see *authority*). That of Scripture stands at the apex, for in Scripture God has revealed saving truth and has done so in a way that the human authors of Scripture could not be mistaken (see ST I.1.9 ad 2). It is indubitably what God intends that the scriptural authors have passed on. Next in authority are the writings of the church fathers who have been deemed by the church to be "doctors," that is, teachers who are learned and skilled in the interpretation of the material that is most important for the church and so worthy of the respect of the church. Accordingly, while recognizing the difference between Scripture and postscriptural Christian reflection on Scripture, Aquinas makes considerable, and respectful, use of the writings of the Fathers in the construction of his own teaching. He quotes the Fathers liberally to help him advance a theology that with theirs is concerned with the informed proclamation, investigation, and where need be, defense of God's saving truth, as revealed in Scripture.

Aquinas's contact with the Fathers took two forms. First, he learned the Fathers through quotation in more recent works. In lecturing on the Bible, whether in the cursory lectures of the bachelor or the more sophisticated lectures of the master, the scholastic employed a glossed Bible, the *Glossa ordinaria*, a work that achieved relatively stable form over the course of the twelfth century. In the *Gloss*, alongside the biblical words were comments drawn from the Fathers to explicate the biblical teaching. These comments were of various lengths, and could be placed in the text (interlinear) or in the margins. The recognition of the value of the Fathers for grasping the biblical teaching did not elevate them to equal status with the Bible. In format, there was a clear differentiation between the biblical words, put in larger script and centrally located on the page, and the glosses, put in smaller script and perhaps in different color ink. Through the gloss, a scholastic could win a nice acquaintance with the teaching of prominent earlier, Western Christian writers on specific passages. Also important for gaining acquaintance with patristic teaching was the *Sentences* of Peter Lombard, a twelfth-century work that quite early in the thirteenth century took on an important role in the training of the scholastic theologian (see *Scriptum on the Sentences*). The *Sentences* are rife with patristic quotations, illustrating specific theological issues. Especially prominent here is Augustine, who is cited over a thousand times, often at considerable length. Through the *Sentences*, one gained a good sense of the Western patristic heritage.

Yet learning through intermediaries is not an entirely satisfactory thing, especially if that is the sole way that one encounters the Christian past. In compilations, one is dependent on the accuracy of the reporting and quoting; one is also dependent on the range of reading of the compiler. Aquinas in fact was not content with the compilation for his knowledge of the Fathers. There is considerable evidence of his interest in reading patristic works in their integrity, and not simply as conveyed through others. Indeed, his own historical research, especially in the years in Italy between his two Parisian regencies, discloses his keen interest in a direct encounter with the early church fathers. He made important discoveries in those years of works that had passed out of general theological circulation. He made good use of those writings in his own; indeed, those writings helped to transform his teachings on grace and on Christ.

The first discovery has to do with Augustine. At the end of his career, Augustine had written against Christians who in later Christian history have come to be called "semi-Pelagians." They were not full-fledged Pelagians because they allowed a significant role for grace. But they taught that the first step on the path to God must be due to human initiative; it lies within the power of one who lacks grace to do something that will impress God with one's religious seriousness; in response to that first step to God, God, in their telling, will give grace. For Augustine, the huge problem with this analysis of how one gets grace in the first place is its naiveté about sin. The teaching would work if humans, after sin had entered history, were still relatively good. Then they could take the first step to God and so get the grace that would help them the rest of the way to God as end. But humans are born into a condition of sin, and original sin so binds the will that in its exercise, the person bereft of grace will only sin. Hence, in asking of people a first step to God, to get grace, his opponents are asking for what is impossible, given original sin and the actual sins that follow on the sinful inclination to sin provided by original sin. Actually, Augustine's teaching against the semi-Pelagians goes further. In the course of his earlier dispute with Pelagius, Augustine had articulated a teaching on predestination, taken in a causal sense. God has a plan and God works out the plan, through grace. Against Pelagius, Augustine had taught a predestination to conversion. Why does someone move away from sin and into grace? Because that is what God has planned for that person, and God executes the plan by a grace of conversion. Against the semi-Pelagians, the scope of predestination is extended; it is not to conversion but to eternal life, and the execution of the plan comes through operative graces that work conversion and perseverance in grace. Without the grace of conversion, there is no conversion, only a bondage to sin; with-out the grace of perseverance, there is no staying in grace, but instead a lapse back into sin. Both graces work out God's predestining will.

These late writings of Augustine, constituting his final teaching on predestination and grace, had, however, passed out of general theological circulation in the medieval West, at some point in the Carolingian period. The teaching on grace in the *Sentences* is bereft of mention of these works, sticking to what could be found in earlier writings of Augustine. Thirteenth-century theologians also were silent about these writings. This includes the early Aquinas, who in his own *Scriptum* on the Lombard's *Sentences* in fact offers a teaching about conversion that is reminiscent of the late Augustine's opponents. Conversion is due to human initiative (see *Facienti quod in se est*), and perseverance is no big problem. Once in grace, one can stay in grace by using it wisely. But while back in Italy in the 1260s, Aquinas did in fact come across these late Augustinian writings and refined his teaching accordingly. As in the ST (I-II.109ff.), Aquinas insists that conversion and perseverance are not human accomplishments but are worked by God in the person by operative graces (see *grace*); these operative graces are given by God in accordance with God's predestining will.

Aquinas's Christology also reveals the importance of his personal research into the patristic heritage. The early disputes about Christ were conducted in Greek, and the ecclesial determinations about Christ, as at the ecumenical councils, were likewise in Greek. Very early in the Middle Ages, the acts of the early ecumenical councils, along with considerable supporting documentation, were translated into Latin and so in principle available to Western theologians constructing their Christologies. Again, however, such material in Latin translation had passed out of general theological circulation, with the result that theologians proceeded in ignorance of the precise form of the early disputes, as well as of the precise determinations of the ecumenical councils. Early in the 1260s, however, Aquinas had come across this material in Latin translation, with major consequences for his own Christology. First signs of this are in the *ScG*, where he shows a close acquaintance with the history (mostly early, mostly Greek) of Christology and an awareness that christological disputes, as well as conciliar resolutions, were principally over the correct interpretation of Scripture (IV.27ff.). The full effect of this rediscovery is found, however, in the Third Part of the ST, with its rich and copious patristic, Greek and Latin, documentation. In reading from the early ecumenical councils, Aquinas was able to come to distinctive assessment of the Christologies reported by the Lombard in his own third book (see d.6). There, Peter notes that in talking about how the divine and human come together in Christ, his contemporaries offered three opinions. One is the *homo assumptus* teaching, in which a human is taken up into union with the second divine person, with the result being that what is said of the one can be said of the other, and vice versa. Another is the composite person teaching, which holds that the second divine person, who from eternity is a distinct person in God and one and the same God as the Father and the Holy Spirit, without loss to itself takes up a second nature and comes to express that as well. The third opinion reported by the Lombard is the *habitus* theory, which states that the Word takes up the parts of human nature (body, soul) and puts them on, as one would put on clothing. In his *Scriptum*, Aquinas disallows the *habitus* theory because of a later twelfth-century conciliar decision against it. But the other two are "opinions," as the Lombard said, although Aquinas has a strong preference for the second, the composite person theory, as more adequate to the reality of Christ. But by his later writings, he can express himself more forcefully, and does so on the basis of his expanded

reading in the Fathers. From his closer study of the early councils and his keener awareness of what was at stake in the dispute, say, between Cyril and Nestorius, it is clear that the second opinion is not an opinion, but orthodox teaching; it is equally clear that the other two opinions are not opinion but lapses (unwittingly, he allows) of the later masters into teachings long ago condemned by the church meeting in council (ST III.2.6c; see also *ScG* IV.37–38). In effect, through his personal researches, stressing the reading of works in their integrity, Aquinas was attempting to bring scholastic theology into even greater conformity with the patristics, by expanding the repertoire of authorities at the disposal of the scholastics.

Bouillard (1944); Wawrykow (1993); Backes (1931); Bataillon (1993); Elders (1997); Geenen (1946, 1952); Principe (1976); O'Rourke (1992).

Epistemology, Theological The treatise on *God* in the First Part of the ST is divided into two related parts. In the first (qq.2–26), the focus is on the unity of the divine essence, looking in turn at God's existence (q.2), the divine essence, or rather, what God is not (qq.3–11), and the divine operations (qq.14–26), both immanent and those that proceed to an exterior effect. In the second part of the treatise, the focus shifts to the *Trinity* (qq.27–43). Throughout, the subject matter is the Christian God, proclaimed by faith. Into the midst of the first part of his treatise on God, Aquinas has inserted two questions on the human knowing and naming of God (qq.12–13). The second is dependent on the first: We name things as we know them. There are a multitude of names that Christians have for God, a number of claims that Christians make about their God. On what basis are these different names asserted and how are they said of God? At first glance, qq.12–13 might seem out of place. A more modern ordering might put those considerations at the beginning of the treatise or prior to it. Before talking about God, one would more reasonably ask how one knows God and to what extent one can be said to know God, and similarly investigate the connection between names of God and the knowledge of God. And then, in a more modern ordering, one would turn to the existence, essence, and operations of God, and finally to the Trinity, having made clear how far the knower can go given her innate capacities, and how far one is dependent on grace, on God's self-revelation. On further reflection, however, Aquinas's actual ordering has a certain plausibility. As inserted where they are, qq.12–13 have the effect of summarizing the practice in which Aquinas has in fact been engaged from q.2 on; those earlier questions give resonance to his explicit comments in these questions on knowing and naming. In those earlier questions, Aquinas was much concerned to differentiate God from the world. His God is the God who brings things into existence. As God's, the world can be thought to resemble God, on whom the things of the world are patterned. Yet no created effect will be commensurate with its creator. The effects that resemble God fall short of God, and so every effort must be made to make clear that the world is not God and that God is not to be reduced to the things of the world. The cause of all, while intimately involved in the world and present to it, transcends it. Hence the observation in explaining the project of qq.3–11: He will be discussing the divine essence, or rather, what God is not. In those questions, Aquinas will show resolutely how God differs from the world. Questions 12–13 restate the point succinctly, and make clear what has been involved in Aquinas's practice in those questions. At the same time, qq.12–13 advance Aquinas's project by being even more explicit about what is involved in talking about God.

Most of q.12 is given over to the knowledge of God in the next life (see *beatific vision*). At that time, those who have successfully navigated the present life and lived in accordance with God's will, will attain to the direct vision of God. Then they will know God face to face, and come to know the essence of God. Throughout these articles (aa.1–10), there is an implicit contrast with what is possible in the present life. Can one know the essence of God in this life? Questions 3–11 have prepared us well for the answer. One does not know the essence of God in this life, and one must remove from God anything creaturely, which would bespeak imperfection and so be inappropriate of the Christian God. But in the next life, God will raise those who have come to God to a new state; gifted with a light (of glory), they will see God as God is. In the final articles of q.12, Aquinas then turns explicitly to the knowledge of God that is possible in the present life, here making good use of his sense of God as creator (as indicated above). What is made by God looks like God, although it falls short of God. The creator God is not to be confused with the things of this world. Hence, as in a.12 of q.12, Aquinas asserts that God can be known, through creaturely effects, to exist, and that there is a resemblance between creaturely effects and the God who creates them but that this resemblance is wholly insufficient to render knowledge of the divine essence. The essence of God transcends our present capacity to know.

In q.13, Aquinas turns to the names that are affirmed of God; these names are revealed in Scripture, although some were also proclaimed by those who lacked scriptural revelation, attained through the sustained use of reason by arguing from effects to God (see *preambles of faith; sacred doctrine*). A good portion of q.13 is devoted to the classification of these names. Some will have to do with removing from God something inappropriate to God (see *negative theology*), by denying to God something that pertains to creaturely existence. Other names will testify to God as cause, as the cause of perfections in creatures. But are there any names that pertain to the divine essence? If we name things according to our knowledge of them, it would seem not, at first glance. Aquinas insists that people do not know the essence of God in this life; how then could any name apply to the divine essence? In fact, some who have reflected on the matter have argued that even names that seem to bespeak perfections (not explicit creaturely deficiencies) in truth are to be taken negatively, as denying to God something inappropriate. Others have suggested that there are only two categories of names given to God: one, negative, the other, having to do with God as cause. Thus, in saying that God is good, one would be saying that God is the cause of goodness in creatures, and leave it at that. Aquinas, however, does think that there is a third category of names. In addition to names that indicate remotion, or naming God as cause, he thinks that names that refer to perfections do affirm truthfully of God and of the divine essence. "God is good" means more than God is the cause of goodness. It is not that God is good because God causes goodness. God is good and therefore causes goodness. Such perfections exist in God prior to their communication to creatures, and they preexist in God in a supereminent way, differing from what is found in creatures.

In his discussion of names said of God that pertain to the divine essence, Aquinas negotiates a middle path, between those who would say that such names are used of God and creatures univocally, and those who say that such names are used equivocally. In equivocal predication, the same term would be used but would mean completely different things as used of different beings. In univocal predication, the term means exactly the same as used of different subjects. Univocity is excluded because this would be to reduce God to a thing of this world, to be talked about in exactly the same way that one talks about a creature.

But perfections found in creatures must exist in a supereminent way in the source of all perfections. Equivocal predication is excluded because this would be to deny the resemblance between creatures and the One who has brought them into being. Hence, in charting a middle path, Aquinas refers to analogical predication; there is continuity between the perfection term as used of a creature and of God, but not exact identity. In some respects, the claim as about God differs from the claim as about a creature. The perfection found in the creature exists in a preeminent way in God. In teasing out this middle position, Aquinas makes good use of the distinction between the *res significata* and the *modus significandi*, between the thing (perfection) signified and the manner of signifying it. In this regard, Aquinas notes two different sequences. One has to do with how we come to know a perfection; this is first through creatures, and only then is the perfection affirmed of the God in whom the perfection originates and exists supereminently. The other underscores that what is found in creatures in fact originates in God and so exists first in God. Thus, to use the language of *modus/res*, the *res* first exists in God and does so in a supereminent way. The *res* is in God in a way appropriate to God. Since we do not in this life know the divine essence, we do not know the mode of being of the perfection as in God; we do know, however, that the perfection is in God. In terms of the *modus*, we know the perfection as it is in the creature. That mode of being is not the mode of being in God. Hence, the perfection is affirmed of the creature according to its mode of being and our perception of the perfection in that being. The perfection is affirmed of God according to the divine mode of being, to which, however, we have no direct access. By analogical predication, the perfection is affirmed of both God and the creature, first of God and then of the creature; the perfection is affirmed of each according to the mode of being of each, which is not the same. We know the affirmation of God to be true, but do not grasp how the perfection is in God.

Aquinas's teaching about analogy has been subjected to severe criticism. Does it in fact steer a middle course? Some have suspected that it is simply univocal predication but by another name. If the same concept is applied to different beings, there must be something in that concept that holds true of these different beings, that is, a univocal core to a perfection term. However, it would appear that in this teaching, analogy is a matter of judgment, of making claims about different sorts of being. In the making of these claims, as suggested by the *modus/res* distinction, one will have to attend to the different ways of being of those of whom perfection claims are made. "God is good" and "This human is good" are claims that stand in continuity; the goodness of the human is patterned on that of God. But there is a crucial difference between the two claims, inasmuch as one is made of a creature and the other of the transcendent source of all things, whose existence and essence are not to be reduced to what we meet in the things of this world.

Rocca (2004); Burrell (1979, 1986); McInerny (1996).

Eschatology The ST was to have concluded with an account of the end things. As Aquinas envisioned the Third Part of the ST, eschatological considerations would have followed the treatment of Christ (qq.1–59) and of the sacraments (qq.60ff.). However, Aquinas gave up writing in December 1273, breaking off the ST at III.90, in the midst of the discussion of penance. His secretary subsequently compiled what is commonly called the "Supplement" to the ST, out of his other writings. But while we lack a treatise on the end things in the ST from Aquinas himself, he devoted considerable attention to eschatology in other writings, and the main lines of his teach-

ing can be gathered from these. Hence, following the Lombard's lead, in his *Scriptum on the Sentences*, distinctions 43 through 50 of the Fourth Book consider in turn the principal points of eschatology (and the Supplement to the ST as it deals with the end things is in the main taken from the *Scriptum*). So too, in the *ScG* (IV.79–97), Aquinas looks at the end, and here, as in the *Scriptum*, he is concerned to do justice to the New Testament teachings on the topic as mediated by the succeeding Christian traditions. As occasion warrants, Aquinas will enter into reflections on the end in the biblical commentaries, as in the lectures devoted to 1 Corinthians 15. In his homilies on the Apostles' Creed (see, e.g., *Collationes Credo in Deum* XIV–XV), he also presents his understanding of the end in straightforward, accessible fashion, all the while rooting his proclamation in the scriptural accounts. In sum, even absent a treatise in the ST on the end, Aquinas's views can be retrieved from the corpus as a whole.

In actual fact, even the ST is a rich source of information on the main lines of Aquinas's teaching in eschatology. Aquinas conceptualizes the Christian faith in terms of the calling into existence of all being, and the calling of some beings, rational creatures, to union with God, to entry into the life of knowing and loving God directly that is proper to God. This is the end of human existence, its point and goal, as freely and graciously established by God. In proceeding through the main topics of theology, Aquinas will therefore keep prominent God's gracious calling of humans to God as their end, and show how this end, freely established as gift of God, provides the point, the final meaning, to the various things considered in theology: the activities of God in the world, the activity of the God become human who is Christ, and the activity of the human person who responds to God's calling in Christ and lives out of the appropriate virtues (see *theological virtues*) in moving to God as end. In doing the work of the *theologian*, in considering God and all things with respect to God, Aquinas will always remember what is the ultimate purpose of the human journey (see *viator; beatific vision*) as established and promoted by God in Christ.

Aquinas's teaching in eschatology can be distinguished into three parts: what he says about the final state, when the human person will, finally and irrevocably, have reached the end to which his affections and activities in the present life have inclined him; the role of Christ in the realization of the final state; and the intermediate state, between the end of life in this world and the attainment of the final state, which some who will at last reach God as their end must first undergo.

In describing the final state of those who will in fact enter into God's own life as the term of their journey, Aquinas notes the following.

Eternal life is a reward as well as a gift. It is principally a gift, for it presupposes that God has loved the rational creature in a special way, willing to some rational creatures the end which is God (see *creation*). Thus, entry into eternal life marks the term of a process that is initiated and sustained by God's causal love, creative of all of the good in the person's life. But God has also made provisions for *merit* and so for eternal life as reward. Journey in this world can be distinguished into two states, one in which the person lacks grace and the other in which the person exists in grace. The movement from nongrace into grace is gift, pure and simple. God moves the person away from sin and toward God; God converts the person. Staying in the state of grace will require the unmerited grace of perseverance. But God has also ordained that the good acts issuing from grace and the theological virtues will be meritorious of the end to which the person aspires. Thus, given this ordination, what the graced person does is deserving of the end to which the person will come in the next life (ST I.23.5c).

Eternal life involves the whole human person, body as well as soul. In his *anthropology*, Aquinas rejects versions of the human that would reduce the human person to soul alone (see ST I.75.4, where he rejects the claim that the soul alone is "the man"). Body as well as soul is essential to being human, and the body as well as the soul has been involved in the journey of the person in this life to the end set for humans by God. Hence, it is fitting that the body participate in eternal life with God.

In describing the heavenly state, Aquinas refers to what the soul, and then the body, comes to experience by virtue of completing the journey to God. In terms of soul, a typical characterization of eternal life—as "beatific vision"—tells us much. As the term of the journey, the soul enters into direct contemplation of God; the faith of the journey here yields to direct vision. Hence, what was believed—about God, about God's workings to bring the person to the end through Christ (see *articles of faith*)—is now known. In this direct knowing of God, the deepest instincts of the human person come to their fruition and rest. People desire to know; by the gift of God and God's supernatural ordering, the end of the human person is to know God. Thus, when the person comes into the immediate presence of God and knows God face to face, the person as a knower is fulfilled, and radically; in this knowing, God comes to shape—finally, eternally, and irrevocably—the human person. In turn, we love what is known, and so in this immediate and intense knowing, the love that has driven the person on the journey itself comes to its highest, fullest, and final pitch. The human before God is confirmed in the orientation to the good that has propelled the journey; the vision, with its attendant love and joyfulness and satiation, will be never ending. The person is now joined forever to God.

Beatific vision fills the soul, but it also has a dramatic impact on the body. There is an overflow, as it were, from the soul, in its enjoyment in contemplation, to the body. With the tradition, Aquinas can speak of four endowments (*dotes*) of the body that come to it in eternal life, by virtue of the soul's contemplation, directly, of God. These are clarity, invulnerability, agility, and subtlety. Through the ascription of these endowments, Aquinas proclaims the final transformation of the body of the blessed in a way that is appropriate to the body and to the greatness of the gift of God's immediate presence. Thus, by *clarity* he is saying that the body is granted a transcendent beauty that mirrors that of the soul, both of which are due to God's presence to the person and each of which, in its own way, shows the beauty of God. By *agility* and *subtlety*, he is suggesting that the beatified body takes on a style and a grace that is befitting heaven, while also indicating that the body at this point is irrevocably fully subordinate to soul and in full agreement, as it were, about the end and the enjoyment of the end. And by asserting *invulnerability*, Aquinas can say that the body is no longer corruptible but is instead immune to passing away or suffering diminution; it no longer can suffer harm. While the language of *dotes* may sound arcane, as such texts as *ScG* IV.86 and *Collationes Credo* XIV make clear, the teaching itself is offered as a reading of Scripture on the final state.

That the body participates in eternal life, and that the body that is glorified is identifiably the same as that of the person in the present life, also means that for Aquinas heaven is a place and not simply a spiritual state; body retains its dimensionality, and the human person who is beatified is in a specific place.

In putting the final state as the completion of a journey, Aquinas can nicely underscore the continuity between the present and the future life, although the fulfillment itself marks a transcendence over the present state. There are ways, however, that the life of the beatified self will differ from the earthly self. For one thing, there will be neither food nor sexual activity in heaven (*ScG* IV.83). Aquinas can support this position by reference to specific Scripture texts (on the matter of sexual activity, e.g., see Matt. 22:30, cited at *ScG* IV.83.13). But he also is convinced of the wisdom of such cessation. Food in this life is needed to replace what is lost through exertion, but in the next life there will be no loss, and hence no need for food to allow for a restocking of the body. As for sexual activity, it is geared to procreation, and that has the end of maintaining the species. But entry into heaven means eternal life, and that for the individual; hence, there is no danger to the species of passing out of existence and so no need for sexual activity. Aquinas does address some doubts about both food and sex. Didn't the risen Jesus eat (*ScG* IV.83.16)? And since Jesus' raising is the model for ours (see below), doesn't that mean that his followers too will rise, and to a life in which they too will eat? As for sexual activity, there is pleasure associated with it; if eternal life is to bring full enjoyment, why not imagine a scenario in which people engage in sex for the sheer pleasure? Aquinas finds neither objection especially compelling. The risen Jesus ate to attest the reality of his being and to confirm the truth of his human nature; in heaven, no one will contest the genuine existence or humanness of those who are in the presence of God. And Aquinas is in no mood to view sexual activity in terms of simply pleasure. Rather, that there is pleasure attached to sex is for the purpose of making the procreative function in this life more inviting. Pleasure is subordinate to procreation; absent the procreative need, the sexual should pass away. To imagine sexual activity merely for the purpose of pleasure would seem to bespeak a distorted view of human goods and their proper ordering.

For the most part, Aquinas discusses heaven in terms of the fulfillment of the individual. Yet Aquinas is aware of the corporate dimension and can also put heaven in terms of communion and community. In coming to God as their end, humans will achieve more than the full harmony and coordination of their essential parts, as body is perfectly subordinate to soul and the whole person is perfectly subjected to God. There will also be a full harmony among all of God's people, who realize the completion of their corporate identity as this has been intimated and initiated by their participation, in this life, in Christ's mystical body. The people on the way become in heaven the people who have completed the journey, and whatever has divided God's people will be overcome in the presence of God. There is in this regard the completion and perfecting of charity. By charity in this life, one loves God above all things and loves other things in reference to God. The love of God in the present life is not complete, in the sense of total and unceasing; neither is the love of others. The end, however, brings such perfection, as those who reach God as their end are confirmed in their loving orientation and give themselves totally to the knowing and loving of God. In this connection, then, they will be perfected in their loving of each other, for God's sake, and will delight in the perfecting and enjoyment of God to which other members of Christ's people have attained.

The other possible final state is hell, and hell is imagined for the most part as the reverse of heaven, as the fitting final deviation from the good. Hence, as with heaven, hell is eternal, and in coming to hell, the person is receiving what the person deserves for sin in this life. By *sin*, the person has deviated from the good set for her by God, and has replaced God with some other, who becomes for that person "god." By sinful action, the person has gone off track, and onto a path that takes her farther and farther away from God. Hence, when such a person reaches the cessation of earthly existence, she is introduced to the appropriate end of such a journey. She is totally distant from God, and God is totally absent from her and known as absent, as the fitting culmination of the sinful journey. Both body and soul, each implicated in sin, receive their due in hell.

Aquinas can in fact assert endowments of the damned body that are the opposite of those enjoyed by the blessed. Thus, in place of clarity, there is darkness in the damned, as is fitting for one whose soul does not grasp the glory of God. So too the damned are burdened by clunky bodies, slow and ponderous in movement, and certainly not in the subordination and right ordering to soul that characterizes the blessed. The damned person is a seriously divided person, whose body and soul remain at odds, and eternally so.

In describing the suffering of the damned—and, while their fate is an eternal, nonending one, they are in fact vulnerable, again a point made in contrast to the blessed—Aquinas can speak of three major penalties. First, there is the punishment of separation from God and awareness that this separation, brought upon oneself by sin, is total and final. Second, there is the punishment of remorse of conscience. The damned know themselves to have failed God and so failed themselves and they regret that, but theirs is not the repentance that, if done in this life, would have provided a reorientation of the person away from sin and toward God as end. The remorse is real, but to no good effect; it simply increases the despair at the final state. Finally, there is sensible punishment. Aquinas takes seriously talk of hellfire, and thinks that such is appropriate, given the person's overattachment to sensible things in the present life, which has made this person qualified for hell. Hell is a place where sinful people suffer in a tangible way the consequences of their actions.

The final state of heaven or hell is not, however, the state of the human person immediately after the end of life in this world. Aquinas in fact posits two stages in the afterlife, one for the soul, and one for the soul with the body. Death means the separation of soul from body. As immortal (for God has so made it), the soul continues to exist, and immediately after the death of the body-soul entity, the soul can receive its due from God. To the souls who have died in their mortal sinning, hell is immediately given; their distance from God is complete and confirmed as final. To some souls who die in the state of grace, heaven is immediately given; for others, however, there can be an intermediate state (see below), and the entry of the soul into heaven will be deferred. The body, however, dissolves with the death of the person. At the end of time, there will be the general resurrection of the dead, which means that bodies will be reconstituted, raised, and reunited with their souls. At this point, the person will enter into the final state. The beatitude of the soul will become perfect; the separated soul has yearned for its body, and as reunited with the body can rest fully in the enjoyment of God. The body too comes to share in beatitude, elevated by the overflow of beatitude from the soul to its final transcendent state. As for the condemned, their risen bodies will come to share in the punishment that the separated soul has endured since the death of the human person.

There is a profound christological dimension to Aquinas's account of the end (ST III.53–59). In keeping with his teaching that as human Christ is the way to eternal life (see the prologue to ST I.2), Aquinas of course sees the journey to God in this life as a life of discipleship to Christ and of imitation of Christ. But he also reads human death and resurrection in the light of Christ. Christ's dying and rising serve as both the efficient and formal cause of the dying (to sin) and rising to life of those who follow Christ and so come to heaven. Christ's resurrection is the pattern and promise of our own (here echoing 1 Cor. 15, a text that Aquinas, not coincidentally, cites in ST I.1.8c in the course of his reflections about the use of argument in *sacred doctrine*), and God raises the dead as God has done in Christ.

There is a strong continuity between the earthly and the raised body. They are numerically the same; there is no creation of a different, "spiritual" body that

substitutes for the person's body as possessed in the earthly life. Male and female will remain, for so God has created people. However, the body will be raised in a form that expresses the body at the height of its perfection. Thus, the age of people will be neither too young (when people would still have to come to maturity) nor too old, when people are in decline. Rather, taking his cue from Christ, Aquinas concludes that the age of the risen will be thirty or thirty-three, when human growth has reached its term and the possession of natural powers is at its strongest and before the decline of old age has set in.

Christ will also act as judge at the Last Judgment, a role that he has merited through his own good actions on earth. The judgment will be of all humans, the wicked and the good, and Christ as judge will state definitively the form that the final state will take for each human, whether heaven or hell. The soul has already received a judgment, immediately after the death of the person; at the Last Judgment, the soul reunited with its body receives the judgment from Christ, in accordance with the person's actions while alive, and the body comes to enjoy, or suffer, along with the soul. In this judgment, Christ will be assisted by the saints (*ScG* IV.96), and the Last Judgment will be followed by a consuming fire that will purify the world of the remnants of sin.

As a final point in his eschatology, Aquinas posits an intermediary state, falling between the death of the person and the entry of the soul into heaven (eventually to be reunited to its body), for some good souls. While the souls of mortal sinners are consigned to hell immediately after the dissolution of the body-soul entity, not every good soul immediately proceeds to heaven. Some people die in venial (not mortal) sin, not having repented for that sin; some die also having failed to do the set satisfaction for the mortal sins that they have confessed and repented (see *penance*). To pay the remaining debt of sin, such souls are consigned for the while to a middle place, to purgatory. Western theologians had long posited a purgatorial fire and increasingly came to designate a separate space that is purgatory; Aquinas is thus traditional in this affirmation. As Aquinas also recognizes, the affirmation of purgatory was one way in which the Latin church differed from the Greek (*ScG* IV.91.11).

Leget (1997).

Esse   Literally, "to be," *esse* may be translated "act of being," or even "being," provided that it is not confused with *ens*, which is used to render "being" in the different sense of an individual, one who has being. Aquinas makes considerable reference throughout his theology to *esse*, and even those with the most casual acquaintance with Aquinas have an awareness of *esse*'s significance for him. As one of his earliest writings discloses (*De ente et essentia*), Aquinas exhibited a healthy interest in *esse* from the very outset of his career. What exactly *esse* denotes or how it might least inadequately be analyzed is, however, a matter of considerable discussion among scholars of Aquinas. Even as indicated by its form (it is a verb), it is not an essence for Aquinas and on that score alone cannot be defined; it is met, in thought, by reflection on its functioning. In what follows, *esse* is taken as an analogous term that designates the act of being. Act of being differs from creature to creature. To give an example, the *esse* of a particular squirrel is not the *esse* of a particular human. Rather, *esse* in each case is proportioned to the individual given the kind of nature that it has. Aquinas employs *esse*-talk also of God, and in fact links the affirmation of God's *esse* to God's self-designation in Exodus 3:14 (see ST I.13.11). *Esse*, of course, will play out differently in God than it does in different sorts of created beings; it is employed analogously of different levels of being.

The importance of *esse*-talk for Aquinas can be gauged by considering how he employs it in three regions of his theology: his depiction of created reality, the articulation of divine transcendence, and the affirmation, in Christology, of **hypostatic union**. There is in creatures a real distinction between essence and *esse*. "Essence" designates what a thing fundamentally is; in identifying the essence of a thing, one is saying what sort of thing it is and so identifying the nature that makes that thing what it is. But to define some thing is not to establish or to say that that thing actually exists. Essence is not self-actualizing, but comes to be, in an individual as the bearer of the nature, by *esse*. *Esse*, then, gestures at the "to be" of the individual who is defined as the bearer of a particular essence. Aquinas's point in positing the real distinction is to insist that there is composition in every created being (or substance, taken in the sense of individual). The nature or essence stands as the potential, which is actualized by *esse*. And to complete the point, it is not as if for Aquinas the nature, apart from its instantiation, is out there somewhere, existing; it exists only as the potential that is the nature is actualized in the individual through *esse*.

The real distinction becomes in turn a handy way of characterizing what is involved in creating (see **creation**). To be a creature means to receive everything from God. The "everything" can thus be parsed both in terms of nature (the creature is the sort of thing it is by the gift and design of God) and in terms of *esse* (the creature receives as well its *esse* from God, the *esse* proportioned to its nature that actualizes the potential of the nature, so that the nature comes to be, individuated, as this existing creature).

There is, however, no real distinction in God. There is no composition of any sort in God (see ST I.3, on the divine simplicity). The God with whom Aquinas is concerned to do justice to in his theology has no potential, as if his God were to develop and grow into the job. Rather, whatever perfections God has, God has eminently and eternally; God is fully actual from eternity; God is not actualized. To secure the point, Aquinas insists on the real identity of essence (what God is) and *esse* in God (ST I.3.4c). The essence—all of the perfections that on the basis of Scripture one will ascribe to God, and preeminently and eternally—is the same as God's "to be." The affirmation of real identity in God thus fits nicely into Aquinas's strategy of distinguishing God from the world, of not confusing God with what God brings into existence in granting creaturely essence and *esse*. And the affirmation of real identity in God gives force to Aquinas's comment very early in the ST as he is about to embark on the treatise on **God** (see the prologue to ST I.2). In treating God, he is not concerned with what God is, but rather "with what God is not." He could convey what God is only if human beings had in this life direct access to God and so were able to see the divine *esse* (with which the essence is identical) as it is. This, however, lies beyond our natural powers; vision is restricted to the next life, when the blessed see God as he is.

We name things as we know them, and our language is well-suited to discussing the things that lie within the human's natural cognitive powers. Sentences, with subject and predicate, replicate the composition that humans encounter in knowing things of this world, that is, those things that are susceptible to composition and in whom it makes sense to distinguish between essence and the act of being. Our language, however, is eminently unsuited to talk about what lacks composition, or potential, or a real distinction between essence and *esse*. But it is all we have, and so Aquinas, with the tradition, insists on formulations that sound odd but are less inadequate to the Reality about whom Christians need to affirm. Thus, for example, one can say of a human that she has a nature (human nature) and has an *esse*. By this way of talking, one is acknowledging that a human is not the nature but an instantiation of the nature, which is possessed in common with others of her sort (i.e., with other humans), and that that human has come to be by God's granting of *esse* to her. She is not her essence, nor her *esse*. But in light of the identity of essence and *esse* in God, and the denial of composition to God, one can stretch the language and say of God that God is (not *has*) the divine essence, that God is (and not *has*) the divine *esse*, and that the essence and *esse* of God are identical. The affirmations are true, but how they are in God lies beyond our ken (see **negative theology**).

Esse also makes a crucial appearance in Aquinas's account of **Jesus Christ**. Aquinas's is an incarnational Christology. It involves the act of the second person of God. The second person—who from eternity is a distinct person in God and fully God, one and the same God as the Father and the Holy Spirit—without loss to itself as fully divine Word takes up a second nature, human nature, and realizes the potential for a second form of life. The Word as incarnate is fully human. In the second person, a second nature has been joined to the first that the second person eternally is; the Word as incarnate has human nature, is a human. In proclaiming Christ as of two natures, Aquinas uses a variety of verbs: The Word "takes up" or "assumes" human nature; in the Word two natures "are united." He also puts the act of incarnation in terms of *esse*, of the conveying of *esse*.

At a number of points in the Thomistic corpus, Aquinas asks whether there is one or two substantial *esse* in Christ. If such *esse* follows on nature, then there would be two; if it is based on person, then there would be one. The latter is in fact the teaching of all but one of the texts in which over the years Aquinas addressed the issue. Here, ST III.17.2 ad 2 can be taken as representative: "The eternal *esse* of the Son of God, which is the divine nature, becomes the *esse* of man, inasmuch as the human nature is assumed by the Son of God to unity of Person." The second part of the statement is familiar by this point in the treatise on Christ in the ST: The act of incarnation involves a taking up, and what is taken up is human nature, such that the Word as incarnate instantiates human nature. It is the first part of the saying—the "eternal *esse* of the Son of God, which is the divine nature, becomes the *esse* of man"—which is a new way, for the treatise, of stating the assuming. This part of the statement itself stands in need of some unpacking, trading as it does on what Aquinas has taught about the Trinity in the ST's First Part. When it is a question of the divine *esse*, *esse* is not treated at the level of the divine person; otherwise, there would be not three divine persons, but three divine beings, each of whom would have a proper *esse*. Rather, *esse* is found at the level of the divine essence, which, as already noted, is not distinct from the *esse* but is identical with *esse* (there is no real distinction in God). Hence, in the present instance, Aquinas says that there is one substantial *esse* in the case of Christ, for the divine Word has shared with the human nature the divine *esse* that pertains to it as God (the eternally actualized divine essence). This divine *esse* in the taking up of human nature becomes the *esse* of that nature; there is one, and only one, *esse* in Christ.

Elsewhere in the treatise, Aquinas inquires into the "creatureliness" of Christ. Christ as God is, of course, not a creature. To deny the full divinity of the Logos, the person of Jesus, would be to lapse into the Arian heresy (see, e.g., ST III.16.8). But Christ is also human; the Word was made flesh, the Word took up and instantiated human nature, with the result that this man, Jesus, has come to be. Therefore, Christ is also a creature, when one takes into account the humanness of the incarnate Word. The present passage (ST III.17.2 ad 2) can and should be linked to that earlier discussion, and it sheds light on the extent, as it were, of Christ's creatureliness. In every other human, to be a human creature means to receive everything from God (see above), both one's nature and one's *esse*.

Neither human nature nor human *esse* is divine; rather, each is patterned on the divine nature and the divine *esse*, and the *esse* that is granted to every other human is proportioned to that nature. From ST III.17.2 ad 2, it is clear that Christ as creature is unlike other human beings. With other human beings, the incarnate Word shares human nature. But Jesus does not have a substantial *esse* that would be akin to the *esse* of other human beings. Theirs is a creaturely *esse*, proportioned to the human nature; Christ's *esse* is that which pertains to the Word as God. Christ's one *esse* is divine; it is this *esse* that in the taking up of human nature actualizes that nature.

There is a certain power to this Thomistic take on hypostatic union. It underscores the identity of Jesus as the Word who from eternity is fully God and is a distinct person of God and who in incarnation is also human. There is a single subject of the two natures. By talking of the sharing of *esse*, Aquinas puts well the real union of the natures. The teaching, however, is controversial and open to attack, especially in light of the claim, about God, of the real identity of *esse* and essence: If in God *esse* and essence are one, isn't the assertion of the sharing of divine *esse* to the human nature of Christ tantamount to the monophysite position? The objection has a surface attractiveness, although it seems to falter inasmuch as Aquinas consistently subscribes to the distinctiveness as well of the natures, of their maintenance in Christ of their integrity as different natures (that is, there is no confusion of the natures; each is possessed and expressed by the Word incarnate). In the present passage, Aquinas talks about the conveying of *esse*, not a mixing of the natures, which retain their integrity and are each fully affirmed of the Word incarnate.

The teaching about Christ's substantial *esse* is controversial, however, on another score. The teaching of ST III.17.2 ad 2 is Aquinas's usual teaching on the matter; he holds it as well, for example, in the early *Scriptum on the Sentences* (III

Sent. d.6 q.2 a.2). But in one text, Aquinas on first reading (at least) seems to be teaching something different. In his disputed question *de Unione Verbi Incarnati* (a.4), he seems to be saying that there are two substantial *esse* in Christ, one each for the human and the divine natures of Christ. Did Aquinas change his mind on a matter of such fundamental import? The intrigue is compounded by the fact that this disputed question is roughly contemporary with ST III.17.2 ad 2. It has been difficult, to say the least, for Thomists to square the two teachings, such that the disputed question would only seem to deviate from the usual view. On the other hand, it is difficult to accept that on such a crucial matter Aquinas would have changed the teaching and then introduced the changed teaching in such a casual way. There is in fact a great deal that is riding on the more usual attribution to Christ of but one substantial *esse*. That teaching goes well with what can be deemed Aquinas's resistance to a Nestorian Christology, in which it would make eminent sense to posit a double substantial *esse*, one per the two persons who for Nestorius (as received by the medievals) are united in Christ. In discussing creatures, Aquinas is consistent in teaching that natures have *esse* only as instantiated in individuals. Thus, if in the disputed question Aquinas is allowing a discrete substantial *esse* for the human nature, that would seem to open the door to a Christology that asserts a pairing of discretely existing subjects. Given his concern for the identity of the person of Jesus and the insistence on the union of the two natures in precisely that person, that would seem to be a mistake that Aquinas would be unlikely to make.

Patfoort (1964); Brown (1998); West (2002); Weinandy (2004); Gilson (1968); Bonino (1993); Cross (2002), ch. 12.

Eternity of the World   *see* **Philosophy**

Eucharist   *see* **Concomitance; Real Presence; Sacrifice, Eucharistic; Transubstantiation**

Evil   With the Augustinian tradition, Aquinas insists that evil is not a thing, that it has no being. Rather, it can be understood only in terms of what does have being, namely, good. Evil is a deviation from the good, an absence or privation of the good. In terms of human acting, in doing something, the person is pursuing a good, a perfection. The good that is pursued may be a real good, truly perfective in some way of the person. But it may be only an apparent good, the person's judgment having been clouded by some previous bad acting, or the will, unduly influenced by the passions, seeking their own good inordinately—that is, as not regulated by the reason—eliciting or commanding some act that will not be truly perfective of the person.

In terms of God's acting, God cannot be mistaken about the good. God always wills what is authentically good. God's will is causal; God wills, and there is good (see *creation*). Aquinas will develop the point in exploring *predestination*. God predestines some to eternal life; God wills to them the good that is life with God in heaven. And God accordingly wills to them the *grace* that will bring them to that end. But does predestination to eternal life require a parallel predestination of all others to hell, the total absence of God? If God is not for someone, does that not mean that God is against that one, and so wills an end appropriate to those whom God hates? Aquinas refrains from positing such a second predestination. God does not cause people to go to hell in light of a decision to send them to hell. Rather, there is an asymmetry between salvation and damnation. In the former, God decides in eternity and works out the decision by grace, communicating good in a special way to some rational creatures. As Aquinas makes clear in his talk about the compatibility of predestination in a causal sense and the affirmation of *merit*, those who are called to God as end and who reach God as end by virtue of the divine decree and the execution of that decree through grace also contribute to the reaching of their end by their good actions as aided by grace. And so in their case, heaven is, radically, a gift, due to the free decision of God to communicate God's goodness in a special way, but it is also a reward by God, rendered to the person for the graced actions that the person does in attaining the end set for her by God. But in terms of others, going to hell is their own accomplishment. They *sin*, and so become worthy of eternal punishment. Eternal punishment has not been willed for them from eternity, nor caused in them by God. God does not cause evil. But God is able to retrieve good from evil by rendering to sinners what they deserve, in justice, for their sin. They sin, and God responds by imposing the apt penalty; in this way, God shows the good of justice by giving them what they deserve for sin, namely, hell.

In discussing evil, Aquinas uses some terms in his moral theology, as well as his account of God's sovereign and just rule, that have technical status. The *malum culpae* refers to sin and the guilt before God that the sinner has. *Malum poenae* refers to what sin brings about, the penalty for sin that God imposes on sinners that thereby retrieves good from the sinner's evil.

In denying the being of evil and describing sin as due to human willing (see *original sin*), Aquinas has followed Augustine's lead. As was the case for Augustine, the teaching is presented with a view to countering dualist assertions. For Augustine, his teaching involved the rejection of Manichaean dualism. For Aquinas, the foil is contemporary Cathar religion, which involved a resurgence in Western Europe of a dualist view that asserted the existence of evil, tied it closely to the physical and material, and ascribed the material, and so evil, to the malicious, creative activity of a god separate from the true God, the God of spirit. This other god was thought to bring the material into existence in order to trap spirits and remove them from allegiance to the true God. The Augustinian account adopted by Aquinas permits the recognition of evil, without granting it equal ontological status to the spiritual, while also putting the blame for evil where it truly belongs—in the wrongful exercise of the human will.

————

Te Velde (2005); Sweeney (2002).

Existence of God   *see* **Preambles of Faith**

Exitus-reditus   Literally, "going out and returning." The organization of the ST reflects the pattern of going out from God and then returning to God. Hence, in the First Part Aquinas considers God and the procession of creatures from God as from their creator. In the Second Part, he looks at the movement through moral action of the rational creature to God as end (see *moral theology*). In the Third Part, he treats Christ, the way to God as end (see *viator*), and the sacraments of Christ, which convey the grace needed for the successful journey to God. The motif of *exitus-reditus* nicely corresponds to what Aquinas insists, in the very first question of the ST, is the main focus of *sacred doctrine*, namely, God and other things inasmuch as they are related to God as to their beginning and end (ST I.1.3 ad 1). In organizing the ST according to this pattern, Aquinas was hardly innovative. Although Peter Lombard himself offers another explanation for his organization of the *Sentences*, it had been suggested in the thirteenth century, prior to Aquinas, that the *Sentences* themselves were organized according to this pattern (see *Scriptum on the Sentences*).

Exitus-reditus nicely captures the essential structure of the most important Christian things. It pertains to the good to want to diffuse itself, as Aquinas reminds us, echoing Pseudo-Dionysius. God is the ultimate good, and so it is most pertinent to God to diffuse God, to proclaim the goodness of God in sharing that goodness with others. Thus, God creates, goes out from God, as it were, in bringing what is not God into being, to show in the ways determined by the divine wisdom the goodness of God (see **creation**). So too, God freely wills to rational creatures the special good that is God. By their natural powers, themselves given by God in establishing the nature expressed in such beings, human beings can attain to a proportionate, natural good. But God has called rational creatures to a higher end, to God's own life (see **beatific vision; predestination**), and so communicates God's good in this special way. As the very first article of the ST's Third Part states, it is very much in keeping with God's goodness for God to become incarnate, in order to facilitate human salvation and so the reaching, in the next life, of the good that is God. In all of this, there is an *exitus*, a going out from God that is productive of good and of which humans are the beneficiaries. So too, woven into the structure of Christian things is the *reditus*. God is the final end of human beings, as established in God's goodness. By acting in accordance with their God-given nature, and through the help of the grace communicated in Christ, people will move back to God as to their source. By entering into communion with God in the next life, human beings will be fulfilled, but in a way that far transcends what they of themselves would have been capable of accomplishing.

Exitus-reditus is in itself not a Christian innovation. Aquinas would have known of non-Christian uses, as in various Platonists whom he would have encountered by report or by direct reading. To the extent that his own sense of the value of *exitus-reditus* would be honed through the study of such other uses, he owes a debt to **philosophy**. But in employing the motif to put the relations and dependence of creatures to the triune God who is their beginning and end, Aquinas needed to modify significantly the motif as used by

others. In Platonist invocations of *exitus-reditus*, there can be a pronounced emanationism: Things proceed from the highest being not by choice but as a necessary consequence of that being's self-contemplation, as an overflow. The return to that being as to their end can have a necessitarian undertone, as those who proceeded now return, as swept up in a movement of ebb and flow. Creating in Aquinas, however, is the free action of a free God, and while it is fully in keeping with God's character as good to create, God did not have to create. A noncreating God would have been as much God as God is. Creation, this *exitus*, is radically a gift. Nor did the triune God have to establish God's self as the end of rational creatures in a special way, or provide the means, in Christ, to reach that supernatural end. Rather, in saving as in creating, the Christian meets the fully free God whose love goes out to what is not God in so many ways.

———

Johnstone (2002); Rorem (1992); O'Rourke (1992).

Facienti quod in se est   As a way of systematically presenting the respective contributions of God and of the human person to the person's first entry into grace—that is, conversion from sin toward God as end—twelfth-century theologians had formulated the *facienti quod in se est*. In its full form, it reads, *Facienti quod in se est, Deus non denegat gratiam.* Literally this means "To one who does what lies in him/her, God does not deny grace," but it can also be translated, "To one who does one's best, God gives grace." In its original formulation, the saying stresses the responsibility of the human person. God makes a general offer of grace to all people. But it is up to the individual to take up that offer by showing God his seriousness in changing his life in such a way that he will get on the right track to God as end. When the individual does something to show God the seriousness of the intention to reach God as end ("does one's best"), God grants the grace that marks the term of conversion. God does so on the basis of a promise: God has committed God's self to a course of action, by which God rewards with grace those who take the right first step.

In his early **Scriptum on the Sentences** of Peter Lombard, Aquinas affirms the *facere* in this straightforward way (see, e.g., II *Sent.* d.28 q.1 a.4 sol.; IV *Sent.* d.20 a.1 sol. 1). The beginning of the spiritual journey is due to the correct activity of the individual, which is acknowledged by God in granting the grace that justifies. Whether Aquinas thinks of this taking of the first step as "meritorious" is not exactly clear. He explicitly rejects a condign merit in this case; after all, whatever a person without grace does can in no way be equal to what God might do in response. Yet there may be a place for a congruent merit here, inasmuch as God does respond, and infallibly, to any such doing of good that inaugurates the spiritual journey to God, by granting justifying grace (see **merit**).

The teaching is rather different in the ST. Aquinas continues to use the *facere*, but in effect stands it on its head, insisting that the initiative in conversion belongs to God. In his reinterpretation of the *facere* in ST I-II.112.2–4, Aquinas makes good use of the developments in his general teaching on **grace**, as well as his increased recognition that the giving of grace is to be linked to predestination, taken causally. As earlier questions in the ST's treatise on grace make clear, Aquinas notes two forms of sanctifying grace: habitual grace and the grace that is *auxilium*. When in ST I-II.112.2 he asks whether one must prepare for grace, it is about habitual grace that he is asking; the answer is yes, for the infusion of any form (which habitual grace is) requires that the matter be prepared. Yet he immediately adds that this preparing of the "matter" of the human person for the infusion of habitual grace is not the accomplishment of the person, but

rather is worked in the person by the other grace, that of *auxilium*; one does not prepare for *auxilium*, which is simply given by God. Thus, the preparing for habitual grace, the doing of one's best, is itself a work of God, done in the person.

Aquinas continues the reinterpretation of the *facere* in the next article, where he explicitly invokes the language of the *facere*. The question in I-II.112.3 is whether God has to give habitual grace to one prepared for it. In the corpus, Aquinas states that there are two ways of looking at the preparation for habitual grace: as done in the human person and as done in the human person by God's *auxilium*. When one looks at the preparatory act as worked in the human person, there is no need for habitual grace to follow. The idea here is that nothing created (the human person) can necessitate God. But when one looks at the preparatory act as worked by *auxilium*, then there is a necessity for the granting of habitual grace. God does nothing idly, and so when God prepares the person for habitual grace through *auxilium*, that is because God wants to give habitual grace to that person; so the conversion inaugurated by *auxilium* comes to its term in the infusion by God of habitual grace.

ST I-II.112.4 completes the reinterpretation of the *facere* by asking whether one person might receive, in conversion, more habitual grace than another. Yes, if one person is more prepared for habitual grace. Such would occur if that person received more *auxilium*, which would work a greater preparation of the matter of the soul for the infusion of habitual grace; more or less *auxilium* is up to God. Again, one cannot prepare for *auxilium*; it is simply given in accordance with God's will. And so the article in effect points us back to the ST's First Part and its discussion of **predestination** (ST I.23).

It is likely that the major impetus for Aquinas's innovative interpretation of the saying came from his discovery and close reading of certain of Augustine's late writings. In combating the Massilians (designated in later Christian history as the "semi-Pelagians"), Augustine disagreed with what might fairly be termed an incipient form of the *facere*. The Massilians had insisted that the beginning of salvation comes from the individual, whose earnest efforts at emendation of life would be rewarded by God in grace. For Augustine, this undermined grace as grace and failed to acknowledge the decisive role of God's predestining will. God gives grace to those to whom God wills to give grace. In reading such works as *The Predestination of the Saints*, Aquinas likely saw his early teaching on conversion, as in the *Scriptum*, as falling under Augustine's strictures, and so revised that teaching accordingly.

Bouillard (1944); Wawrykow (1995), chs. 2–3.

Faith   Faith is the first of the theological virtues, in the sense that its act is generated first and is the foundation for acts of hope and charity (see *theological virtues*). Before one can hope—that is, aspire to a future good that is difficult yet possible to attain—or love the highest good for its own sake, one must know, through faith, one's end and the way to this end. For Aquinas, faith is a "habit of the intellect, by which eternal life is begun in us, which makes the intellect assent to things which are unseen" (ST II-II.4.1c). As are the other theological virtues, the virtue of faith is infused with habitual grace in the first justification of the person. As a habit, faith establishes in its bearer a steady disposition to acts of a certain kind, to acts of faith, acts of believing (*credere*). Faith is perfective of the intellect, extending its capacity, as is proper to the theological virtues, to the supernatural level. It orients the believer to God as supernatural end (". . . by which eternal life is begun in us"), and it anticipates the vision of the next life, although it falls short of that vision in the way that believing something to be true differs from seeing that thing for oneself. By faith, one comes to hold the truths

that are necessary for salvation: about God, about Christ as the way to God (see *articles of faith*). One assents to things that are unseen; one sees as if in a glass darkly. In the next life, one will see God face to face, and so reach one's fulfillment (see *beatific vision*). Faith is not salvation, but without faith, one would not reach one's end in God.

Drawing on diverse statements of Augustine, Aquinas notes three acts of believing that pertain to the virtue of faith: *credere Deo, credere Deum, credere in Deum* (ST II-II.2.2). The first refers to the authority on the basis of which one believes; one believes these truths as revealed by God, the First Truth. The second refers to the material content of faith. One believes certain things about God—for example, that God is one and triune and that God is the source of all being and the end of the rational creature in a special way. One also believes that God has become human in order to render possible human salvation, and that Christ is the way to eternal life. Hence, by *credere Deum*, one believes these truths, as referred to the God who establishes God as our end and provides for the successful movement, through Christ, to this end. Finally, by *credere in Deum*, Aquinas acknowledges the role of charity in the act of faith, and so the role of will in believing. For justification and correct relationship to God, it is not enough to simply believe certain claims about God. One must love the one who reveals these truths. In this connection, Aquinas will distinguish unformed from formed faith (II-II.4.3–4; 5.2–3). The latter is faith as shaped by love. The former lacks love, and is the simple affirmation of these truths. Such does not justify, for one is not correctly related to the God who is to be loved above all things and for God's own sake. Unformed faith is that which is held by the demons (see Jas. 2), and they are not justified. In initial justification, the three theological virtues are infused together, and so the act of faith that is made possible by this perfecting is formed by charity. But charity can be lost by mortal sin, while faith remains—as unformed. For Aquinas, faith is the first of the virtues. It is the basis for the other virtues, the theological as well as the infused moral virtues (see *virtue*). It is also the last virtue that may be lost, when after the loss through sin of the other virtues that rest on it, it finally too may pass away, as the sinful person turns to unbelief.

Faith is the beginning of eternal life, not eternal life itself. Aquinas can thus also second the definition of faith offered in Hebrews 11:1 (cited in II-II.4.1): "Faith is the substance of things hoped for, the evidence of things not seen" (KJV). By faith, one has the first glimpse of the end and what pertains to that end: It is the "substance of things hoped for." But what is hoped for is not possessed; if it were, there would be no need for hope, an aspiration for some future (not present) good. There is, then, a not-yet quality to faith. One is provided in faith with a certainty and confidence; after all, faith rests on the word of God, and God's word is most certain (*credere Deo*). Faith and vision are not the same, however, and one must move toward vision. One does that by faith, by acts of faith, by which one both grows in faith and comes closer to the end that is God. In the augmentation of faith, as in the first giving of faith, the divine contribution is essential. The simple possession of a virtue does not ensure acts of the virtue. The intellect that is inclined to faith must be moved to the act of faith. This occurs at two levels. The will as well as the intellect is involved in believing; the will must move the intellect to affirm the truths of faith. As itself shaped by charity, perfective of the will, the act of faith will be informed, shaped by charity (*credere in Deum*). But the will itself must be reduced to act. This occurs by God's prompting, by the divine instinct that is the grace of *auxilium* (see *grace*). The person who stands in correct relationship to God is rendered more receptive to the divine promptings by additional habits that are themselves also given by God,

namely, the *gifts of the Holy Spirit*. In the case of faith, these gifts are understanding and knowledge, discussed in ST II-II.8–9. In growing in faith, the person is dependent on God; from the beginning of the process, in the unmerited granting of habitual grace and the theological virtues, through the acts of faith themselves, to the final attaining of God, the divine contribution is crucial, without rendering the human contribution (it is, after all, the human who believes) inconsequential.

Bourgeois (1974); Brown (2002); Jenkins (1997).

Fittingness   Aquinas's writings on the truths of the Christian faith are rich in arguments for fittingness. Often indicated by the Latin *convenienter* or *conveniens*, the argument for fittingness aims at making manifest the meaning and wisdom of the Christian dispensation. In pursuing the wisdom of the revealed order, Aquinas's practice is different from what came to prevail among later scholastics. In later medieval writers, the dialectic of the two powers of God, the ordained and the absolute, came into greater prominence. By contemplating what lies within God's power absolutely and suggesting how a different course of action was possible to God and may have been preferable to what God in fact has done, later scholastics could disclose the contingency of the actual order and underscore God's freedom before the world. God could have acted otherwise; what is revealed as Christian truth, in terms of God's dealings with the world, could have been otherwise. Aquinas himself knows the dialectic and uses it in moderation (see, e.g., ST III.3.5–7). But such use is geared to showing the wisdom of the actual Christian order. Much more frequently, Aquinas sticks to the revealed order and through the argument for fittingness tries to show how different facets of the Christian message make sense. The "making sense" is most typically uncovered by demonstrating the coherence of the Christian message, by showing how basic convictions about God inform claims about people and how what is proclaimed about Christ, meaningful in itself, informs and reflects essential Christian claims about God and people. The argument for fittingness thus goes well with a view of theology as "faith seeking understanding" as geared to the understanding of the faith that is actually held by Christians.

In the construction of the argument for fittingness, Scripture enjoys great prominence, as mediated to later generations through the interpretations of the church doctors (see *Scripture; doctors of the church*). As Aquinas reminds us, Scripture is the revealed will of God (see, e.g., ST III.1.3c) and is the surest guide to God's actions and motives for so acting. The church doctors will help, for they have been principally concerned in their work with the grasping of God's word in Scripture and meditation on the scriptural message. They have, in the judgment of the church, been typically successful in their reading of Scripture; later readers of Scripture can thus benefit from their aid.

An example is in order. Near the beginning of the treatise on Christ in the ST, Aquinas asks whether the incarnation of the Son of God was necessary for the restoration of the race. The posing of the question in this way may be misleading, as if Aquinas's intention were to show that the second divine person "had" to become incarnate, that there was no other way for the effects associated with the incarnation to be brought about. The corpus of the article immediately counters such an initial perception. There are two senses of "necessary." A thing is said to be necessary in the first sense when an end cannot be had without that thing. Hence, food is necessary for the preservation of human life. The second sense is when an end is attained better and more conveniently, as a horse is "necessary" for a journey. It is in the second, not the first, sense that the incarnation is neces-

sary; it is more fitting for the restoration of the race that it occur through the incarnation of the second divine person.

Having established the sense of "necessary" in play, Aquinas then goes on to proclaim ten reasons for the fittingness of the incarnation of God to work out human salvation, making especially good use of writings of Augustine in the process. These ten reasons are divided into two groups of five: those that have to do with "furtherance in the good," and others that have to do with "withdrawal from evil." (Not incidentally, the headings are reminiscent of what Aquinas says in ST I-II of natural law; by the use of such terminology here, he is underscoring the overlap between natural and divine law while also indicating that the latter, definitively and finally revealed in Christ, has a higher end, namely, the supernatural end that is the triune God who makes possible reaching this end through the grace of Christ. See *law*.) In advancing the first group of five, on furtherance in the good, Aquinas expresses his view of human life as a journey (see *viator*), a journey that must be viewed in terms of God and God's plan for humans. Indeed, God's plan is the starting point and setting of this inquiry. God did not have to create anything and did not have to create human beings, who in their rationality imitate, without replicating, God's knowing and loving. God did not have to call rational creatures to the special good that is life with God in heaven. Yet, granted God's wise ordering of rational creatures to God, the incarnation makes sense and provides further evidence of God's wise communicating to humans of God's good. To get to God as end involves a journey of the affections and of doing; so has God determined to render those who will enter into eternal life, to enter into the direct contemplation of God, qualified for the vision. To be more precise, by acts of the theological virtues of *faith, hope*, and *charity*, one gets closer to the end that is God and one engages in a training that readies one for God. So too, good actions, done in grace, are like steps on the path to God (see *merit*).

In the first group of five in the present article, Aquinas points to the *theological virtues* and moral action to explain why the incarnation is "necessary" in the second sense, that is, fitting. To reach the end, one must know the end and the way to the end; this comes by faith. And faith is made more certain by believing God, who speaks. Hence, in becoming incarnate, God is able to establish faith by proclaiming what must be believed. So too, the incarnation greatly strengthens hope; God's becoming human is strong proof of God's great love for us. In like fashion, the incarnation should arouse love in response to God's great love in taking up our lot and working for our salvation. In the fourth reason, Aquinas turns to moral action, and in the process shows that creating and redeeming in his theology are closely linked (see as well III.3.8). All things are made in accordance with God's Word. By sin, the *image of God* has been obscured in people, and people have gone off track. Who better to get people back on the path to God than the Word according to whom they have been made? By becoming human, the Word made flesh can thus provide the example for our own moral behavior, by showing us as humans how to live and so come closer to God. To cap off the first list of five, Aquinas echoes a venerable patristic saw. Why become human? So that humans can become God. That is, in the union of the two natures in the person of the Word, there is a foretaste of the end to which God has called people and to which people aspire, and by the *hypostatic union*, God provides the one who is the path to that end. In sum, God acts wisely in calling people to eternal life; God facilitates the working out of that plan by becoming human, as a goad to faith, hope, and charity and as the model for emulation, by showing what can occur for the person through Christ at the end time.

The second group of five stands in nice continuity with the first, although arguably the focus has shifted, from God's wisdom in willing eternal life and executing God's plan, to the human beings who are the beneficiaries of that plan. In the first four of the reasons having to do with withdrawal from evil, Aquinas is urging people, on the basis of the incarnation, to stay on the correct path. At the same time, in these reasons we meet a nuanced, Christian understanding of what it means to be human. In the first two, the great dignity of the human is to the fore. People have been made by God for God, and God has shown God's great love for people by becoming human. People should not sell themselves short by honoring the *devil* through sin (the first reason). So too in the second reason: Human beings hold a high place among creatures, and this is underscored by the incarnation, by which God becomes, precisely, a human being. Thus, by virtue of the dignity of the human in God's plan, people should stay away from sin. In the next two reasons, Aquinas points to specific sins as particularly threatening the movement to God as end, in accordance with God's plan. Yes, people have great dignity. But they should not be presumptuous. They are not the source of their dignity or the cause of their elevation. Rather, all that they have, they have from God, not least the grace that comes through Christ that makes attaining eternal life possible. People too are prone to pride; the incarnation—the lowering, that is, of one who is God to human form—should provide, in its humility, an effective remedy. Finally, in the fifth reason, Aquinas turns to one of his ways of accounting for the great salvific importance of Christ's work on the *cross*, namely, satisfaction. By sin, people owe a debt to God, but they cannot pay the debt; they cannot make up for the infinite offense that their sin has done to God. What God does is of infinite value. But God does not owe the debt of sin. And so God has become human, and in the voluntary death on the cross pays the debt owed for sin. Justice is maintained, and God's mercy and love are also shown; God as human has acted wisely. Again, in all of these reasons in the second group of five, the journey motif is prominent; the withdrawal from evil that is promoted by the incarnation advocates the staying on the correct path to God. And, as with the first group, the affirmation of incarnation is shown to go well with crucial Christian beliefs without thereby necessitating God (in the first sense discussed in the article).

Narcisse (1993); Wawrykow (1998).

Gifts of the Holy Spirit   God's love is transformational. As shown in the teaching on grace and the infused virtues (see *grace; theological virtues*), the entry into correct relationship with God that is brought about by God's love is productive of new being in the individual. The love that God shows that stands as the foundation of correct relationship to God transforms the individual, healing the sinful self and producing new capacities in the individual by extending the scope of the powers of the soul. Through the grace that is habitual, the essence of the soul is healed and elevated; by the theological virtues that flow from habitual grace, the powers of the soul are extended in their reach, as they are also by the moral virtues that are infused in justification. Justification brings new capacity, a new potential for actions pleasing to God. By the theological virtues, one can believe in God and affirm what God reveals; by hope, one can aspire to God as end; by charity, one is able to love God for God's own sake. By the acts that emerge from these virtues, as willed by the individual, one comes closer to God.

The transformation is real. The person who lacks them surely looks different from one who has been granted habitual grace and the theological virtues; the latter can do more. Yet the human person remains a work in progress. It is one thing to have a power, but quite another

to use that power, or use it promptly, or unfailingly use it well. In this sense, one has to become what one is; otherwise put, one has to grow into the new life that has been provided by God, come to actually live as one now can live, by God's grace. It is in this connection that Aquinas affirms the great value of the gifts of the Holy Spirit. Habitual grace and the infused virtues provide the potential. As he makes clear in the discussion of grace, in affirming the sanctifying grace that is *auxilium*, in the journey of the habitually graced individual to God as end, additional grace is needed— the grace of *auxilium*, which is the movement of the Holy Spirit who prompts the use of the habits. The gifts of the Holy Spirit are themselves habits, distinct from the infused virtues, which are given by God to facilitate the use of the infused virtues (II-II.68.2–3). As are the infused virtues, the gifts are the signs in the individual of God's love; they are gifts worked in the person by the Holy Spirit. They are habits designed to make the person endowed with the infused virtues amenable to the promptings of the Holy Spirit; they render more likely the realization of the potential constituted by the infused habits. They are the means by which the Holy Spirit moves the graced person possessing the virtues to the inheritance promised to the elect.

The discussion of the gifts is put by Aquinas in the midst of that of the virtues, in both parts of the ST's Second Part. In ST I-II.68, he offers a brisk review of the gifts in general, showing, among other things, the basis of their affirmation in Isaiah 11 (I-II.68.4 sed contra; a.7), their origin in the Holy Spirit (e.g., a.2), and their close connection to the virtues, in particular to charity—indeed, those who lack charity, as is the case of those whose faith is only unformed (see *faith*), also lack the gifts; those who have charity, the form of the virtues that perfects the will that elicits or commands human acts, have all of the gifts (I-II.68.5c). In the ST II-II, Aquinas underscores the close connection between virtues and gifts by assigning each gift to the virtue that it makes amenable to the promptings of the Holy Spirit. Thus, he discusses in the course of the account of the theological virtue of faith, the gifts of understanding (II-II.8) and knowledge (q.9); in relation to hope, fear (q.19); and the gift of wisdom (q.45), in relation to charity. Gifts are attached to the cardinal virtues (see *virtue*) as well: The gift of counsel (q.52) is linked to prudence, that of piety (q.121) as perfective of justice, and the gift of fortitude (q.140) in connection with the cardinal virtue of the same name. Only temperance lacks its specific gift, although the gift of fear (q.19), attached to hope, does double duty in this regard.

Horst (2001); Nicholas (1992).

God   After its opening question on *sacred doctrine*, the ST devotes a series of questions to God (ST I.2–43). It is most appropriate to open a work such as the ST with the treatment of God. As ST I.1 has insisted, sacred doctrine, the body of truths required for salvation, has principally to do with God, and with other things as they are related to God as to their beginning and end. It is with these truths that the *theologian* is concerned, in doing the *theology* that pertains to sacred doctrine. Hence, before turning in his *summa* of theology to the procession of creatures from God as their creator (ST I.44ff.), and the movement of the rational creature to God as end through moral and supernatural activity (ST I-II, II-II), as made possible by *Jesus Christ*, who as man is the way to God as end (prologue to ST I.2; ST III), Aquinas offers the present reflections on God. At two main points, Aquinas offers comments on the organization of the treatise on God. At I.27 he characterizes the preceding questions (qq.2–26) as concerned in the main with the unity of the divine essence; the questions that follow deal with the *Trinity* (qq.27–43). Some readers of Aquinas have imagined that the two parts of the treatise on God correspond to the two kinds of truth contained in sacred doctrine. The one kind, the *articles of faith* as they deal directly with God, would come in qq.27–43; the other kind, the *preambles of faith*, would be the focus of the earlier questions (qq.2–26) and, in this reading, treated under the formality of the demonstrable rather than the formality of the revealed. His organizational comments in I.27 would seem to indicate, however, that that proposal is faulty as a rendering of what Aquinas is doing. Rather, it is one and the same God who is the focus of the inquiry throughout both parts of the treatise on God, the Christian God who is revealed as one God in three persons. The scriptural revelation governs the inquiry throughout; Aquinas in interpreting and representing that revelation will call upon all of the resources at his disposal: the postbiblical readers of Scripture and the philosophers whose terms, concepts, and reasonings may help in retrieving the scriptural message (see *authority*). In qq.2–26, the discussion revolves around the unity of essence of the Christian God; in the subsequent questions, it revolves around the Trinity. Both aspects are important, and neither is to be privileged at the expense of the other. God is one and God is three; there are things that are common to the three persons, and others that are peculiar to each. Aquinas discusses them all.

Both parts of the treatise are required in order to speak responsibly about the Christian God; the ideas that figure in the first part of the treatise prepare for the second main part, there turned to good effect. Hence, the discussion of the perfections that exist in God in a supereminent way lay the foundation for the consideration of the distinction of persons in God. God is rational, and is so in a way that surpasses our own rationality. God has an intellect and has a will appropriate to God. Such exist in God in an eminent way, as is proper to the one who is the cause of such perfections in creatures. The discussion of divine intellection (I.14) and willing (I.19), appropriate in the part of the treatise given over to the unity of the divine essence and what is true of God as God, prepares for the reflection on the divine persons. It is not a stretch to say that the discussion in I.14 and I.19 is teleologically sculpted, with an eye to the presentation of the persons who, distinct from each other by the eternal acts of God's self-knowing and self-loving, are identical with the divine essence (see *Trinity*).

In his other main organizational reflection, at the head of ST I.2, Aquinas offers a characterization of the first part of the treatise on God. There are three sections of questions on the divine essence: one on the existence of God, comprised of a single question (q.2); a second on the manner of God's existence (qq.3–13); and a third on the divine operations, namely, God's knowledge (qq.14–18), the divine will (qq.19–21), and what pertains to the divine intellect and will jointly (qq.22–24), including providence (q.22) and *Predestination* (q.23). He brings this third section of the first main part of the treatise on God to a close with a consideration of the divine power (q.25) and beatitude (q.26). Aquinas immediately qualifies the second section by commenting that qq. 3ff. have to do with the manner of God's existence, or rather, he interjects, what is *not* the manner of God's existence. To offer a description of the divine essence would require a direct knowledge of the divine essence, but such is not possible in this life, given the way that humans know and their dependence for knowing on the evidence of the senses (see *anthropology; epistemology, theological*). God lies beyond our natural cognitive experience and so beyond our ability to describe. And so, in dealing with the manner of God's existence, Aquinas is in fact engaging in a lengthy moment of *negative theology*, of making clear the divine otherness by showing how God is not to be confused with the things of this world and not subject to their conditions. Hence, to give one example: God is simple, is not composed

in any way; this includes God's *esse* and essence, which in God are not to be distinguished but are identical (I.3.4). The recognition and articulation of difference between God and world in qq.3–11 condition the entire discussion of God in both parts of the treatise. Aquinas's account of God is not exclusively negative. On the basis of Scripture he does affirm certain truths about God that are to be taken positively. But even in such affirmation, Aquinas is aware of how God differs from what we know directly in this life and so how we name what we know. He knows that such claims about perfections in God are true, but he is also aware of how these perfections in God nonetheless escape us. The apophatic tempers the cataphatic in Aquinas; he is keenly aware of the mystery of God, of how God eludes even the most painstaking analysis. Indeed, a great goal of the treatise is to help his readers become even more attentive to the divine transcendence.

There are in fact two motifs that course their way through the entire treatise on God. One has already been noted: the concern for articulating divine transcendence. The other is the conviction of the divine immanence. Each is pursued in such a way that the one does not contradict the other. In gesturing throughout these questions at divine immanence and transcendence, Aquinas discloses his grasp of the import of the doctrine of creation, taken broadly. That doctrine will be subjected to close analysis in the questions that immediately follow the treatise on God (in ST I.44ff.). But his affirmation of God as creator informs the present questions on God and subtly shapes the presentation of God. God is the creator of all; all things are effects of God. No effect is identical or equal with its maker. Hence, when we speak of God and perforce must use terms of God that we know first of all through creatures, we must attend to the ways that God eludes our categories, to the ways that God is not to be reduced to a thing of this world. Aquinas has various strategies for articulating the divine transcendence: by removing from God anything that bespeaks imperfection and by affirming all perfections found in creatures as in God, but in a supereminent way that escapes our capacity to grasp. At the same time, God's effects are not utterly unlike their maker. God creates intentionally, in order to proclaim the divine goodness. Things "look like" God, are made after God in such a way that they can proclaim, outside of God, God. Thus, while not the effect, God can be said to be present in the effect, and so susceptible to the kind of knowing that is possible through effects. God is the source of being—of all being, and of the entirety, essence and *esse*, of each being. In this connection, Aquinas becomes almost lyrical in affirming divine immanence; as the subsistent *esse* who is the cause of all being, God is "most innermost in all things" (I.8.1c). God is also present to the world through God's power. God brings things to be and sustains them in their being and directs them to the end established for them by God. To come at the divine immanence from the other angle: While humans can come into the immediate presence of God and know God face to face only in the next life, at the end of their journey to God, they can be united, as it were, with God now, through their own operations (I.8.3c). In particular, they are united to God and God is present to them as the object of *faith, hope*, and especially, *charity*, all of which are rooted in the sanctifying grace that is the *mission* of the Holy Spirit (I.43). Again, there is no confusion of immanence and transcendence, or subverting of the claim of divine transcendence by the insistence of divine presence in essence and power and operation. Rather, the difference is maintained, while showing the world in its dependence on the God who transcends it.

Dodds (1986, 1993); Burrell (1979, 1986, 1993); Sokolowski (1982); Emery (1998, 2003, 2004); Hankey (1987).

Grace   The final questions of ST I-II, on the movement of the rational creature to God as end, are devoted to grace (qq.109–14). Grace is absolutely essential for the successful completion of the journey to God (see *viator*). Grace overcomes the obstacles that separate people from the transcendent end that is God, and renders them fit for their direct encounter with God in the next life. In Aquinas, grace brings not only forgiveness but transformation of the person as well. Grace establishes correct relationship with God and makes possible the good actions that God seeks of those called to eternal life. In working out his mature teaching on grace, Aquinas has learned much from the apostle Paul and from Augustine. His closer engagement with the Pauline epistles and with certain later writings of Augustine led to the formulation of a teaching that insists on the divine contribution, by grace, throughout the successful journey of the person to God as end. Through grace, as rooted in God's predestining will (see *predestination*), God takes the initiative in the salvific process and leads the person to the end to which the person has been freely and lovingly destined by God.

Running through the questions on grace are three basic distinctions and pairings. These pairings are first introduced in the opening question of the treatise (I-II.109), whose topic is the need for grace. In each of the ten articles of the question, Aquinas asks whether grace is needed for this or that. In the opening article, he asks whether grace is necessary in order to know truth. To answer that question, he invokes the first of the pairings, the distinction between the natural and the supernatural. If the truth that is to be known is natural, then grace is not necessary. By "natural," Aquinas means what falls within the scope of a being given its nature. In the case of human beings, truth is natural when it has to do with intelligible species that can be grasped through abstraction from the evidence provided by the senses, as retained in phantasms. For such truth, the endowments of the person as human will suffice. However, if a truth lies beyond the human's natural powers—as is the case with whatever is not corporeal or necessarily attached to body—then grace will be necessary. To do anything, one must have the capacity for that. Thus, to know supernatural truth, which is not accessible through the senses, one will need grace, which is seen as boosting or elevating the capacities of the person to allow for supernatural action. In the remainder of I-II.109 and throughout the treatise on grace, Aquinas will repeat the point that acting supernaturally, as in acts of *faith*, *hope*, and *charity*, will require added supernatural endowments (the *theological virtues*) that are rooted in God's grace granted to a person.

The opening article of the treatise may seem to be authorizing a clear division of the natural and the supernatural, each apparently integral and separate from the other. Grace will deal exclusively with the supernatural; natural capacities suffice for the natural order. While perhaps a plausible reading when restricted to this first article, Aquinas immediately complicates matters. In the second article, he asks whether grace is needed in order to will the good. A first move is to ask whether the good in question is natural or supernatural; if the latter—that is, God as God is to be willed if people are to reach their end in God—the answer is yes, grace is necessary. But Aquinas points out that even with regard to the natural good, which in principle lies within the grasp of the person as human, humans experience great difficulty as a result of the fall. *Original sin* has greatly complicated matters, throwing the person out of allegiance to God and setting the self against itself. The lower parts of the human person are at war with the higher, rational self, and so are not susceptible to its lead. Thus, even with regard to the natural good, people need grace. Without grace, they can do some things; Aquinas mentions here building dwellings, planting vineyards, and the like. But to the good that

is proportionate to the person as human, grace is required. The effect of introducing the problem of sin, then, is to show that the division between natural and supernatural, useful as an analytical tool, does not authorize viewing the one in isolation from the other. If there had been no sin, grace would have been necessary only with regard to the supernatural good; no one attains God as end without grace. But after sin, grace is also needed in order to do the good that is natural to people.

This same article introduces the third distinction that is important for the treatise on grace. There are in fact two kinds of grace: habitual grace and the grace that is *auxilium* (lit., "aid" or "help"). As its name indicates, the first kind of grace is a habit, a steady disposition to act in a certain way. It adds power to the person, thus rendering possible acts of a certain kind. The other grace, *auxilium*, bespeaks God's active involvement in human acting. A power is needed for an action. But a power does not reduce itself to an act. Rather, something already in an act must reduce the potential to act. For Aquinas, when talking about the movement of rational creatures to God as their end, this something in an act is God. God reduces the potential constituted by habitual grace, the added endowment of the person, to act, by *auxilium*.

Aquinas invokes the third pairing in giving his more complete analysis of the second distinction, that between the pre-fall and the post-fall state. Does the human person need grace in order to will the good? In terms of the supernatural good, the human person has always been in need of grace. To reach the transcendent end that is God, the person needs to be raised, as it were, to God's level. The grace that bridges the ontological gap between the rational creature and the God who is the creature's end, by divine decree, is both habitual and the grace of *auxilium*. Habitual grace boosts the capacities of the person to the supernatural level. It provides the potential for supernatural activity. But habitual grace does not reduce itself to action. For that, the other grace, of *auxilium*, is needed. By *auxilium*, God reduces the person to supernatural action. Both graces were needed in the pre-fall state and, obviously, now as well. Is grace necessary for the natural good? After the fall, definitely; and again, both graces are in play. Habitual grace not only elevates the person to the supernatural level; habitual grace heals the fallen and disrupted self, restoring correct order within the self just as it restores the whole person to subjection to God. But, again, habitual grace does not reduce itself to action. Moreover, while the healing of the self is real, it is not complete in this life. The person still lives in a fallen world, and the subordination of the lower self to the higher, and of the whole person to God, is not final or complete. The graced person is still a work in progress, as the person strives to grow in conformity to God's will. The person is still bombarded by **temptation** to sin, from without from sinners and from the **devil**, who is envious of God and wishes to prevent humans from coming to God as end; from within, by the remnants of sin, both original and actual, that seek to reassert themselves and wring the person away from God. When first introduced in I-II.109, there is a fundamentally metaphysical need for *auxilium*: to reduce potential to act. But, as the question continues, Aquinas inserts a moral need for *auxilium* as well. *Auxilium* reduces to supernatural action; it also reduces the person to morally correct action, realizing the potential reconstituted by habitual grace and its attendant virtues. Grace both elevates and heals; both graces, habitual and *auxilium*, are involved in both functions of grace.

A little later in the treatise on grace, Aquinas makes a final point of consequence about habitual grace and *auxilium*. As he states in I-II.111.2c, each can be further divided into operative and cooperative. The definitions of "operative" and of "cooperative" differ when used of *auxilium* and of habitual grace. In the case of habitual grace, operative refers to "being," to the new being that is provided by the infusion of habitual grace. As operative, habitual grace makes its recipient pleasing to God by healing the self harmed by sin and elevating the person to God's own level. As cooperative, habitual grace has to do with "operation," in the sense that it disposes its bearer to actions that will lead the person to God as end. Aquinas devotes rather more attention to the other grace, *auxilium*, as operative and cooperative. In terms of *auxilium*, "operative" indicates when the will is moved by God and the will is simply moved. The example that Aquinas gives in the present article is conversion. In conversion, someone who is a sinner is moved by God's grace away from sin and toward God as end. But that is not the only example that Aquinas might have provided. From the final articles of I-II.109, he could also have cited the operative *auxilium* responsible for perseverance in the state of grace once one has entered that state. In the state of grace, one continues to be tempted to sin, and habitual grace does not suffice for the overcoming of new temptation. Rather, God must keep the person in grace; God does that by *auxilium*, which in light of I-II.111.2c can now be identified as operative. God moves the will, and the will is simply moved. As for cooperative, when used of *auxilium*, this means that the will is moved, and is moved in such a way that it also moves itself. Aquinas undoubtedly expects his reader to recall what he has written on God's causing, especially in the discussion in the First Part of providence and predestination. In ST I.22.4, he states that the effects of providence are certain and infallible, because they are worked by God. But God uses secondary causes to achieve these effects. When God uses a secondary cause that is necessary, the effect will be certain (because it is caused by God) and necessary, because it is caused by God through a secondary cause that is necessary. When God uses a secondary cause that is contingent, the effect is certain and contingent, because it is caused by God through a secondary cause that is contingent. Aquinas makes the same point in the next question, on *predestination* (I.23.6). In executing God's predestining will, God employs the causality of human beings to bring them to the end set for them by God; their effects will be certain and contingent. God's causing is not at the expense of the genuine causing of human beings; in causing, God brings about the authentic, life-promoting causing of humans. That God is able to do so—that is, that God's causing is not at the expense of genuine human causing—is testimony to the divine transcendence. The successful causes that are contained in the world are often successful at the expense of those through whom they work. God is not to be reduced to such a cause; God, the transcendent cause of being, can cause in such a way that the human also is cause. In I-II.111.2c, Aquinas is restating the point, now in terms, especially, of cooperative *auxilium*.

In that article, Aquinas links his talk of operative and cooperative *auxilia* to what he has written very early in the same part of the ST (I-II.6ff.) on the human act. Operative *auxilium* matches up with what he here calls the interior act, while cooperative *auxilium* matches up with the exterior act. The discussion of the complete human act earlier in the I-II is detailed and complex. But here it can be noted that the complete human act is said to fall into three parts: the intention of the end, the choice of the means, and the execution of the act. While it is a matter of some debate among scholars of Aquinas, it is likely that the latter two parts of the human act should be ascribed to cooperative *auxilium*, and the first, to operative *auxilium*. Thus, when a person wills an end, and this is really conducive to reaching the end that is God, this is due to operative *auxilium*. When the person deliberates about means to the end, opts for a particular strategy, and then performs the act, that is to be ascribed to cooperative *auxilium*. Later in the treatise, Aquinas

will come at the main effects of grace. One is justification, being set right with God, which is the effect of operative grace (ST I-II.113). The other is *merit*, which is the effect of cooperative grace (I-II.114). Thus, for each good act of the person, God gives, by operative *auxilium*, good intention. God then cooperates in the choice of means and execution of the act, which can be termed meritorious of the end to which the person has been called by God.

In the different questions of the treatise on grace, Aquinas employs the model of life as journey. The end of that journey is in the next life, with God. The present life can be, and should be, the path to God as end, although by sin people go off the path and unless they repent, will end up in final separation from God, in hell. The present life itself can be divided into two states: the state of sin, which is prior to conversion, and, after conversion, the state of grace. In the light of I-II.109 and 111.2c, it is possible to limn the following sequences of grace: Conversion to the state of grace is due to an operative *auxilium*, by which the will is moved and does not move itself. In conversion, the person is turned away from sin and toward God as ultimate end. At the completion of the conversion process, habitual grace is infused, providing new being (operative habitual grace) and the possibility for operation that is morally and supernaturally good (cooperative habitual grace). This habitual grace is the only habitual grace that is infused. However, this habitual grace is susceptible to growth; it is augmented when the person in fact acts out of this grace and the theological virtues given with it. Or it can be lost, and is, through mortal *sin*. To the person in the state of habitual grace and who in fact has been destined by God to eternal life, additional *auxilia* will be given. These *auxilia* figure in the morally and supernaturally good actions that the graced person does in reaching God as end. There will be as many *auxilia* as there are good acts done in the state of grace that further the progress to God as end. As operative, these *auxilia* will provide good intention and so perseverance in the state of grace; as cooperative, they will work with the person in adopting appropriate means for realizing these ends, oriented to the ultimate end that is God, and in executing the exterior act.

The teaching on grace complements, and presupposes, that on predestination. Predestination is God's plan to bring some rational creatures to share in God's own life, in heaven; secondarily, it is the execution of this plan, by grace. In ST I.23, in discussing predestination, Aquinas is content to speak generally of grace, although he is clear (as in 5c) that sometimes grace moves and only moves (the example given there is conversion) and sometimes moves in such a way that the person moved is also an agent (as is the case for acts done in the state of grace). He leaves to the treatise on grace in the I-II the further specification of grace as both *auxilium* and habitual, and of each as operative and cooperative. The discussion of both grace and predestination is resumed in the Third Part, when talking of adoption and Christ's predestination. In III.23–24, Aquinas nicely completes the discussion begun in the First Part and continued in I-II, by making clear the Christic dimension of predestination and grace. God's predestining in eternity is "in Christ." Those who are called to eternal life will come to eternal life through Christ, through the grace that God makes available in Christ. In coming to eternal life through Christ, humans who have been joined to Christ as their head (see **church**) will come into the inheritance promised to those who are children of God. They will be treated as heirs, and their receiving of the inheritance will be patterned on the sonship of the Word, who has become human as Jesus. What pertains to the Word as the natural Son of God will be given to humans, the adopted children of God, to those who will enter into eternal life, into God's self-knowing and loving that constitutes salvation, through union with and discipleship to Christ.

Aquinas's teaching on grace underwent considerable development over the course of his scholarly career. An examination of the teaching presented in his early *Scriptum on the Sentences* of Peter Lombard reveals some prominent differences with that in the ST. In that early work, the first entry into grace is ascribed to human initiative. In the *Scriptum*, Aquinas offers a fairly straightforward and conventional reading of the saying, *Facienti quod in se est, Deus non deneget gratiam* (to one who does her best, God will give grace). It is up to the human person to take the first step to God, and the person can take this step. Once that is done, God will infuse grace. Correspondingly, in the earlier writing, perseverance is no big problem. Once one has entered into the state of grace, staying in that grace is a matter of acting out of habitual grace, in accordance with it. When one wills in accordance with that grace, one stays in that grace. In the *Scriptum*, grace is exclusively habitual; at this stage, Aquinas does not affirm a separate grace, that of *auxilium*. Sin is acknowledged, but its effects are hardly as severe as they are in the ST. Sin can be overcome and the right thing done. That would be, for the person not in the state of grace, the first step to God, which will be met by God's granting of habitual grace. For the person in habitual grace, there is no need for a separate grace, the grace of *auxilium*, that would overcome temptation and keep the person on the way to God as end by providing good intention. Finally, the connection between grace and predestination in the *Scriptum* is loose. Moving into grace seems to be possible for all; it is up to each person to act correctly, which each can, and so impress God and so receive habitual grace. In the ST, on the other hand, the entire salvific process, the entire journey to God, falls under God's predestination. God wills salvation for some rational creatures. Therefore, God executes that plan by giving the operative graces that work conversion and perseverance in grace, to bring those people to that end. And God provides the habitual grace, in accordance with predestination, that boosts the moral and supernatural capacities of a person and inclines her to good acts. In affirming merits, the good acts of the person deserving as a reward of the end to which God has predestined some as a gift, the person will be aided by the grace given to the elect.

In revising his teaching on grace, playing up the consequences of sin that must be overcome by grace, and linking inward grace to God's predestination, Aquinas is showing his closer acquaintance with Paul as mediated to him by Augustine. Aquinas did study Paul at first hand and prepared commentaries on the Pauline epistles; his commentary on Romans is especially detailed. Aquinas in mid-career had come across writings of the very late Augustine, writings that had passed out of theological circulation after the Carolingian period. In reading those texts of Augustine— such as *The Predestination of the Saints* and *The Gift of Perseverance*—Aquinas saw that Augustine's target were monks who insisted on the need for the human person to take the first step to God and so to initiate conversion. In rejecting that teaching, Augustine had insisted that taking the first step is an impossibility. By the bondage to sin, one would only, if left to one's own devices, sin the more. To break the captivity to sin, an inward grace is needed to transform and reform the sinful self; such a grace is given in accordance with God's predestining will. And since one continues to be tempted to sin, in order to stay in grace an inward grace of perseverance is needed, again given in accordance with God's predestining will. For this late Augustine, God's predestination is in fact to eternal life, and is executed by operative graces of conversion and perseverance. Thus, in the ST, Aquinas is showing himself the beneficiary of this reading of Augustine, incorporating and restating the Augustinian lessons in terms (habitual grace, *auxilium*) accessible to his own readers.

———

Bouillard (1944); Lonergan (1971); Wawrykow (1995, 1991, 2005a); Laporte (1973); Pesch (1967); Somme (1997).

Gratia non tollit naturam sed perficit   *see* Nature and Grace

Gratuitous Graces   In the course of his treatise on *grace*, Aquinas divides grace into two basic kinds (ST I-II.111). One is *gratia gratum faciens*, commonly translated as "sanctifying grace." This is the grace that sanctifies an individual, granting the person a participation in the divine nature and ordering him to God as to one's supernatural end. It is this grace that receives the much greater part of the attention in the treatise on grace. The other kind of grace is *gratia gratis data*, commonly translated as "gratuitous grace." The phrase is not altogether happy; after all, the first kind of grace is also gratuitously, in the sense of "freely," given by God. This gratuitious grace, in the technical sense, is given not for the sanctification of the recipient, but to allow the recipient to help others to God (I-II.111.1c).

In positing this second kind of grace, Aquinas has in mind the words of Paul in 1 Corinthians 12:8–10, quoted in I-II.111.4 sed contra: "To one is given through the Spirit the utterance of wisdom, and to another the utterance of knowledge according to the same Spirit, . . . to another the working of miracles, to another prophecy, to another the discernment of spirits, to another various kinds of tongues, to another the interpretation of tongues." Some of these graces have to do with knowledge. The faith that is a gratuitous grace is not the virtue of faith, but a gift of special certitude about the invisible things of faith, by which the recipient can instruct others about what belongs to the faith (ad 2). The wisdom and the knowledge of the

Pauline text are not to be confused with the *gifts of the Holy Spirit* of the same names; these graces imply such a fullness of knowledge and wisdom that a man may not merely think aright of divine things, but may instruct others and overpower adversaries (ad 4). The word of wisdom that is the gratuitous grace provides the recipient with an exceptional knowledge of divine things and with a sound grasp of human things, as these pertain to the Christian religion.

Other of the Pauline graces have to do with doing or operating, confirming or proving what the recipient says. One way of confirming is when the recipient does what God alone can do, as when she performs miracles, including miracles of healing. Another way of confirming is by stating something that God alone can know, whether future contingents (and here there is the grace of *prophecy*) or the secrets of the heart (which is the grace of discerning spirits).

The final category of gratuitous graces given in I-II.111.4c is speech, and has to do with the fitting presentation to listeners of what the recipient knows. There is the gift of tongues, which allows the use of an idiom that a hearer can understand; the interpetation of tongues permits clarifying the sense of what is said.

Aquinas returns in II-II.171–78 to the graces that are gratuitous. In the prologue to q.171, Aquinas repeats the principal categories listed in I-II.111.4, of knowledge, speech, and operating or doing. Two questions (qq.176–77) are devoted to the graces having to do with speech; the final question of the treatise deals with the gratuitous grace of miracles (q.178). Most of the questions (qq.171–75), however, are given over to prophecy, looking in turn at prophecy in itself—its cause, mode, and principal kinds. This opening part of the treatise on prophecy concludes with a consideration of rapture, especially that of Paul (II-II.175.3–6), a discussion that also sheds light on the cognate topic of the *beatific vision*.

The teaching of the treatise on these graces (II-II.171–78) is recognizably of a piece with that in ST I-II.111, for the most part simply adding detail to that earlier presentation. However, the treatise does mark an advance in explaining even better how this kind of grace differs from sanctifying grace and from the virtues (see *theological virtues*) that arise from sanctifying grace. Sanctifying grace includes habitual grace, which heals a person of the effects of sin and elevates him to the supernatural order. It provides a stable disposition to him to act in a way pleasing to God. So too, the theological virtues provide a stable disposition to acts pleasing to God; by the virtue of faith, for example, one is inclined to acts of faith. The gratuitous graces, however, are not habits, stable dispositions to act in a certain way. Rather, they are transient actions of the Holy Spirit in a person that allow that person to act for the benefit of others, whether through special graces of knowing, of doing, or of speech. In these graces, God gives what will be helpful for another, and through the recipient works toward the salvation of those with whom the recipient will come into contact (see, e.g., II-II.171.2).

Bonino (2002); Berchtold (2000).

Holy Orders   *see* Sacrament; Character, Sacramental

Hope   The second of the *theological virtues*, hope is defined as the expectation of future good that is difficult yet possible to attain (II-II.17.1c). The future good to which hope aspires is God as final end; Aquinas thus is reinforcing the point that the theological virtues are to be viewed in the context of the movement of the human person to God as end. This future good is difficult to attain; not everyone, after all, reaches God as end. Yet it is possible to attain to God; otherwise, there would be not hope, but despair.

In examining the possibility of hope, Aquinas nicely draws on his mature teaching on grace, and in particular the grace of *auxilium* that is distinguished from habitual grace (see **grace**). *Auxilium* is God's help that moves people to act; it bespeaks a certain dynamism on God's part, as God prompts, inwardly, the human person to what leads to God as end. For Aquinas, something is possible in one of two ways: by one's own resources, or by the aid of another. The possibility of hope is not grounded in the first option; rather, as will be noted shortly, one looking to oneself would not hope, but would despair. Rather, the possibility of hope is due to the help of a friend, of God, who helps people as they move toward their transcendent end (II-II.17.1c; 21.1c).

Talk of *auxilium* leads Aquinas to posit, in turn, a double object of hope. The first has already been noted in the definition of hope: the God who is the end of the human journey. The second object is God's *auxilium*, which renders success in the journey possible. It is this *auxilium* that imparts to hope a confidence. What is impossible to one left to her own resources is possible because of God, and since God is most certain, one can be confident of reaching, with God's help, the end set for the person by God. While the agreement is not total, there is a similarity between Aquinas's teaching about the confidence of salvation as rooted in hope, and what the sixteenth-century Reformers would say of faith. In affirming the two objects of hope, Aquinas can designate these objects variously, in different writings. In the ST (II-II.17.4c), he speaks of the primary object, God in heaven, as the final cause of hope, and of *auxilium* as the efficient cause. In the disputed question *de Spe* (a.1c), he can call the first the material, and the second the formal, object of hope.

In the rest of the treatise on hope in the ST (II-II.17–22), Aquinas nuances the teaching by considering the vices opposed to hope and the gift of the Holy Spirit that is attached to the virtue of hope that makes it more susceptible to God's prompting. The first vice opposed to hope is despair (II-II.20). Here the attention of the person shifts from God as the second object of hope to oneself, and in looking at oneself, one perceives the huge gulf between oneself and God, both ontologically and morally. One may think that one is too unworthy to come under God's word of forgiveness in Christ (II-II.20.2 ad 2; 3c). Thus, in looking to oneself, one despairs of reaching God as end. The other vice opposed to hope is presumption (II-II.21), and this considers the resources by which one might reach God as end. It is possible to make too much of oneself, to presume on one's own powers; such would be an insult to God, whose aid is absolutely required in order to come to God as end. But it is also possible to presume too much on the help of a friend. That the help of God is required for the successful journey is evident. But as is also evident in his teaching on **merit**, God has ordained that those who have come into grace will then be led by grace to good actions that will deserve the end to which people have been graciously called, as a reward. One would be too presumptuous if one left it all, in effect, to God—if, that is, one did not work out of grace and do the acts that are pleasing to God and that contribute to the working out of one's salvation, as God intends (II-II.21.1c). God deserves the principal praise for human salvation, and without God's grace there is no salvation. But God works out the person's salvation not despite the person's own causality, but through and with it. To be presumptuous in the second sense would be to abdicate one's God-given responsibility to pursue the good as this leads to God as end.

Fear is the gift of God that accompanies the virtue of hope (II-II.19) and makes its possessor more pliable to the promptings of divine grace. There are in fact different kinds of fear. In servile fear, for example, one would refrain from evil out of fear of punishment. This is not the fear with which Aquinas is concerned. Rather, he is thinking of filial fear, and the evil to which this fear responds is not punishment, but rather the threat of estrangement from God. In filial fear, one fears the separation from God that comes through sin (II-II.19.1c). Thus, filial fear perfects the virtue of hope by making its possessor more prompt to trust in the God who makes it possible to come to God. Since one does not want to be separated from the heavenly Father, one gives oneself ever more in hope to the God who sustains the movement back to God (II-II.19.9 ad 1).

Bernard (1961); Conlon (1947); Pfürtner (1964); de Couesnongle (1974).

Hypostatic Union   As part of his incarnational Christology (see *Jesus Christ*), Aquinas affirms hypostatic union (e.g., ST III.2). The divine and the human natures are united in the hypostasis of the divine Word, the second person of God. The Word from eternity fully expresses the divine nature; the Word is one and the same God as the Father and the Holy Spirit. Without loss to itself as fully divine Word, the Word in the incarnation has taken up to itself a second nature and come to express it as well. The union of human to divine nature occurs in the second divine person, who as incarnate is the person of Jesus. While truly united, the two natures retain their integrity. The Word incarnate is fully God, fully human, and neither nature is to be reduced to or confused with the other.

In articulating hypostatic union, Aquinas is concerned to differentiate this orthodox position from various others that have been proposed in Christian history. For example, he rejects a monophysite position (e.g., in ST III.2.1). Such a teaching is susceptible to three formulations, all of which fail. It may be that the human nature is absorbed by the divine, or vice versa, or that out of two natures a single one, a mixture of the

two, comes to be. In any of these scenarios, there is a loss of nature, of at least (in the first two formulations) one nature, or as in the third, of both natures, which give way to a third. But this is to put in jeopardy human salvation. In the orthodox position, that the Word of God becomes human without loss to itself as Word, this means that there is an essential community between the Savior and the God who saves, and the Savior and those who need the redeeming from sin. If either nature or both recede, such essential community in nature will be forfeited. It will not be God who saves (and God alone can save); or it will be the humans, who need saving, who will be represented in the Christ who saves. If the natures are fused, the Savior will be neither God nor human.

Aquinas is in fact more concerned with the opposite error, as reflected in the teaching of Nestorius. The monophysites bring the natures too close together. Nestorians keep the divine and the human too far apart. With the orthodox, Nestorians affirm two natures. But as rendered in the tradition from Cyril of Alexandria on, the Nestorians affirm as well two persons, two subjects of action in the one Christ. Thus, there is not simply a union of the natures, but as well a union of persons, with one person expressing one nature and the other person the other nature, and the two persons coming together to form a partnership, Christ, whose goal is human salvation. There is a surface attractiveness to the Nestorian position, of which Aquinas (e.g., ST III.2.2 ob. 2, 3) is fully aware. Is there a human person in Jesus in the sense that there is a human person for every other instance of human nature? Does there not have to be a human person in that sense for there to be the essential community between the Savior and the race that even the orthodox acknowledge as crucial to Christology, concerned as it is with soteriology? Hence, Nestorius provides for a human person in the case of Christ, one that is the same as the human person in every other human being. The problem with this position, however, is that it insufficiently accounts for the unity in the Savior. In the Nestorian formulation, one person would do one sort of thing when it comes to Christ, and the other person would do other sorts of things. In the orthodox position, as formulated by Aquinas, there would not be such a distribution of labor, according to different subjects of action. Rather, as shown in detail in his Christology, there is a single subject in Christ, of whom all things, whether divine or human, are affirmed. The Word is the person of Jesus. The Word from eternity is the second person of God, who is one and the same God as the Father and the Holy Spirit. Some things will be said of the Word as distinct person, others as fully God. And the Word was made flesh. So still other things will be said of the Word—and it is the Word of whom these are said—as incarnate. The Word is the true subject of the human doings and sufferings of Jesus. Who is this who dies on the cross? In a Nestorian Christology, it is the human subject who dies, the human subject who has entered into a partnership, at the moment of conception, with the fully divine Word. The Word does not die on the cross; the Word is not the subject there. In Aquinas, on the other hand, it is the Word—as human—who suffers and dies for our salvation. God so loved the world that God sent his only Son; it is the Word of the Father who, as human, dies on the cross.

To return to the surface attractiveness of the Nestorian position, there is, in fact, in Aquinas's teaching a "human person" in the case of Christ, although that person differs from "human person" in the usual sense. A second nature has been joined to the first precisely in the Word. The Word is a person. From eternity, the Word is the second divine person. That does not change in incarnation. But the divine person also becomes human as instantiating the human nature in the case of Jesus. In Nestorius, there is a human being independently of the work

of "incarnation" of the Word. In Aquinas, there is no human in the case of Jesus apart from the work of incarnation of the Word. The Word takes up the human nature, and a human comes to be. The Word as incarnate is the human person. Does the absence of a human person in the usual sense mark a loss? So Nestorius. Or rather, does it mark a gain, inasmuch as in Aquinas's Christology there is a person, the second divine person, who as incarnate truly is human? As Aquinas puts it, it is better in this regard to exist in something nobler than oneself—that is, for the human nature to be instantiated by the Word—than to exist by oneself (ST III.2.2 ad 2). As the true bearer, the subject, of the humanity in the case of Jesus, the Word is truly human, who does and acts as other human persons can.

In the mature writings—*ScG* as well as ST—the principal foil of the affirmation of hypostatic union is Nestorius. But it is Aquinas's sense that more recent Christologies have lapsed into the Nestorian position. In the *Sentences* of Peter Lombard (III.d.VI), Peter reports three contemporary (that is, twelfth-century) positions on the union of the divine and human in Christ. One of these is called by the scholastic commentators the *homo assumptus* or two supposit theory. In this opinion, a human at the moment of its conception has been assumed into union with the divine Word, such that the two are closely related, and what is said of one can be said of the other, and the Word supplies its person to the human, a distinct supposit, so that the Word is the person of that supposit. Hence, in this opinion, there would be one person and two natures, but because the Word is supposit and person, the human also a supposit, there would be two supposits as well. In the light of his historical research in the early 1260s (see **doctors of the church**), Aquinas came to reject the designation of this position as an "opinion." Rather, it is a heresy, one long ago condemned by the church meeting in council, into which holders of the position have unwittingly lapsed (ST III.2.6c)—unwittingly, because they had worked out the position in ignorance of the early christological disputes and determinations as at Ephesus (431). For Aquinas, "hypostasis," "person," and "supposit" are all synonymous. And so to say that the union of the two natures in Christ is hypostatic is the same, for him, as saying the union is personal (that is, in the person of the Word) or in the supposit of the Word. In *homo assumptus*, however, that person and supposit are synonymous is not acknowledged, and as a way of escaping the charge of "Nestorian" in an obvious sense (that is, does it affirm two *persons*?), this position had distinguished person and supposit (a person is a supposit that has come to full perfection). Hence, in his own discussions of hypostatic union, given this position reported in the *Sentences*, the textbook of scholastic theology (see **Scriptum on the Sentences**), it was incumbent upon Aquinas to make the point explicit. Thus, right after the insistence on personal union (ST III.2.2), he adds (a.3) that this is the same as saying, therefore, a union of the two natures in the hypostasis, in the supposit, of the Word.

Gorman (2000a, b); Wawrykow (2005b); Stump (2002); Weinandy (2004).

Image of God   In the course of his discussion of the creation of the first humans and their original state, Aquinas examines the biblical teaching (Gen. 1:26) of the human person as made "to the image and likeness of God" (ST I.93). The image of God, in fact, stands at the heart of Aquinas's theological anthropology, and confirms the link he alleges repeatedly between God's creating and saving activity (see **creation**). By the assertion of the human person as made to the image and likeness of God, Aquinas is making clear that his understanding of the human person is not confined to or principally concerned with what pertains to the human by virtue of human nature and the powers of soul that it provides. The vision of the human conveyed by "image of God" is, rather, dynamic. The full sense of the possibilities of the human is intimated only when the human is set against the backdrop of God's sapiential plan for communicating God's goodness and the living out of the life, made possible by God, that will bring one to God as end.

In parsing "image of God," Aquinas notes three related senses that are in play (ST I.93.4c). One in fact has to do with the nature. All creatures are made by God to proclaim, in the way appropriate to each kind of creature, the goodness of God. Rational creatures, however, can proclaim the goodness of God in a distinctive way, by their rational capacities of knowing and willing. Although human knowing and willing fall short of God's eternal willing and knowing of God, in the very structure of its being, the human proclaims God in a way that transcends what is possible to a creature that lacks rationality, and merely is or lives. Hence it is that while in other creatures there can be, by virtue of God's intentional creating, a trace or vestige of God, in rational creatures there is the image of God, provided by the patterning by God of human nature on the divine. In this copying of the divine found in the human, there is not a perfect likeness; such is reserved to the second person of God, who is the image of the Father and one in nature with the Father (I.93.1 ad 2). In the case of human beings, there is an inequality, not identity. Nonetheless, all rational creatures, unlike lower forms of being, do resemble by their natural capacities God in a way deserving of the tag, "image."

The second sense of image has to do with the orientation of the human to God and to the acts that relate the human person to God. While all humans can be called in the image of God in the first sense, only those who are in grace are the image of God in this second sense. Grace, and the virtues that it brings, provides this conformity. People here not only have the natural aptitude for knowing God; in their elevation to the supernatural order and reception of the virtues that orient them to God as end and that allow for the knowledge that faith brings, the aspiration and desire given by hope, and the love of God as friend involved in charity, they are more to the image of God. There is, in fact, a significant dynamism in this. Powers of soul are one thing, as are the habits that perfect the soul. But in the actual use of the powers, as perfected by the habits, in the way intended by God, we meet, says Aquinas, the image of God in the primary and chief sense (I.93.7c). The image of God found in the powers of soul and these habits is secondary. God is not static. God is in act, eternally contemplating and loving God; thus, as the person knows and wills, and in particular knows and wills God (I.93.8c), the person is more to the image of God. The preposition "to" itself nicely indicates the dynamism of this principal sense of image. People are in the image of God; graced people in their acts are *in* the image of God and also *to* the image of God—meaning that they are not finished products, but by their willing and knowing God not only imitate divine acting, on which their knowing and willing is patterned, but come closer to the God to whom they aspire.

In the third sense of image of God, one comes in fact to the human person as at the end of the journey that is human existence (see *viator*). In heaven, the blessed will come face to face with God and will know and love God perfectly (I.93.4c). Hence, they will have reached the term of image of God, will have come to the fullest expression of the image that is possible to humans, namely, the knowing and loving of God that is proper to God, as rendered in a human key. The progression, then, in the three senses of image of God is from natural resemblance, as provided by the nature and so common to all human beings, through growing resemblance, through

the graced acts that imitate God's eternal acts, to the life of glory, where one enters into the life of knowing and loving that is proper to God.

There is a profound Trinitarian dimension to Aquinas's account of the image, as is clear from the fifth article of ST I.93. For the acts of knowing and willing in God are in fact the acts constitutive, from eternity, of the persons of God. In knowing Godself, the Father speaks the Word, and in loving God, the love that is the Holy Spirit proceeds from both (I.93.6c). Hence, the knowing and willing of God of the graced person (image in the chief sense, in this life) is itself Trinitarian, recalling and proclaiming that knowing and loving that is the Trinity.

As part of his analysis, Aquinas considers in passing a difficulty created by some words of the apostle Paul. In 1 Corinthians 11:7, Paul writes, "[Man] is the image and reflection of God; but woman is the reflection of man." Does this mean that only the male is the image of God (I.93.4 ob. 1)? Aquinas, however, is adamant about the universal application of the image of God, to include women as well as men. To explain Paul, he has recourse to a point that he has made in the question immediately proceeding (I.92.2–4), where he discusses Genesis 2:22. There it is stated that God made the woman out of the rib taken from Adam. That does not address the image of God in its principal import, but deals with something only secondary, tangential. "Image" in this sense is found only in men, not women, for just as all creatures proceed from God as beginning and end, so woman proceeds from man. But in the bulk of his response to this objection (I.93.4 ad 1), Aquinas insists that in its primary force, image applies as much to women as to men. "Image of God" as discussed in this question has to do with natural aptitude and the graced use of the aptitude, and such is found equally in women and in men. Indeed, the words of Genesis 1:26ff., the foundational text for the image of God, says as much. Right after the words "In the image of God he created him," it is added, "'male and female he created *them*" (RSV), and as Augustine observes, "them" is used in the plural lest it be thought that both sexes were united in one individual. By their graced knowing and willing, all humans, men and women, imitate God and come closer to the God that is their end.

Merriell (1990); Dauphinais (1999); Geiger (1974); Pelikan (1978).

Instrumental Causality

Instrumental Causality An instrument is employed by a principal agent to do something. Instruments are of various sorts. The pen with which I write is an instrument that is separate from me and inanimate; it is not alive and works only as moved by me. The ambassador who negotiates a treaty on behalf of the president is an instrument that is separate (that is, is not the president) and animate, herself a living agent. The hand that holds the pen that writes these words is a conjoined instrument, a part of the one who is responsible for this intentional action and who employs the hand in writing.

Aquinas refers to instrumental causality throughout his theology, and in a variety of settings. Instrumental causality figures, for example, in his discussion of *Jesus Christ*, and of the *sacraments* (for other examples, see *prophecy* and *grace*, with regard to operative and co-operative *auxilia*). In his Christology, Aquinas affirms **hypostatic union**. Two natures have been united in the person of the Word. The Word is thus the bearer of the divinity (as has been the case from eternity; the Word is a distinct person in God who is one and the same God, and fully so, as the Father and the Holy Spirit). The Word as incarnate is thus also the bearer of the humanity in the case of Jesus. To shed additional light on the union of the two natures, on how they stand in relation to each other, Aquinas cites, as in *ScG* IV.41, a more accessible model. As suggested in the *(Pseudo-) Athanasian Creed*, "Just as rational soul and flesh are one man, so God and man are one Christ." In turning to the human composite to figure the relation of humanity and divinity, there is some danger, as Aquinas immediately notes in this passage. Soul is related to body in two ways: as form is related to matter, and as to an instrument. The former cannot be in play here; divinity is not the form of the humanity (such a view might be plausible in a monophysite Christology, but not in Aquinas's). Rather, in likening the humanity-divinity relation to that of body and soul, one must think in terms of instrument. The body is the instrument of the soul; the humanity is the instrument of the divinity. The body is conjoined to its soul of which it is the instrument; the humanity of Christ is the conjoined instrument of the divinity. Here, in the specification of the reading of the Athanasian model, Aquinas is in fact showing his debt to his Greek patristic predecessors, for whom as well the humanity is the organ of the divinity in the case of Christ. In Christ, the subject is always the Word; the Word incarnate employs its humanity to bring about human salvation.

Sacraments too are instruments. They do not of themselves possess spiritual power. Rather, they convey the power of Christ on the *cross*. The principal agent is the God-man who suffers, dies, and is raised for our salvation. The Holy Spirit of Christ conveys this grace to others through the sacraments. These are the sacraments of Christ's saving humanity. They are not that humanity, but are separate from it. The sacraments are thus separate instruments, employed by Christ and the Holy Spirit to convey grace.

Actually, in discussing the sacraments, Aquinas extends the point to cover the ministers of the sacraments. They have been designated through their ordination to act on Christ's behalf (see *character, sacramental*). But in saying the words of the sacrament and performing the actions of the sacrament, they do not create the grace that is given in the sacrament. Rather, through their work as representatives of Christ, it is Christ and the Holy Spirit who grant grace and so apply the work of Christ on the cross. Here the example of the ambassador of the president is not exactly parallel. Presumably, in negotiating the treaty the ambassador will draw on her personal qualities—tact, sense of the appropriate, knowledge of the situation—to accomplish the president's goals. The personal qualities of the minister of the sacrament are a matter of indifference in the giving of sacramental grace. As long as the minister is in fact Christ's delegate (as established in the receiving of priestly character in ordination) and the minister in celebrating the sacrament intends what the church intends in so celebrating, the sacrament will do what it is supposed to do. Christ, the principal agent, will offer grace through the sacrament.

Tschipke (2003); Reynolds (2003, 2004); Mansini (1998).

Jesus Christ   Aquinas offers lengthy reflections on Jesus Christ in many of his works. He presents his Christology in the first twenty-two distinctions of the third book of his *Scriptum on the Sentences* of Peter Lombard, discussing those topics that the Lombard had but adding a number of others. The *Summa contra Gentiles* is a more personal work, in which Aquinas enjoys even more discretion in selecting and treating theological issues. Aquinas discusses Christ in the fourth book, beginning with a consideration of the second divine person (IV.2–14) and then looking at incarnation (chs. 27–49) and the salvific effects that arise through the work of the incarnate Word (chs. 50–55). In its Christology, the *ScG* is thoroughly historical and scriptural. Dogmatic formulation (e.g., the *Trinity, hypostatic union*) is rooted in Scripture and shown to provide the only adequate rendering of the scriptural witness to God and to Christ. Orthodox reading of Scripture on the pertinent points of christological doctrine is contrasted in the fourth book with various heretical misreadings, described in more or less chronological order. Theological history in fact provides the structure of many of the chapters. In chs. 2–9, he shows the finer delineation of Trinitarian doctrine as this has to do with the second divine person against the backdrop of various heretical misreadings of Scripture; in chs. 27–39, he does the same with regard to the incarnation of the Word. In the *ScG*, in the presentation of orthodox teaching with its scriptural roots and of heretical distortion of Scripture, Aquinas shows himself the beneficiary of his closer acquaintance, subsequent to the *Scriptum*, with the Greek patristic discussions and determinations about Christ as he came to know them in newly recovered Latin translation (see *authority*).

ST III.1–59, however, is the most sustained and detailed of Aquinas's christological pieces. Throughout, his mastery of the preceding tradition and of the intricacies of christological doctrine is palpable and inspiring. The treatise on Christ falls into two main parts, each susceptible to further division. In the first of these parts (qq.1–26), he offers a thorough reflection on *hypostatic union*. After an opening question on the *fittingness* of the incarnation (q.1), he investigates in turn the mode of union (qq.2–15) and what follows on the union (qq.16–26). The discussion of the mode of union itself is distinguished into three subgroups of questions. Question 2, on the mode of union in general, stands on its own, as a kind of overture to these questions (qq.2–15). Question 3 also stands on its own, devoted to the person who assumes human nature, the second person of God. Questions 4–15 are on the human nature that is taken up by the Word. Actually, these questions can be distinguished again, into the human nature itself (qq.4–6) that is assumed (in its constituent parts of body and soul, and the order of their assuming by the Word), and what is designated as the "coassumed" (qq.7–15). The coassumed do not fall under human nature and so are not part of the definition of what it means to be human, as given by the nature. Rather, the coassumed cover those perfections and defects that actual human beings may have, as affecting or modifying the nature. In qq.7–15, Aquinas asks which coassumed perfections and defects the Word become human had. He is guided in this inquiry by Scripture: what does Scripture indicate about various perfections and defects when it comes to Jesus? He is also guided by his sense, formed by the reading and meditation on Scripture with the aid of the mediating tradition, about what is appropriate to the Savior. The Savior will take on those perfections (see qq.7–13) and those defects of body and soul (qq.14–15) that will further, not hinder, his salvific work. In qq.7–13, Aquinas asks about Christ's grace, both personal (q.7) and as head of the *church* (q.8); qq.9–12 are given over to the *knowledge* that *Christ* had; and q.13 looks at the extent of the power of Christ's soul. The category of coassumed is valuable, for it does allow one to describe a human in her historical actualization without being prone to confuse what is not essential with what is essential to being human. To take two examples dealing with imperfections: Does dying fall under the definition of the human? That is, is the human as human mortal? As Aquinas has shown already in his account of *original justice* and *original sin*, dying is not part of human nature, but a penalty imposed in response to the misuse of something that is essential to being human, namely, the human will which gives the human control over her actions. So too, sinning and the inner disruption to the self that is brought by sin are not essential to being human, but rather what results from the misuse of the will. Hence, it is possible to talk of Jesus' absolute sinlessness, as required by Scripture, and not put his genuine humanity in doubt. To complete the point, as sinless, Jesus did not have

to die; that he did die indicates the willing acceptance of this sentence imposed on sinful humans in order to achieve their salvation. Or to take a perfection: Jesus did have the fullness of grace. Hence, he was moved by grace perfectly, so that in the exercise of his human will, he willed what was good and appropriate to human nature and in conformity with God's will. His moral success was not due to the fact that he is God, but to his fullness of grace and openness to that grace; that he received the fullness of grace was fitting, however, precisely because the person of Jesus is the Word of God.

In the third subgroup (qq.16–26) within the first main part of the treatise on Christ, the focus is on what follows on the union. A wide range of points having to do with consequences is covered in these questions, allowing Aquinas to further specify the grammar of incarnation, what is involved in saying that the Word became flesh. There is a threefold division within qq.16–26, with questions in turn on Christ in himself (qq.16–19), including on what sort of statements can and cannot be affirmed about Christ (q.16), and the being of Christ (q.17; see *esse*); questions on what belongs to Christ in relation to the Father (qq.20–24); and finally, things pertaining to Christ in relation to us (qq.25–26). In these final two questions of the first main part of the treatise on Christ, Aquinas looks at the adoration of Christ and of Christ as mediator.

With the second main part of the treatise on Christ (qq.27–59), there is a shift in focus and tenor. As Aquinas states in the prologue to q.27, after the treatise on the union of God and man and the consequences thereof, it remains to consider what things the incarnate Son of God did or suffered in the human nature united to the Word. Questions 27–59 look at what the incarnate Word did and suffered, in four main stages. Aquinas considers first those things that relate to the Word's coming into the world (qq.27–39), beginning with some questions on *Mary*, the

Mother of God (qq.27–30) as part of the consideration of the Word's conception as human (qq.27–34), followed by a discussion of his birth (qq.35–36), his circumcision (q.37) and his baptism (q.39, preceded in q.38 by a discussion of the baptism of John). In the second section of the second main part of the treatise, Aquinas considers the incarnate Word's life in the world; qq.40–45 treat his mode of living, his doctrine, and his miracles, including a consideration of the *Transfiguration* (q.45). The third section is devoted to his departure from the world, including a close consideration of the effects of Christ's death on the *cross* (qq.48–49). The treatise on Christ concludes with a consideration of those things that concern his exaltation after this life (qq.53–59); he looks in turn at the *resurrection of Christ* (qq.53–56), his ascension (q.57), his sitting at the right hand of the Father (q.58), and his judiciary power at the Last Judgment (q.59; see *eschatology*).

The ST is innovative in its Christology precisely in terms of this second main part of the treatise on Christ. Previously, scholastic treatises on Christ had been content to treat the material covered in the first main part, where the grammar of incarnation was to be limned. In the ST, however, Aquinas adds a complement to that material, by turning directly to the Gospel accounts of Jesus, now read with the aid of that grammar. Aquinas in the ST was the first to make the retelling of the story of Christ, from the beginnings to its culmination, integral to a scholastic treatise on Christ. By this move, he was able to show concretely the value of the close articulation of the grammar of Christ. With a firmer grasp of that grammar, he could engage, as in ST III.27–59, in a retelling of Christ's story that would highlight who this is—the second person of God become human—and make ever clearer why it is important to the faith that Jesus be fully God and fully human. As God, he can save; as human, he has identified with those who need

saving. In his acts and sufferings, he works out human salvation and shows other humans how they are to live, as they journey to God as their end, through Christ (see *Omnis Christi actio nostra est instructio*).

Although the ST in this particular regard marks an advance over his other writings on Christ, there is a remarkable consistency in the basic understanding of Christ offered by Aquinas from the beginning to the end of his career. The main points of his Christology are as follows.

Aquinas's Christology is resolutely incarnational. Incarnation is to be taken in two, related senses. First, there is the act of incarnation, an act of the second divine person, who takes up human nature. Second, by virtue of the act it is possible to provide a description of the reality that results from that act. The incarnate Word is fully God and fully human.

The person of Jesus is the Word of God. In taking up human nature and instantiating that nature, there is no loss to the Word. What is true of the Word from eternity continues to be true in the act of incarnation. Because of incarnation, something else comes to be true of the Word as incarnate.

The Word takes to itself a full human nature. Everything that pertains to being human is to be affirmed of the Word incarnate. Hence, the Word incarnate has a human body and a complete human soul, by virtue of which the incarnate Word can sense and know and will as human.

There are, then, three sorts of statements that can be made of Christ. Some of these statements pertain to the Word as God. Whatever is true of being God is true of the Word, who is one and the same God as the Father and the Holy Spirit. Some of these statements pertain to the Word as a distinct person in the Godhead. The Word is not the Father and not the Holy Spirit; the divine persons are distinguished by relations of origin, and each has properties peculiar to itself. Thus, it pertains to the Word to proceed from the Father, and in the *creation* of all things, as patterned on the inner-Trinitarian relations, each of the divine persons exercises its peculiar causality. Some of these statements pertain to the Word as incarnate, as truly human. Thus, it is the Word as incarnate who lives and learns (see *knowledge, Christ's*), who acts and suffers, and does so through the instrumentality of the human nature that the Word truly possesses and bears (see *instrumental causality*). Throughout, there is the same subject: the Word. But it is important not to confuse these different sorts of statements. To do so will be to run the risk of heresy, as shown in the Arians, for example, who took scriptural statements that have to do with the Word as incarnate as if they had to do with the relations between the Word and the Father.

Accordingly, as in ST III.16, Aquinas employs a reduplicative strategy in interpreting statements about Christ. It is important to specify in what respect (*secundum quod*) one is speaking about Christ and so referring to the Word who is the person of Christ: as God, or as Word, or as human? Can one say, for example, that Christ is a creature (a.8)? If the statement is taken as about the Word as Word or as God, then the answer is no. That is the position of the Arians, who did not talk about God as triune and who imagined that in proceeding from the Father, the Word proceeded as do creatures from their creator—and so the Word, in that rendering, would be ontologically distinct from, and inferior to, the Father, who alone is God. But the human nature that is taken up by the Word in the act of incarnation is creaturely, and so if it is specified that it is to that nature that reference is being made—Christ is a creature according to the Word's human nature—then the statement would be acceptable. However, if in the reduplication there were an addition that attracted the predicate to the hypostasis or person that bears the nature, then the statement would not be

acceptable or true. "Christ inasmuch as he is human" is acceptable; "Christ inasmuch as he is this human" is not, because the "this" makes the statement to be directly about the Word who takes up the nature and expresses it, not to be directly about the nature taken up; and the Word is not a creature (a.10).

In reflecting on Christ, Aquinas does not favor one nature at the expense of the other. It is sometimes claimed that an incarnational approach will be insufficiently attentive to the humanness of Jesus. Whatever the truth of this appraisal as made of other theologians, it hardly applies to Aquinas. On the basis of Scripture and the mediating tradition, Aquinas does insist on the divine personhood of Jesus and the full divinity of Jesus, and from the outset of the story of Jesus. But his insistence on the full humanity and its centrality to the account of Jesus and his work is equally significant; the Word is human, and the Word as human works out human salvation. Recall in this connection the number of questions in ST III.1–59 that are devoted to or have as their principal focus the true human nature of Jesus and the various perfections and defects attached to his nature: qq.4–15 and the entire second main part of the treatise on Christ. The human is in a profound way the medium of expression and action of the Word, and in no way incidental to the activity of the Word on our behalf.

The Christology is closely woven with other parts of Thomistic theology. Trinitarian discourse nicely complements the Christology; that Aquinas in ST III needs to devote only one question to the person who assumes (q.3) is due to the close attention in the First Part of the ST to the second person who is one and the same God as Father and the Holy Spirit and a distinct person. ST III.3 builds on and evokes ST I.34–35, which deals with the second person as Son and image of the Father. So too, the account of the Word in the Word's humanity builds on and completes the *anthropology*, as this is begun in the First Part of the ST and continued in the Second Part, which deals with the movement of the rational creature to God as end. That movement is through Christ, who inasmuch as (*secundum quod*) he is human is the way to God as end (prologue to ST I.2). For Aquinas, as in the Fathers, Christology and soteriology are intimately linked. The insistence on the union of the two natures in the person of the Word is no idle or merely speculative claim, made for its own sake. One must get the Christology right in order to secure salvation. God has called rational creatures to God's own life in the next world (see *beatific vision*); the call is made through Christ. To underscore the connection, Aquinas distributes the account of what Christ does for salvation over both main parts of the treatise on Christ in the ST. Questions 48–49, on the *cross* and qq.53–56, on the *resurrection of Christ*, have to do with the precise actions of the God-become-human that make possible the successful journey of God of those who will be linked to Christ by faith and charity. But Aquinas prefaces the entire treatise with a question on the *fittingness* of the incarnation (q.1), and what he has in mind is the soteriological implications of the Christology. It is fitting for the Word to become incarnate in view of the call of humans to God and the need to overcome sin in order for that end to be realized.

Finally, when affirming the soteriological end of the incarnation, Aquinas is thinking of both senses of incarnation, not simply the first. It is not simply incarnation as act that is in play, as if the mere fact of God becoming human established the possibility for human salvation. Rather, it is what the Word become human does and suffers as human that provides the way to God as end. Hence, it is incumbent on us to study the actions of the human person, to learn how we should behave in order to come to God as end (see *Omnis Christi actio est nostra instructio*). We must acknowledge, in faith and charity and the actions that arise from these virtues, that it is

precisely in the genuine death and real raising of the Word become human that God has taken decisive action for human salvation.

Potvin (1973); Ruello (1987); Wéber (1988); Schoot (1993); Torrell (1999); Tschipke (2003); Scheffczyk (1986); Lohaus (1985); Wawrykow (1998, 2005b); Gondreau (2002, 2005); Mostert (1978); Corbin (1978); Morard (1997); Boyle (1996b); Laporte (2003); Crowley (1991); Morris (1982); Principe (1974); Swierzawski (1984); Reynolds (2003).

Knowledge, Christ's   In the ST, Aquinas affirms of Christ four different types of knowledge: one of Christ as God and three of Christ as human. In positing these many types, Aquinas is working out the logic of incarnation, that is, what is to be said in light of the scriptural testimony about the knowing of the Savior who is fully God, fully human. There is an added importance to the discussion in ST III.9–12. We find here one of the relatively few places in his theology where Aquinas explicitly acknowledges a change of position (ST III.9.4c; 12.2c), rejecting what he had earlier held, in the *Scriptum on the Sentences* of Peter Lombard (III *Sent.* d.14, a.3; d.18 a.3), about Christ's empirical or acquired knowledge.

Human beings are liable to many different forms of knowledge. One is the empirical knowledge of which they are naturally capable. Such knowledge is won through the use of the capacities that belong to the person as human. This knowledge is rooted in sensation, and eventually the active intellect, working on the phantasms that arise from sense evidence, abstracts intelligible species from the phantasms. These intelligible species are in turn stored in the passive intellect and can subsequently be combined in order to form judgments. The process is discursive, step-by-step, from sensation through phantasm to the work of the active and passive intellects. It is discursive as well in marking a movement from an imperfection—not knowing something—to the perfection of knowing.

Human beings have a supernatural calling, and Aquinas is attentive to the knowing that figures at different stages of realizing the call to God as end. In the next life, when a person has successfully completed the journey to God as end, he will be in the immediate presence of God and know God directly. In knowing God, the person will have been granted by God a special light, the light of glory, that perfects the human and allows the direct knowing of God. God in God's essence will be seen. In this life, there is no face-to-face encounter for the Christian (with the exception of a few rare instances, as in the momentary rapture of Paul; see ST II-II.175). Rather, people live by *faith*, and by the light of faith, the *theological virtue* that perfects the intellect at the supernatural level, they can affirm certain truths about God: that God is the end of human existence, that Christ is the way to that end, and so forth (see *articles of faith*). Faith makes possible a successful journey to God; to reach an end, one has to "know" about it and how to get there. But once the person is ushered in the next life into the presence of God, faith gives way to vision. One does not believe what one sees; the beatified see God, and so there is no need any more for faith.

Christ had four kinds of knowledge. As God, he had the full knowledge that belongs to God eternally. As God, the Word incarnate who is Jesus knows God directly and all things in God, both those things that actually come to be by God's will as well as other ways by which God's existence might have been participated by creatures. In this affirmation, Aquinas is giving expression to his belief that the act of incarnation does not entail loss to the Word as God. In the act of incarnation, what is true eternally of the Word as Word and as God (distinct person in the Godhead and fully God, and so perfectly expressing the divine nature, with all its perfections) remains true.

By virtue of the incarnation, something else comes to be true. The Word became flesh, took up all that pertains to human nature and came to express that as well. The Word as incarnate has a human body and a complete human soul, including the nutritive, sensitive, and intellective powers of soul. In Christ, all of the powers of soul are fully functioning.

Three of the kinds of knowledge that Christ had pertain to him as human. These confirm his true and complete humanity; they also gesture at the supernatural calling of humans and the role of Christ, as Savior, in facilitating the realization by others of this calling. Two of these kinds of knowledge may be termed "supernatural," although one also has to do with the capacities that Christ had as human. First, for Aquinas, Christ enjoyed as human the beatific vision from the first moment of his human conception (ST III.9.2; q.10). Christ always had, even while engaged in his earthly existence, the full and direct knowledge of God that is promised to the blessed; this direct knowledge while in this life was not momentary, as it was for Paul, but persistent. For Aquinas, this is a prerogative of the one who is called to be Savior. In himself, Christ in effect shows the end to which people are called and to which they will come when they are joined to him by their faith and charity and move through him as the way to God (see *church*; *viator*). Correspondingly, Christ did not have the virtue of faith; such is needed only by those who have not reached the direct knowledge of God (ST III.7.3c).

Christ as human also had a second kind of knowledge, one that might be termed "supernatural" in the sense that it lies above the knowledge that humans by their natural capacities might attain. This is the infused knowledge that the angels have, which grants to them a full knowledge of all intelligible species, of all things that potentially might be known. All such things were known by Christ, as imprinted on his soul by the

Word (III.9.3c; q.11). Yet this knowledge does have to do with a capacity of soul that is natural to a human, namely, the passive intellect. That stands potentially to the knowledge of all intelligible species. What is merely in potential has a certain imperfection, and the Savior should be perfect. In order to remove that imperfection, and to grant to the passive intellect its perfection, the Word imprinted that knowledge, proper to the angels, on the passive intellect at Jesus's conception.

Empirical or acquired knowledge, with its habit of knowledge of intelligible species built up through abstraction from phantasms, is the third kind of human knowledge possessed by Christ (ST III.9.4; q.12). Here Aquinas moves away from a position announced in the *Scriptum*, having in the meantime more firmly grasped the logic of incarnation. The Word takes up a full human nature, including the active intellect, which is responsible for abstraction. There is nothing in Christ that is in vain. What has not its proper operation is useless. The proper operation of the active intellect is to make actual intelligible species. Thus, by virtue of the affirmation of incarnation, it is necessary to say that in Christ there were intelligible species received in the passive intellect by the action of the active intellect. So Christ, as do the rest of us, had empirical or acquired knowledge (ST III.9.4c; q.12). In the *Scriptum*, Aquinas had wondered about the need for a habit of acquired knowledge, in light of the affirmation of the infused knowledge of intelligible species imprinted on the passive intellect. Here he moves away from that position as inadequate to the true humanity of Christ. It is in growing in knowledge that we find proof of that genuine humanity. Jesus really did learn; he really did move from ignorance to knowledge, as Scripture in fact tells us (see, e.g., Heb. 5:8, as quoted in ST III.9.4 sed contra).

More recent theologians have questioned the ascription of the beatific vision to Christ from conception. The scriptural testimony may not require the affirmation, and it would seem to remove Christ too far from the normal experience of other human beings, whose model he is to be. After all, faith is required of all others; why would Christ not show them how to believe and how to act on that belief? This may be, however, an instance of a prerogative that is appropriate to the Savior, who need not be like those he saves in every respect (think here, for example, of Christ's sinlessness). There are multiple other ways in which Aquinas's Christ acts wonderfully as a model for emulation (see *Omnis Christi actio nostra est instructio*), including in the living out of the virtues of obedience, humility, patience, and, especially, charity that characterize the Christian life.

Torrell (1994); Mansini (1995c).

Knowledge, God's

In the ST's treatise on *God*, once he has discussed that God is (ST I.2) and the essence of God—or rather, what God is not (qq.3–11)—Aquinas turns to the divine operations in order to conclude the consideration of what pertains to the unity of the divine essence. The first of these operations is God's knowledge (I.14). God as knower has the highest object: God. God knows God and knows God perfectly. There is no discursiveness in this knowing, as there is in human knowing. God does not acquire knowledge step by step, moving from the imperfection of not knowing to knowing something. God knows in an eternal act by which God knows all that is in God. This knowing is comprehensive, grasping perfectly God as God is. God in knowing God also knows all that is not God. God knows the ways in which the divine essence is imitable by creatures. In terms of those things that actually are and occur, God's knowledge is called the knowledge of vision. God sees what is. In terms of what might proceed from God but does not, that is called simple knowledge (a.9). In knowing what is not God, God's knowledge does not stop at universals or general causes of things. Just as God creates each and every being, God knows each and every being; God's knowledge extends to individuals (a.11). And it extends to what individuals do. God knows the past and the present. Does God know the future, the future effects that contingent causes may bring about but that as contingent causes do not have to bring about and might not? God's knowledge does in fact extend to future contingents, to what humans may do, and God knows such perfectly—as these do in fact occur. God's knowledge, however, does not impose necessity on things. God is not subject to time, but as standing outside of time, God knows all things as present to God's simple, eternal glance (a.13). God, finally, knows even evil (a.10). Evil, of course, is not a thing the way that an individual is a thing. Rather, evil is deviation from the good, from the real. In knowing the real, God also knows the ways in which there can be, and is, defection from the good.

In discussing the divine knowing, Aquinas is exploiting the lessons that have been advanced in the previous questions of the treatise on God. In discussing what God is not, he has been much concerned with the articulation of the divine transcendence. Aquinas is also aware that perfections must be affirmed of God. Since it is better to be able to know than to be incapable of knowing, knowing is to be ascribed to God (a.1), a point, of course, that Scripture, which reveals God, is concerned to make. But in affirming any perfection of God, it is necessary to remove any imperfections, any creaturely aspects, from that perfection as affirmed of God. Thus, as part of the treatment of God's knowing in I.14, Aquinas will deny discursiveness, subjection to time, limitation in the scope of knowledge, and the like—all as inappropriate to the God who knows, and knows all, and knows all perfectly and from eternity.

The presentation of God's knowing in I.14 figures in other discussions in the ST. In the same part of the treatise on God—that is, as having to do with what pertains to the divine unity—Aquinas treats what has to do with the divine intellect and will, providence and *predestination* (qq.22–23). Those questions will develop a point already made in q.14, that God's knowing is not only speculative but also practical (a.16), that is, productive. In discussing providence and predestination, Aquinas makes clear that knowing is involved but that this is a knowing, as linked with the will, that is productive, causal. Here, I.23.5c is nicely illustrative. The article is crucial for the account of *merit* in Aquinas. In the latter part of the corpus, Aquinas explains how meriting goes with predestination. God has ordained that part of the salvific process, a process that is initiated and sustained and completed by God, has been ordered by God to another part as meritorious of it. Thus, what the elect do in the state of grace will be meritorious of eternal life, by the divine ordination. But before getting to that part of the analysis, Aquinas makes clear how predestination is and is not to be construed. The issue initially raised for discussion in I.23.5 is whether God's foreknowledge of merits is the cause of predestination. This way of putting the question would make sense if predestination were a matter of knowing only; in that case, what Aquinas says about God's knowledge of future contingents could be invoked. But that is a wholly inadequate account of predestination, one that is inattentive to God's practical knowing. Predestination is both a plan that God has and the execution of that plan. God orders some rational creatures to eternal life and then executes that plan through the grace that works conversion into grace and moves the person to God as end, via the graced acts that can be deemed meritorious. Predestination, which pertains to the divine intellect and will, is not a matter of God (fore-) knowing what a person will do and then giving that person what that person deserves, heaven or hell. Rather, the proper sequence is that God knows and wills what God wants and then implements the plan. A person is not first good and then predestined; one is predestined and so made to be good by God. What holds here of providence and predestination will hold as well later in the First Part, in the discussion of *creation*; this is God's act, involving God's loving will and God's productive knowing. God brings into being the creatures that God knows and wills, to imitate the divine being in the ways set by God.

In the second part of the ST's treatise on God, the focus shifts to the *Trinity*. God has revealed in Scripture that God is triune, and in the second main part of the treatise, Aquinas seeks to explicate this revelation, fully aware, however, that whatever he states will fall short of the mystery. What he has written in I.14 sets the stage for the consideration of the distinction between the first and second persons of God. Here, Aquinas follows the lead of Scripture, as in the first chapter of John's Gospel, where we read of the Word who is God and who is with the Father (see too, *ScG* IV.11). That scriptural witness allows the recasting of the presentation in I.14 of God's contemplation of God. In this eternal act, the Father in knowing God speaks the Word, who proceeds from the Father and in the eternal act of proceeding receives divinity from the Father. The essential operation provides the basis for presenting the eternal distinction of these persons, and in attending to that distinguishing, under the guidance of Scripture, that earlier presentation finds its final articulation. The persons in their relations of origin are identical with the divine essence.

The account of God's knowing also makes an appearance in the presentation of Jesus Christ. Aquinas notes that Christ had four kinds of knowledge (see *knowledge, Christ's*). Jesus is the Word made flesh, and in talking about Christ's knowledge Aquinas ascribes three of these kinds of knowledge to the Word as,

precisely, human. In the account of Jesus as knower (ST III.9–12), the greater part of the attention is given to the different kinds of human knowledge of Jesus. But one of his kinds of knowledge pertains to him as God; Aquinas can simply acknowledge that and move on to the human kinds, because he has pursued the account of God's knowledge in sufficient detail in ST I.14.

Even more significant for the theology is the way that God's knowledge shapes the account of human salvation. God has called human beings to enter into God's own life. Life in this world is to prepare those who are called for the direct enjoyment of God in the next. What God promises is the direct knowledge of God, to be taken up beyond merely human capacities—which will be expanded and transformed by God—in order to know God as God is. Aquinas discusses the end of human existence in some detail at the beginning of ST I-II (qq.1–5). But there is a first foray into the *beatific vision* in much closer vicinity to I.14. In the first main part of the treatise on God, Aquinas has interjected— between the treatment of what God is not (qq.3–11) and God's operations— two questions on the knowing and naming of God (qq.12–13; see *epistemology, theological*). The second of these questions looks at the names affirmed of God as received in Scripture and in other sources, both postbiblical Christian and extra-Christian materials. The first of these questions is on knowing. Only the final three articles in q.12 have to do with knowing, in any sense, of God in the present life, on the basis of which (as in the following question), people name God. The greater number of the articles in I.12 (aa.1–10) have to do with the end to which God calls people, have to do, in other words, with the direct knowledge of God that will come to those so called in the next life. Hence, Aquinas in short succession comes at God's knowledge from two perspectives: in q.14, as this knowledge belongs to God; in q.12, as this knowledge can become that of the human person, brought to salvation and having entered into God's own life. As these two discussions make clear, there is significant overlap between the two accounts: When people know God in God's essence, they will be engaging in the knowing that is proper to God. But there will be, as well, significant differences. That knowing is in fact proper to God. For humans, it is a gift. To engage in it people will have to receive an added light, the light of glory, that will replace the added light, of faith, by which people in the present life are oriented to that end in the next. Finally, while the beatific vision will be directly of God and the beatified will know God as God is, their knowledge, in contrast to God's eternal self-knowing, will not be comprehensive; they will not in a single swoop grasp God completely, as God is. Such lies beyond even a creature raised to God's level. That one is still a creature. Comprehensive knowledge of God is possessed by God alone (I.12.7).

———

Hankey (1987).

Law   The lengthy treatise on law (ST I-II.90–108) holds a prominent place in the presentation of *moral theology*, Aquinas's account in the ST's Second Part of the movement of the human person to fulfillment. Having reflected on beatitude and on what alone—the vision of God—can bring complete blessedness to humans (I-II.1–5), human acts and their goodness (qq.6–21), and the passions of the person (qq.22–48), Aquinas turns to the principles of human acts. Of such, there are two main kinds, intrinsic and extrinsic. There are two principles that are intrinsic: the powers or natural capacities of the person (discussed, however, by Aquinas in the First Part of the ST, as part of his theological *anthropology*), and habits, both good (virtues) and bad (vices) (I-II.49–89). Aquinas also discusses the external principle of good human acts, which is God. God acts as external principle in two ways. The sec-

ond is by *grace* (I-II.109–14); the first is by law. In discussing law where he does, Aquinas is thus especially concerned to show how by law God instructs the person on how to act in order to reach fulfillment.

Although intelligently worked into the moral theology, the discussion of law presupposes and builds on the discussion of *God* that is found in the First Part of the ST, in particular of God's providential rule. Indeed, the treatise on law is most fruitfully read when done so in conjunction with the questions on God's providence and *predestination* (ST I.22–23). This will be most apparent in the discussion of eternal law, which may fairly be deemed the chief of the kinds of law examined in the treatise on law; it is to this law that the other kinds of law must be compared and related.

The treatise on law is itself well crafted. It begins with a discussion of the main characteristics of law in general (ST I-II.90), and then enumerates the kinds of law (q.91) and their effects, of making people good, and commanding, forbidding, permitting, and punishing (q.92). Finally, in the bulk of the treatise, there is detailed comment on each kind of law: eternal law (q.93), natural law (q.94), human law (qq.95–97), and divine law (qq.98–108), itself divided into Old (qq.98–105) and New Law (qq.106–8). In constructing his teaching on law, and relating it to God's plan for created reality and to the movement of human beings to God as end, Aquinas draws on a rich range of sources. He acknowledges and exploits classical, non-Christian teachings about the meaning and point of law; he turns as required to law texts, both civil and canon; he makes good use of the teaching of his Christian predecessors (Augustine has an especially prominent role in this regard); and he has learned a great deal from Scripture, in particular. Indeed, in his handling of divine law, to which a healthy portion of the treatise is devoted, as well as of natural law, Aquinas has shown himself faithful to the principal insights of the apostle Paul in Romans and Galatians. Quotations of these Pauline epistles are frequent enough; Aquinas has attempted, with considerable success, to make the teaching of Paul his own.

The opening question of the treatise identifies four principal characteristics of law; these features will figure in each kind of law. In sum, law is a dictate or ordinance of the practical reason, promulgated by the one who has charge of the community, for the common good (I-II.90.4c). First, law is an ordinance of the practical reason. Here Aquinas is trading on the distinction between speculative and practical reason. The latter has action as its point, rather than the contemplation of truth for its own sake. Thus, law has to do with what is to be done, and so is suitably ascribed to the practical intellect. Second, this dictate of the practical reason pertains to the one who has care for the community. Individual people, of course, can offer advice about what to do and what not to do, but such is private, and lacks the status of law. In the case of human communities, only the people, or those who act on their behalf and as the people's representative, can issue law. Third, law must be promulgated; it must be issued in the appropriate form so that those to whom it is directed know about it. Finally, law is for the common good, understood formally as the final cause that is common to the whole (I-II.90.2 ad 2), not a peculiar good that may be proper to this or that individual. Law deals with action that is geared to what is fulfilling of all.

In discussing the first kind of law (I-II.91.1; q.93), Aquinas expressly identifies eternal law with divine providence (91.1c). What he teaches about providence in the First Part holds of eternal law. Providence is all-encompassing, covering all of God's creatures. It is the plan that God has in bringing creatures into existence, ordering different kinds of creatures to their appropriate ends, and providing for different kinds of activities by which different sorts of creatures might realize their God-determined ends. Eternal law thus pertains to God as lawgiver, the God who has care for all of created reality (the "community" in play here) and who brings, through divine government (see ST I.103), things to their God-appointed ends.

In affirming natural law (I-II.91.2; q.94), Aquinas is taking account of the distinctiveness of the human creature while also insisting on the continuity of humans with other creatures. There is a law of nature, as it were, for each kind of creature brought into being and ordained to an end by God. But human beings are distinctive in possessing a sort of providence of their own, as intended by God in bringing this sort of creature, with its characteristic activities and end, into being. Human beings are rational and possessed of a will that gives them control over their own actions. It is in this light that Aquinas defines natural law as the participation of humans in the eternal law. Natural law involves the law of human nature as ordered to its end, as inclining humans to the acts proper to them and leading to their good; it involves recognition of this law, and the attempt to work out and grasp its implications for life in the world (91.2c). All those things that the human has a natural inclination to are naturally apprehended by reason as being good and consequently as objects of pursuit, and their contraries are apprehended as evil, and so are objects to be avoided. As presented in 91.2 and q.94, natural law is fairly rudimentary, in the sense of containing but a few general precepts imprinted on the practical reason. The most fundamental is "to do good and to avoid evil." When people act, it is with a view to their flourishing, not to their destruction; in their actions, they are pursuing their good.

In light of the complexity of being human (that is, while there are aspects of being human that are proper to the human, other aspects are shared with other created beings), this fundamental principle is teased out to a few others (ST I-II.94.2c). In this connection, Aquinas mentions what humans share with all substances, with animals, and then what is proper to them as human (that is, rationality). By natural law, there is an inclination to maintain oneself in the good of being and to ward off all obstacles (an inclination shared with all substances). There is also the inclination shared with animals; hence the inclination to sexual activity as procreative, and to educating offspring, and the like. In terms of what is proper to being human, there is the inclination to the good according to the nature of one's reason. Thus, humans have an inclination to know the truth about God (and so an orientation to the transcendent), as well as an inclination to live in society (the human as social animal) and so to form associations beyond the family unit. Thus, it pertains to the natural law for humans to shun ignorance and to avoid offending those among whom one has to live. These fundamental precepts help to explain moral action, which enacts, as it were, these principles in concrete action; they also allow for evaluation of practices. Do such conform to these fundamental inclinations as provided by the Establisher of the nature? As Aquinas puts it in a subsequent article, these basic principles, which serve as axioms of moral behavior, cannot be obliterated. But there can be faulty application of the principles in particular circumstances, and so they can be obscured in actual activity (I-II.94.6). For example, practical reason may be hindered by concupiscence or some other passion in acting from the general principle in a particular practice. Aquinas can also come at the point from another angle by writing of other precepts of the natural law that he terms "secondary" (I-II.94.4, 6). The secondary precepts stand to the primary as conclusions to their premises; they are the term of the practical reasoning by which the fundamental axioms are applied in the lived circumstances of human existence. As Aquinas insists, the success of the move from primary to secondary is by no means guaranteed. In the secondary precepts, the natural law can be blotted out (to use the language of 94.6c) from the human heart, either by evil persuasions or by vicious customs and corrupt habits, as among some men, theft and even unnatural vices, as Paul says (Rom. 1), were not esteemed sinful. Sin does, in other words, have its consequences.

Aquinas's invocation of natural law has been celebrated by many, who see in it the possibility for dialogue between Christians and non-Christians and as the basis for the working out of strategies for courses of action that people of goodwill, regardless of specific religious commitment, might jointly take for the betterment of humans. Does natural law, common to all humans, not make it possible to envision ever more just ways of living in community and of fostering the acquisition of the goods sought by all? There is something to be said for this reading of Aquinas, for Aquinas does think that natural law is of universal application (that is, holds for all people), although many today would question the notion of a "human nature" and would dispute the role of teleology in accounting for human action. But in so approaching Aquinas on natural law, there is also the possibility of distortion. He inserts the discussion of natural law in a larger account of the movement of the human person to God as transcendent end. As such, natural law can make a contribution to reaching that end, although (as will become clearer in the discussion below of divine law) its role is subordinate. It is concerned with the natural, not with the supernatural. Aquinas himself seems little inclined to extract natural law from the other laws that figure so prominently in his depiction of the movement of people to God as end. He insists on the linking of natural law to eternal law, on the one hand; he highlights the necessity of divine law, and by implication the insufficiency of natural law, in the attainment of the final good of human beings, as determined by God, on the other.

The third law that Aquinas discusses, human law (I-II.91.3; qq.95–97), follows on natural law. Here the emphasis has shifted to human lawgivers, to those who govern human communities and who should seek to establish and promote conditions in which the community and its members might flourish. As Aquinas states in I-II.95.2c, there are two ways in which something may be derived from the natural law. First, as a conclusion from premises: in this regard, Aquinas says that from the principle that "one should do harm to no man," one can conclude that "one must not kill." The other way has to do with particularization, with specifying how a general principle is to be observed. Thus, as an example, he notes that the law of nature has it that the evildoer should be punished, but that he be punished in this or that way is a determination made in human law. The different derivations have different status. In the latter, the derivation has the status of human law alone; in the former, the derivation has the status of natural law as well. As indicated by I-II.96.4, Aquinas is concerned with the justice of human laws. A law is just when it is geared to the common good, the lawgiver does not exceed his power, and the law is fairly applied. In contrast, a law can be unjust when it contravenes one of these criteria or when it is opposed to the divine good (as would be the case for a law requiring idolatry). In that article, Aquinas offers a nuanced account of law as binding on conscience, and of the circumstances in which unjust laws should not be observed (this is the case with laws that contravene the divine good).

Aquinas's analysis of natural and human law is sympathetic and realistic. Natural law may be obscured by sin or ignorance in its application; not all human law is just. Yet natural law is never effaced and provides the fundamental orientation to the human person as human. Natural law instructs in what pertains to the nature, and it is geared to the fulfillment of the person at the natural level. To the extent that it is based on natural law, human law is just and does provide for the flourishing of human community.

Natural law, nonetheless, is insufficient. Human beings have been called to a transcendent end. Natural law may provide an orientation to the transcendent, but it does not identify that end as the Christian God nor give instruction on how to reach the transcendent end of entering into God's own life of knowing and loving. Thus, beyond the natural law, there is need for a final type of law, the divine law, which also is rooted in eternal law and which has to do with instructing humans about the transcendent end and the way to this end. In the course of the treatise on law, Aquinas offers in this connection a variant on the adage so closely associated with him: "Grace does not destroy nature but perfects it" (see **nature and grace**). In the treatise on law, it appears in the form, "Grace presupposes nature" (I-II.99.2 ad 1). What this means is that grace does not eliminate nature, but works on it, extending the power of the self beyond its natural capacities and orienting the person to the transcendent end that is God. In terms of law, the natural law is not removed by the revelation of the divine law. It remains as a fundamental orientation of human being. But it is not the only law nor even the principal; it is extended, perfected by a higher law: the divine law by which humans are guided to their transcendent end.

In introducing divine law (I-II.91.4), Aquinas in fact offers a number of reasons why there was need for a divine law. The first has already been noted: Humans are ordained to an end of eternal happiness that is disproportionate to their natural capacity. The other reasons trade more directly on the limitations of natural and human law. Because of the uncertainty of human judgment, especially on contingent and particular matters, different people form different judgments on human acts; whence also different and contrary laws result. Thus, in order that people may know without any doubt what they ought to do and what they ought to avoid, it was necessary for people to be directed in their proper acts by a law given by God, for it is certain that such a law cannot err.

Next, Aquinas notes that people can make laws in those matters of which they are competent to judge. But people are not competent to judge interior movements, which are hidden, but only exterior acts. Yet for the perfection of virtue it is necessary for people to conduct themselves aright in both kinds of act. Consequently, human law could not sufficiently curb and direct interior acts; thus, it was necessary for this purpose that a divine law should intervene.

Finally in this vein, Aquinas notes that human law cannot punish or forbid all evil deeds, for in aiming at doing away with all evils, it would do away with many good things and would hinder the advance of the common good. Thus, in order that no evil might remain unforbidden and unpunished, it was necessary for the divine law to supervene, whereby all sins are forbidden. In the same passage (I-II.99.2 ad 1) in which he offers the "grace presupposes nature" claim mentioned above, Aquinas nicely indicates the continuity of, and difference between, natural law and divine law, here referring to the part of the divine law that is the Old Law. The Old Law "is distinct from the natural law, not as being altogether different from it, but as something added thereto. For just as grace presupposes nature, so must the divine law presuppose the natural law." In terms of I-II.91.4c, the "added" may be parsed in terms of the transcendent end, the greater certainty of the divine law, the extension by divine law to interior acts, and the identification and threat of punishment of all, not just some, evil acts.

The divine law that is revealed by God to order people to God as transcendent end falls into two parts. In his initial introduction of the Old and New Law (I-II.91.5c), Aquinas follows the lead of Paul's comments in Galatians 3. The two laws that make up the divine

law are addressed to people at different stages of development. The state of man under the Old Law is that of a child under a pedagogue; the state under the New Law is that of a fully grown person who is no longer under a pedagogue. The Old Law, then, can be said to stand to the New Law, with which it makes up the divine law, as the imperfect stands to the perfect. The rest of this corpus explicates the Pauline teaching by drawing a series of contrasts that underscore the imperfection of the Old and the perfection of the New. Hence, law orders to a common good. In the Old Law, as befits the state of those under it, what was promised was sensible and earthly, a kingdom of this world. The New Law, on the other hand, orders humans to an intelligible and heavenly good: the kingdom of heaven, life with God as eternally enjoyed by God. So too there is a difference in reach: The New Law goes beyond the Old by directing our internal acts. Finally, in this connection, the two parts of eternal law had different inducements to observing its commandments. The Old Law did so by fear of punishment, while the New Law does so by love, which is poured into human hearts by the grace of God that is bestowed in the New Law. The present passage highlights the contrasts; with the coming of the New Law there is a move to a greater perfection in law. Yet as the treatise on law proceeds and Aquinas engages in closer analysis of the Old (qq.98–105) and New Laws (qq.106–8), the continuity becomes more apparent, as does the value of the Old Law. The two parts of divine law are given by the same God, and the Old Law is meant to prepare for the giving of the New Law, by readying the people from whom Christ would come for his appearance (I-II.98.4). Although imperfect, the Old Law is indispensable. It foretells the Christ who is to come, to offer salvation. It readies the Jewish people for that coming, by showing them how to live and how to be in correct conformity with God (I-II.98.2). And it prepares for Christ in the fundamental sense of showing the need for Christ by identifying sin and disclosing the inability of those under the law to keep the law of their own resources. Human salvation is not a human possibility if one looks only at human capacities, as established in the nature. Human salvation requires grace, and that comes in the New Law (I-II.98.1c).

The large number of questions devoted to the Old Law (qq.98–105) disclose Aquinas's interest in it, both for its own sake and in relation to the Christ who would come from the Jewish people to bring salvation to all. Following a traditional division, Aquinas distinguishes three sorts of precepts in the Old Law. The moral precepts are meant to order the people correctly to God and to others, or as he puts it in I-II.99.2c, to establish friendship between the people and God. The moral precepts of the Old Law are reducible to the precepts of the Decalogue (I-II.100.3), and there is significant overlap between these moral precepts and the natural law (q.100.1). The other two kinds of precepts are the ceremonial and the judicial, and Aquinas sees both as geared specifically to the Jewish people, to ready them for the coming of Christ. The ceremonial precepts (I-II.99.3; qq.101–3) are determinations of the worship of God and are meant to call the people away from idolatry and to the correct worship of the true God. They cover sacrifice, sacred things, sacraments, and observances (101.4). They have a special value in prefiguring Christ and the full worship of God that Christ makes possible. Hence, once Christ comes and fulfills the law, the ceremonial precepts cease to be in effect; to observe them after Christ would in fact be a mortal sin (I-II.103.3–4). The judicial precepts (I-II.99.4; qq.104–5) cover relations among the members of the people and further specify the moral precepts that promote justice among humans. While with the coming of Christ they no longer are in effect, observing them, inasmuch as they are designed principally to promote correct interpersonal relationships, would not be a sin (I-II.104.3c).

With the discussion of the New Law (I-II.106–8), Aquinas brings the treatise on law to its climax. The discussion of New Law at the same time marks the beginning of the treatment of the other way in which God, the external principle of human action, helps people in the movement to God as end. For the New Law is, principally, grace, the grace that is brought by Christ and conveyed by the Holy Spirit to those who believe in Christ. Only secondarily is the New Law something written, disposing people to the grace of the New Law and to the use of that grace (I-II.106.1c). In the discussion of the New Law, the theme of perfection/imperfection reemerges. The Old Law could not justify. The Old Law prepares for Christ. The New Law of grace, however, does justify and in this sense fulfills the Old Law (I-II.107.2). It sets people right before God and orders them to the end that is God. It brings forgiveness. It is new power, moving people to the end that is God. The New Law as the law of grace is a law of justification and sanctification, themes that Aquinas will pursue in the treatise on grace itself (I-II.113–14). Through the grace that is the New Law, people are positioned to do the virtuous acts, both inner and outer, that God seeks from those who would enter into God's own life in the next world (I-II.107.4). With grace, they will do what is otherwise not possible for them and yet needed in order to reach God.

Porter (1999); Tonneau (1970); Brown (1981); Hall (1994, 2002); Kossel (2002); Hood (1995).

Mary Aquinas's teaching about Mary is incorporated into his Christology. In the ST, Aquinas discusses Mary in four questions at the beginning of the second main part of the treatise on Christ (III.27–30). In the group of questions to which the account of Mary belongs, the principal topic is the entry of the Son of God into the world (qq.27–39); it is thus appropriate to consider Mary at this point. Aquinas investigates in turn her sanctification in the womb (q.27), her virginity (q.28), her espousals (q.29), and the annunciation (q.30).

Mary's importance is derived from her intimate relationship with the Word become human. She is the Mother of God (the title is used throughout q.28 and appears elsewhere in these questions), for from her matter the Holy Spirit had formed the humanity taken up by the Word in becoming human. She is thus the guarantor of the humanity of the Word incarnate. The Word was really human; the Word has received this humanity through Mary.

Aquinas does not affirm the Immaculate Conception, a dogma defined by the Catholic Church only in the nineteenth century. He asks instead about her sanctification in her mother's womb (q.27). We meet in this question an interesting application of Aquinas's theological method. The starting point of his inquiry into the truths of the faith is, as a rule, *Scripture*, interpreted with the aid of the mediating Christian tradition (see *articles of faith*; *authority*). Aquinas also shows a great interest in arguments for *fittingness*. Such do not demonstrate Christian truth—in the case of the articles, that is impossible—but show the meaning and plausibility of particular claims by relating them, usually in the light of Scripture, to other important Christian claims. The present questions on Mary are in fact rich in arguments for fittingness. There is a complication, however, when it comes to the sanctification of Mary. Scripture not only does not mention her sanctification in her mother's womb, it does not even mention her birth (III.27.1c). Yet, Aquinas continues in that place, it may reasonably be argued that she was so sanctified, as Augustine has suggested. Augustine had argued that since her body was assumed into heaven, it was likely that she was also sanctified in the womb. Aquinas agrees

that this would make sense, that she who brought forth the Only Begotten of the Father full of grace and truth would receive a greater privilege of grace than others. Others had been sanctified in their mother's womb—Aquinas mentions Jeremiah (Jer. 1:5) and John the Baptist (Luke 1:15) as two witnessed by Scripture as freed from original sin by grace. So too, then, was Mary. She was conceived in *original sin* and is truly of the race of Adam, but she was immediately cleansed by God's grace (q.27.1 ad 4). And she was cleansed in such a way that she was preserved from all *sin*, whether mortal or venial (III.27.4c).

Mary's virginity was perpetual. That she was a virgin in conceiving is attested by Scripture (Isa. 7:14 is quoted in the sed contra of q.28.1). She was a virgin as well in Christ's birth (a.2) and for the rest of her life (a.3). In making each of these assertions, Aquinas engages in extended arguments for fittingness—why it made sense for Mary to be and remain a virgin. Those for the final of these claims—that she remained a virgin after Christ's birth—can be given here as representative. After noting that Helvidius is in error in saying that Mary, after Jesus' birth, was carnally known by Joseph and bore other children, Aquinas gives four reasons why she remained a virgin. First, Helvidius's error is derogatory to Christ's perfection. As he is the Only Begotten, being the Father's son in every respect perfect, so it was becoming that he should be the only begotten son of his mother, as being her perfect offspring. Second, that error is an insult to the Holy Spirit, whose shrine was the virginal womb wherein the Spirit had formed the flesh of Christ; it would be unbecoming that it should be desecrated by intercourse with a man. Third, that error is derogatory to the dignity and holiness of God's Mother, for thus she would seem to be most ungrateful, were she not content with such a Son and were she of her own accord to forfeit by carnal intercourse that virginity which had been miraculously preserved in her. Finally, it would be tantamount to an imputation of extreme presumption to Joseph to assume that he attempted to violate her whom he knew by the angel's revelation to have conceived by the Holy Spirit. As for the large number of objections in this article—six, rather than the more usual three or four in articles in the ST—Aquinas knows of comments made in passing in Scripture that might raise doubts about the continued virginity, but he does not find them compelling and is able, in the responses, to turn them to the account offered in the corpus.

While they did not engage in sexual intercourse, the marriage of Joseph and Mary was true. Wedlock is said to be true by reason of its attaining its perfection. The perfection of anything is twofold. The first perfection of a thing consists in its form, from which it receives its species. The second perfection of a thing consists in its operation, by which in some way a thing obtains its end. The form of matrimony consists in a certain inseparable union of souls, by which husband and wife are pledged by a bond of mutual affection that cannot be sundered. And the end of matrimony is the begetting and upbringing of children. The first of these is attained by conjugal intercourse, the second, by the other duties of husband and wife, by which they help one another in rearing their offspring. Hence, in terms of Mary and Joseph, the first perfection was there beyond doubt. Both consented to the nuptial bond, but not expressly to the bond of the flesh, except on the condition that that be pleasing to God. This is why the angel calls Mary Joseph's wife (Matt. 1:20). But as to the second perfection, if this requires carnal intercourse, then this marriage was not consummated and Mary remained a virgin after Jesus' birth. Nevertheless, the second perfection of marriage was here, in terms of the upbringing of the child (III.29.2c).

As part of the consideration of the annunciation in III.30, Aquinas notes some of Mary's virtues. She was truly humble (III.30.4 ad 1), she was obedient,

and she offered to God, in the response to the angel, the free gift of her obedience (III.30.1c). Elsewhere, Aquinas is more obviously exuberant in his praise of Mary as one who saw herself in relation to God and did not try to put herself in God's place, but offered herself to God to do as God willed through her. Thus, as in the fourth of his homilies on the creed (*Collationes Credo in Deum*), Mary can be presented as a fitting model for emulation in her constant faithfulness to God in Christ.

Nichols (2004); Ols (1991); Mullaney (1954).

Matrimony   *see* **Sacrament**

Merit   The final question of ST I-II is devoted to merit, which Aquinas identifies as the effect of cooperative *grace*. The final question in the treatise on grace, ST I-II 114 makes good use of the preceding questions on grace, to locate merit in the movement of the human person to God as end (see *viator*), the overarching topic of the I-II.

Question 114 is divided into two, unequal sections. Articles 2–10 investigate the possible rewards for merit. The opening article asks about the possibility of merit before God. At first glance, merit before God seems improbable. Merit and reward fall under justice, and justice applies only to those who are equal. But there is the greatest disparity between God and the human person, between the Creator and the creature (1c). How then can there be merit before God? How can we meaningfully talk of the human person doing something that elicits a response, a reward, from God? Why would God have to respond with a reward to what the rational creature voluntarily does? The objections to the first article heighten the case against merit, and so against the contribution through the good action that is voluntary of the human person to that person's attainment of God as end. To merit means to put another in one's debt; the one for whom one works must respond, in justice, to what the first does. But God is debtor to no one. Likewise, to merit means to do something that benefits another, to give that other something that the other needs. But our works could not possibly benefit God, who is in need of nothing from us. In affirming merit, Aquinas in fact grants the fundamental insights of the arguments against merit in the corpus and in the objections. There is the greatest inequality between humans and God. God derives no benefit from our meriting. Meriting could not possibly put God in our debt. Nonetheless, Aquinas does affirm merit, the voluntary action of the person as deserving reward from God, as a way of explicating scriptural comments about salvation as a reward for human action (see a.1, sed contra), and does so in such a way that he is faithful to his consistently expressed insight into salvation—that it is utterly dependent on God's will and is fundamentally the gift of God to those whom God loves in a special way.

In ST I-II 114.1c, Aquinas asserts that the ground of merit is the divine ordination. "Ordination" is a sapiential term, referring to God's wise communication of God's goodness. It is first encountered, in terms of meriting, in the First Part of the ST, in the discussion of *predestination*. When the present article is read in conjunction with ST I.23.5c, it is possible to discern three basic meanings of the ordination that ground merit. First, God has ordered one part of the salvific process to another as meritorious of it. Life is a journey. The journey comes to its term in the next life, in the presence of God. To reach eternal life, one must prepare for it in the present life, through morally and supernaturally good acts, which are made possible by grace. To qualify for eternal life, one must end one's earthly life in grace. This presupposes having moved away from sin and toward God in conversion. As I.23.5c makes clear, there is no merit in conversion. Here the human person is simply

moved, by God's grace, to the faith that justifies. But God has ordained the acts of the person done in the state of grace as meritorious of the end of eternal life. By God's decree, what one does in grace will be meritorious of that end, construed in this connection as reward.

But, secondly, the whole process stands under God's predestining will; by "ordination," Aquinas is also referring to predestination. In eternity, God has willed to show God's love in a special way to some rational creatures by ordering them to eternal life, to entry into God's own life. There is no meriting of this divine willing; indeed, God wills to so communicate God's goodness prior to the existence of any being. Rather, predestination to eternal life is a gift, and only those who have been destined to that life will attain it. While predestination is primarily God's plan for the sapiential communication of God's goodness in this special way, it is secondarily also the execution of this plan. The execution is through grace. God has determined that only those who end their earthly existence in grace will make it to eternal life. Thus, in executing predestination, God works conversion into grace in the first place; in this, as Aquinas makes clear in I.23.5c and in the treatise on grace (see *Facienti quod in se est*), the person is simply moved by God. The person does not move herself; there is no expression on her part of the will, and so there is no place to talk of merit at the point of conversion. But once moved into grace, it is possible to talk about the voluntary agency of the human person and the correct expression of that agency by grace. And so, once in the state of grace, there is room to talk about merit, about merit of the end to which God has called that person as a gift. In this sense, given the ordering of acts in grace to eternal life, it is possible to say that eternal life is both gift and reward.

To return to ST I-II.114.1, the ordination that makes meriting before God possible involves predestination, grace, and the ordering of one part of the journey to another as meritorious of it. The meriting that comes under consideration in ST I-II.114 is therefore the meriting of the elect, of those called by God's love into special relation to God and ordered to share in God's own life. That meriting will be restricted to the state of grace; meriting of conversion is excluded. In meriting there will be a contribution of the human person, in the correct use of the will in eliciting or commanding acts that will be pleasing to God. But that there is such correct use is itself a sign of grace, given to those predestined by God to God as their end. There will be justice here, a justice that is contextualized and established by God's ordination. God's ordination provides for the "equality" called for by justice. In meriting, the person will not be putting God in one's debt. Rather, by the ordination, God has voluntarily put God in God's debt, and in rewarding the person for what the person does by the aid of the grace that is given to the elect, God is keeping God's promise to God. In meriting, one is not doing something for God, as if God were in need of what the elect do. Rather, meriting and rewarding, by virtue of the divine ordination, proclaim God's goodness, as determined by God (ad 2). God is able to bring the elect to their freely granted end through the correct use of the natural endowment of the will, as this correct use is made possible by God's grace. In the salvation of the elect, we meet, and principally, the good of God's love, which initiates and sustains the movement of the elect to God. We meet as well the good of God's justice, in the rewarding of the elect for the good that they do by God's grace.

In the rest of q.114, Aquinas asks about possible rewards for merit. Articles 2–10 can be grouped according to different possible rewards, all plotted according to the model of life as a journey. Can one merit eternal life, the end of the journey to God (aa.2–4)? Can one merit grace in the first place (aa.5–7)? Can someone in grace merit more grace and staying in grace (aa.8–9)? Can one merit temporal rewards (a.10)? In pursuing these inquiries, Aquinas repeats the lessons of ST I.23.5 and of the earlier questions in the treatise on grace, while adding nuance. Can one merit conversion in the first place? No, meriting presupposes grace, and by definition one in the state of non-grace lacks grace. Conversion is simply worked in the person by God (a.5). Can one merit eternal life? Only those who are in the state of grace can be said to merit eternal life as a reward. The voluntary actions of the person in grace will be evaluated in two ways. As the act of a creature, there is the greatest disparity between what the person does and what God might do in response. And so there is no place in this regard to talk of condign merit; such merit requires equality in value between what is done and what might be given in response. Rather, in terms of the act as human, there can be but a congruent merit; it is congruent, fitting with God's generous nature, to reward the person for the correct use of the will. But the same act can be evaluated in terms of the grace in which it is done, and then there is space for condign merit. Grace is the activity of the Holy Spirit in one's life, moving and prompting the graced person to actions in keeping with the calling to eternal life. As stimulated by the Holy Spirit, there is the desired equality between act, as graced, and the reward of eternal life (a.3). Can one in grace merit more grace and perseverance in grace (aa.8–9)? Yes to the former, but no to the latter. Read by themselves, these articles can be quite puzzling. If one can merit more grace (a.8), why does that not mean that one has merited perseverance in grace (denied in a.9)? But read in conjunction with the earlier questions on grace, with their discrimination between habitual grace and the grace of *auxilium*, and the further articulation of each of those graces into operative and cooperative, the problem disappears. In ST I-II.114.8, Aquinas refers to habitual grace. One can, through morally and supernaturally correct action, merit more of that grace. That grace is a habit, and *virtues* once possessed are increased by actions in accordance with such habit. In I-II.114.9, it is an *auxilium* that is operative that is in question. As discussed earlier in the treatise on grace, perseverance in grace is a gift of God, given to those whom God has predestined to eternal life in order to keep them in the state of grace by enabling them through this operative *auxilium* to overcome **temptation**. Finally, can one merit temporal goods (a.10)? Here Aquinas is reflecting on the fact that the good do not always prosper in this life and the evil definitely do not receive, in this life, their due. All will, however, receive what they should in the next life, when the discrepancies and injustices of history will be resolved and God, the Lord of history, will give all what they truly deserve.

An upshot of the entire inquiry into merit in ST I-II.114 is to acknowledge that human beings do contribute to the working out of their salvation. Their acts are their own and will receive their due from God. God does not work out a person's salvation in spite of or without regard to what distinguishes the human from other beings, namely, the rational capacities of soul displayed in intellection and willing. But by working into the discussion what cannot be merited— conversion in the first place, perseverance in grace—Aquinas nicely reminds us that the affirmation of merit does not put the one who merits on a par with God, or detract from the crucial claim that salvation is, radically, a gift. The meriting that is affirmed is the meriting of the elect, and that they can merit is due to God's predestination and the grace, given freely, that moves the person into correct relation with God and makes possible the correct use of the will. Meriting also involves God's ordering of the state of grace to the end of the journey as meritorious of it. Without the divine contribution—as summarized by "ordination" and further specified in the treatment of the operative graces that work conversion and perseverance and that fall outside of merit—there is no

meriting. In the hands of Aquinas, talk about merit becomes a way to proclaim God, principally, while also according to the person a real role in the working out of that person's salvation as due to God.

Wawrykow (1995); Lynn (1962).

Miracle   *see* **Transfiguration**

Missions   Aquinas brings the treatise on *God* in the ST to completion by considering the divine missions (ST I.43). Mission refers to ways in which the triune God acts in the world. All three divine persons are involved in the missions, although one is not sent. The Father, the principle who is not from a principle, is not sent, but sends the Son. The Father and the Son send the Holy Spirit. The sending of the Son is the incarnation, by which God takes decisive action for human salvation. As incarnate, the second person of God makes possible the salvation of others through his acting and suffering on behalf of others. The Holy Spirit, sent by the Father and the Son, conveys the grace that is made available in Christ, moving people to *faith* and the other *theological virtues* by which they can attain to the triune God as end.

The missions are patterned on and reflect the inner life of the Trinity. The sending of the Son and of the Holy Spirit into the world does not constitute the Trinity of persons. Rather, sending presupposes the divine persons and reenacts, in history, the eternal processions. The Son proceeds eternally from the Father; the Father, as Father, as source of divinity, generates the Son, who receives divinity from the Father in this eternal act of generation. In being sent, the Son offers to what is not God the way to eternal life and participation in the inner life of the Trinity. The Holy Spirit proceeds from the Father and from the Son (*filioque*) and is the mutual love of the Father and the Son. In being sent, the Holy Spirit makes those who are called to God as end into lovers of God (see *charity*); it is by their moral and supernatural affections, granted to them by the Spirit, that they can reach their end in God. The economic Trinity presupposes the immanent Trinity, and neither is to be reduced to the other. In the missions, the economic Trinity manifests the triune God, who eternally is, in a way that is suited to humans and their call to God as end.

The question on mission in the First Part of the ST is but a first foray on mission. The discussion is taken up and extended later. The Third Part can be said to continue the discussion of the mission of the Son, first in the Christology (III.1–59), where Aquinas reflects in detail on the incarnation and what *Jesus Christ* does for human salvation, and then in the account of the *sacraments*, through which the Son's work in the flesh is applied to those who come after the *cross* and *resurrection* and who follow Christ. The continuation of the discussion of the mission of the Holy Spirit is also found in the Third Part; it is by the Spirit that the spiritual benefits of Christ's death and resurrection are extended to others. But the mission of the Holy Spirit is prominent as well in the Second Part of the ST—in the general discussions in I-II of the virtues, both *theological* and infused (see *virtue*), worked in a person by the Spirit by which that person may strive toward God as end; of the *gifts of the Holy Spirit*, which perfect the infused virtues and render that person more susceptible to the prompting of the Holy Spirit who seeks to bring the person to God as end; of *grace*, which is for Aquinas the grace "of the Holy Spirit" (I-II.106.1), which moves the person to God by reducing the virtues to act; and, then, in II-II in the detailed and specific discussion of each of the theological virtues (faith, hope, charity) and the infused moral virtues, as well as their particular gifts, all of which attest to the Holy Spirit's activity in the world, according to Aquinas.

Emery (2004).

Moral Theology   The entire Second Part of the ST (I-II; II-II) may fairly be characterized as an extensive exercise in Christian ethics. Its overarching theme is the movement, through moral activity, of the human person to God as end, in accordance with God's will to share God's own life with rational creatures. In I-II, Aquinas provides a general overview of moral theology, opening with a consideration of the end of human existence as this has been set by God (qq.1–5), that is, sharing in the next life in the life that God eternally enjoys, of knowing and loving God directly (I-II.3.8; 5.8). This is a supernatural goal, one that lies beyond the natural capacities of the human person and that requires grace and other gifts of God to attain (see *beatific vision*). By putting this set of considerations about the end of human existence in God right at the beginning of this part of the ST, Aquinas is thus nicely underscoring that his is in fact a *theological* ethics, one fully in keeping with a work called the "Summa of *theology*." Aquinas then looks at the structure of the human act (qq.6–17) and the goodness or badness of a human act (qq.18–21), and then at the passions of the soul, the concupiscible and the irascible, which should be susceptible to the rule of reason but by sin may not be, and so stand in need of reform (qq.22–48). The rest of I-II is given over to the principles of human moral action. In I-II.49–89, the focus is on the *intrinsic* principles of human acts, the habits, the stable dispositions that incline, but do not necessitate, the powers that they perfect to acts of a certain kind. (The other intrinsic principle, the powers themselves, have already been treated in the First Part of the ST, in qq.77ff.). After some general comments about habit (qq.49–54), he considers good habits (qq.55–70), that is, the *virtues*, and bad (qq.71–89; for vice, see *sin*). ST I-II comes to a close with an examination of the extrinsic principle of human acts, which is God. Since God instructs and aids, in these final questions Aquinas looks in turn at *law* (qq.90–108) and *grace* (qq.109–14).

In II-II, he looks more closely at the virtues that will figure so prominently in the successful movement to God. The first forty-six questions are devoted to the *theological virtues*, which give the capacities for activity that is on the supernatural plane and is oriented to God as transcendent end. Hence, in qq.1–16, he looks at *faith*, in qq.17–22 at *hope*, and in qq.23–46 at the greatest of the theological virtues, *charity*. Questions 47–170 treat the cardinal virtues, as well as virtues closely associated with them (see *virtue*). In qq.47–56, he focuses on prudence, in qq.57–122 on justice, and in qq.123–40 and 141–70 on the two cardinal virtues that perfect the passions, fortitude and temperance, respectively. ST II-II concludes by looking at acts that pertain especially to certain humans, for example, in some detail (qq.171–74) at the *gratuitous grace* that is *prophecy*, as well as the different states (the active, the contemplative) of perfection in the church on earth (qq.170ff.)

In developing his teaching about the virtues, Aquinas builds on the psychology introduced in the ST's First Part, with its detailed rendering of the human person in its basic psychosomatic unity and classification of the soul in its various parts (nutritive, sensitive, rational; see *anthropology*). But, more fundamentally, Aquinas's ethics is thoroughly theological, put in the light of God, as suggested itself by the placement of the moral considerations in the second place, after the detailed consideration in the ST's First Part of God and the processions of creatures from God. The ethical considerations of the Second Part will find their completion, in turn, in the Christology of the Third Part, in which he treats of Christ, who as human is the way to God as end (see *viator*). This includes reflections on Christ as the perfect human who is the moral exemplar of others (see *Omnis Christi actio est nostra instructio*). It may be, as Leonard Boyle has suggested, that in constructing the ST as he did, Aquinas was indicating a dissatisfaction with the way ethics had hitherto been taught in his order. Previously, Dominicans had considered the moral life in terms of the virtues and vices set off on their own, and without reference to the basic christological and theological convictions that must, in Aquinas's view, inform thought about a moral agent who is called to God as his proper end. By this ordering and placement, Aquinas in contrast intended to make clear that ethics must be both theological and christological, based on the belief in God as beginning and end of human existence (see *sacred doctrine*) and in Christ as the one who makes possible the successful completion of the moral journey to God. In such a view, the core of ethics will be expressed in the Second Part of the ST, but it will be complemented and extended in the First and Third as well. To get his teaching about morality, one will also have to read what Aquinas says about God and Christ, and so draw the connections among all three of the ST's parts.

Pope (2002a, b); Schockenhoff (1987); Wadell (1991); Boyle (1982); Pinckaers (2002).

Natural, Supernatural   *see* Grace

Nature   *see* Person

Nature and Grace   For Aquinas, performing an act presupposes the capacity for that act. What lacks the capacity, cannot perform the act. In Aquinas's rendering, salvation involves knowing God face-to-face, participating in the inner life of God that is proper to God. The knowing of God directly lies beyond the natural capacities of the human. Humans can naturally come to know only what is accessible through the evidence provided in sensation; such is hardly the case with God. Hence, in discussing the *beatific vision*, Aquinas speaks of the light of glory, an added power given by God in the next life that

makes the human capable of the direct vision of God in God's essence. Likewise, in talking about the movement in the present life of the person to God as end (see *viator*), which involves not only morally good but supernaturally ordered acts, Aquinas speaks of other added capacities, appropriate to this life as ordered to God as end, that make supernatural action—action that has the triune God who is the end of humans as its object—possible. These are habitual **grace** and the **theological virtues**. Grace and these virtues extend the capacities of the person. What was not possible to the person as human, as endowed with the powers of soul contained in human nature, is now possible to the person as graced and elevated by the virtues.

In a handful of places (e.g., ST I.1.8 ad 2), Aquinas invokes a saying that captures well his most fundamental ideas about the relations between human nature and grace: "Gratia non tollit naturam sed perficit," literally, "Grace does not remove nature, but perfects it." By this saying, Aquinas is intent on holding in correct balance two important points. The first has already been mentioned: Grace marks a perfecting or extending of the capacities of the person. Without that perfecting, the supernatural life—a life in this world that is in fact ordered to God as end and that can bring one to the fuller perfection that is life with God in heaven—would not be possible for the human. There is, in fact, a huge gap between the human and the God who is the human's end, the gap that separates what is not God from God. Through grace and the theological virtues, God has bridged the gap by raising the person to God's own level. Acting out of this grace and these virtues will bring the person to the end promised by God, namely, God.

Grace and glory involve a radical transcendence of the self. By grace, one is raised up to a share in the divine nature that is appropriate to life in this world. By glory, in the next life, one is elevated to God directly and enters into God's own life. There is nonetheless a genuine continuity between the person as graced and the person as human. "Grace does not destroy nature." The human has been called to know and love God, and this knowing and loving certainly transcends what the human is naturally capable of; hence the need, first for grace and then for the light of glory. But knowing and loving is natural to the human, albeit discursive knowing, the knowing natural to the human, surely differs from the intuitive grasp of God that will come in the vision of God. It is a human being, a knowing being, who has been called to the beatific vision. The perfecting that grace and then glory brings is in keeping with that nature, although, again, bringing that nature to a perfection is simply impossible for it on its own. If, in contrast, a stone were called to the beatific vision, or to a form of existence in this world that required intentional activity in grace, then grace would not perfect but would perforce destroy the nature, making the stone into something that it is not by nature—a thinking, loving being who moves to God as end by its intentional acts. Thus, along with the discontinuity, marked by God's granting of elevation to the divine plane, there is, in Aquinas's rendering of nature and grace, a real continuity as well.

The same interpretation may be applied to the depiction of the human being as *capax Dei*, or *capax gratiae*, or *capax gloriae* ("capable of God," "capable of grace," "capable of glory"). One is not capable of seeing God directly of oneself, and one does not acquire grace through one's own efforts, through the use of one's natural capacities (see **Facienti quod in se est**). Grace is a gift, given to those to whom God wills eternal life (see **predestination**); so too, the vision of God in the next life is a gift, the end to which God predestines some, and does so freely, as the ultimate expression of God's love. But grace works with the nature and does not destroy or eliminate it; grace perfects the nature, healing it of sin and the effects of sin and raising it to the supernatural level. And the end to which grace orders the graced person is in keeping with the natural capacities of the person as elevated by grace and the theological virtues, although the vision of God in God's essence perfects the person in a way that simply outstrips the person's natural capacities.

Stoeckle (1962); O'Neill (1974).

Negative Theology

Negative Theology As part of his *theological epistemology*, Aquinas advances a sophisticated negative theology. Resting on certain positive affirmations about God—in particular, as the transcendent source of all being, God is pure act—this negative theology is threefold. It denies, in the first place, some qualities to God as entirely inappropriate to God (qualitative negation); second, it affirms certain perfections of God while denying to God the mode in which these perfections are evident in creatures (objective modal negation); and third, attending to the way in which humans know and name, it denies to God what is integral to our manner of knowing (in particular, in forming judgments humans compose and divide) but that cannot be present in the God who is utterly one and simple. Thus, by the first, Aquinas would deny that God is a body or is material; the transcendent God who is the source of all being is immaterial. By the second, he would affirm that as the source of such perfections as goodness and wisdom, God "possesses" such perfections, but transcendently, and not in the manner in which such perfections appear in what God makes. And by the third, he denies composition in God while also insisting on the need, when talking about God, of using both concrete and abstract terms. God is wise, but is also wisdom itself. In this way, Aquinas differentiates God from creatures, who may be termed "wise," for example, but are not at the same time wisdom itself or subsistent wisdom. While rooted in a sense of divine transcendence, including the utter and primary richness of God's being, this negative theology in turn helps to secure and refine that sense. God is not to be confused with creatures, and the various denials in his negative theology render such confusion more difficult. This "negative" knowledge is not quidditative, as if yielding God's essence as it is. As Aquinas repeatedly reminds us in his theological epistemology, such quidditative knowledge will come only in the next life, when God, with God's aid, is seen directly by the human as God is. But in facilitating the denial to God of what is inappropriate, Aquinas's negative theology helps one get a better sense of truths that must be affirmed *about* God. The complement of this negative theology is the more positive (yet similarly modest) knowledge associated with analogical predication.

Rocca (2004), part 1; Johnson (1998); Humbrecht (1993–1994); Wissink (1994).

Omnis Christi actio nostra est instructio

Omnis Christi actio nostra est instructio Literally, "every action of Christ is for our instruction." This saying appears at ST III.40.1 ad 3 and nicely conveys Aquinas's conviction about the importance of Christ as moral exemplar. The saying trades on the close link that Aquinas draws between creating and saving; it also confirms the soundness of Aquinas's decision to include in the ST's treatise on Christ the material covered in III.27–59.

For Aquinas, ***Jesus Christ*** is the Word of God incarnate. Without loss to itself as fully divine second person of God, the Word has taken up human nature and come to express it, instantiate it. The Word as incarnate is fully human, and the Word is the true subject of the human activities of Jesus. There is a special fittingness of the Word becoming incarnate. While it certainly lies within the divine power for one of the other divine persons to be the term of the assumption of human nature in the incarnation, it made sense for assumption to terminate in the Word. Here Aquinas can point to the Word as the wisdom of God and to the distinctive role in creating (see *creation*) played by the second divine person. The Word is the plan of creation. All things have been made in accordance with the Word, have been patterned on the Word, in order to proclaim the goodness of God. Rational creatures have a special likeness to the Word, by their rationality. But rational creatures have marred the image by their sin. Who better, then, to become incarnate in order to overcome sin and restore the image than the Word according to whom rational creatures were made (ST III.3.8)? The Word incarnate is a true human, in the sense that the incarnate Word has everything—body and soul—essential to being human. But the incarnate Word is true human in a moral sense as well. Jesus was without sin, and so Jesus was not subject to those consequences of sin that destroy correct order within the self, or that disrupt the correct order of the human to God as the rule of action (see *original justice; original sin*). Jesus also had the fullness of grace (ST III.7), and so the Word in the Word's assumed humanity was fully subject to the promptings of grace and so correctly exercised his capacities as a human. The Word as human acts correctly, in accordance with God's plan for human beings. Thus, in his actions, one finds the model for emulation, a calling to the form of living that was rejected in the fall but rendered possible anew by God's faithfulness and in the sending of the Son, to remove the barrier of sin and to provide the way to God as end (see *viator*).

Until the ST, scholastic treatises on Christ focused on the grammar of Christ, on the *hypostatic union* of the two natures. Establishing the grammar would be useful in reading the Gospels properly. But apart from occasional references in earlier treatises to specific incidents in the Gospels (especially with regard to the passion), scholastic treatises did not engage in a full-scale retelling of the story of Christ, as rendered in the Gospels, in the light of the grammar of Christ. The innovation of the Christology of the ST is that Aquinas has brought such material into the heart of the scholastic account of Christ. He begins the treatise on Christ with a consideration of hypostatic union and what follows on that union (III.2–26). Then in the second main part of the treatise (qq.27–59), he reviews the story of Jesus, from the entry of the Word into the world, through the life and activities and the passion and death, to, finally, the resurrection and the departure from this world. In the actions of the God become human, human salvation is made possible, for by his *death* and *resurrection* Christ overcomes the sin that keeps humans from God and makes available the grace that will bring one to a successful completion of the journey. In the actions of the God who becomes truly human, Christ shows other humans how to act out of grace and so to live as God wills for those who will attain to God. In this connection, then, it is well worth the effort to study the story of Christ and to attend to its details, to see how he worked in grace in given circumstances and to learn those virtues that he wishes his followers to emulate. It is in this study that Aquinas himself engages in III.27–59 and to which he exhorts us by the present saying.

Schenk (1990); Gillon (1959); Hibbs (1991); Torrell (1991).

Original Justice As part of his theological *anthropology*, Aquinas considers the first people in the original state, prior to the fall (ST I.94ff.). The original state is marked by full harmony and right order. The human person was subject to God and open to God's promptings, although not necessitated by God's grace. Within the human self, the different powers of the lower soul—the sensitive powers, which provide for sensation and for the passions—were subject to the rule of the higher soul, and so rational, in the sense that they observed the rule of reason, which in turn was subject to God. Correspondingly, the body and the soul were in full harmony; the needs of the body were met without exaggeration and without allowing them to govern the life of the human. Due proportion among the parts of the soul, and between soul and body, was observed. Finally, the first human stood in harmony with others—with the other person, made from him, and with the rest of the creation, which was made for the human and observed the right order toward the human.

Crucial to Aquinas's depiction of the original state is the insistence that the first humans were made in grace. By grace, the first people were ordered to eternal life and the vision of God that that would bring. By grace, their natural capacities were extended to the supernatural order. It is grace that was responsible for this original harmony, not only of the person before God, but within the person, and of the person with various others. That the different powers of the soul are in equilibrium, and that the body is subject to the soul, is not a human achievement, due to the powers of the nature or due to the human nature. Rather, God made the person in grace, and this grace kept the powers of the soul in their due ordering, the lower subject to the higher, which itself was subject to God.

In light of this rendering of the original state, Aquinas has an easy enough time depicting *original sin* and its consequences. He can do so in great detail, corresponding to the different forms of the original harmony, but ultimately it comes to loss and disruption: the loss of grace and the disruption that that entails. The depiction of the original state also lends resonance to his account of the human person as made in the *image of God*. In describing the image, there are three stages or parts: the human's natural capacities, which make the person like to God as a knower and lover; the actualization of these capaci-

ties through grace and the graced acts of knowing and love (faith and charity) that grace facilitates; and, in the next life, the realization of the image in the state of glory, by knowing and loving God as God knows and loves God, by the culmination of grace. In talking about the original state, Aquinas replicates the first two of these meanings of the image: All humans are made in God's image, in terms of their natural capacities. And some humans, as aided by grace, grow in the image by their graced activities. The first people had the image in both of these senses and would have reached the third level, if they had done what God asked, as was possible in their grace. If they had done God's will, they would have received more grace and eventually would have been confirmed in that grace, and finally given heaven, the image in the third sense. But they did not; they rejected God's will, substituting their own, and as a consequence forfeited grace, the image in the second sense. All that remained to them was image in the first sense; even then, given the disruption of the nature and its inner ordering by sin, the image was not full.

Talk of the original state is also helpful for the light that it can shed on the end times (see *eschatology*). There is, for Aquinas, a huge difference between the original state and the *beatific vision*. It is the difference between the image of God in the first two senses, and the full achievement of image in the third sense, when the blessed reach God and come to live God's own life. Heaven is not, in Aquinas, a return to paradise, but something that transcends it, in the way that glory is greater than grace. The first people did not enjoy the vision. Rather, by grace they were ordered to the vision, such that if they acted correctly, in grace, they would have attained to the vision of God. But they did not; they sinned, and as consequence of that sin, they were subject to *death*. The rest of us, who also sin and so are subject to this penalty, also die. But in Christ, death is overcome (see the *resurrection of Christ*), and those who have been joined to Christ (as the mystical body of Christ; see *church*) will also overcome death. They will be raised up in their bodies in the end times, and the full person will come to enjoy the end to which God has called people in their original constitution—the end, that is, that would have been theirs if they had not fallen from God and that the original state anticipated, although imperfectly.

———————

Kors (1922).

Original Sin   Original sin is discussed at two points in the ST: in I-II.82ff., in the course of the review of sin and the vices, and in II-II.163ff., as part of the closer examination of the sin of pride. The presentation of the effects of original sin plays nicely off the account of the original state found late in the First Part of the ST (especially qq.94–96). There Aquinas depicted the original state as one of thorough harmony: within the human, as pertains to the relations among the different parts of the soul, and between soul and body, and of the person with others—with God, first of all, but of the first human with his helpmate, and with the rest of creation as well (see *original justice*). This thoroughgoing harmony was established by the grace in which the first human was created, a grace that oriented the human person to God as end, provided the correct ordering within the self, and made for equilibrium in the person's dealings with the outer world. Original sin brings about the forfeiting of grace, and so introduces disharmony and lack of order into the self and the world. The reason is no longer subject to God, the lower parts of the soul are no longer subject to reason, the body is at war with the soul, and human beings are at odds with each other. The withdrawal of grace allows what Aquinas terms "concupiscences" in the person (I-II.82.3; 83.4). Each part of the self has its proper good, its proper perfection. In the well-ordered self, each part is allowed its due, but no more, and

the lower self is subject to the rule of reason, whose own good should be the standard for the aspiration to and attainment of lesser goods. In the disordered self, things run rampant. Each part of the self seeks its own good, and inordinately; these are the concupiscences that arise through original sin.

Original sin also has the consequence of making people guilty before God; subsequent sins, in light of the concupiscences, will increase the guilt before God. Or to put the same point in different fashion, here employing the metaphor of "journey" favored by Aquinas (see *viator*): In original justice, the human person was correctly ordered to God as end, and if the person would have obeyed God's will, the person would have been confirmed in grace and eventually in glory (that is, the end of the journey, which is life with God in heaven), and that would have been the inheritance of those who would come after Adam. They would have been born in original justice. But by original sin, the human person has gone off track, is going in the wrong direction, is not approximating to God as end through his acts. And the more that the person acts in the wake of original sin and as in accordance with the concupiscences, the more off track he will go and the closer he will come to what will be his end, namely, the eternal punishment that is absolute and irrevocable distance from God (see *eschatology*). By original and actual sins, the person becomes liable to this punishment. In giving that punishment, God is rendering what is due that person. And so, as a final consequence of original sin, people are liable to death, taken in a twofold sense. By the sin that offends God, one qualifies for spiritual death, ending up in hell, completely apart from God. But one also now is subject to physical death (see *death*). If the first person had not sinned, that person would not have physically died. The grace in which the person was made prevented the corruptible part of the human from corrupting, and the confirmation in grace that would have followed keeping

God's will would have removed the possibility of corruption. No sin, no death. But after the fall, there is physical death, as a reminder of the seriousness of sin.

Sin entered the world through one man, and Adam's sin is the sin of all other humans. Later humans do not themselves sin originally, but by receiving their human nature to which original sin and its consequences are attached, they are born into original sin. In trying to account for the ascription of that man's sin to others, Aquinas uses the figure of a single body. All humans born of Adam may be considered as one man, inasmuch as they have one common nature. The multitude of humans born of Adam are as so many members of one body. And they have received their nature from Adam. In talking about this reception, Aquinas gestures at the biology prevalent at his time, in which in human generation the woman was thought to provide the matter and the man the formal aspect of human nature to the offspring. Thus, as the active principle of all those who would follow in the species, Adam passes on original sin and the consequences of that sin. By all being in Adam virtually, all others generated in the normal manner of human generation come to share in that sin and its consequences (I-II.81.1, 3). Hence, if someone were generated in an atypical way—say, by a miraculous forming from human flesh (a.4)—that person would not contract original sin, because the usual active principle would be missing, and so Adam would not be the active principle of one so miraculously formed. The importance of Adam as the active principle of all other humans and so the conveyor of this sin of origin is underscored in a counterexample that Aquinas provides (a.5). What if Adam had not sinned, but Eve had? Would there have been an original sin that would be passed on as a legacy? No, for the woman provides only the matter, not the active principle of generation. What if Adam had sinned but Eve had not—would there have been original sin passed on to those generated

in the typical way? Yes, for, again, the male is the active principle of generation, and so those generated in Adam (as the first in the series, in the race, of active principles) would have contracted Adam's original sin.

In II-II.163, Aquinas specifies that the first sin was a sin of pride. Pride (*superbia*) is so called because by it, a human aims higher (*supra*) than he is; that one is proud who wishes to overstep beyond what he is (II-II.161.1c). The fall involves an inordinate coveting of a spiritual good, above the measure of the human (II-II.162.1c). To clarify this point, Aquinas has recourse to his depiction of the original state. The first human was endowed with his natural capacities, and made in grace. By that grace, the person was ordered to glory, and if he had willed as God wills, he would have been confirmed in grace and in glory. He would have attained to God as God intends, through the grace that God had freely provided. But in the fall, he willed a spiritual good—the knowledge of good and evil—that pertains to the divine nature. He willed to attain this, not by grace, but by his own natural powers, that is, by bypassing grace. The person aspired to a likeness to God, and to a likeness that would be gained by the exercise of his natural powers, as unaided by God. This is how the person is proud, has an undue estimation of himself, and so acts in a way that contravenes the divine will and puts him at odds with God. In pride, the person has overreached.

The discussion of original sin and the origination of the human predicament in the act of Adam, transmitted by Adam to those who share the nature, owes much to Romans 5. By one man, sin and death have entered the world, and all of those who are generated in the normal fashion have this sin and suffer its consequences. The dependence on Romans 5, in turn, establishes the possibility of Aquinas advancing, as a subtheme of his Christology, the view of Christ as the Second Adam. Just as by one man sin and death have entered the world, so by the Second Adam sin and death are overcome, by Jesus' death and resurrection (see *cross*; *resurrection*). And just as the race has suffered by the act of the First Adam, which is their act also, so humans will thrive when they are united to Christ by their faith and charity (see *church*) and make the death and resurrection of Jesus their own, through the faith that justifies. In Christ, they die to sin, and the consequences of sin are overcome in principle. In Christ, they receive the promise of eternal life in the presence of God. And their own physical death will not be the final word when it comes to the existence of the body-soul composite (see *anthropology*). Those who belong to Christ will physically die, by virtue of their natural union with the First Adam, but they will rise again, as patterned on and made possible by the resurrection of the Second Adam, and will come to enjoy, in both soul and body, the richness of life in the presence of God.

Kors (1922); Dubois (1983); Labourdette (1985); Te Velde (2005).

Penance   Aquinas had intended to discuss in the Third Part of the ST Christology, sacraments, and eschatology. He completed only the treatise on Christ and part of that on the sacraments. The questions on penance (III.84–90) are in fact the final ones that Aquinas crafted before giving up his academic work after his experience in early December 1273. He did not cover all that he had wished on the sacrament of penance, but he wrote enough to make clear the main points of his teaching.

Aquinas locates penance in a double context. One is the depiction of human existence in terms of a journey that has God as its end (see *viator*). God initiates the journey by calling some rational creatures to the end that is God, promising to these creatures participation in God's own's life (see *predestination*; *beatific vision*). God can also be said to

initiate the journey by giving the *grace* and the *theological virtues* that direct a person to God as end and make possible the morally and supernaturally good actions that bring her closer to God as end and prepare her for entry, in the next life, into the immediate presence of God. Especially important here is the teaching about *charity*. As a theological virtue, charity is given, infused, by God as a gift. Through this gift, one obtains the capacity to respond in kind to God, that is, in love. Charity establishes a community between its recipient and God, and is the basis of the friendship that pertains to God and to those who are by God's grace in correct relationship to God.

Charity and grace, however, can be lost through *sin*. Grace and the virtues incline the person to good action, but do not compel good action. The person is a voluntary agent, and it lies within the power of the human will to act against these good inclinations provided by God, and to sin. Mortal sin takes the person out of correct relationship to God and destroys the friendship that had existed between them. By sin, one offends God; one disrupts the self and becomes prone to *temptation* and further sinning; one becomes guilty before God and subject to God's punishment. However, it is possible to overcome sin and to enter anew into correct relationship with God. One does this through penance, described in the treatise on penance in terms of both a virtue and a sacrament, which are closely related for Aquinas. By the virtue, one is truly sorry for one's sins and seeks reconciliation with God. In repenting, one will do as God wills, which is to confess one's sins, for which one is truly penitent, to the priest, who here serves as the minister of God. The priest in turn will speak God's word of forgiveness to the penitent, and the penitent will be restored to correct relationship to God. The friendship will be renewed, and the person, having repented and confessed for past sins, will be on the way again to God as end.

In discussing the sacramental restoration of friendship and the overcoming of sin, Aquinas invokes certain lessons from his treatise on grace (ST I-II.109ff.). For one thing, conversion away from sin and toward God is not a human accomplishment. Rather, conversion is worked in the sinner by God through a grace that is operative (see *Facienti quod in se est*). This holds whether one is talking of first conversion or a conversion subsequent to sin with the attendant fall out of grace. So too, the repentance called for by penance—the new movement away from sin and toward God that must follow on the sin that has removed one from correct relationship to God—is worked by operative grace (III.86.4 ad 2). In the same passage in the treatise on penance, Aquinas also refers to cooperative grace. Operative *auxilium* moves the will, and the will is simply moved. Cooperative grace moves the will in such a way that the will moves itself (ST I-II.111.2c). In the sacrament of penance, contrition and confession and absolution will bring forgiveness of sin, and the restoration of friendship with God. Penance also changes the debt that is owed to God. Mortal sin establishes an infinite debt. The sacrament of penance converts that eternal debt into a temporal debt, which is paid for by the act of satisfaction assigned by the priest. Cooperative grace, Aquinas notes in this passage, facilitates the act of satisfaction, making it easier to bear the punishment that makes up for the remaining debt of sin.

The other context in which Aquinas places penance is, of course, the sacraments of the New Law. What he teaches about the **sacraments** generally, and about particular sacraments such as **baptism** and Eucharist, holds for penance. The principal agent in this sacrament is God, to whom alone the forgiveness of sins and the granting of grace belongs. God works through the priest (III.84.3 ad 3), who by his ordination (and so reception of the priestly **character**), has been delegated to act in the person of Christ, in the conveying of the grace made available by God through the **cross** of Christ. The priest

here, as in the other sacraments, serves as an **instrumental cause** of God, applying to repentant sinners the grace that has been offered by God through the conjoined instrument that is the humanity of Christ, in which the Word become human has suffered to overcome sin (see **Jesus Christ**). Aquinas employs as well the threefold sacramental formula used to analyze the other sacraments (III.84.1 ad 3). In penance, the *sacramentum tantum* (the sign only) are the actions performed externally by the repentant sinner (going to the priest to confess, performing the act of satisfaction) and by the priest (hearing the confession and absolving of sin, in the name of God). The *res et sacramentum* (the thing and the sacrament) is the sinner's internal repentance; the external actions signify that the person is truly sorry for sin and wants to move away from sin and back to God. The *res tantum*, the result of contrition, is the forgiveness of sin, which is removed by the infusion of grace. In terms of the middle part of the formula, Aquinas insists on genuine repentance as this is worked by God in the sinner. Unlike some later theologians, who speak of attrition, or sorrow for one's sins out of a fear of punishment, as adequate, with the subsequent transformation of attrition into contrition in the sacrament, Aquinas holds that contrition is required for the sacrament to be effective. If there is sham at this second level, such that the external actions do not signify repentance, there is no reception of the *res tantum*; the spiritual effects will be blocked by an impediment in the one who is confessing (III.84.3 ad 5). Finally, as in other sacraments, Aquinas shows in his discussion of this sacrament an attraction to the language of form and matter. In discussing the Eucharist, for example, he will devote a series of questions (III.74–77) to the matter of that sacrament—ranging from the bread and wine, the stuff used in the sacrament, bread and wine, through the real presence that comes about by transubstantiation, to the remaining accidents of the bread and wine; he gives as well a question (q.78) on the form, that is, the sacramental formula which describes the presence as well as effects it. In penance, the part taken by the penitent serves as the matter, both the words or deeds of the penitent, all having to do with past sin; the penitent grieves over sin, confesses sin, seeks to atone for sin (III.84.2–3; 90.2c). The form of the sacrament has to do with the part taken by the priest (III.84.3c), who speaks the words of absolution that have been established by Christ as the instrument for the forgiveness of sins. Both the form and the matter are required for the sacrament.

The person whose sins have been repented of and forgiven by God in this sacrament must do penance in the sense of performing an act of satisfaction assigned by the priest. In insisting on the need for the person to satisfy, Aquinas is witnessing to the importance of Christ's work on the cross. Apart from that work, it would be impossible for anyone to satisfy for sin. Mortal sin puts one into an infinite debt to God; for those who are joined to Christ, through the faith and charity that God's grace makes possible, that infinite debt is changed into one that is manageable, into a temporal debt that is satisfied through the works assigned by the priest (III.86.4c). By suffering in atonement for sin, the person is also growing in discipleship to Christ, taking up the cross of Christ to overcome, in this modest and wholly derivative way, the remnants of sin. In insisting on satisfaction, Aquinas witnesses to the great harm that sinning does: It disrupts community, with God chiefly, but with others as well. Paying in this moderate way a price for sin is a salutary reminder to the person of the seriousness of sin, and a way for that person to repair through this action the fabric of community damaged by sin.

Valkenberg (1996); Wissink (1996).

Person   Aquinas employs the term *persona* at a number of places in his theology: in his discussion of human beings, angels, Christ, and God. As used of such divergent beings, *persona* is used analogously. There is continuity among these diverse affirmations, but difference as well. "Person" does not mean exactly the same thing as said of God and as said of a human being.

Aquinas's starting point is the definition of "person" provided by the sixth-century author Boethius, in his treatise against the Christologies of Nestorius and Eutyches (*Contra Eutychen et Nestorium*). Boethius defines "person" as "the individual substance of a rational nature." Nature makes a thing the sort of thing that it is, allowing for classification. A person is an instance of the nature, one who expresses that nature. It pertains to the individual substance to exist in itself, and not in another; here the contrast is with accidents, which do not exist of themselves, but exist in another. In terms of substances that are corporeal, accidents exist in the substance as in their subject and modify and proclaim their subject, revealing what sort of thing it is. When a being of nonrational nature is in question—as in the case of a tree or an animal—the word "person" will not be used of the individual who possesses and expresses such a nature. The word "person" is reserved to an individual who possesses *rational* nature. And so, says Boethius, we can use "person" to speak of the human being, possessed of rational intellect and will; of the angel, who has and expresses a higher form of rational nature; and of God, who is supremely rational. As Boethius continues in that treatise, one will use "person" to speak of Christ, in whom two natures are united in the incarnation.

In speaking of the human as person, there is no great problem for Aquinas in adopting the Boethian definition as is. A human being is an individual of human nature. Human nature is a possibility for a certain form of life, which is realized when an individual comes to be. The nature does not exist apart from its instantiation in the human person. The being is human because all that falls under the nature (body, the human soul, including the capacity for discursive thought and rational willing) is found in this being. There are others of this type, and each human is a human person, each realizing by its being the potential constituted by the nature. These different human persons share the same nature (identity in species), but the nature is numerically different in each case, in accordance with the difference in person from case to case. I am a person, as is the reader of these pages, and my person is distinct from the person of the reader; we are different persons, each of whom has realized the possibility constituted by the nature. As a person, the human is the subject of doings and sufferings ascribed to that person. Those are peculiar to that person; they are not those of another person, who is a different subject.

In applying the terms "person" and "nature" to God, however, certain modifications must be made (see ST I.29). Or rather, the need for modification will have been acknowledged in the light of the scriptural revelation of God, and the modifications will have been acknowledged prior to Aquinas, by his important theological predecessors in the faith, who saw the value of using "person" and "nature" to organize and present the scriptural witness to God but were sensitive to the divine transcendence. First, as to nature, there is no potential in God; thus, one must guard against imagining, in referring to the divine persons and divine nature, of an actualizing of the nature, or of a person coming to be who realizes a potential for the divine form of life. Rather, God eternally is, and is perfectly, from eternity. There is no distinction between what God is and the "to be" (*esse*) of God. Along the same lines, there is no difference between a divine person and the divine nature. The divine persons are identical with the nature, and eternally and perfectly so. While it is helpful to distinguish between identity in species and identity in number when talking of human nature, the distinction

is lacking when it comes to God. Each of the divine persons is perfectly God and each is equally the same God from eternity. "Person" too can help organize reflection on God, but here too modification of the usage as for humans has been required. As used of humans, "person" indicates distinctions among humans; one human is not another, and the distinction between one human and another is complete. They share the same nature, which each has realized, but not numerically the same nature. One human is distinct, in being, from another. There are, to be sure, distinctions in the Godhead; Scripture reveals this, with its talk of Father, and Son, and Holy Spirit, and its insistence that the Father is not the Son, who is not the Spirit. And each person can be the subject of divine activity. But distinctions among the divine persons cannot run along the lines of distinctions among human persons. If that were the case, and divine being pertained to each of the persons, each of whom was marked off from the others in this way, the affirmation of three divine persons would be tantamount to the affirmation of three gods, which of course cannot be, as again ruled out by Scripture. Aquinas's application of person-talk to God follows the manner of the distinctions in the Godhead. The distinctions in God, which are not absolute although real, have to do with the divine processions, the eternal act by which the Son proceeds from the Father, who speaks the Word in knowing God, and the eternal act by which the Holy Spirit proceeds from the Father and the Son in their mutual love. Relations of origin differentiate the divine persons, and such is to be indicated when using "person" to speak of God. "Person" as used *in divinis* refers to subsistent relation, allowing for difference in God but insisting on the relatedness of the persons that stands at the core of the immanent Trinity. This relation differs from the relations that can exist between human persons; there, relation is an accident, pertaining to

beings that exist independent of the relation. In God, however, relation subsists,
and eternally so, and the divine person
is the subsistent relation that distinguishes that person from the others, to
whom, however, the person is decisively, and eternally, related. That relation subsists in God, and so is taken in
the mode of substance, shows the continuity between divine person and human
person, and so the pertinence of the
Boethian definition; but there is also difference, and "person" is used analogously in the two cases.

The transformation of "person"
when used of God informs Aquinas's
account of *Jesus Christ*. In his Christology, Aquinas affirms *hypostatic* or personal *union*. It is the second person of
God who becomes incarnate; it is in the
second divine person that a second
nature, the human nature, has been
joined to the first eternally expressed by
the Word—the divine nature which the
Word is. There is an existing subject in
the case of Christ. But the person in
Christ is to be construed along the lines
of person in God, not person in other
humans. In others, the possibility of the
nature is realized in a person coming to
be, a person who is an independent
agent and who differs in person from
other human persons. In Christ, there is
a person, who definitely differs from
other human persons. But the person of
Christ is the second person of God, who
proceeds from the Father, who receives
from the Father divine nature in an eternal act of generation, and who is the relation by which the second person differs
from the first. In this sense, then, in
assuming human nature, the Word has
taken up humanity, as it were, into the
inner life of the Trinity, as a foretaste and
as the firstfruits of the end to which the
triune God has called human beings, the
attainment of which is made possible
through the work of Christ, the Word of
God who as human is the way to God.

Seidl (1987); Hipp (2001); Emery (1998).

Philosophy   Aquinas's ideas about
philosophy find expression in the course
of his exposition of *sacred doctrine*. He
stresses the distinction between the two,
while also allowing for some overlap as
well as for the possible contribution of
what is originally philosophical to the
theological enterprise.

Sacred doctrine proceeds from above.
God is its principal teacher, and at its
core are the *articles of faith*, truths that
exceed the ability of reason to demonstrate but that are required for salvation.
Philosophy, however, is built up by reason. Humans observe the world and
build up various bodies of knowledge
(sciences) that treat of distinct areas of
philosophical discourse, from the lower
sciences to the highest philosophical discipline (i.e., metaphysics, also called
"theology," although in a different sense
than the *theology* that figures in sacred
doctrine; see ST I.1.1 ad 2). On the basis
of the different starting points of sacred
doctrine and philosophy, Thomists can
refer to the "autonomy" of each; neither
derives its principles from the other (see
ST I.1.5 ad 2 and 6 ad 2), and neither is to
be reduced to the other. Moreover, reason has a different status and scope in
each. While reason does have a place in
sacred doctrine—although it cannot
demonstrate the articles, it can investigate them, interpret them, show their
links, and defend them from attack—it is
revelation that provides the decisive
perspective in sacred doctrine. In philosophy, however, reasoning and argument
are to the fore. While the highest science
will not argue to its principles but rather
assume them (ST I.1.8c), arguing to new
conclusions and so building up the particular science stands at the heart of
philosophical work.

Aquinas gestures at three principal
ways in which philosophy and sacred
doctrine might interact. First, if need be,
sacred doctrine can judge philosophy
and find it deficient and in need of refor-
mation. Such is the case when philosophy
makes claims that are at odds with reve-

lation (I.1.6 ad 2). Although the major truths (articles) of the faith exceed the capacity of reason to demonstrate them, they are not contrary to reason (see ST I.1.8c), and so any claims that have been derived through the use of reason that contradicts the articles can themselves be shown to be in error. Second, there is some overlap in terms of content between sacred doctrine and philosophy. Here it is a question, not of the articles of faith but of the *preambles of faith*. Such truths, Aquinas acknowledges, have been demonstrated by philosophy, independent of Christian revelation. Such truths have also been revealed, as part of sacred doctrine (I.1.1c). Readers of Aquinas can differ on the manner in which the preambles of faith enter into his own project: as revealed, or as demonstrable? If the latter, then when Aquinas argues to the existence of God, or God's oneness, he would in effect be proceeding as a philosopher. And if he were so proceeding, then the arguments for God's existence and the like might very well have a foundational status, setting the stage for the subsequent, distinctively theological engagement with the articles of faith.

In considerations of sacred doctrine, perhaps the most important way in which philosophy and this doctrine can interact turns around the "handmaiden" status of philosophy (see ST I.1.5 sed contra). Philosophy can serve sacred doctrine and its theology; it can be called upon to help in the elucidation and defense of the faith. Thus, what has been developed by philosophy in accordance with its own methods and ambitions can be turned to the use of sacred doctrine. Early in the ST, Aquinas puts this possible contribution in terms of the saying, *Gratia non tollit naturam sed perficit* ("Grace does not destroy nature but perfects it"; I.1.8 ad 2). Natural reason, as he says there, should (and can) minister to faith, just as *charity*, oriented to God as end, can perfect the natural will. The appropriation of philosophical terms and arguments must be governed by divine revelation and the

needs of Christian argument, which will enable the theologian to discern what is useful and what is not in pagan philosophy, and to make whatever modifications to the philosophical that might be called for to be true to Christian truth (e.g., the insistence on God's utter transcendence). Aquinas was himself the beneficiary of a fine training in the philosophies, apart from and prior to his advanced training in theology, and was adept in deploying arguments and terms of originally philosophical derivation. But in making use of philosophy for Christian ends, Aquinas was hardly an innovator, a point that emerges in his own consideration of such terms as *person* and "nature," so useful in Trinitarian and christological discussions (see, e.g., I.29). In supplementing through philosophical means the resources of the Christian traditions in his own presentation of the faith, Aquinas is following the lead of the great Fathers of the early centuries of the Christian movement.

Scholars of Aquinas have disagreed about the status of philosophy in Aquinas's own Christian intellectual project. Are portions of the corpus of writings to be described as "philosophical"—in particular, the numerous commentaries on the writings of Aristotle? And to push the point, are parts, at least, of works that might fairly be termed "theological" in fact "philosophical," such that it would be appropriate, as many scholars have done, to try to extract the philosophy of Aquinas and to consider his debts to various predecessors and its continued relevance, apart from its theological applications? In this regard, might not ST I.2–26, the first part of the ST's treatise on *God*, be an exercise in philosophy, as a prelude to the second part of that treatise, to the *theology* that begins with q.27, with the consideration of the *Trinity*? In like fashion, much of the *Summa contra Gentiles* might from this vantage be termed "philosophical." While its final book certainly is concerned with specifically Christian matters, the first three books arguably are principally concerned with those truths that the philosophers first discovered through the apt use of reason; in treating those truths, Aquinas himself would have proceeded as a philosopher (see Kretzmann 1997).

As has been frequently noted, however, Aquinas tends to think of "philosophy" as something that is pre-Christian, not something that is currently being pursued. He himself seldom seems concerned with the "philosophical" for its own sake. Rather, he brings in Aristotle and others for Christian purposes: to clarify, interpret, and defend the faith. The principal truths of the faith are revealed, and the articles seem to relativize, contextualize, and "christen" those truths that are also accessible to philosophy. To put it bluntly, it is one thing to argue for God as one; it is another to make that affirmation of the God who is held, on the basis of revelation, to be three. In his commentary on Boethius's De trinitate (q.2, a.3 ob. 5 and ad 5), Aquinas invokes the biblical image of some water mixed with a larger amount of wine to figure the relation between philosophy and theology. For those who think that Aquinas at times proceeds as a philosopher, the water (philosophy) will retain its character in the mixing (see Owens 1993). For other readers, however, the water will be thoroughly transformed (Jordan 1993), arguably making the search for a "philosophy" in Aquinas somewhat beside the point and even contrary to Aquinas's own practice and intention.

Scholars also are in dispute about which of the major pre-Christian philosophers Aquinas prefers, or better, finds more useful for Christian ends. Quite typically, it is Aristotle who is thought to be so privileged, and some would go so far as to term Aquinas a "Christian Aristotelian." That seems excessive, and given Aquinas's statements about sacred doctrine and the theology that pertains to it and the hierarchy of *authority* in sacred doctrine, puts the stress where Aquinas would not put it. He is not an Aristotelian, if that is meant to characterize his principal outlook and ambitions in his intellectual work; he is a theologian, one who makes use of Aristotle and others in doing his theological work. A good deal of the extant Thomistic corpus is tied to his profession as a scholastic theologian. Some of the writings have to do with his training for work in the theological faculty; here the *Scriptum on the Sentences* is especially important. Other writings issue from his responsibilities as a master of the sacred page. One could mention here such biblical commentaries as those on John and the Pauline epistles, reflecting his classroom lecturing; one can also mention the various disputed questions on topics of interest to Aquinas, which he originally disputed in the school. Commentaries on specific works of Aristotle also figure prominently in the Thomistic corpus. But such do not arise from his responsibilities as, or training to be, a scholastic theologian. The sole text on which the bachelor and then master of theology lectured is Scripture; neither the novice theologian nor the theological master lectured on Aristotle. Aquinas's commentaries on Aristotle are, rather, extracurricular offerings, not required by his mandate as a school theologian but prosecuted out of personal interest. For most of the Middle Ages, Aristotle had been known only through those logical works translated by the sixth-century author Boethius. The twelfth and thirteenth centuries had seen a burst of translating activity, and other works of Aristotle became available to the largely Greekless West. (Aquinas himself knew no Greek and was thoroughly dependent on translations from the Greek, whether for Aristotle or for the early Greek church fathers.) Aristotle came to be known as "the Philosopher," and what he wrote on various topics, from soul through ethics to natural philosophy and metaphysics, exerted an enormous influence. The high medieval intellectual reception of Aristotle, however, was not even. Aristotle's works were often accompanied by commentaries, and some of what Aristotle or his commentators said could be seen to be hostile to the Christian faith. For example, is there personal immortality? A single intellect, whether active or passive, common to all humans? Some thirteenth-century theologians reacted to the newly recovered Aristotle with suspicion, wanted to limit access to his ideas, and certainly questioned his theological value. Aquinas, for his part, was more open to the possible benefits that Aristotle could bring. Without subordinating Christian faith to Aristotle—to the contrary, his reading of Aristotle could be as calm as it is precisely because he could evaluate it from the solid perspective of his faith and his theological sense of what the faith is about and what it promotes—Aquinas thus subjected specific writings of Aristotle to close study, to discern what was true in them, to isolate and reject what was false, and thus was able to call upon Aristotle for his own theological work, to do the things that the theologian must do: investigate and clarify the main truths of the religion, show their connections, ponder their implications, and defend them from attack.

Aquinas's serenity when it comes to Aristotle can be seen in a debate that broke out at the University of Paris about the eternity of the world. Is the world eternal? So Aristotle teaches, concluding this, apparently, through demonstrable argument. Yet this flies in the faith of what Christian revelation proclaims: The world is not eternal, but is called into existence, with a beginning in time, by God. For some, Aristotle's teaching was proof of his basic incompatibility with Christian faith; the Christian doctrine of *creation* is not an incidental matter, but is fundamental to the faith and to the depiction of the relations between God and the world. Others saw in the Aristotelian teaching the disclosure of the limitations of Christian faith and the needs for its supplementation by extra-Christian,

philosophical sources. If Aristotle could show that the world is eternal, this would at the same time show that the faith is wrong, and reason in this case should be preferred. Aquinas's own position, as articulated in a treatise devoted to the topic (*On the Eternity of the World*) and echoed in the systematic writings, is more nuanced, falling in the middle. Aquinas proceeds by showing what does and does not fall under the Christian notion of God's creating. Creation is *ex nihilo*, meaning that everything that a creature is has been received from God. God does not employ preexisting material in order to form any creature, but rather creates from nothing. Contrary to what the theological opponents of Aristotle taught, beginning in time is not intrinsic to the notion of creation. It is possible, says Aquinas, for God to create eternally, for what is created to have eternally existed. What is intrinsic to creating is that created things are brought to be by God; it lies within God's power and under the divine will to have created eternally. That creating had a beginning, in the sense that the coming to be of creatures had a beginning in time, is a matter of revelation. Christians assert a temporal beginning on the basis of revelation. This is to be numbered among the articles of faith. This leads Aquinas to chastise the theological opponents of Aristotle. They think they can demonstrate that creating has a beginning. Such would confuse what is an article with what is a preamble, and it would be to expose Christian truth to ridicule, for the arguments that they allege are simply not demonstrative. Yet what about the apparent demonstration, by Aristotle, that creation is eternal? Here, acting out of a considerable hermeneutical charity, Aquinas states that the arguments that Aristotle has brought forward in the *Physics* (8) are not meant to be taken as demonstrative; they are, rather, probable, and so can be rejected, as they must be, in the light of faith. Aquinas's differentiation between an eternal and a temporal creation is difficult, and the vast majority of his contemporaries were unable to follow his analysis.

In this theological work, Aquinas found in Aristotle a valuable contributor, though he always evaluated this contribution according to Christian norms and needs. Aquinas calls upon Aristotle, in a less problematic way, in a variety of contexts in his own theological writings. For example, he invokes Aristotle in his *anthropology*, with regard to the depiction of the human person as a unity of body and soul, each of which is required for the human. Aristotle helps Aquinas in clarifying how people know, and to what their knowledge, as unaided by grace or supernatural light, can and cannot extend (see *epistemology, theological*), and his reflections on *virtue* make a nice contribution to Aquinas's teaching about the moral life.

Without denying the Aristotelian contribution, other scholars have pointed to the debt that Aquinas also has to Plato and the Platonists. The debt has been obscured by the presence of harsh comments in the corpus about the root errors of Plato: for an epistemology that is insufficiently attentive to the origin in sensation of human knowing, and for the hypostatization of universals, which reflects a confusion of the ontological with the epistemological. Aquinas's direct access to Plato would have been limited. Only a very few of the dialogues were available in Latin translation (including the *Meno* and the *Timaeus*), and even then it is doubtful that Aquinas had read them. Yet avenues for indirect access to Plato were considerable, not least through the writings of the church doctors (Augustine, Pseudo-Dionysius) who shaped Aquinas's theological sensibilities in a not inconsiderable way. In depicting more positively Aquinas's relations with Plato, these scholars point to Aquinas's sense of the hierarchical character of reality: There are different levels of being, each of which stands in relation to and dependence on others. In the working out of divine providence through government, God will execute God's plan through intermediaries, and bring the lower beings to what is higher through the work of middle levels of being. Most notably, Aquinas's ideas about *esse*, about its analogical character and the ways that different sorts of being participate in *esse*, may suggest as well an indebtedness that for the most part has been left without explicit acknowledgment.

Wippel (2000); Jordan (1986a, 1992, 1993); Owens (1993); Booth (1983); Hankey (2002); Jenkins (1996); Dod (1982); Bonansea (1974).

Pope Christ is the head of the *church*, which consists of those who have responded in faith and charity to the gracious offer of salvation made by God in Christ. However, Christ has appointed others who by derivation may also be called "heads," to serve as his representatives on earth (ST III.8.6). Thus, bishops have charge of the church in their diocese. The pope has been designated by Christ as head of the church throughout the world during the time of his pontificate. For Aquinas, the jurisdictional primacy of the pope is grounded in the doctrine of Petrine primacy. The promise to Peter is made through Peter to those who stand in Peter's succession.

In designating the pope the head of the church, Aquinas does not intend to suggest that the pope is the source of grace or the principal medium of grace. God alone can grant participation in God's own life (i.e., grace), and God does this through Christ. However, God conveys grace through the sacraments, which are viewed as *instrumental causes* of grace, and God employs priests, who act *in persona Christi* also as instrumental causes of grace. In terms of the distribution of grace, inasmuch as the pope is also a priest, he is an instrumental cause of grace. But grace does not originate in the pope, nor do other priests receive their power as instrumental causes through the pope. That comes to them directly from Christ, in their ordination by their bishop.

As exercising the principal jurisdictional authority during his pontificate, the pope bears responsibility for maintaining the church on earth in its conformity to God's will and for promoting the movement of the people of God to the end to which they have been called. It is the charge of the pope to keep order in the church and to ensure that the faith that saves is well-known and observed by those in his charge. In times of crisis, when heresy threatens the faith, it lies with the pope to see to it that orthodoxy is upheld. In this regard, the pope can call a council of bishops to affirm the faith clearly, so that the heresy can be rebuked and the faithful confirmed in their correct orientation to God. It may be necessary to give the faith in this circumstance a new, more precise articulation (see *articles of faith*), to make explicit, in the light of the challenge to faith, what was previously only implicit. The pope in turn will confirm the determinations of the council and publish, if there is one, the new statement of faith that might emanate from that council.

Whether Aquinas affirms papal infallibility is a matter of scholarly discussion. The formal teaching on papal infallibility is, of course, much later (1870). But even in Aquinas's time, there were some who insisted on the infallible judgments of the pope in matters of faith. A Franciscan proclaimed the infallibility of the pope as a way of ensuring that later popes would not undercut decisions of earlier popes favorable to the Franciscans (that is, later popes would be bound to the infallible judgments of their predecessors). Aquinas's position is more difficult to assess. However, as when thinking of the Petrine primacy, Aquinas does think that the faith of the pope is indefectible, and so can guarantee the endurance in time of the one faith that saves. In calling a council and confirming its decisions, themselves rendered under the guidance of the Holy Spirit, the pope too is guided by the Holy Spirit, who will ensure that the church is kept faithful to God's word in Christ.

———

Congar (1974b); Bonino (1986); Ryan (1989).

Prayer In ST II-II, Aquinas subjects the virtues (see *theological virtues*; *virtue*) introduced in I-II to closer analysis. From II-II 58–122, he examines the cardinal virtue of justice, noting in the process those lesser virtues that might be associated with justice. Justice has to do with rendering to others what is due to them. Among the virtues annexed to justice is religion (II-II.81), which has to do with rendering to God what is due to God. As part of that discussion, Aquinas observes that prayer (II-II.83) falls under religion. Prayer is the unfolding of the will to God; it is the interpretation, before God, of the desires of the human person. The definition allows for an expansive notion of prayer, to include one's inner wants as well as the external expression, through deeds, of one's desire for God. It also allows for varieties of prayer, including thanksgiving to God for all that God is and does (see II-II.83.17). However, in the detailed discussion of prayer in II-II.83, the emphasis is put on the internal character of prayer, and prayer is seen principally (although not exclusively) as petition to God by the human person.

Aquinas nicely locates the prayer of petition in his account of the human person as made by God for God, and as reaching God as end through the morally and supernaturally good actions that prepare the person for life with God in heaven. Aquinas's skill is disclosed well in his consideration, in the heart of II-II.83 (see a.9), of what he terms to be the perfect prayer: that taught to people by Jesus. In his reading of the Lord's Prayer, almost all of the petitions have to do with the journey of the person to God and the overcoming of the obstacles that would keep a person from God. In the Lord's Prayer, one asks to reach the end set for people by God, and for the grace that frees one from temptation by allowing one to do what is good and is in keeping with the person's nature and end as set by God.

Aquinas discusses prayer elsewhere in the ST, in conjunction with other important theological topics. The treatment of prayer elsewhere conforms nicely with these *ex professo* comments about prayer. Prayer is treated as part of the consideration of **predestination** (I.23.8) and **grace** (see, in particular, I-II.109.9–10). Predestination is God's plan to communicate God's goodness to certain rational creatures in a special way, by ordaining those creatures to eternal life. The implementation of this plan comes through grace, which works conversion to God and moves the person to God as end through the person's acts. In such a view, is there room for prayer? As in I.23.8, Aquinas says there is, for God has ordained that by prayer the person will receive the grace necessary for the successful journey to God. Thus, prayer is fruitful when it is in accord with God's will, when one prays for what is suitable and when God has ordered that prayer to the obtaining of grace. Prayer, then, becomes the vehicle and occasion for the giving of grace; it itself is made possible by grace. In I-II.109, Aquinas picks up the thread, in the process showing his debt to the very late Augustine (see **grace**; **doctors of the church**). Once in the state of grace, does one need more grace, that is, grace in addition to the habitual grace infused as the term of conversion? The answer is yes, and here Aquinas shows his sense that while grace does morally transform, the transformation is not complete in this life. One continues to be assailed by **temptation** to sin, both from without (see **devil**) and from within, from the remnants of the sin, both **original sin** and actual **sin** from which grace frees. Under such attack, one would succumb to temptation and sin, and so lapse from the state of grace, unless new grace were given. This additional grace is the operative grace (*auxilium*) of persever-

ance, which leads a person from temptation and delivers her from evil, so that she can continue to the end set for her by God. Again in I-II.109 we meet the Lord's Prayer, repeating the analysis of Augustine in such later works as *The Gift of Perseverance*, in which Augustine links the petitions of this prayer to the giving of the grace needed to continue on the right path to God.

Aquinas discusses prayer in the Third Part of the ST as well, in the course of his account of **Jesus Christ**. Jesus himself prayed, and he taught us how to pray. In III.18.6 ob. 1, Jesus' prayer in the garden comes in for special scrutiny. What should be made of Jesus' asking for the chalice to pass from him, and the subsequent declaration that it is not his will but God's that should prevail? Aquinas's analysis is subtle and complex, drawing upon his **anthropology** and his sense of the correct relation and hierarchy within the human self (see **original justice**; **grace**), and showing nicely his grasp of the logic of incarnation. The human person is a composite of body and soul, and within the soul there are different levels of power (nutritive, sensitive, intellective). The human person was originally made in grace, which subjected the first people to God as their principal object and provided for the right hierarchy within the self. Just as reason, the highest part, was in perfect subjection to God, so the lower powers were perfectly subordinate, by grace, to reason. They do have their proper goods, but in giving expression to the appetite for these, the lower powers observed the dictate of reason and so what is fulfilling of the human person at his highest level. Sin has disrupted this ordering, removing grace, and so removing the subjection of the person to God and the harmony within the self. Now the self is at odds with itself, as different powers seek peculiar goods inordinately, that is, without regard to the highest needs and end of the person. For sinful humans, grace restores subjection to God and harmony in principle within the self, although by virtue of the remnants of sin, one must always guard against temptation. Grace allows the overcoming of temptation.

To turn to the case of Jesus: What holds in general of the anthropology, with regard to composition, holds of Jesus. In becoming incarnate, the Word really did take up a full human nature, including body and the full range of powers of the soul. And what held of the first humans in the original state, holds of Jesus. He was born without original sin, and did not himself sin. He had the fullness of grace. He as human is in complete subjection to God, and there is the originally intended harmony in him, by grace.

In this particular praying of Jesus, Aquinas observes that Jesus is fully human as well as fully divine; thus, he speaks of two wills. He also underscores that Jesus really did pray. This is what humans who are correctly related to God do, in proclaiming themselves as in correct relationship to God. In the utterance of his wish that the cup pass from him, Jesus' prayer gives utterance to the desire of his sensitive part, which seeks, as is proper, the preservation of the being of the human. But in the immediate addition of the recognition and acceptance of God's will, he shows that his self is in perfect harmony, by his grace, and that he as a complete and single entity seeks what is the highest and true good of the person as a whole, namely, God. And so in his prayer he concludes with his willingness to do the will of God.

Maidl (1994); Ryan (2000), chs. 3–4; Torrell (2004); Tugwell (1988), pp. 363–523 (for the principal texts in the Thomistic corpus on prayer).

Preambles of Faith   There are two kinds of truth found in *sacred doctrine*, the teaching of God that is necessary for salvation: the *articles of faith* and the preambles of faith. Both kinds of truth are revealed by God. The articles must be held by faith. They transcend the natural capacity of the human person to know. The preambles of faith can be demonstrated by reason, although most hold them by faith on the basis of revelation. That they can and have been demonstrated permits Aquinas to see a certain overlap between Christian teaching and non-Christian philosophical achievement. The best of the philosophers have attained, through the use of reason, to these particular truths held by Christians. That God has nonetheless seen fit to reveal the preambles—the existence of God, the oneness and goodness of God, and the like—makes sense. Only a few have been able to demonstrate them, and only after a long time, and even then with an admixture of error (ST I.1.1c).

This second category of truth in sacred doctrine has been a matter of considerable scholarly disagreement. These truths are revealed, but they can be demonstrated. How then do they enter into Aquinas's intellectual project? If as demonstrated, then when Aquinas turns to these truths, he will be proceeding as a philosopher among the philosophers (see *philosophy*). He will go as far as reason can take him, and then, but only then, turn to specifically Christian matter, that is, to the articles, which although not susceptible to demonstration, can be thought about and elucidated through the use of reason ("faith seeking understanding"). In dealing with the articles of faith, he will perforce be working as a theologian. To give an example from early in the ST, some scholars believe that the treatise on God (I.2–43) follows the distinction between the two kinds of truth, and so reflects two successive methodological approaches to truth that is Christian. In the discussion of the unity of God, of what pertains to the divine essence (qq.2–26), Aquinas in this view proceeds as a philosopher, showing what can be said about the divine essence, or better, given the otherness of God that reason can acknowledge, what cannot be said. But when he arrives finally at the

Trinity (q.27ff.), he will shift gears, and proceed as a theologian, dependent on revelation and guided in his reasoning and arguing by the scriptural revelation. To continue the point, for some who take the preambles in this way, the philosophical arguing that will yield a knowledge of God will itself be preparatory for the act of faith, for the acceptance in faith of what God reveals about God—that is, that the God whose existence and basic characteristics of intellection and willing can be demonstrated—is in fact triune. Argument will lead, in this reading, to the act of faith.

There are considerable problems, however, with this take on the preambles. The treatise on God is found in a *summa* of *theology*, and Aquinas in the ST's first question (I.1.1 ad 2) explicitly distinguishes the **theology** that pertains to sacred doctrine from that which is found in philosophy, that is, metaphysics. They are not the same; the former proceeds on the basis of revelation, and Aquinas does not say that that proceeding is restricted to the articles. The treatise on God in the ST constitutes a unity, moreover; the distinction of that one treatise into two parts hardly warrants positing differing methodological approaches, a philosophical to be followed by a theological. If that were what Aquinas were attempting in I.2–44, he probably would have told us that. To return to the commonality of claim, between the philosopher and the Christian when it comes to the preambles: Both may say that God is one, but the Christian says that together with another claim, or better, as part of one and the same claim, namely, that God is one-and-three. Surely there is a difference between the one god of the philosophers, and the one God of Christians who is three. And in reviewing Aquinas's treatise on **God** from beginning to end, it seems to be the same God, the Christian God, whom he discusses. The focus in one part of the treatise differs from that in the other, but it is the Christian God—first in that God's unity of essence, and then as a Trinity of persons—who is the topic throughout the treatise. Finally, with regard to argument's supposed capacity to prepare for the act of faith, that particular claim shows a serious ignorance of the psychology of **faith** for Aquinas. Faith is not an accomplishment of the person, as if one could move oneself, or have another human move one, to faith. Faith, rather, is a gift, moved in the person by God through an inwardly operative **grace**. The preambles, in the ST at least, would seem to enter into the project as revealed, and as connected to the other truths of the doctrine, that is, the articles. In borrowing from the philosophers, Aquinas has not ceased to be a theologian, for he is dependent principally on the divine revelation.

On the face of it, an earlier work of Aquinas, the **Summa contra Gentiles**, would seem to lend more support to the claim of a philosophical approach by Aquinas to the preambles. In his lengthy introduction to the entire work (I.1–9), Aquinas notes the distinction between the articles and the preambles, observes what reason can do with regard to the preambles but cannot with regard to the articles, and then proposes to organize the matter of the *ScG* in a distinctive way, looking first at the preambles (books I–III) and then at the articles (book IV). Much has been made of Aquinas's organizational comments and apparent description of his methodology in the different books of the *ScG*. Some have even called the *ScG* Aquinas's *summa* of *philosophy*, at least in its first three books, where Aquinas proceeds as a philosopher. More modestly, the opening books have been termed an extensive exercise in natural theology, the finest example of its kind in the history of Western philosophy. In these books through the use of reason, Aquinas has shown what reason can prove without recourse to revelation, which, however, would confirm the truths established rationally.

That the *ScG* has a distinctive ordering is beyond doubt, and the distribution of topics is, roughly, as Aquinas promises.

Yet there are considerable problems with the claim that the preambles are incorporated philosophically and that the use of Scripture in the opening books, which is considerable, is merely to confirm what reason has established. For one thing, the order of the first three books of the *ScG* is hardly philosophical; the philosopher would work up to a consideration of God, not begin with that. Beginning with God, on the other hand, befits *theology*, which considers God and all other things in relation to God as their beginning and end. Likewise, there is considerable specifically Christian material found in these early books, ideas that on Aquinas's telling cannot be established by reason. The third book, on providence, includes considerable mention of the extent of providence; it covers all humans and all of their acts. Yet Aquinas states in the prologue to the contemporary commentary on Job that human speculation on providence could not reach that truth; hence the need for the book of Job. Similarly, the third book concludes with a lengthy discussion of *grace* and God's predestining of some rational creatures to a participation in God's own life, ideas that would fall among the articles, not the preambles. It may be a dubious move, moreover, to isolate the first three books from the fourth. While he does have an organization, and three of these books do go together, there is the fourth book, and that book is integral to the entire project of the *ScG*. It is preferable to seek a characterization that would be applicable to the entire work. Such is, it would seem, provided by Aquinas among the organizational comments that introduce the book, in I.9, where he states that in this work he will examine what "the faith professes" and will employ reason as it can be used with regard to the kinds of truth that fall under sacred doctrine. Thus, in the fourth book, only probable argument can be used. In the first three books, probable argument will complement demonstrative argument, as derived from the writings of the philosophers and of the church fathers, and from

Scripture. It is also crucial, to continue along this line, to recall the heading of the entire work, provided by the saying from Proverbs 8:7, about proclaiming the truth and defending it. In taking up the office of the wise man, following here in the footsteps of wisdom incarnate (see *theologian*), Aquinas investigates truth—Christian truth—proclaiming it and defending it, and doing both all the way through the four books of the *ScG*. Defending it takes many forms, including the correction, where need be, of the philosophers, otherwise helpful in the presentation of some aspects of Christian wisdom. As a reminder, the preambles were revealed—and revealed together with the articles—because the truths about God that can be demonstrated were known only by a few, and then only after long effort, and even then as mixed with error. In employing the demonstrative arguments in books I–III, along with Scripture and probable arguments, it is necessary for Aquinas to correct the philosophers; such is done on the basis of revelation.

Or it may simply be that when he began the *ScG*, Aquinas thought it was possible to segregate the truths of sacred doctrine and treat the one (as in book IV) in explicit dependence on scriptural revelation and with a contextualized use of reason, but treat the other (in books I–III) philosophically, and aim at demonstrating, with the philosophers, the truths to be placed in those books. Aquinas did have a concern to find a more effective way of organizing and presenting the truths of the religion; there is a different organization of these truths in the ST compared with the *Scriptum*. Hence, the *ScG* may be an experiment in systematic theology that seeks to discover whether the truths of the religion can be pursued in two different ways, first philosophically and then theologically. If this is an experiment in systematic theology, then as he proceeded in the writing, he discovered that the organization would not work, as witnessed by the inclusion of revealed matter even in these first books.

Most fundamentally, the experiment would not work because in the end the division would prove artificial, inadequate to the integrity of the faith. Hence, Aquinas would continue his experimenting in systematic theology, as in the ST, where the articles and preambles are treated together and in the way suggested above.

De Broglie (1953); Shanley (2002), chs. 2–3; Kretzmann (1997); Hibbs (1995, 1998); Wawrykow (2001).

Predestination　Predestination is a part of providence. Providence is God's plan for creatures, by which God orders creatures to their appropriate ends (ST I.22). Providence is comprehensive; by providence, all creatures are ordered by God, their maker, to their proper fulfillment. There is a secondary aspect to providence: While it is principally God's plan, it involves as well the execution of this plan. God brings creatures to the end set for each by God. The execution of providence is divine government, which Aquinas discusses in detail toward the end of the ST's First Part (qq.103–19).

A part of providence, predestination is the plan that God has to communicate God's goodness in a special way, by calling some rational creatures to God's own life. Predestination is God's decision in eternity to bring some rational creatures to heaven. Predestination is of these rational creatures to eternal life. God's will is utterly efficacious; those who are ordained to eternal life will attain eternal life, will enter into the immediate presence of God and know and love God as God knows and loves God (see *beatific vision*), in accordance with God's will. As with providence, there is a secondary aspect of predestination. God not only wills this special end for some rational creatures; God executes God's plan, by grace. In discussing predestination of some to salvation in ST I.23, Aquinas makes some mention of grace as required

to fulfill God's plan, although the focus remains on predestination as ordination, as plan. The fuller treatment of *grace* comes in I-II.109–14; in those questions, Aquinas thus also completes the presentation on predestination.

As with providence, predestination pertains to the divine intellect and will. God's predestination is not capricious, although the reasons for predestining this particular one rather than another are known to God alone. God's predestining is a matter of intellect; it is purposeful and intentional. But it is a matter of the will as well. In this connection, in talking about predestination, Aquinas is continuing his reflections on God's loving (ST I.20), which pertains to the divine will. God's loving is causal; it establishes good. That something exists is the result of God's willing of good. That something exists as a being of this sort, with the capacities associated with a nature of that sort, is the result of God's loving. That something exists as having an end proportionate to the nature and with acts that can fulfill the nature by approximating that natural end is the result of God's loving. That some rational creatures— brought into existence, and into existence as rational, with acts appropriate to a rational nature that can fulfill the rational creature in terms of the human nature— are called to eternal life, and brought to eternal life through grace is also due to God's loving. God in love wills to these rational creatures the good that is proper, natural, to God. Such good transcends the natural capacities of rational creatures; it is "supernatural." One cannot act in a way unless one has the capacity to act in that way; hence the need for grace, to boost the capacities of the person, to make the person capable of what will bring that person to the special end willed to that person in love by God; hence the willing of that grace, in love, by God, to fulfill God's will for that person. As will become even clearer in the treatise on grace in I-II.109–14, there is more to grace, more to the functioning of grace and the need for grace. There Aquinas plays up even more the need for grace to overcome sin. One who is predestined to eternal life will receive the grace that elevates to the supernatural level and heals, in principle, the person of the effects of sin. Grace allows the overcoming of the obstacles that would prevent one from reaching God as end; grace executes, in the temporal order, God's plan to share God's own life with those whom God loves in this special way.

For Aquinas, the affirmation of the predestination of some to eternal life due to God's special, sapiential loving does not entail the affirmation of the predestination of all others to eternal death, to hell. Only if God's causing were productive of evil could that be the case for Aquinas. But God never wills what is *evil* in itself or what is only apparently good. God only wills what is actually good. Hell in itself is an evil, the ultimate and final defection from the good that is God. The sin that qualifies the person for hell is not good but evil, a deviation from what would really fulfill the person. Hence, when people go to hell, that is their own accomplishment. God does not cause their sinning, nor destine them in eternity to hell. God does, however, respond to what sinners do, and in the process retrieves good from their evil. Hence, in sending them to hell, God shows the good of justice, giving to sinners what they deserve for their freely performed sin.

In affirming single predestination, the ordering of some rational creatures to eternal life, Aquinas is concerned to locate human action in the movement of the predestined to God as end. His concern for human action is expressed in two questions. The first asks about *merit*. Is there a place for merit in an account of salvation that is rooted in God's predestining will? When he raises this question in I.23, his initial formulation is not altogether promising. He asks (a.5) whether God predestines someone to eternal life on the basis of a foreknowledge of that person's merits. If that were the case, God would be reactive. Someone would be good in action, God would see that this is the case, and God would give that person eternal life. For Aquinas, however, that messes up the sequence. Someone is not first good and then "predestined" in the attenuated sense of foreknown and so rewarded. Rather, first God predestines that person to eternal life, and then in the giving of the grace that executes that decision, the person is good. Human goodness follows on divine willing. But as Aquinas continues in that article, there is a place for merit, not as the cause of predestination but as the result. God has ordained that those who will attain the eternal life willed for them will do so through their merits, through their morally and supernaturally good acts. Such acts will deserve a reward from God. Aquinas is quite specific about where, in the movement of the destined to God, these meritorious actions will fall. Eternal life comes in the next life. The present life is, at it were, the path to God. The present life can be divided into two stages: preconversion and post-conversion. Can one merit conversion, that is, the entry into grace in the first place, the reception of the grace that heals and elevates and makes one worthy to attain to God as end? No, there is no merit at this stage; conversion is gift, pure and simple, worked in the person in accordance with God's predestining will. God has ordered that person to eternal life; no one in sin is qualified for eternal life; one must be in the state of grace in order to be qualified for eternal life. Hence, God works the conversion and infuses the grace that is needed to qualify for eternal life. But once the person is in the state of grace, God has ordained that the acts of that person that are done in and by grace will be meritorious of eternal life. Again, there is no idea here that merits occasion the predestining. Rather, merits follow on the predestining. And the context for meriting is quite precise: The elect can merit, for they have received the grace that moves them to acts pleasing to God and, on the basis of the divine ordination, deserve eternal life. In this telling, eternal life is both gift and reward. It is gift, principally, because it is due to God's predestining will, which is not occasioned in any way by human acting. God predestines those whom God loves in a special way. But, secondarily, eternal life is a reward, given by God in justice for the meritorious actions that the graced person, called to God as end, performs. In giving eternal life, God's love and justice are both in play. In damnation, by contrast, only justice is to the fore; God responds, justly, to what people, by the misuse of their will, do to qualify for hell.

Aquinas poses the question of the relation between God's predestining and human acting in a second way in I.23.6. That article in fact mirrors I.22.4, where Aquinas raises the same question in terms of providence. God's will is totally efficacious. What God wants to happen, does happen, as God wants it to happen. Elsewhere, Aquinas talks about the human person as in control of her actions; this control is afforded by the basic endowment of the human will. The human, unlike the plant or the animal, can and does will, and pursues goods in accordance with her own light. Can one have both real human willing that lies in the person's power and a totally efficacious God? Would not God's success as a cause have to be at the expense of the human as genuine agent, reducing the person to a puppet in the hands of God, moved this way or that in accordance with God's predestining will and the execution of the divine plan for the elect? In I.23.6, Aquinas offers a first go at this problem. He is convinced that it is meaningful to affirm both God's success as a cause of human action and human action as genuine. As caused by God, the effect is certain, infallible. As caused by God through a secondary cause that is contingent, a secondary cause that is a real cause of its own effects, the effect is contingent as well. In offering the judgment, Aquinas reflects his sense of God's

utter transcendence. Those causes in our experience that are utterly successful tend to be so at the expense of the real causing of those through whom they act. (Think, for example, of the army general who wants to take the hill and whose soldiers do take the hill; it is not what they want or would like to do that matters, but the general's will alone. In being successful, such a "first" cause imposes restrictions on those through whom he acts.) But God is not to be reduced to the causes that we normally experience. God is on a different ontological plane. And so in God's causing—through those whom God has brought into existence and endowed with their natural powers—God can be successful, and utterly so, without eliminating the real causing of those through whom God acts. To the contrary, they really cause, as moved by God to act; God respects and deploys their causing, for God's ends. In the treatise on grace (see ST I-II.111.2), Aquinas continues his reflections along this line, nuancing the teaching by bringing into account what he had written earlier in I-II about the different parts of the human act (from intention, through choice of the means, to actual execution). That teaching as found in I-II.111.2 is in continuity with the present teaching as a refinement of it, but it adds to the present teaching by being even more attentive to the different forms that God's interaction with the human will take.

Paluch (2004); Arfeuil (1974); Goris (1996); Hoonhout (2002); McGinn (1975); Chardonnens (1997).

Prophecy   Counted among the *gratuitous graces*, prophecy is a knowledge that is revealed by God to select individuals for the benefit of others. Although the revelation may include truths that are accessible to human reason, the truths revealed by God in prophecy are for the most part supernatural. They are known naturally by God and are imparted by God through the mediation of the angels employed in revelation (ST II-II.172.2) so that humans may come to know through the prophets truths that are important for their salvation. Prophecy allows of degrees and has various possible ingredients. It may involve the mere granting by God to the prophet of a supernatural intellectual light that gives apprehension and judgment of the truth(s) revealed by God; such is the case of Joseph, who interpreted the dream of another. It may involve the simple granting of forms or species, whether intellective or imaginary, by which supernatural truth is manifested, without the granting of intellectual judgment. Prophecy in the fullest form, however, has both the judgment and the species, as is the case with Moses and those designated "prophets" in the Old Testament. In describing prophecy, Aquinas is concerned to distinguish this knowledge from others. The prophetic light that gives judgment of what is revealed is supernatural, and so unlike the natural light possessed by all people as human (the agent intellect that abstracts intellectual species from the evidence provided by the senses). The prophetic light is not to be confused with either the theological virtue of faith or the light of glory. The virtue of *faith* is a habit, a stable disposition to believe; the prophetic light is transient, involving a momentary elevation of the individual by God to grasp supernatural truth (ST II-II.171.2). So too, the light of glory is permanent, and this light makes possible the vision of the essence of God. In prophetic vision, it is not God's essence that is seen (II-II.173.1), but a species given by God to convey a truth known by God that is needed for human salvation.

Prophecy has to do principally, but not exclusively, with future contingents. In the questions on prophecy (ST II-II.171–75), Aquinas makes good use of his account of God as knower found in the First Part of the ST (see *Knowledge, God's*). An effect is contingent when it proceeds from a cause that is not always causing and does not always produce the same effect; the contrast, then, is with necessary causes, which when posited do produce the same effects. In discussing God's knowledge of future contingents, Aquinas makes two basic points. First, these contingents are future only with regard to humans, as seen from our perspective. As such, they are indeterminate (i.e., the same effect does not always follow from a contingent cause). But all things—whether past, present, or future, for us—are as it were present to God, and so contingents are not future to God, but present. In God's perfect knowledge, God knows what occurs, what in fact follows on contingent causes. Second, God also knows these contingents as in their causes, inasmuch as God knows the order of causes in relation to their effects. In God this twofold knowledge of (future) contingents is united. But it is not always united in the prophetic revelation. Hence, sometimes the prophetic revelation is an imprinted likeness of the divine foreknowledge, insofar as the latter regards future contingencies in themselves and such things happen in the same way as foretold. The example that Aquinas gives is the prophecy in Isaiah 7:14: "Behold, a virgin shall conceive" (KJV). Sometimes, however, the prophetic revelation is an imprinted likeness of the divine foreknowledge as knowing the order of causes to effects; then at times the event is otherwise than foretold. Yet this does not mean that the prophecy covers a falsehood, for the meaning of the prophecy is that inferior causes, whether they be natural causes or human acts, are so disposed as to lead to such a result. This is the case in Jonah 3:4: "Forty days more, and Ninevah shall be overthrown." In Aquinas's restatement, this reads, "Its merits demand that it should be destroyed" (II-II.171.6 ad 2).

Later in the treatise on prophecy, Aquinas endorses a saying of St. Jerome as providing a fitting division of prophecy (II-II.174.1 ob. 1). Jerome had written that prophecy is of three types. The first, the prophecy of divine predestination, has to do with God's plan; this prophecy must be fulfilled, and its accomplishment is independent of our will. The example that he cites is the virgin birth, as found in Matthew 1. The other two types mentioned by Jerome are the prophecy of foreknowledge, in which the human will can enter, and the prophecy of denunciation, which is significative of God's disapproval. Aquinas fleshes out the saying of Jerome by invoking the twofold knowledge involved in God's foreknowledge (II-II.174.1c). The future is contained in the divine knowledge in two ways: first, as in its cause; thus, we have the prophecy of denunciation, which is not always fulfilled. This foretells the relation of cause to effect, which is sometimes hindered by some other intervening occurrence. Second, God foreknows certain things in themselves—either as to be accomplished by himself, and of such things is the prophecy of predestination, or as to be accomplished through human free will, and such is the prophecy of foreknowledge.

While principally about them, prophecy is not restricted to future contingencies. Prophets know things that are far removed from a man's knowledge (II-II.171.1c). There are three ways in which things may be apart from our knowledge (II-II.171.3c). The highest in fact has to do with future contingents. Such lie beyond the knowledge of all humans, for they are in themselves indeterminate. Hence, in prophecy God especially reveals what is future to us. But something may be remote from the knowledge not of all men, but of a particular man; such may also be known prophetically, as is the case reported in 2 Kings 5, where a master knew in this way what his disciple had done in his absence. Other things may be removed from the knowledge of all humans due to a defect in human knowledge, although the things in themselves are not unknowable. The example given here is the mystery of the Trinity, which transcends human powers of knowing, limited in range to what can be established on the basis of the evidence provided by the senses. Here Aquinas echoes a point made in the First Part of the ST, to the effect that God is most knowable in himself, but not to us (I.2.1c). Such truths can and do fall under prophetic revelation, as shown in Isaiah 6, where the seraphim reveal the Trinity by saying, "Holy, holy, holy."

Given the expansive scope of prophetic revelation, Aquinas can give a fairly detailed account of the progress of prophecy over time (II-II.174.6). Prophecy is directed to the knowledge of divine truth, which not only instructs people in the faith but also guides them in their actions. In terms of action, prophetic revelation did not vary over time. At all times people were divinely instructed about what they were to do, according as it was expedient for their spiritual welfare. But in terms of instruction in the faith, there was variety and progress. Aquinas recalls the distinction he had made when talking about the object of faith (in ST II-II.1) and the principal categories there of the *articles of faith*. Our faith, he reminds us in II-II.174.6c, consists chiefly in two things: the true knowledge of God and the mystery of the incarnation, by which the Son of God became human. Aquinas then charts prophecy's progress according to each of these headings. If we speak of prophecy as directed to the Godhead as its end, prophecy progressed according to three divisions of time: before the *law*, under the law, and under *grace*. Before the law, Abraham and the other patriarchs were prophetically taught things pertinent to faith in the Godhead. Under the law, prophetic revelation of things pertinent to faith in the Godhead was made in a yet more excellent way, because then not only certain special persons or families but the whole people had to be instructed in these matters. Here Aquinas notes that Moses was more fully instructed in the divine simplicity, as recounted in Exodus 3:14 ("I am who I am"). Afterward, in the time of grace, the mystery of the Trinity was revealed by the Son of God himself. Aquinas adds that in each state (before the law, under the law, and under grace), it is the first revelation that is the most excellent. That to Abraham surpasses that to Isaac; that to Moses was more excellent than that to the prophets, and that to the prophets was founded on that to Moses. In the time of grace, that to the apostles, about the God who is one and three, is the foundation of the entire faith of the church.

As for faith in the incarnation, it is evident, Aquinas says, that the nearer people were to Christ, whether before or after him, the more fully were they instructed on this point, and after him, as Paul says (Eph. 3:5), more fully than before.

The importance of Aquinas's questions on prophecy extends beyond the details they provide about what seems to be the chief of the gratuitous graces. For Aquinas, saving truth is revealed by God in Scripture (see *sacred doctrine*). Scripture, as the first question of the ST insists, is the revealed will of God. Aquinas does not discuss divine inspiration in the opening question of the ST. That discussion is deferred until these questions on prophecy; accordingly, they have received close study from scholars interested in the closer grasp of the Thomistic teaching about revelation and the respective roles of God and the human authors in the formulation of Scripture. In these questions, Aquinas confirms that it is God who plays the principal and decisive role. It is God's truth that is conveyed through the prophets; it is God who lifts the prophet above himself to a grasp of truths that are important for human beings as they seek their fulfillment. It is a human being who knows these truths, who proclaims them to others, who works miracles in confirmation of these truths (II-II.171.1c). But these humans stand to God as instruments (see *instrumental causality*) to the principal cause (II-II.173.4c). It is God ultimately who reveals these truths and has them pro-

claimed and who works the miracles. It is through these humans that God's truth is revealed. And since God reveals to them not all the truths known by God but only those that God chooses to reveal to them, and these humans, even in their momentary elevation, remain humans and so limited in their capacity, Aquinas adds that even true prophets know not all that the Holy Spirit means by the things that the prophets see, or speak, or even do. The comment is telling, and helps to complete the analysis in the final two articles in the ST's opening question, on the language and meaning of *Scripture*. The truth that the human authors of Scripture proclaim may be fuller and deeper than they know.

———

Bonino (2002); Berchtold (2000).

Providence   *see* Predestination

(Pseudo-)Athanasian Creed   Creeds are normative. They are constructed by the church meeting in council, under the guidance of the Holy Spirit, to articulate the faith (see *articles of faith*). They are closely related to *Scripture*, of which they offer definitive interpretation when it comes to the truths necessary for salvation, as against the misreadings of various Christian heretics. A creed thus serves as the rule of faith, proclaiming in clear summary form (ST II-II.1.9 ad 1) the same truth as does Scripture.

In his writings, Aquinas makes considerable use of two creeds that meet fully the criteria for creed. He accepts the apostolic origin of the Apostles' Creed, and he thinks of the Nicene Creed, which he more usually calls the "Creed of the Fathers," as later than the Apostles' Creed and as a further specification of the faith, necessitated by subsequent heresy. In both cases, the church, guided by the Spirit, has spoken authoritatively about the faith.

Aquinas also knows of the so-called Athanasian Creed. He accepts the great bishop of Alexandria as the author of this creed. But for that very reason, as the work of an individual, it does not of itself have creedal status for Aquinas. Rather, Athanasius drew up this declaration of faith as an exposition of doctrine, as is clear from its form. Since, however, it contained in brief the whole truth of the faith, it was subsequently accepted by the pope, to whom it belongs not only to call councils but to confirm their decisions as binding (see *pope*). In this sense, this creed too can be considered as a rule of faith (ST II-II.1.10 ad 3).

Aquinas employs one of the sayings in this creed to good effect in his Christology. As in ST III.2.1 ob. 2, the Athanasian phrase can be used to complicate the Christology. The topic in that article is the locus of the union in Christ. With the orthodox tradition, Aquinas holds to a union in the person. In the person of the Word, who from eternity is God, a second nature, the human nature, has been joined to the Word's divine nature. The natures are not joined directly, as if forming one nature; that is the monophysite position, which ultimately removes either the full divinity or the full humanity or both by confusing, in such a direct union, the two natures. But in his creed, Athanasius states that the union of the two natures is to be likened to the union of rational soul and flesh in any human being. Just "as the rational soul and flesh are one human being, so God and man are one Christ." Doesn't this creed affirm the natures as the locus of the union, and do so in a way that is congenial to the monophysites? In other words, in this quoting, the Athanasian words in effect provide the opportunity for a clarification of orthodox teaching, by allowing Aquinas to clarify what is and what is not meant by these words (ad 2).

In another use of these words from the Athanasian Creed (*ScG* IV.41.9), the contribution ultimately is more positive, in the sense of more directly contributing to Aquinas's reflections on the union of the natures in the Word. But again, in making use of the saying, Aquinas is aware that they might mislead. Divinity

does stand to humanity, in the case of Christ, as soul stands to body. But, Aquinas quickly adds, soul is related to body in two ways. One of these is completely inappropriate for figuring the relation of divinity and humanity, and is not what Athanasius has in mind. Aquinas, following Athanasius's lead, is not thinking of soul as the form of the body; divinity cannot be the form, the actualizer, of humanity in the case of Christ. Rather, it is the other relation that is in play here: Body stands to soul as its instrument. The soul employs the body that is joined to it. So too, the humanity of Christ is the instrument of the divinity; the Word employs the humanity conjoined to it as the organ of the divinity. It is the Word who acts; in his human acts, the Word employs the humanity that it has taken up and come to express (see *instrumental causality*).

Real Presence As a sacrament, the Eucharist signifies sacred reality (e.g, ST III.73.4). It recalls the Last Supper, the final gathering of Jesus with his chief disciples, at which the sacrament was instituted. It recalls especially the *cross* and Christ's redemptive suffering, and passes the *grace* of Christ on, as a cause (see *causes; instrumental causality*). It also signifies the end to which people are traveling, to the eternal banquet with God in heaven.

Yet the Eucharist does more than signify and cause grace. In company with his chief theological predecessors and contemporaries, Aquinas affirms that in this sacrament, Christ is really, truly present after the consecration of the elements of bread and wine.

Employing language of philosophical origin, Aquinas says that real presence is a substantial presence. Two senses of "substance" are in play here. First, "substance" refers to an individual, one that exists as a subject. Second, it can be taken as synonymous with "essence" and "nature." "Nature" is what makes a thing the sort of thing it fundamentally is; to give the "essence" of a thing is to identify its nature and to define it. In discussing the eucharistic conversion, Aquinas speaks of the starting point of the change, the substance of the bread, and the end point of the change. This is the substance of the body of Christ. To parse this in terms of the two senses of substance: Prior to the consecration, when one points to the bread and asks what this is, the answer is that it is, and essentially so, bread. After the consecration, however, the answer is different, for by the power of God that accounts for the conversion (see *transubstantiation*), the substance of the bread has been changed into the substance of the body of Christ. And in like fashion, the wine has been changed by God's power into the substance of Christ's blood. Pointing to what formerly had been bread and wine, the answer of faith is that these are in truth the body and blood of Christ (ST III.75.1; q.76).

In applying the language of substance to express Christ's eucharistic presence, Aquinas, as were other medieval theologians, was careful to distinguish this substantial presence from other substantial presences. For example, corporeal substance is modified and typically manifested by accidents. Accidents do not exist in themselves but in another, in substance. By its accidents, the substance is proclaimed (allowing for the judgment of its essence) and related to place (as this piece of bread, prior to the consecration, is related to the altar on which it is found by its dimensions). Similarly, Jesus as active in Galilee had bodily accidents that also revealed he was human and permitted him to be seen and touched and to relate to place. The same holds for the risen Jesus, now enthroned in heaven. In proclaiming the eucharistic change, of substance (of bread) into substance (of Christ's body), there has been in effect a double distancing, as it were, of substance and accident, corresponding to the starting point and end point of the conversion. It is the substance of the bread that has been converted into the substance of Christ's body, not the sub-

stance as modified by its accidents or with its accidents that has been changed. The accidents of the bread and wine remain after the eucharistic change, signifying that the Christ who is present is present as spiritual food and drink. And the term of the conversion, the body of Christ, is not present as substance modified by accidents or with its accidents, at least in their proper mode (see *concomitance*); the accidents of Christ's body and blood remain, after the eucharistic conversion, in heaven, in their proper place. In stating the presence as substantial, Aquinas has no place for what would amount to a transaccidentation that would accompany transubstantiation.

While he employs a philosophical term to express the presence, the affirmation of substantial presence is made on the basis of Scripture, in particular the institution narrative. The words "This is my body" and "This is my blood" preclude any merely symbolic presence (ST III.75.1). Rather, at the Last Supper, Christ makes the promise to be present in this sacrament when it is correctly performed—by his due representative, the priest, who acts in the person of Christ (see *character, sacramental*) in stating the words of consecration. When the priest states these words, Christ keeps his promise; by the power of God, what was bread is changed into Christ's bodily substance, and what was wine is now the substance of Christ's blood. The statement "This is my body" is both performative (ST III.75.7 ad 1 and 3; q.78)—it achieves the promise—and is descriptive: this really is (not bread but) Christ.

Aquinas alleges a range of reasons why Christ renders himself in this sacrament. Perhaps the most moving involves friendship (ST III.73.5; 75.1). Friends want to be together. And Christ offers himself, with God, as the reward to his friends for faithful, Christian striving toward God as end. But as he was about to go to his death and so remove himself from the company of his disciples, he wanted to provide them with solace and support as they continued on their path to God as end.

Thus, while these friends will not be with him irrevocably and without cease until they join the risen Christ in heaven, in the meantime he becomes present to his followers, on a regular—albeit momentary—basis, whenever this sacrament is celebrated, thus maintaining and deepening the communal relationship of disciples to their head that will come to full fruition in the next life.

Brock (2001); Power (1993); Morard (1995); Emery (1997).

Resurrection of Christ   The treatise on Christ in ST III comes to its term with a consideration of Christ's exaltation after this life (ST III.53–59). That discussion is itself divided into four subsections, the first of which is on Christ's resurrection, which Aquinas covers in four questions. He asks in turn about the resurrection of Christ in itself (III.53), the quality of the person rising (54), the manifestation of the resurrection to the various witnesses mentioned in Scripture (55), and its causality (56). The analysis of resurrection is thoroughly theological, giving nice testimony to the significance of Christ's human nature and the ways in which Christ's humanity figures into the working out of human salvation and the inauguration of God's eschatological kingdom (see *eschatology*).

Dying involves the separation of soul and body, and such had occurred in the death of Christ. The soul and body, taken up by the Word in becoming incarnate, had separated in his death on the cross, although each continued to be in union with the Word (III.53.4c). In the resurrection of Jesus, body and soul were reunited. Resurrection, however, is much more than the overcoming of death by reversing the division that it brings about, although it surely is that as well. It entails a raising up of the human to a new level, to the level of glory. There is, then, a profound continuity between the earthly Jesus and the risen Jesus (they are one and the same). But at the same time, there is a transformation of Jesus to a new, spiritually glorified form of life. Jesus' true body was glorified, receiving the endowments, and irrevocably, that befit the beatified (54.2), such as clarity and agility.

From the beginning to the end of the ST's questions on Christ's resurrection, the tenor of the discussion is insistently scriptural. Scripture sets the stage for the discussion of resurrection by affirming it of Jesus and by affirming that Jesus' resurrection will serve as the model and cause of our own (e.g., 54.2c; 56.1). It provides the details of the account of resurrection that Aquinas offers here, and Aquinas puts forward his analysis precisely by referring repeatedly to what Scripture has to say about the resurrection of Christ. And the issues that Aquinas raises here, due to apparent discrepancies in the different scriptural witnesses on the matter, find their resolution through Scripture, through Aquinas's close treatment of the pertinent scriptural material. What we meet in these articles is a series of successive arguments for the fittingness of resurrection in its various aspects (see *fittingness*). Aquinas does not imagine that he can argue for resurrection in a philosophical way, as if he could establish through demonstrative argument its absolute necessity, or as if he could show by rational argument that only by Christ's resurrection could God bring about our resurrection (56.1 ad 3); such lies beyond the scope of reasoning, and would call into question God's power and freedom. But granted the resurrection of Christ, as revealed in Scripture and held by faith, Aquinas, convinced of the soundness of God's ways and the wisdom of what God has done in Christ, attempts to plumb the meaning and the riches of this particular set of affirmations about Christ. He is asking here the "Why?" Why, for example, a resurrection? Why a resurrection on the third day (53.2)? Why a resurrection that was manifested to the witnesses named in

Scripture, and not to others (q.55)? Here the opening article of this group of questions can be taken as representative of Aquinas's mode of proceeding, and of the scriptural tenor of the analysis. Did Christ have to rise again (53.1)? On the face of it, this might seem to predict a quest for necessity in the strict sense, but the corpus quickly disabuses that notion. There are five reasons, he states, why it made sense for Christ to rise again. First, to commend the divine justice, to which it belongs to exalt those who humble themselves for God's sake; and so, since Christ humbled himself even to death on the cross, out of love and obedience to God, it behooved him to be uplifted by God to a glorious resurrection. Second, for our instruction in the faith, since our belief in Christ's Godhead is confirmed by his rising again. Third, for the raising of our hope, since through seeing Christ, who is our head (see *church*), rise again, we hope that we likewise shall rise again. Fourth, to set in order the lives of the faithful, so that dying with Christ we might rise with him to life in God. And fifth, in order to complete the work of our salvation; just as for this reason did he endure evil things in dying that he might deliver us from evil, so was he glorified in rising again in order to advance us toward good things. In putting forth each of these points, Aquinas trades heavily on Scripture. To confirm the first point, for example, he cites Luke 1:52 and a psalm; he argues the next point by weaving together 2 Corinthians 13:4 ("He was crucified in weakness, but lives by the power of God"), 1 Corinthians 15:14 ("If Christ has not been raised, then our proclamation has been in vain and your faith has been in vain") and a psalm read christologically. So too, in discussing the third point, on the raising of our hope, we meet a neat juxtaposition of 1 Corinthians 15:12, which moves from Christ's to our future resurrection, and Job 19:25, 27 ("I know that my Redeemer liveth . . . and in the last day I shall rise out of the earth. . . . This my hope is laid

up in my bosom"). Through Aquinas's adroit use of Scripture, one emerges from each discrete argument for fittingness, and from these questions as a whole, with a better grasp of the meaningfulness and wisdom of what is affirmed in faith.

In these questions, Aquinas forcefully restates the Pauline point about the significance of the resurrection of Christ for other humans. Christ's resurrection, he stresses, causes both efficiently and formally. In terms of the latter, Christ's resurrection is the exemplar cause of the resurrection of those who have followed Christ in this life and so have prepared correctly for entry into eternal life, that is, entry into the inheritance that is theirs as children of God and that comes to them through God's Son become human (see, e.g., 56.1 ad 3). Thus, in the general resurrection, the resurrection of his disciples will conform to Christ's own, and so in their case, as in his, there will be profound continuity (materially the same body, joined anew to its soul) and discontinuity, in the sense that they will be raised to a perfection and to a manner of life appropriate to the blessed. Christ's resurrection is the efficient cause of all others, of the wicked as well as of the good. Here (56.1 ad 3) Aquinas makes nice use of his teaching about the humanity of Christ serving as the conjoined *instrumental cause* of his divinity. God raises Christ from the dead; Jesus in his divinity raises himself, his body and soul, separated at death, into new life. Through Christ, God will raise all others; the humanity of Christ will serve as the instrument of this raising.

The eschatological consequences of Christ's resurrection are clear: His resurrection is the firstfruits and the promise of what will come for others at the end of time, when they too are raised from the dead. But Christ's resurrection has present consequences as well; here, drawing on Paul, Aquinas points to the moral implications of resurrection. Hence, to return to ST III.53.1c, Aquinas makes Romans 6 and Romans 4 the scriptural basis for the fourth and fifth points, respectively, for the claim that Christ's resurrection makes eminent sense. The resurrection makes sense to set in order the lives of the faithful. As Romans 6:4 states, "As Christ was raised from the dead by the glory of the Father, so we too might walk in newness of life," and then goes on in verses 9 and 11 to add: "Christ, being raised from the dead, will never die again. . . . So you also must consider yourselves dead to sin and alive to God in Christ Jesus." The fifth point in the corpus turns to Romans 4. The fifth point is expressed succinctly in verse 25: "[Jesus] was handed over to death for our trespasses and was raised for our justification." Aquinas's teaching, echoing Paul, thus offers a corrective to those who speak only of the cross as providing the possibility for human salvation. That Aquinas takes the *cross* seriously is beyond doubt. But for him it is complemented, as in Paul, by the resurrection of Christ, which completes God's work in Christ and which is also required for all others to be saved, to stand in right relationship to God and to be on the right path to God as end. As Aquinas puts it in 53.1 ad 3, "Christ's passion wrought our salvation, properly speaking, by removing evils; but the resurrection did so as the beginning and exemplar of all good things." In Christ, we both die (to sin) and rise to new life—morally now, ontologically at the end of time.

In putting Christ's resurrection into such prominence, Aquinas is quite innovative when compared with the teaching found in Peter Lombard's *Sentences*, which was so important for the training of the scholastic theologian. In the *Sentences*, Peter's treatment of the resurrection of Christ in the treatise on Christ (bk. III, dd.1–22) is kept to a minimum, to some comments about Christ in the tomb and the overcoming of death by the resurrection. Peter also makes some comments in passing about Christ's resurrection in the fourth book, in those distinctions (bk. IV, dd.43–50) that have to do with eschatology. Already in the

Scriptum on the Sentences, Aquinas saw the value of inserting a separate distinction on the resurrection (see d.21). And, as already noted, in the ST's treatise on Christ, he offers a well-defined and closely articulated discussion of Christ's resurrection, in four questions, playing up its present soteriological as well as eschatological significance. The effect is to give in scholastic discourse the resurrection of Christ its due.

Valkenberg (2000), ch. 2; Holtz (1951); Crotty (1962); Torrell (1996a).

Revelation   *see* **Scripture; Sacred Doctrine; Prophecy**

Sacrament   Aquinas offers extended discussions of the sacraments, both of the sacraments in general and of individual sacraments, throughout his career and in a variety of writings. He treats them in such occasional pieces as *De articulis fidei et ecclesiae sacramentis* as well as in the scriptural commentaries as prompted by given passages. The sacraments especially receive their due in the systematic writings. There are lengthy treatises on the sacraments in the *Scriptum on the Sentences* of Peter Lombard (bk. IV dd.1ff.), the more personal *ScG* (IV.56–78), and ST III.60–90, although that treatise was left unfinished in the middle of the discussion of *penance*, due to the cessation of his writing after his experience in December 1273. By the *ScG*, the teaching on the sacraments had reached their mature and final form. Sacraments are set under the category of sign. Sacraments are signs of something else, to which they point. To be more precise, sacraments are signs of a sacred reality that sanctifies.

The sacred reality that sanctifies is Christ. In his analyses of the sacraments, there is a relentless consistency. The spiritual power of the sacraments, Aquinas insists repeatedly, is rooted in the *cross* of Christ; by the sacraments, Christ's grace is proclaimed and conveyed. The centrality of the cross is underscored in Aquinas's comparison of the sacraments of the Old Law (that is, the symbolic practices of the Jews as rendered in the Hebrew Bible) and those of the New Law. Could the Old Law sacraments justify? They could, in the sense that they provided the opportunity for the expression of faith in the Christ who was to come and to die for human sin. But those sacraments do not justify in the sense of causing or conveying grace. Only when Christ has in fact come and has died for sins (and been raised unto our salvation) can sacraments both signify and cause what they signify, that is, both proclaim Christ as sanctifier and confer his grace on the recipients of the sacraments. Causing grace, then, is reserved to the sacraments of the New Law, which come after Christ and are employed by Christ to convey the spiritual effects of the cross.

That there are seven sacraments of the New Law was a given by Aquinas's day. Twelfth-century theologians had come to this conclusion by mid-century, and the affirmation of the seven sacraments was adopted by Peter Lombard in the *Sentences*, which became the textbook for later scholastics. In discussing the seven sacraments as a group, Aquinas draws a parallel between the sacramental life and corporeal life. In corporeal life, a human comes to be, grows in strength, uses food to sustain life and to grow, faces difficulties that need overcoming, and forms associations for mutual support and to aid in coming to perfection. So too by baptism, the individual enters into being, spiritual being, by dying to sin and being joined to Christ. Confirmation facilitates the individual's spiritual growth, by giving the fortitude and strength to remain true to Christ. The Eucharist is spiritual nourishment, for in this sacrament, Christ offers himself as sustenance to the person who is journeying to God as end (recall that among the many names for this sacrament is *viaticum*, food for one on the way; ST III.73.4). **Baptism**, confir-

mation, and Eucharist all have to do with the proper movement of the person to God as end. Sometimes, however, the Christian goes off track, through sin; it is through penance that one gets back on track, by confessing one's sins and receiving the grace of forgiveness. The fifth of the sacraments geared to the individual, extreme unction, provides support to the person at the time of death; the anointing of the body and asking for forgiveness of the sins associated with the different parts of the body is meant to provide both spiritual and physical comfort to one whose activities in this life will soon be judged. The remaining sacraments, in Aquinas's reckoning, are more communal in intent. By holy orders, priests are delegated as representatives of Christ, who are to proclaim Christ in their preaching, provide for the governance of the church, and perform the sacraments—all to the benefit of the members of the church. By matrimony, which is a sign of the unity of Christ and his church (Eph. 5:32; *ScG* IV.78.3), there is provision for the material growth of the church. As he puts it in the *ScG* (IV.78.2), matrimony consists in the union of a husband and wife for the purpose of generating and educating offspring for the worship of God.

In every sacrament, there is matter and form. While at first glance this might seem to be an observation that would be due principally to the decision to employ Aristotle in analyzing Christian things, Aquinas is in fact here showing his allegiance to Augustine. As Augustine had stated, "Word is added to the element and then there is a sacrament." Hence, as he works through each sacrament, Aquinas goes to some length to show both the form/word and the matter, taken in a broad way to include not simply the material element that is employed but physical gesture as well. To offer but a few examples: In baptism, the water used to signify washing is the matter of the sacrament, while the words of the baptismal formula provide the form, specifying how the washing action signifies and so causes what is signified. Likewise, in the Eucharist, the matter of the sacrament is the bread and wine, whose status as typical food and drink has been adopted to signify the spiritual eating that can occur in the sacrament, when by the words of institution, these elements are transformed into the body and blood of the Christ who has freed people from their sins and who provides them with the sustenance to continue on the journey to God as end.

The insistence on the element, on materiality, reflects Aquinas's sensitivity to the implications of the doctrine of *creation*. What is not God has been made by God and so is good. Thus, material things can fittingly be adapted by Christ, in the sacraments, to spiritual ends. Aquinas also stresses the suitability of the use of material things in the sacraments in terms of the human condition, parsed in two ways. Human beings are dependent on the evidence of the senses for knowing; thus, in using sensible things to signify and convey grace, Christ has acknowledged our typical way of knowing, and so facilitates the grasping of spiritual truth by having material things point to spiritual truth. Aquinas also knows that integral to sin is an extreme or wrong attachment to the things of this world. There is then a moral, pedagogical function to the sacraments as employing material things, for they wean people from such wrong attachment and show how material things are to be rightly ordered to God and so used in the movement to God as end.

The causality of the sacraments is diverse. The sacraments, in the first place, are discussed in terms of final causality: God employs the sacraments to bring people to the end set for them, freely, by God. The sacraments promote the successful completion of the journey to God as end (see *viator*). Efficient causality is also prominent in the analysis of the sacraments, and at two levels: that of the principal and that of the instrumental efficient cause. There was, in fact, some movement in Aquinas's thinking in this

connection. In the *Scriptum*, the only efficient cause of grace is God. Grace, after all, is participation in the divine nature, and only God can grant such participation. At this point in his theological development, Aquinas saw the sacraments simply in terms of dispositive causality; they exercised a moral force, preparing the recipient for the infusion of grace by God. Eventually, however, Aquinas came to see the sacraments as possessed of an efficient causality, inasmuch as they were the instruments by which God conveys grace. Actually, given how he roots the sacraments in the cross, Aquinas's treatment of efficient causality is even more nuanced. Jesus Christ is the second person of God who, without loss to itself as fully divine Word of God, has taken up and come to express everything (body and soul) required to be human (see *hypostatic union*). Thus, as God, Jesus grants grace as the principal efficient cause of grace. In this granting, the human nature of Christ stands to the divinity as its conjoined instrument, through which, efficiently, grace is caused and conferred. The sacraments, too, stand in this sequence. They are *instrumental causes*, not as conjoined instruments of the divinity (as is Christ's humanity), but as separated instruments, through which the grace of the fully divine Son-of-God-become-human causes and confers grace. Finally, formal causality also figures in the mature treatment of the sacraments as secondary causes of grace. The material elements employed in the sacraments retain their proper character and form, which has accounted for the choice of these elements as apt signs of the sacred reality that sanctifies. Every sacrament of the New Law conveys grace. But each sacrament thus conveys grace in a manner suited to itself, as indicated in the comparison above of the sacramental with the corporeal life.

In reflecting on the sacraments, Aquinas successfully strikes a balance between the objective efficacy of the sacraments and the need for the proper personal disposition of the recipient to benefit from the sacrament. Do the sacraments of the New Law always signify the sacred reality that is Christ the sanctifier and infallibly cause grace? When the sacrament is correctly performed—that is, when the delegated representative of Christ uses the elements and states the words that Christ has designated for the sacrament—the answer is yes; participants in the sacrament should not worry on this score. But this is not to say that everyone receives the spiritual effect intended by Christ through a given sacrament; the offer of grace can be, in a word, turned down. The actual reception of grace offered in a sacrament presupposes that the recipient stands in a correct relationship to Christ. To employ here the ecclesiological language favored by Aquinas (see *church*, on the "mystical body of Christ"), to receive grace one must belong to Christ, be joined to Christ by the faith and love that Christ seeks. Those who are not members of Christ's body act fictively when they receive the sacrament; by their action, they are claiming what is in fact not the case. And so, while grace is always conveyed through the sacrament, it is received only by those who are in fact Christ's. For others, their separation from Christ—their lack of faith and charity, and their mortal sin, which precludes community with Christ—blocks the reception of sacramental grace. In his discussion of specific sacraments, Aquinas goes into more detail in how this plays out (say, for *baptism*, Eucharist, or *penance*), but he is consistent in rejecting a mechanistic or automatic bestowal of grace through sacramental performance.

Aquinas makes good use of a threefold sacramental formula in analyzing the sacraments, not least in insisting on sacramental efficacy and personal quality. Put together by his medieval predecessors from patristic sayings, the threefold formula—*sacramentum tantum; res et sacramentum; res tantum*—was well established by the time Aquinas started writing on the sacraments. By *sacramentum tantum* ("sign only"), Aquinas

refers to the material (taken broadly) employed in the sacrament. Hence, in baptism, the "sign only" is the water as used in washing; in the Eucharist, the bread and wine used in eating and drinking. By the *res et sacramentum* (lit., "the thing and the sign") is meant what is signified by the sign only. But at this level, what is signified also signifies (the *res* is also a *sacramentum*), and so what is the *res et sacramentum* signifies what is *res tantum*, what is "thing only." With this last, we are before the spiritual effects of the sacrament, the particular form in which grace is conferred by a discrete sacrament, with its proper formality. In terms of the Eucharist, the *res et sacramentum* is the body and blood of Christ that are truly present at the term of the consecration of the bread and wine. The body and blood of Christ in turn points to the spiritual effects of this sacrament: new grace and further incorporation in the mystical body of Christ. And what is *sacramentum tantum* in this particular sacrament also points to the *res tantum*; just as one bread is made from many grains, so from many people, one body of Christ is made when individuals come to Christ as their head by their faith and charity and receive the Holy Spirit who binds them to Christ and to each other. In terms of baptism, the *res et sacramentum* is baptismal character (see *character, sacramental*), an indelible mark on the soul that qualifies one for subsequent full participation in the sacramental life of the church. This character in turn points beyond itself, to the *res tantum* that is the spiritual effect of baptism: forgiveness of sins and entry into Christ's only body.

In light of this threefold formula, what then is obtained when one receives the sacrament? Whether one is talking about a recipient who is correctly disposed or incorrectly indisposed, all recipients receive the *sacramentum tantum* and the *res et sacramentum*. In terms of the Eucharist, the Christ who is really present at the term of the consecration (*res et sacramentum*) is received or encountered by all humans who receive the consecrated host. But only those who are correctly disposed receive the *res tantum*; those who receive fictively—that is, who lack, because of mortal sin, the formed faith that binds them to Christ as head—have in effect rejected the offer of grace, the *res tantum*, that is offered in this sacrament. So too in baptism, in the case of adults (for the case of infants who are baptized, see **baptism**) who are correctly disposed, they are the full beneficiaries of this sacrament—not only washed as a way of signifying Christ's cleansing from sin (*sacramentum tantum*), not only receiving the character that marks them as Christ's (*res et sacramentum*), but also, and especially, receiving the grace that covers original sin and sets one right before God. Those adults who are incorrectly disposed will go no further than the second level. In their case, the *res tantum* will be rejected.

King (1967); Walsh (1993, 2005); Gallagher (1965); Chardonnens (1999); Yocum (2004).

Sacred Doctrine   The ST opens with a consideration of sacred doctrine, holy teaching, setting the stage for the theological inquiries that constitute the rest of the work. There is a double sense of "teaching" that governs the reflections in ST I.1. First, "teaching" is taken in the sense of what is taught. Sacred doctrine is the body of truths necessary for salvation (a.1c). The **theologian** is thus concerned with those truths that must be affirmed, in faith, in order to come to eternal life. Second, "teaching" points to the act of teaching, and thereby to the one who teaches. The principal teacher of sacred doctrine is God, and in his various discussions of sacred doctrine, Aquinas keeps the focus resolutely on God. God reveals the truths necessary for salvation, doing so in **Scripture** and in a way that takes account of the way that humans come to truth (a.9c). The

role of human beings in this teaching is thoroughly subordinated to that of God. Human beings enter into sacred doctrine as agents of God in passing on the truths necessary for salvation, through the writing of the Scripture in which God's saving truth is proclaimed and, subsequently, in the ongoing interpretation of scriptural teaching and application of its lessons to the contemporary scene.

There are two categories of truth that make up sacred doctrine. Both kinds of truth are revealed. The first, commonly called the **articles of faith**, exceeds the reach of reason and so cannot be demonstrated. In ST I.1.1c, Aquinas gives as the example of an article of faith the human person's transcendent end. God has established God as the end of the human person, promising participation in the next life in God's own life and activity to those who are correctly disposed in this life by their *faith, hope,* and *charity,* and morally good actions that are performed with the aid of *grace.* Apart from revelation, human beings would not be aware that this is their end, nor, for that matter, of the way to this end. The other kind of truth in sacred doctrine is sometimes called (although not expressly so designated in ST I.1) the **preambles of faith**. These truths—such as the existence of God—are revealed by God and are held by faith by most people. However, these truths are susceptible to demonstration. Why then has God also revealed them? Only a few have in fact demonstrated them, and only after a long time, and even then with error (a.1c).

Throughout the first question in the ST, Aquinas enters into a series of comparisons between sacred doctrine and other doctrines or sciences ("science" being taken in an Aristotelian sense). He relates sacred doctrine to the knowledge that God has of God and that God shares with the blessed as the end of their journey (a.2). This is to know God directly. Sacred doctrine is not that knowledge—in this life, one proceeds by faith—but is rooted in that knowledge. Sacred doctrine is patterned on that knowledge, revealing God and all things in relation to God in the way that is accessible to humans in this life, thus facilitating the movement to God as end. Aquinas also compares sacred doctrine to the philosophical disciplines, to those sciences that are built up through observation of the things of this world and through the exercise of reason. Aquinas offers a variety of ways in which sacred doctrine is like and unlike the philosophical disciplines and of the ways that it is distinguished from them, while also allowing some interaction between sacred doctrine and these other disciplines (see *philosophy*). Here it can be noted that Aquinas is convinced of the superiority of sacred doctrine over the philosophical disciplines. Philosophy can be distinguished into two types: speculative and practical, the former having to do with contemplation and the perfection of the intellect, the latter with action. For Aquinas, sacred doctrine is both speculative and practical (a.4), and in both ways outstrips the philosophical disciplines. It is the supreme contemplative science because of what it contemplates: the God who by God's gracious decision is the transcendent end of human beings and who will be known directly in the next life by those who will have successfully completed the journey to God and who now, in this life, believe what God has revealed and reflect upon it. It also reigns supreme among the practical disciplines, for it leads to action and affections that will in fact, as designed by God, be conducive to reaching the highest end, namely, eternal life.

Aquinas turns repeatedly throughout his corpus to the topic of sacred doctrine. Hence, he looks at sacred doctrine in his opening to his *Scriptum on the Sentences*, as well as the opening to what he had planned as a revision of the *Scriptum*; in his commentary on Boethius's *De trinitate* (q.2); and in the opening chapters of the *Summa contra Gentiles* (I.1–9), as the context of the treatment there of the wise

man and his activity in pursuit of Christian wisdom (see *theologian*).

Chenu (1957); Van Ackeren (1952); Persson (1970); Congar (1960); Weisheipl (1974); Jenkins (1997).

Sacrifice, Eucharistic   In his discussion of the Eucharist, Aquinas focuses on the Eucharist as *sacrament*. However, at points in the treatise—as in his treatment of the use of the sacrament (ST III.79.5, 7), the minister of the sacrament (e.g., 80.4, 6, 10), and the ritual of the eucharistic liturgy (83.1)—he notes that the Eucharist is also a "sacrifice." The eucharistic sacrifice, the sacrifice of the Mass, has been a matter of considerable controversy in Christian history. Some worry that the sacrifice of the Mass puts in doubt the sufficiency of the sacrifice of Christ on the *cross*, as if Christ had not done enough through the cross to make human salvation possible, or that a eucharistic sacrifice might involve a resacrificing of Christ that would be distinct from that of the cross. In providing a theology of eucharistic sacrifice, Aquinas makes clear the intimate connection between cross and sacrifice and the dependence of the latter on the former. To make his case, he makes adroit use of his teachings about *real presence*, about the *instrumental causality* of the sacramental formula and that of the human minister of the sacrament, and about the *church* as the mystical body of Christ, actual membership in which is required for fruitful encounter with the eucharistic Christ in both sacrament and sacrifice.

Sacrifice entails an offering. In any sacrifice, something is offered by someone to another, for some purpose (ST II-II.85). In describing a sacrifice, it is thus important to designate who or what is sacrificed, the one who makes the offering, the recipient of the offering, and the point or goal of the offering. In the sacrifice of the cross (see ST III.48.3), the principal offerer is Christ, the second person of God who without loss to himself as a distinct, fully divine person, has taken up and come to express human nature as well. On the cross, Christ offers his life up to God. In this offering, he expresses his praise and thankfulness to God, as is proper through morally correct action, but he offers himself up as well for the remission of sins. Thus, this sacrifice, made to God, sets things right between the sinful race and God; its benefits are applied to those who accept the value of this offering, as done by the Savior on their behalf before God.

The eucharistic sacrifice is in effect identical with Christ's sacrifice on the cross. It is not just that the Eucharist proclaims the passion and signifies it as a memorial, although it is surely that. Rather, the Eucharist contains Christ himself, the Christ who becomes present when Christ's words at the Last Supper are said, in Christ's person, by Christ's representative, the priest. A telling designation of the Christ truly contained in the sacrament is "Christ crucified" (e.g., ST III.73.5 ad 2); it is, therefore, because the sacrament contains the Christ who died on the cross as sacrifice to God for our sins that the Eucharist can also be designated a "sacrifice" (ST III.79.5 and 7). There is no resacrificing of Christ here, if by that is meant a new slaying of Christ, as on the cross. Such, in any case, would be impossible for Aquinas, given his understanding of the mode of Christ's eucharistic presence and the sense that the bodily accidents of Christ are present by *concomitance* and not in their proper mode. Hence, as present in the sacrament, Christ is not passible (e.g., III.81.3). This is a sacrifice because in this sacrament, Christ by the power of the Holy Spirit becomes present, the same Christ who was sacrificed on the cross. And it is Christ who offers himself up to God.

Christ's offering in the Eucharist is in a secondary way also the offering of Christ's people, here acting in discipleship to Christ and acting in a way made possible by their union to Christ as their head. In this connection, the comments that Aquinas provides about the priest are illuminating. In terms of real presence, the priest does act *in persona Christi*, and the contribution of the priest is that of an instrumental cause, through whom Christ and the Holy Spirit act in bringing about Christ's real presence in this sacrament. Yet the priest in the liturgy also acts on behalf of Christ's people, and in the prayers of the liturgy he offers up on their behalf their sacrifice of praise and thanksgiving (III.83.4 and 5). In this sense, then, they too in the Eucharist are offering Christ to God—not as the principal agent (which is always Christ) but as joined to Christ and following his lead in his offering to God. True sacrifice, however, always involves Christ, and the effectiveness of this sacrifice is wholly derived from Christ.

As the sacrifice of the cross, this sacrifice is sufficient to overcome all sin and to reunite all people to God as their source and end. But this does not mean that all people benefit from the sacrifice of the Mass. In making the point, Aquinas draws an exact parallel between the Eucharist as sacrament and as sacrifice. In the Eucharist as sacrament, there is a tremendous opportunity for spiritual growth, for this sacrament contains Christ himself, who is the source of all spiritual good. But only those who are correctly related to God in Christ, by their faith and charity and as moved by the grace of the Holy Spirit, actually benefit from the encounter with the eucharistic Christ. In terms of the threefold sacramental formula that Aquinas employs so well, all who receive the sacrament receive the *sacramentum tantum* (the remaining accidents of the bread and wine), and the *res et sacramentum* (the Christ truly present). But not all receive the *res tantum*, the spiritual effects that the eucharistic Christ offers; only those in the correct spiritual disposition, living members of Christ's body, so receive. The same holds for the Eucharist as sacrifice. It may be offered for the intention of specific individuals. But it will benefit those individuals—that is, those individuals will actually receive the effects of the Eucharist as sacrifice—if they are in fact living members of Christ's body, are moved by the Spirit, and are joined to Christ by faith and charity. If such is lacking, the effects of the Eucharist as sacrifice are not received (see, e.g., III.79.5c). Thus, in the treatment of the Eucharist as sacrifice, as in that of the Eucharist as sacrament, Aquinas is concerned to put in the proper balance the objective efficacy of the Eucharist and the requisite spiritual dispositions of recipients.

Humbrecht (1998); Wawrykow (1993).

Salvation *see* **Cross; Sacred Doctrine; Prophecy; Beatific Vision; Eschatology; Grace**

Scriptum on the Sentences An important part of the training of the scholastic theologian was the preparation and delivering in a public setting a series of lectures on the *Sentences* of Peter Lombard (d.1160). Aquinas's lectures on the *Sentences* were given in 1252–1256, and were made available for copying shortly thereafter. In preparing his lectures, Aquinas drew on the commentaries of others, including those of Bonaventure and Albert the Great. Aquinas's *Scriptum* (lit., "writing") is extensive, numbering almost one and a half million words; this is the first of Aquinas's forays into systematic theological writing, the last of which, the ST, is only slightly longer.

The *Sentences* of Peter Lombard, compiled in the early 1150s, fall into four books, each of which is comprised of chapters. Peter had identified the theological topics that need to be discussed in a comprehensive presentation of the Christian faith, and then amassed authoritative sayings of the Fathers, almost exclusively Latin (with Augustine at the head), on these topics. In a chapter, Peter would describe what is involved in that particular topic, note if there were disagreements on the matter, and bring in pertinent patristic sayings to support whatever positions were stated in the chapter. Subsequent to the Lombard, and by the third decade of the thirteenth century, his chapters had been further grouped into "distinctions," and in their lecturing, Bonaventure, Albert, and the like would refer to the distinction (rather than to the chapter or group of chapters).

The adoption at the medieval university of the *Sentences* as a training device is due to a number of features of this work. It is relatively comprehensive, and its ordering of topics had a certain plausibility. In its patristic documentation, it offered the budding scholastic theologian with a good exposure to the Latin patristic tradition. The Lombard was relatively sober in his own theological judgments and in the reporting of the views of others. And the text left plenty of opportunity for commentators to show their own theological acumen. At times in discussing a teaching, the Lombard may express puzzlement about what needs to be stated definitively on a topic. His commentators could thus try to rise to the challenge.

In his own *Scriptum*, or commentary, on the *Sentences*, Aquinas follows the same basic pattern for each distinction. For each distinction, Aquinas offers a division of the text, a question or set of questions, and an exposition of the text. In the division, he explains the organization of the distinction, reviews its basic content, and locates it in the treatise (that is, in the group of distinctions of which it is a part, as well as in the book as a whole). In the exposition, he looks at the words or terms that call for explanation or interpretation. The second part, the questions, constitutes the core of the teaching. The style in this part of the distinction will be familiar to readers of the ST. A question is divided into articles, each of which consists of objections, a sed contra, a solution or body of the article, and responses to the opening objections. Here the Lombard has occasioned the inquiry in the sense of broaching the theological topic, but there is no perceived need in the questions to explicate his wording. In posing the questions, Aquinas enjoys great freedom. The number of questions, and their thrust, is for him to decide, and it is not unusual for Aquinas to introduce, in a question or article, considerations that the Lombard had simply left out of account in his own presentation. In such adding, one can get a sense of the distance between the twelfth-century compiler and the thirteenth-century theologian who uses the Lombard as an occasioning text for his own theologizing.

Peter had distributed the principal topics of Christian theology over four books. The first treats of God; the second, of the creation and then of the fall, sin, and the need for grace; the third book, of Christ and the virtues; and the final book, of the sacraments and the end things. Near the beginning of the first book, Peter had explained the principles of distribution. In organizing the four books, he had employed Augustine's comments about *res* (thing) and *signum* in *De doctrina christiana*. For Augustine, a sign is a thing that has reality but also points beyond itself, to another thing. On this basis, for Peter, book four of the *Sentences* has to do with signs (as is obvious in the case of the sacraments). The first three books have to do with things. Augustine had also noted that there are things to be enjoyed (relished and willed for their own sake), things to be used (employed in the coming to reach what is to be enjoyed), and things that are to be enjoyed and used. In these additional comments, Peter found the justification for the organization of the first three books. The first treats of the triune God, who alone is to be enjoyed and in whom alone can human beings find fulfillment. The second treats of the creation and the things of this world, which cannot be enjoyed (to do so would be to sin) but are to be used in the movement to God. And the third looks at Christ, who as God is to be enjoyed but as human is to be used, as the way to God as end. Later scholastics wondered if there was not

more to Peter's overall organization. One suggestion was that he had adopted the *exitus-reditus* motif (that is, "going out and coming back"). In this view, books one and two go together, discussing God and the procession of creatures from God; and books three and four go together, as discussing the movement of rational creatures to God as end through Christ and Christ's sacraments.

Aquinas was not unsympathetic to this proposal, but in the prologue to his own commentary, he makes another about the overall organization, which is striking for its christological tenor. The *Sentences* are concerned with Christian wisdom. Wisdom, says Aquinas, pertains especially to the second person of God, who is wisdom itself. The Word as wisdom is involved in all that is covered in a Christian theology. It is by the Son as wisdom that the hidden things of God are manifested, especially that the God of Christians is triune; this is the focus of the Lombard's first book. The very creating of things is a work of divine wisdom. God has made all things in wisdom, and so the second book of the *Sentences* is devoted to creation. Wisdom has to do with recreating and with perfecting. Through their sin, human beings have fallen from God and have distorted God's creation. Who better than the one according to whom all thing things were made, God's wisdom, to become incarnate in order to restore fallen creatures to their correct order to God? Hence, the third book of the Lombard's *Sentences* examines the incarnate Son of God and his work for our salvation. Finally, the fourth book has to do with perfection, with the applications of the grace of Christ, through the sacraments, to those who aspire to God as their end. This prologue, from the very beginning of Aquinas's theological career, thus provides a nice response to those who would imagine that Aquinas's understanding of Christian things is insufficiently shaped by Christ.

While in Rome in the mid-1260s, Aquinas began a revision of his *Scrip-*

tum, perhaps in the hope of making it better suited to the needs of newcomers to the discipline. He reworked part of the first book before abandoning the project. Instead, he took up work on the *Summa theologiae*, intending it to be a more streamlined and efficient investigation of the truths of the Christian faith.

McInerny (1998), pp. 51–54 (for the prologue to the *Scriptum*); Synan (1974); Boyle (1983); Biffi (2001); Lohr (1980).

Scripture   To say that Scripture is the principal source of Aquinas's theology is to risk understatement, perhaps even distortion. Aquinas draws on a wide range of writings in constructing his theology. But in insisting that Scripture is the principal authority (ST I.1.8 ad 2), he means more than that Scripture is to be counted among the written sources on which he draws, or that it is the first among these sources. Rather, Scripture is authoritative in a unique way, which distinguishes it from his other sources. Scripture is the revealed Word of God. It is in Scripture that God has revealed the truths necessary for salvation. It is in Scripture that the God of Christians is revealed definitively, as triune, and as the beginning and end of all things. Revelation is not made by God in any of the other sources called upon by Aquinas— not in the church fathers, or more recent Christian tradition, and certainly not in the philosophy that Aquinas can so adroitly employ for Christian ends. Scripture is the unique locus of God's revelation. Scripture thus enjoys a foundational status for Aquinas—for the Christian life, which is rendered possible by God's revelation in Scripture; and for Christian theology, whose chief responsibility is to respond to God's Word, to plumb its depths, to interpret it for the present age, to defend its truth from attack. Scripture thus is *the* source, and it provides the framework for Thomistic theology with its use of a variety of sources in order to grasp more adequately God's Word. As Aquinas puts it elsewhere (ST II-II.1.9 ob. 1), Scripture is the "rule of faith," the deposit of truths required for salvation, but also the measure by which all else is to be judged, whether Christian action or the claims of the other sources quoted alongside this principal authority.

There is, as is evident, a very close relation between **sacred doctrine** and sacred Scripture. They are not, strictly speaking, identical. The latter is the medium of the former, where the body of truths needed for salvation as revealed by God are expressed. Yet, in treating sacred doctrine, Aquinas at times underscores the centrality of Scripture by writing as if the two were synonymous. Is a sacred doctrine, in addition to the philosophical disciplines, necessary (ST I.1.1)? Yes, as he puts it in the sed contra of that article, for "all scripture is inspired by God and is useful for teaching, for reproof, for correction, and for training in righteousness" (2 Tim. 3:16), and, Aquinas adds, the scripture inspired of God is part of no philosophical science, and so is part of another, the additional doctrine that is necessary. Is there a place for argument in a doctrine whose main truths (see **articles of faith**) lie beyond the capacity of reason to demonstrate (a.8)? As part of his analysis here, Aquinas notes how it is that sacred *scripture* will argue with those who oppose it, whether in whole or in part.

This high estimation of Scripture as the locus of God's revelation does not, however, cause Aquinas to posit an inerrancy that would apply to every word in the Bible. Rather, in his praise of Scripture and in his work on it, he keeps the focus resolutely on the articles of faith, those truths that are needed for salvation. Such have been revealed by God to the human authors of Scripture in a way that does not allow for human distortion (ST I.1.9 ad 2). But the human authors of Scripture can be responsible for illustrations or reports that may reflect, say, contemporary science and that may subsequently be shown to be false. In affirming Scripture, Aquinas has no interest in defending or maintaining such faulty illustration. Again, Scripture is important not because it endorses an outmoded science or a questionable history, but because in it God reveals God's self and the way to God as end, as established by God in Jesus Christ.

By virtue of the close connection between sacred doctrine and sacred Scripture, Aquinas accordingly gives to Scripture considerable attention in his account of sacred doctrine and the theology that pertains to it. In the opening question of the ST, the final two articles of the ten on sacred doctrine examine scriptural language and meaning. In ST I.1.9, the starting point is an observation about much of scriptural language. It tends to be figurative. One thing is spoken of in terms appropriate for another. Sacred doctrine is teaching in a double sense; it is not only what is taught, but the mode or act of teaching as well. And it is God who is the principal teacher of this doctrine. Shouldn't God teach in the most efficient and reasonable way? Why then is there figurative language in Scripture? Doesn't such language obscure and confuse, hide the truth rather than manifest it (ob. 2)? And specific figurative expressions seem especially inappropriate—those, that is, where divine things are spoken in terms of material things that are lowly (ob.3). If God, through the human authors of Scripture, was going to write figuratively, shouldn't God at least have used higher things to express God's self (speak of God's self in terms of the angels, say, rather than a lion)? In his response, Aquinas plays up the suitability of figurative expression and the wisdom of God teaching divine truth in this manner. As in the corpus, he ties the use of figurative expression to the way that human beings know. Humans come to knowledge on the basis of evidence provided by the senses; hence, in manifesting divine truth through sensible things, God shows God's self to be a prudent

teacher, tailoring the presentation of the message to the intended audience and the way that all humans come to know. In the rest of the corpus and in the responses to the objections, Aquinas pursues the theme of God's wisdom in teaching spiritual things through material figures, by noting differences among human beings. Among those he mentions are the simple, the more intellectually advanced, and the impious. As for the impious, figurative expression does in fact confuse or conceal, as the objectors worry, but that shows God's good judgment in putting spiritual truth in terms appropriate to material things (ad 2). In the case of those who refuse to open themselves to God's message and find it trivial or wish to deride it, the veiling in figures does serve to preserve the truth from them (lying behind this part of the analysis is the biblical injunction to "cast not your pearls before swine"). But for others, figurative expression is apt and confirms God's skill as a teacher. The presentation in Scripture of Christian truth in figurative terms is well suited to the simple, those of good disposition who seek God, for they are more easily able to grasp truth when put in such terms (corpus). The more intellectually advanced, however, need and appreciate the challenge of trying to grasp what may not be immediately evident in a given passage because of a figurative expression (ad 2). The idea here is that what one has to work for, one appreciates the more. Nor is the choice of particular figures inept. It is indeed better to have used lowly material things, for one is less likely to think that such expressions are affirmed of God in their proper terms (as if God were a lion, not likened to one). The use of higher things, such as angels, to speak of God would run that risk (ad 3). Finally, there is no possibility that anything crucial to the Christian message will be lost or left out of account by the use throughout Scripture of figurative language. As Aquinas puts it (ad 2), here echoing both Pseudo-Dionysius and the Augustine of De doct-

rina christiana (II.6), whatever is said in one passage of Scripture that poses a difficulty in interpretation will be stated more clearly at some other point in Scripture, and so the point of the first passage can be grasped by referring to others. In referring to passages in which Christian truth is more clearly stated, Aquinas may be thinking of nonfigurative expressions of that truth, or he may be thinking of other figurative expressions that are more immediately accessible to a reader than the problematic passage. At any rate, the revelation of God and all that is necessary for salvation are consistent in Scripture, and the use of figurative expression does not put the proclamation of the message at risk.

In ST I.1.10, Aquinas turns to the levels of meaning in Scripture. With the tradition, he insists that Scripture has more than one level of meaning. The fundamental distinction is between the literal sense and the spiritual sense. That Scripture has more than the literal sense is due to the divine authorship. The literal sense is what the words convey. The literal sense in Aquinas covers not just words as used in their proper meaning, but metaphor too, when the meaning that is conveyed is written of in terms appropriate to another (10 ad 3). But it lies in God's power to signify his meaning not only by words but also by things themselves. God is the Lord of history, and so can, and does, order the realities signified by the words (the literal meaning) to point to other realities. Hence, in sacred Scripture, the literal meaning is in turn foundational of other, spiritual meanings by God's arrangement; that signification whereby things signified by words have themselves a signification is the spiritual sense. The spiritual sense is itself divided into three senses: the allegorical, moral or tropological, and anagogical. As Hebrews 10 notes, the Old Law is the figure of the New Law (see *law*), and as Pseudo-Dionysius has added, the New Law is itself the figure of future glory. Moreover, in the New Law, whatever the head does is a type of what his members

ought to do (see **church**, as the "mystical body of Christ"). Therefore, Aquinas states in I.1.10c, so far as the things of the Old Law signify the things of the New Law, there is the allegorical sense; so far as the things done in Christ, or so far as the things that signify Christ are types of what we ought to do, there is the moral sense. And so far as they signify what relates to eternal glory, there is the anagogical sense.

The response to the first objection of ST I.1.10 is especially effective in making clear what is and what is not at stake in the affirmation of multiple levels of meaning in Scripture. First, it is not as if God has expressed some saving truth at the literal level, and other parts of that truth only at the spiritual level. All of the truth necessary to the Christian faith has been expressed by Scripture at the literal level; at the spiritual level, it is the same truth that is recovered, not a different or additional truth. Second, this implies that there is a built-in check on extravagant interpretation at the spiritual level; the same truth as found someplace in Scripture at the literal level will be uncovered by a spiritual reading. Third, in terms of his systematic theology, Aquinas's preference is for the literal sense; it is from that level of meaning alone—conveyed by the word—that argument, so essential to the scholastic theological enterprise, can be drawn. This does not mean that, having affirmed it, Aquinas simply ignores spiritual meaning. He is principally concerned with discerning, interpreting, and conveying God's teaching in the words, but he not only allows spiritual reading to those who are properly prepared for it (to be precise, those who know and adhere to the rule of faith and are shaped by it), he practices it himself, even in the ST. Thus, as in ST I-II.102, where he considers the ceremonial aspects of the Old Law, he notes both how those precepts were known and used by the Jews, and how they point to and teach about what was to come in Christ. On the whole, however, it is correct to say that in his actual exegesis, the literal meaning holds his attention.

Scholars of Aquinas have debated whether Aquinas thinks there can be multiple meanings at the literal level. As in I.1.10 ad 1, where he insists that positing many levels of meaning in Scripture (literal and spiritual) does not lead to confusion because it is only from the literal level that argument can be drawn, it would seem to be implicit that there is only one literal teaching in a given passage of Scripture. The interpreter would grasp that meaning and then employ it, as needed, in argument. Yet there are passages in Aquinas where he seems to aver a multiplicity of literal meanings. The corpus of this same article is one example. At the very end of the corpus, he states that since the literal sense is what the author of Scripture intends, and since the author of Scripture is God, it is not unfitting, as said by Augustine in the *Confessions*, if even according to the literal sense, one word in Holy Scripture should have several senses. Aquinas makes a similar comment in the disputed questions *De potentia* 4.1, where different patristic interpretations of the account of creation in Genesis are considered. It is not easy to see how the affirmation of many literal meanings can be squared with the insistence that since argument is drawn only from the literal level and not from the spiritual levels, there will be no confusion in sacred doctrine. Perhaps all that Aquinas is doing at the end of the corpus is repeating the teaching of the earlier part of the corpus, although putting that teaching a bit clumsily: There are several senses in Scripture "according to the literal sense," in that the spiritual senses, distinct from the literal, are based on the literal sense. Yet, the positing of Aquinas's affirming multiple literal meanings may help to make sense of a feature of his biblical commentaries. In interpreting a passage, he can offer a variety of ways of taking the passage. There is a recognizable limit to these possible interpretations, but each in its own way would be making a point about the faith, although not necessarily the same point. Aquinas will at times not indicate a preference for one or the other of these literal interpretations; if he does think that there are many literal meanings, he would not have to. Each of these in its own way would contribute to the grasping and building up of the faith; all meanings would be conveyed by the words and intended by the divine author of Scripture. The positing of many literal meanings may be Aquinas's way of proclaiming the inexhaustible riches of Scripture, calling forth and authorizing ever new, faithful attempts to grasp God's saving teaching.

In the discussion of Scripture and sacred doctrine in ST I.1, Aquinas is content to restrict his comments to scriptural language and meaning. Elsewhere, in one of the lectures that he gave on the occasion of his elevation to a magisterial chair, he offers a pithy description of Scripture, dividing it into its main divisions. There are two main divisions of Scripture, the Old and the New Testaments. The former is concerned with God as commanding. Here the law is given; its keeping is advocated, with the consequences for failure to keep it stressed; and examples of how to conform to God's will are provided. There are, then, in Aquinas's reckoning, three main divisions in the Old Law: the law books (Exodus, Leviticus, Numbers); those of the prophets, who urge conformity to God's will and explain why this is good and threaten those who fail to observe God's will; and the hagiographical works, where good advice as well as personal example are offered to facilitate the keeping of the law. In terms of the prophets, Aquinas adds that there is another way to characterize them: as having to do with Christ. Thus, in Isaiah we meet the mystery of the incarnation (and this is why Isaiah is read in church in Advent), Jeremiah has to do with the mystery of the passion (and this is why Jeremiah is read in Passiontide), and Ezekiel is concerned with the resurrection.

The New Testament helps people to eternal life, the end set for people by God. It proclaims God's grace, required by humans to make it to eternal life. The New Testament books are subdivided into three categories. First, the Gospels deal with Christ, the origin and source of grace. Second, the Pauline epistles testify to the power of grace. Third, the remaining books deal with the living out of grace through the virtues that emerge from grace and are stimulated in their expression by grace. Both Old and New Testaments are canonical, and they deal with God's saving teaching each in their distinctive ways.

Aquinas's interest in Scripture had ample opportunity for professional expression. Indeed, the proper designation of the scholastic theologian in the thirteenth century was *Magister in sacra pagina*, "master of the sacred page." The text of the theology faculty at the university was Scripture, and lectures, always text-based at the medieval university, were always on Scripture (see *theologian*). Accordingly, in the training of the scholastic theologian, Scripture stood front and center. The student would attend the lectures of the masters, but would also eventually give lectures on Scripture himself, attended by other bachelors. The lectures of the biblical bachelor are ordinarily termed "cursory"; they involve a quick running over of a book in the Bible, to convey its basic teaching and to interpret, in a sprightly fashion, problematic words or verses. The lectures of a master were meant to be more complex and sophisticated. The analysis was to be more sustained, to get even more into the difficulties and possibilities of the text of a given book in the Bible. At Paris in the thirteenth century, the practice was for a master to lecture one semester or a year on a book of one testament, and then the following academic unit on a book from the other testament.

Given Aquinas's professional duties, it should not be surprising that biblical commentaries form a substantial part of the Thomistic corpus. In his two stints as a master of the sacred page at Paris, he would lecture in the academic year on a book of the Bible, and the lectures would be made available for copying. Even when he was not at Paris but back in Italy in the service of his order, he seems to have devoted a fair amount of his lecturing to the Bible, although he enjoyed more freedom in deciding his curricular offerings to the Dominicans in his charge. The biblical commentaries constitute between one-fifth to one-fourth of his extant writings. From his student days, we have his commentaries on Jeremiah, Lamentations, and Isaiah; that on the first eleven chapters of Isaiah is in fact quite dense, not what one would expect from a "cursory" exposition. There are also lengthy and insightful commentaries on the Gospels of Matthew and John, and on the Pauline corpus, and part of one prepared on the Psalms.

Two of the commentaries, both from the years in Italy in-between his two stints as regent master at Paris, deserve special comment. At the request of the pope, Aquinas set about to offer, through sayings culled from the church fathers, a running commentary on the four Gospels. This work is the *Catena Aurea*, the "golden chain." For the first Gospel, Aquinas was content to draw from the Latin fathers alone. But, as he states in the dedication to the commentary on the second Gospel, he in the meantime had had translated sayings from the Greek fathers that he wove together with sayings from the Latin fathers in the commentaries on the remaining Gospels. In an age where knowledge of Greek among Latin intellectuals was rare, Aquinas's commissioning of translations, and his use of the translated material to explicate the gospel, was a contribution of the first order. This translated material also later found its way into the Third Part of the ST, which stands out among thirteenth-century writings for its close acquaintance with Greek patristic Christology.

The commentary on Job is also an important work. In his preface, Aquinas acknowledges the commentary on Job of Gregory the Great (d. 604), who was very influential in the Middle Ages. Gregory had pursued the spiritual meaning of Job, and had done an excellent job. But a study of Job was needed that would attend to its literal meaning; this is what Aquinas offered in his commentary. For Aquinas, Job has to do with divine providence, more precisely, with its extent. As Aquinas notes, the philosophers were able to come to some knowledge of divine providence; he offers in this regard a quick history of their speculation on the matter. But they had not come to the recognition that divine providence extends to human beings and covers each and every human act. Rather, this is what is revealed in Job. What the philosophers could not discover, the full extent of providence, is here revealed by God. The commentary on Job is contemporary with the third book of the *Summa contra Gentiles*, a rather controversial work. Is this a work of Christian theology, from beginning to end? Or are its first three books an exercise in natural theology, with Aquinas, in the company of the philosophers, showing what reason can discover of the truths that pertain to God and others in relation to God, prior to turning, in the fourth book, to exclusively Christian material, obtainable only by revelation? In the third book of the *ScG*, the focus is on providence. His comments in the preface to Job help give a better feel for what he is doing in the *ScG*. He may be proceeding in the company of the philosophers, but the truth that he is considering in these books is not simply or exclusively philosophical truth. As in the discussion of providence, it is the Christian teaching on providence, including the extent of this providence as revealed in Scripture, that is the focus of Aquinas's efforts.

McInerny (1998), pp. 5–12 (for the inaugural sermon, "Commendation of and Division of Sacred Scripture"); Valkenberg (2000); Arias Reyero (1971); Van der Ploeg (1947); Torrance (1962); Boadt (1985); Elders (1990a, b); Aillet (1993); J. Boyle (1996a); Berchtold (2000); Prügl (2005); Pesch (1974).

Sin   For Aquinas, sin is contrary to nature; it is an act or a habitual disposition that runs contrary to the fulfillment of the person as human. Sin is at the same time an offense against God, a failure to do what God seeks of people. While this may make it seem that for Aquinas there are two distinct standards for evaluating sin—namely, in terms of human nature and in terms of God—for Aquinas there is significant overlap between the two, and the first is included in the second. It is God who creates the human, endowing this being with the sort of nature that it has, ordering the human being to the end set for it in accordance with its natural capacities, and providing for the acts that would fulfill its nature and bring it closer to the good proportionate to the nature. In this sense, to act against the nature—that is, to do what is not in accordance with the nature and will not lead to natural fulfillment—is at the same time to offend against the will of God as creator of the human. There is, of course, more to offense against God. God has ordained rational creatures to a supernatural end, one that transcends the natural capacities of the human. By God's grace, reaching such an end is possible, and the movement to this end is by correct affections, of believing, hoping, and, principally, loving. In sinning, one does not reach this end. One goes off track and, absent repentance and return to the path to God as supernatural end, the eventual result will be hell, the just payment for sin. To sin against God in this connection means to reject this end and the path to it, and to adopt some other good, other than God, as the end of one's existence. It is to deny God and to put oneself and the goods of this world, sought in an inordinate way, in place of God.

In reviewing sin as part of the *moral theology* of the ST's Second Part (I-II.71–89), Aquinas acknowledges different ways of classifying sin. Sin may be, for example, actual or habitual. Actual sin is, as the name implies, an *act* that runs counter to the nature and is against the will of God. Habitual sin falls under the category of habit, and is a bad habit. It is vice, which is a steady disposition to act in a way not conducive to fulfillment (I-II.71). The vice is acquired when one does enough acts of a sort to have a steady disposition to act in that way when occasion arises. The counterpart here is *virtue*, which is a steady disposition of the person to act in a way that realizes the possibilities of the originating power of the act. As is the case with virtue, vice does not necessitate. It does not force the person to sin. Rather, the act of sin is due to the will of the person, as eliciting or commanding an act in accordance with the vice. Vice, as does virtue, inclines; it does not compel.

Aquinas also employs a division of sin into mortal and venial (see ST I-II.88–89). As the name suggests, the latter sort of sin is relatively minor. Its lesser force is made clearer by holding it up against the standard of the other sin, mortal sin. Mortal sin kills. That is, mortal sin is destructive of the community that pertains between God and the person who had stood in correct relationship with God, by virtue of the reception of the *grace* that heals and elevates and the theological virtues that provide new, heightened capacity to the self, to make possible the believing, hoping, and loving that God seeks and that bring the justified believer ever closer to the end that is God. Mortal sin in particular is destructive of *charity*, the bond of friendship made possible by God's loving, which establishes in the object of that loving the capacity to love in return. Charity and mortal sin are incompatible. One who sins mortally, who offends God grievously and who acts against proper subjection to God, loses charity, falls from grace, returns to a life that is spiritually unfruitful, inasmuch as acts not done in charity cannot bring one to the God who should be the end of all human acts. Venial sin lacks the destructive force of mortal sin. One way to get the difference is to say that the one (mortal sin) brings full removal of spiritual good or utter destruction of community. Neither is brought about by venial sin, at least not by one venial sin, or a few. Rather, there may be an incremental erosion of community, of subjection of the person to God, through venial sin, which may be preparatory to the full lapsing from the correct relationship needed for someone to reach God as end.

It is possible to grade sins (I-II.72–73). At one level, of course, all sins are of equal seriousness and gravity, for all mortal sins are against God and are offensive to God. But from another angle, it is possible to grade the sins according to the objects that the sinner may substitute for God as end. In sinning, one turns away from God and to some other thing. The gravity of the sin will be taken from the object, what drew the person away from God and has been substituted in God's place. Hence, carnal sins, in which the body or some material thing has been substituted for God, are less serious than more spiritual sins, where it is imagined that some higher thing is the end of the human person, rather than God, and that that thing is where one will find completion. The higher up in the hierarchy of being one goes in this regard, the more serious the sin.

As part of his review of sin in the ST's Second Part, Aquinas discusses *original sin*. He makes clear that that sin is due to the wrong exercise of the will; that the consequences of that sin are many and dire, running from the loss of grace to the wild, immoderate expression of the different parts of the soul pursuing, inordinately, their own goods rather than subjecting them to the highest good of the person, which accords with the reason and the call of the person to God as end; and that all who come after Adam receive this sin and its consequences, inasmuch as the whole nature was in Adam while sinning and Adam, as the active principle of the generation of the nature in those who follow, passes on his sin and its consequences to those who belong to him by nature. The model of original sin and its consequences provides in concise form what sin means to the individual. By original sin, one is taken out of correct relationship to God; the harmony that grace can provide, within the self and in relation to others, is lost; one becomes guilty before God; one is liable to death, both physical and spiritual, for sin leads away from the end that can alone fulfill and to the end of total absence (i.e., hell; see *eschatology*) from God. So too with the individual's sinning. By original sin, one is disposed to further sin; new sinning creates a further disposition or set of dispositions (the habits that are vices) to subsequent sin. The battle within the self, and disharmony with others, is heightened by new sinning. And the more one sins, the more one is liable to the just punishment of God (I-II.87), whose will has been contravened by each and every sin. The guilt of sin will lead to the *evil* of penalty, of punishment. God gives sinners what they deserve. The full payment for sin will be given in the next life, unless the sinner repents in the present life and makes up the debt established by sin.

The one who repents of sin receives by God's grace forgiveness of that sin. And by God's grace that one is set anew on the path to God as end and is capable of the acts that God seeks of those called to God. There is a transformation by grace, although it is not complete at its first moment. With the help of *grace*, and the *theological virtues* and the *gifts of the Holy Spirit* that perfect the virtues, one will be the more transformed, approximating even more what God seeks of the human as moral and supernatural agent. But while past sins are forgiven, the debt associated with them must be paid. The debt is no longer infinite, as it was in the sinning against the infinite God and prior to conversion and repentance. Christ's work on the *cross* pays the infinite debt, and by repentance one is joined to Christ and his benefits are applied to those who believe and hope and direct their love to God through him. The eternal debt is transmuted into a temporal one. This remaining temporal debt attached to past sin must be paid by restoring the good that would have been realized or expressed in morally and supernaturally good action but was not, because of sin. The paying of the debt by the Christian marks a further incorporation of the individual into the community and harmony that has been disrupted by her sin: the equilibrium of the self, relations with others, and ultimately the relation with the God who is the end of human existence. Again, in talking about satisfaction for the debt (see, e.g., III.49.3 ad 2), Aquinas is not advocating some sort of works righteousness, or putting the value of Christ's work on the cross in doubt. There is a difference between punishment and satisfaction (I-II.87). Punishment is imposed against one's will; it is given as the just response for the wrong that someone has done and refuses to make up for. Satisfaction is the voluntary payment of the debt. In Aquinas's reckoning, only one who is joined to Christ can satisfy; apart from Christ, the debt would be simply overwhelming. Christ must come before and pay the debt of the race to God, and one must be joined to Christ in order to oneself satisfy, to render to God (in manageable form) what has been withheld through sin. The eternal debt has been reduced. The remaining debt paid "in Christ" is a good reminder of the seriousness of sin, of the damage that it has done—to oneself and to others. By restoring through satisfaction, one works toward the healing of community in its many dimensions, repairing as it were the fabric of community torn by sin. At the same time, there is a therapeutic dimension to this work, as one becomes more aware, through the restoration brought by acts of satisfaction, of the damage wrought by sin and, more especially, of the possibility for authentic existence that is available to those correctly related to God.

————

Sweeney (2002); Te Velde (2005).

Subalternation The affirmation of subalternation comes in the course of the treatment of *sacred doctrine* and the *theology* that pertains to it (see ST I.1.2c). Is sacred doctrine a science, according to the criteria articulated by Aristotle as in his *Posterior Analytics*? It would seem not. An Aristotelian science in the full sense has to do with cause and effect, and in a science, the cause is better known, and the effects are known as proceeding from the cause. In light of the divine transcendence and the inability in this life to know the divine essence in itself, it would seem that sacred doctrine would by necessity fail the test of science. Likewise, a science proceeds from principles that are self-evident, but not everyone who learns of the principles of sacred doctrine—Trinity, incarnation, and the other *articles of faith*—affirm them. The way in which Aquinas develops the account of the scientific character of sacred doctrine, and by extension its theology, discloses nicely one form that the debt to Aristotle might take in the analysis of peculiarly Christian matters (see *philosophy*). In Aristotle, lower sciences can stand in dependence on higher sciences, receiving their principles from the higher. Hence, for example, music proceeds from principles received from mathematics. Sacred doctrine is revealed by God, but is not the knowledge or science that God has of God's self. Rather, it is based on that knowledge, with God revealing God's self and all in the light of God in a way accessible to people in their present state. In other words, sacred doctrine is a subalterned science, standing to God's self-knowledge the way music stands to mathematics (ST I.1.2c).

In the same article that introduces subalternation, Aquinas reminds us of the soteriological import of sacred doctrine. The higher knowing from which sacred doctrine receives its principles is that "of God and of the blessed." The higher knowing is the knowing that is proper to God; it is to this knowing that God has freely called human beings— entry into God's own life and activity in the next life, when God brings the human journey (see *viator*) to its term by sharing with the blessed the knowing and knowledge proper to God (see *beatific vision*). The blessed possess this knowledge now; it is to this that people in this world should aspire.

————

Chenu (1957).

Summa contra Gentiles Aquinas did the bulk of the work on the *ScG* in the first half of the 1260s, while back in Italy in the service of his order's educational needs. Employing the distinction between the *preambles of faith* and the *articles of faith* to structure the entire writing, Aquinas discusses the following theological topics in the four books of the *ScG*: in book I, God, considered in God's existence and essence; book II, creation, with a view to God as Creator and the creatures brought into existence by the divine creative power; book III, providence, including a consideration of grace and predestination; and book IV, such revealed truths as the Trinity, Christ, the sacraments, and the end of human existence which is God. In composing the *ScG*, Aquinas eschewed the question and article form familiar from the ST. Rather, he comprised each book of chapters, in each of which he investigated some truth associated with the principal topic of the book.

Though commonly known as the *Summa contra Gentiles*, an equally venerable title is *Liber de veritate catholicae fidei contra errores infidelium* ("The Truth of the Catholic Faith against the Errors of Unbelievers"). The latter title is more descriptive of the contents and aims of the entire work. *Summa contra Gentiles* as a title would seem to have a principally negative bent; it is a writing against (contra) unbelievers. *Liber de veritate*, however, captures better the spirit of the work, as announced in the saying from Proverbs (8:7) that stands at the head of the work. "My mouth shall meditate truth, and my lips shall hate impiety" (*ScG* [ET 1975]). As teased out by Aquinas, this is an apt description of the work of the wise man, to be taken up in this writing. The work of the wise man is of two kinds: the proclamation (and investigation) of the truth and the defense of the truth against those who would attack or obscure it (I.1.3–4). The alternate title nicely alludes to both of these tasks: it is against errors (so, the defense of the truth), but it is also, and in the first place, a meditation on the truth of the catholic faith. As witnessed by the four books, "infidels" is a rather plastic term. Aquinas does not have the same "unbelievers" in mind in each book, or even within a given book. Unbelief can take different forms, running from those who know or accept little of what falls under the Christian faith, to those who are Christians but who differ from the orthodox on some crucial aspect of the faith (as in book IV, in the consideration of orthodoxy on Christ in tandem with the rejection of various Christian heresies). The alternate title is also more descriptive, finally, because of the use of the word *Liber* (book) in place of *Summa* in the other title. A *summa* aims at comprehensiveness; a book is a more streamlined affair. The *ScG* is lengthy, but not in comparison with the later *Summa theologiae*; it is less than half the length of the ST. And the *ScG* does not aspire to the breadth or the detail of the ST, which is indeed a *summa*. It sticks with the bare bones, the basic elements, of the truths that it covers in its four books.

The *ScG* is a much contested work in the scholarship. On the basis of the organization according to preambles (books I–III) and articles (book IV), some imagine that in the first three books Aquinas is engaging in philosophy; here the pre-ambles would be considered under the formality of demonstrable rather than that of revealed. Only in the fourth book would Aquinas be proceeding theologically. There has also been considerable dispute about the genre of the work and its target audience. Aquinas tells us that he is, despite his trepidation, taking up the task of the wise man in preparing this writing. But he does not state for whom he is writing, and the writing style is distinctive among the writings of Aquinas. One suggestion has been that this can be taken as connected with missionary activity. Aquinas would have prepared this work at the request of a Dominican friar concerned with converting Muslims and other nonbelievers, and so he would have needed from Aquinas a work that would handle Muslim unbelief and disagreement with Christian faith. This seems unlikely; the arguments in each of the books can be quite complex and would be hardly suited to missionary work, and the proposal is rooted in a tale that arose after Aquinas's death. It is probably better to style the *ScG* a work of Christian theology, in which throughout its four books, Aquinas proclaims, investigates, clarifies, and defends Christian wisdom, while urging his reader to pursue the wisdom that is from God and leads to God. In the analysis, he will call upon his considerable learning—in the sources of the Christian faith, as well as extra-Christian writings—to clarify Christian wisdom, differentiate it from lesser forms of wisdom, and to defend it from misunderstanding and attack. This will include using the philosophers for Christian ends, and where need be, in employing philosopher against philosopher.

In the scholarship there has been a special fascination with the first three books, especially when they are seen as examples of Aquinas the philosopher at work. The fourth book, however, is quite remarkable and serves as the crown of this exhortation to Christian wisdom. Aquinas attempts, and accomplishes, much in reviewing the **Trinity**, Christology, the *sacraments*, and the end things in the fourth book. He strives mightily to root dogmatic formulation in each case in Scripture, showing how the affirmation of *hypostatic union*, for example, best captures the scriptural witness to Christ (IV.27, 39). He shows too how various heresies arise from a poor or limited reading of Scripture. And he seeks to clarify what is at stake in the main affirmations of the Christian faith, employing the insights of his great predecessors as well as of *philosophy* in this pursuit. The writing is clear and persuasive, in the sense acceptable when talking about the articles of faith. His arguments will not bring the reader to faith; by definition, that is impossible of the articles. But the arguments can help the reader attain a better understanding of what is proclaimed in faith. The final book nicely brings to a head the search for wisdom that characterizes the endeavor throughout. And as a final recommendation of the final book of the *ScG*, the later ST was left uncompleted midway through the discussion of the sacraments, while the *ScG*, for its part, offers a quick and accessible review of all seven sacraments (chs. 56–78), as well as the principal tenets of a Christian *eschatology* (chs. 79–97).

———

Gauthier (1993); Hibbs (1995, 1998); Kretzmann (1997); Jordan (1986b).

Supernatural   *see* **Grace; Nature and Grace**

Temptation   Temptation is a test of the human person, meant to induce the person to sin (ST III.41.1 ob. 1). God does not tempt, but God does permit temptation, and God will punish the one who succumbs to temptation, thereby retrieving good from the *evil* done by sin. In discussing temptation, Aquinas distinguishes between the temptation of Adam and of Jesus, on the one side, and that of other humans, on the other. What necessitates the differentiation in approach to temptation is the

fall and its consequences for those born into *original sin*. Through the discussion of temptation, Aquinas makes clearer the consequences of sin, as well as the resources available for resisting temptation to sin.

After the fall, humans experience temptation from two sources: from without and from within. The *devil* tempts people from without, employing the things of this world to try to lure people away from God and into sin. Those who are born into original sin also experience the temptation that arises within themselves, from the flesh. Here Aquinas is giving full weight to the disruption that emerges from the forfeiting of *original justice* through original sin. The original state was marked by harmony: of the self before God and within the self; the lower self was subject, through grace, to the rule of the higher self, of reason. Original sin removes that grace, the self is thrown out of its subordination to God, and the harmony and hierarchy within the self are destroyed. Rather than aspiring to their own goods in a moderate way, one that is conducive to the realization of the self in its highest acts (i.e., of reason), now there is a battle within the self, as each power seeks its own good, and does so without concern for the greater good of the person. Such concupiscences provide the temptation to sin, and acting on such inordinate expressions of desire for private goods, sinning, leads to a disposition to further sinning. In a fallen world, the person born into original sin is simply bombarded by temptation: by the devil, through others employed as tools to promote more sin; from the flesh, which inclines, as fallen and disrupted and habituated in vice, to more sin.

Temptation can be strong, but there is no compulsion to sin. It is possible to resist temptation through conscious effort and the correct use of the will. One does not always have to be sinning (ST I-II.109.8c). But it is not possible to resist all temptation, at least not by the exertion of one's natural powers. One will not always be on the alert; one will act out of habit more often than not; one sin will lead to another. To be more successful in the resistance to temptation, *grace* is required. In the ST, in the treatise on grace, Aquinas makes clear that this grace is to be distinguished from the habitual grace that is infused in conversion. That habitual grace provides a basic healing of the sinful self, restoring in principle the harmony lost by original and actual *sin*, and that grace elevates the self to the supernatural order. Habitual grace establishes a disposition to morally and supernaturally good action. But dispositions do not reduce themselves to actions; the will must be applied to correct action, correct working out of a good habit. This is done by an operative *auxilium*, one that moves the will to correct intention and in the process provides for perseverance. The operative grace that works perseverance in grace (ST I-II.109.9–10) cannot be merited by the individual. It is a gift of God, given in accordance with God's predestining will. However, God has so arranged that those in grace will pray for this grace, which may be granted if God so wills to use that prayer as the occasion for its giving, for its giving to bring the person to the end destined for the person by God (ST I.23.8). In this regard, in the treatise on grace (I-II.109.9–10), Aquinas evokes the Lord's Prayer. In the light of the late Augustine (see *doctors of the church*), Aquinas thinks that all but one of the petitions of the Lord's Prayer have to do with asking for perseverance in grace, including the request that God not lead us into temptation. By the grace of perseverance, it is possible to resist temptation, not sin, and to continue on the way to God as end. That the graced person is able to resist the temptations that continue to beset her even as she is healed by habitual grace is itself a grace of God.

For Adam prior to the fall, as in original justice, and for Christ, who lacked original sin, there is no temptation from within. Temptation from within is itself a consequence of sin; hence, those who lack sin, lack such temptation. Rather, they were tempted from without, by the devil. In the temptations of Adam (ST II-II.165) and of Christ (III.41), the devil followed the same basic order, showing how clever the devil is. The devil did not start off with a temptation that addressed the strength of these spiritual men, committed as they were to God and the good. Rather, the devil worked incrementally, offering first a temptation to a lesser sin, then to a greater, and finally, as the object of tempting was, perhaps, worn down, offering the gravest temptation. In each case, the devil began with a temptation that had to do with food, something material that is most akin to a being who is corporeal (so, for Adam, the forbidden fruit; for Christ, turning stones into bread). Then the devil tried to tempt each to vainglory, to which spiritual people may be prone, that is, doing something for show (so, for Adam, "your eyes will be open"; for Christ, casting himself off from the pinnacle of the temple). Finally, the devil led the temptation to the extreme height of pride. With Adam, he promised that he would be as the gods, knowing good and evil; with Christ, he urged him to seek worldly riches and fame, to the extent of holding God in contempt (III.41.4c).

There is, of course, a crucial difference in the two stories of Adam and Jesus. They were subject to the same temptations, in the same order. Both had grace that was sufficient to resist temptation. But Adam succumbed, while Jesus did not. In terms of the First and Second Adam motif that comes to expression on occasion in Aquinas's Christology, Jesus tells the story of the human as it should be told: not as a story of sin, of defection from God's will, but as a story of conformity to God's will, as intended by God in creating humans for community with God and as made possible by grace. To put the same point in slightly different fashion: Jesus was successful in resisting temptation not because he is God; he was successful as a true human who lived in conformity as a human to God's will, with the help of God's grace.

As is typical in the discussion of Christ in the Third Part of the ST, in discussing the temptation of Christ (III.41), Aquinas is very much concerned with *fittingness*. All four of this question's articles ask about fittingness. Was it fitting for Christ to be tempted (a.1)? To be tempted in the desert (a.2)? To be tempted after a fast (a.3)? To be tempted in the order that he was (a.4)? Jesus' tempting was for our benefit. That he was tempted is a warning to those who follow him, lest someone, feeling himself holy, may think himself safe or free from temptation. Likewise, his being tempted gives us an example of how to overcome the devil (see *Omnis Christi actio nostra est instructio*). Finally, his temptation fills us with confidence in his mercy. As Hebrews 4:15 puts it, "We do not have a high priest, who is unable to sympathize with our weaknesses, but we have one who in every respect has been tested as we are, yet without sin" (ST III.41.1c; see also a.3c).

Torrell (1999), pp. 224ff.

Theologian   By the beginning of the thirteenth century, theologians who worked in the schools saw themselves as committed to three basic tasks: lecturing, disputing, and preaching (*lectio, disputatio, praedicatio*). In the second, they promoted, in dialectical fashion, their own research on the important, traditional topics of Christian theology as well as addressed the pressing theological issues of the day. In the third, they passed on the fruits of that research, to the university community in the first place but more generally, through the preaching of their students modeled on their own, to the broader community of Christians. As for the first task, thirteenth-century theologians evinced a sustained, sometimes difficult, encounter with the tradition and a preoccupation with texts. At the university, chief among these texts was

Scripture, and the lectures of the scholastic theologian were given over to the scriptural books, explicated with the aid of the mediating tradition. The proper designation of the scholastic theologian at the University of Paris was in fact "master of the sacred page." These fundamental tasks help to account for a good portion of the extant Thomistic corpus. We have some of his sermons; a considerable number of his disputations, both ordained and quodlibetal, as revised for publication; and numerous commentaries on *Scripture*.

By Aquinas's time, the training of the scholastic theologian had been standardized. The aim of this education was to give the bachelor in theology a grasp of the texts foundational for doing theology, and to develop and hone the skills needed for the threefold tasks of the regent master of theology. Hence, the bachelor participated in the disputations of the master, as well as in disputations run by and for bachelors. The bachelor also lectured on Scripture, although cursorily (in distinction from the more detailed and sometimes speculatively daring readings of the master of the sacred page). And as the culmination of the preparations of the bachelor, the bachelor lectured at length and over a period of time on the *Sentences* of Peter Lombard (see *Scriptum on the Sentences*). Compiled in the middle of the twelfth century by the eventual bishop of Paris, the *Sentences* offered a more or less comprehensive introduction to the major topics in theology, as well as important sayings of the Western fathers on these topics. Some of these sayings could clash, at least at first glance, and so the reading of the *Sentences* gave the bachelor opportunity to hone his dialectical and literary skills as interpreter, as well as to advance his own ideas on the key theological topics.

Entry into the theological faculty presupposed in the student a good grounding in philosophy, as provided by close study of the Aristotelian corpus. Aristotle was the preserve of the arts faculty, not that of the sacred page. Students of theology did not study Aristotle as part of their theological training; they had already done so, and so were able to bring to bear that knowledge in their preparation for, and eventual doing, of theological work (see *philosophy*).

As in the ST (I.1), Aquinas customarily introduces his systematic writings in theology with a consideration of *sacred doctrine*, the body of truths necessary for salvation that are revealed by God, the principal teacher of this doctrine. In discussing sacred doctrine, Aquinas does a number of things. For example, he compares this doctrine to other doctrines: to God's knowledge of God (in which the blessed share), on the one hand, and to the philosophical disciplines, from which it differs profoundly, on the other. The latter are built up by observation and the use of reason; sacred doctrine, for its part, is revealed by God, and deals mostly with the truths that lie beyond the capacity of reason to demonstrate (see *articles of faith*). Yet while not susceptible to demonstration, such truths of the faith can be reflected upon, shown in their plausibility and in their connection to each other, and defended from attack (I.1.8). In his comparisons of sacred doctrine with the philosophical disciplines, Aquinas stresses its special nobility (a.5) and its status as wisdom (a.6). ST I.1.6 is in fact good testimony to Aquinas's skill in exploiting the various sources at his disposal (see *authority*). He quotes, among others, from the apostle Paul's description (in 1 Cor. 10) of himself as a "wise architect" who lays out well the things of faith, and from Augustine the description in *De trinitate* of wisdom as the knowledge of divine things, and he echoes Aristotle in the *Metaphysics* to show why this doctrine is the most deserving of the designation of wisdom. As Aristotle shows, it pertains to the wise man to arrange and to judge, and to judge lesser things in the light of a higher principle. Thus, says Aquinas, sacred doctrine is wisdom most especially, for it is principally concerned with God, as

revealed by God, and with judging and ordering other things viewed in the light of the God revealed in this doctrine.

While wide-ranging, there is a feature of Aquinas's discussion of sacred doctrine that deserves highlighting and pondering. In discussing sacred doctrine as science and as wisdom (aa.2–7) and then (in aa.8–10) the ways and means of this doctrine, Aquinas keeps the focus resolutely on God, the principal teacher of this doctrine. Perhaps as a way of underscoring the revelatory origin of this doctrine, Aquinas as a rule speaks quite formally and, as it were, abstractly. Is there a human practitioner of this doctrine, a theologian, who works in concert with or, better, as subordinate to God, in conveying and teaching and investigating the truths necessary for salvation? We know there is, and in fact the rest of the ST, an extended exercise in doing theology, is the work of a particular theologian. Yet in discussing sacred doctrine, Aquinas shows little interest in the humans engaged in the theology that pertains to sacred doctrine (I.1.ad 2). Rather, he stresses the primary role of God, and he speaks formally of sacred doctrine or sacred Scripture providing the truths necessary for salvation and, as in a.8, of sacred Scripture arguing with those who oppose the faith, in whole or in part, and, as in a.6, of sacred doctrine ordering and judging in light of God as the highest cause. What moderns have come to expect at the beginning of theological texts, an introduction to the theologian with appropriate methodological comments about stance and ambitions, is missing from Aquinas's treatment of sacred doctrine.

For an acknowledgment of the theologian, of the person now engaged in teaching this doctrine, we need to turn to other texts by Aquinas, outside of the ST. Two will be considered here. The first is one of his inaugural lectures from 1256, given on the occasion of his appointment as regent master of the sacred page. As was the custom, Aquinas has organized his lecture according to a biblical verse, in this instance Psalm 104:13, which reads, "From your lofty abode you water the mountains; the earth is satisfied with the fruit of your work." God in eternity has established the law that God will reach what is lowest by way of things that are in between. In terms of this verse from the Psalms and its usefulness for an inaugural lecture of a new regent master in theology, there are three levels in play. At the top stands God ("From your lofty abode"), who reveals saving truth in Scripture. At the bottom are the students with whom the regent master will be concerned ("the earth is satisfied with the fruit of your work"). And in the middle are the teachers who are the mediators to the students of God's saving truth (the "mountains" that are watered by God). Already there is much that will be familiar to readers of the first question of the ST, not least the "downward movement": The starting point of the discussion of the teacher of theology is what God does, namely, reveals saving truth (in Scripture).

The lecture itself falls into four parts, discussing in turn (1) the exalted nature of spiritual teaching, (2) the high standing of those who teach it, (3) the position of those who hear it, and (4) the manner of its communication. (The first, second, and fourth parts are key here.) In terms of the first part—that is, this spiritual teaching's exalted nature—there is nothing that we meet here that we do not also meet in the ST. In short, what the master is concerned with is truth about God that is revealed by God to bring human beings to God's own life, to eternal life. Yet there is a subtle difference in presentation that surely bears noting. In talking about God's revelation, language about "science" has moved to the margin, supplanted by repeated and insistent mention of wisdom, both in this particular part and subsequently when reference is made to God revealing. What waters from above is the wisdom of God, which reveals to the human authors of Scripture the full range of the wisdom that is needed for salvation, including and especially what in the ST are called the

articles of faith. Later teachers of this doctrine are concerned with God's wisdom.

But it is the second and the fourth parts of his lecture that are especially important, for here Aquinas fills in the gap that he will leave in the ST's first question. Why, he asks at the head of the second part, are the teachers of this wisdom appropriately called "mountains"? In short, they are symbolized by "mountains" because the exalted nature of this teaching requires "high standing" of those who teach it. More expansively, Aquinas gives three reasons for the suitability of this particular symbol for the teacher. *"Mountains are high.* They are raised above the earth and close to the sky. In the same way holy teachers ought to make light of the things of the earth and yearn only for the things of heaven." *Mountains "are radiant.* The mountains are the first to catch the sun's rays, and holy teachers are likewise the first to receive radiance in their minds. Like mountains, teachers are the first to be enlightened by the rays of divine wisdom." *Mountains "are a defense,* because mountains protect the land from its enemies. In the same way, the church's teachers ought to protect the faith against error." Having insisted on the appropriateness of the symbolism and so on the high standing required of the university teacher, Aquinas completes the second part of the inaugural lecture by repeating the insistence, but now in terms of the three functions of the university teacher mentioned earlier in this entry: preaching, lecturing, and disputing. All teachers of the sacred page ought to be "high" because of the high quality of their lives, so that they will be capable of *preaching* effectively. As Scripture says (Eccl. 12:11), "The sayings of the wise are like goads, and like nails firmly fixed." Hearts, Aquinas notes, cannot be goaded on or fixed in the fear of God unless those doing the goading are themselves fixed in an elevated way of life, are themselves wise. So too, the teachers need to be *enlightened*, so that they can suitably teach by *lecturing*. And they need to be *well armed* so that they can refute errors by arguing against them. As Luke 21:15 states, "I will give you words and a wisdom that none of your opponents will be able to withstand or contradict."

These comments on the teacher's high standing, emphasizing as they do the need for correct spiritual orientation and moral uprightness in order to do his work effectively, are complemented by Aquinas's further reflections, in the final part of the lecture, on the manner of this wisdom's acquisition. Aquinas's comments here make full use of the three levels at play in the Psalms verse (God, teachers, students), all the while hammering away on wisdom. Aquinas also shows well human insufficiency and the radical dependence of all, including the regent master, on God. As is the case in each of the other parts of this lecture, Aquinas's reflections on the acquisition of wisdom fall into three segments. The first has to do with the manner in which wisdom is communicated, with reference both to the magnitude and to the quality of the gift received. The teachers' minds do not have the capacity to hold all that is contained in God's wisdom; this is why the Psalms verse says *"watering* them from things above" rather than *"pouring* things above onto the mountains" (Tugwell 1998). The point is basically the same as that made in the ST (I.1.2) about the difference between the knowledge that God has of God (and which is promised to the blessed) and the knowledge that is sacred doctrine. Next the biblical text alludes to the manner in which this teaching is possessed. God possesses wisdom by nature, and this is why the "lofty abode" is said to be God's, because it is natural to him. But teachers *share* in this knowledge, doing so abundantly since they are said to be watered from God's "lofty abode." They participate in this wisdom, receiving it, in due measure, from another. Finally, the biblical verse speaks of the power to communicate. Here the teacher is styled as the instrument or minister of God; it is God who is the principal teacher, conveying

saving truth through ministers. Thus, Aquinas notes, God communicates wisdom by his own power, and he is said to water the mountains by himself. But, he adds, teachers can only communicate wisdom in a ministerial role, and so the fruit of the earth is not ascribed to them, but to the works of God.

The closing words of the lecture nicely reflect the balance Aquinas is after in this portrayal of the one who will do the work associated with the position to which he is about to ascend. Who, he asks, is capable of being a minister of God in the conveying of divine wisdom, (otherwise put) of working at the university as a master of the sacred page? What God requires, he answers, is ministers who are *innocent, intelligent, fervent,* and *obedient.* Such will be capable ministers, worthy instruments of God. But of ourselves, he adds, no one is adequate for this ministry, and so it is for God's help, to make him a capable instrument of God's wisdom, that he must pray.

The other text that is helpful in assessing the vocation of the theologian according to Aquinas comes at the beginning of the better-known *Summa contra Gentiles*, a work that falls chronologically between the inaugural lecture (1256) and the ST (1266–1273). As was the case for the Inaugural Lecture, there is much that is familiar in the opening chapters of book I of the *ScG* when they are read in conjunction with the opening question of the ST. Although they eschew explicit mention here of sacred doctrine, these chapters affirm the same basic ideas. God has revealed the truth necessary for salvation. This truth falls into two categories. As is the case with the Trinity, one category of truth is revealed, falls beyond the capacity of reason to demonstrate, and must be held by faith. The other category of truth covers such things as the existence of God. These truths too are revealed and held by most people by faith, but can and have been demonstrated. With regard to the first category of truth, while reason cannot demonstrate such truths, reason can explore or investigate them, and defend them from attack, without claiming to have exhausted their mystery.

In its opening two chapters, the *ScG* marks a genuine advance over what we met in the inaugural lecture. In the first of these chapters, Aquinas discusses the office of the wise man. It pertains to the wise man to order and judge. More particularly, the wise man is concerned with the highest truth, and will pursue a twofold task: Investigate and reflect on this truth, and defend it from attack. In the second chapter, Aquinas then engages in praise of the pursuit of wisdom. Among all human pursuits, he says, the pursuit of wisdom is more perfect, more noble, more useful, and more full of joy. It is *more perfect* because, insofar as a man gives himself to the pursuit of wisdom, so far does he even now have some share in true beatitude. It is *more noble* because through this pursuit man especially approaches to a likeness to God who "in wisdom made all things" (Ps. 104:24). And since likeness is the cause of love, the pursuit of wisdom especially joins man to God in friendship. It is *more useful* because through wisdom we arrive at the kingdom of immortality. It is *more full of joy* because, as is said in the Wisdom of Solomon 7:16, "companionship with her has no bitterness, and life with her has no pain, but gladness and joy."

Most significantly, having defined the wise man's office and praised that work, Aquinas openly affirms that it is this office that he himself is taking up in the present work. As he writes (I.2.2), "And so, in the name of divine Mercy, I have the confidence to embark upon the work of a wise man, even though this may surpass my powers, and I have set myself the task of making known, as far as my limited powers will allow, the truth that the Catholic faith professes, and of setting aside the errors that are opposed to it. To use the word of Hilary: 'I am aware that I owe this to God as the chief duty of my life, that my every word and sense may speak of Him.'" The work of the theologian, then, is the work of the wise man, undertaken with a keen sense of both its value and of its difficulty, and so performed in due humility.

There is, finally, a subtle christological dimension to Aquinas's account of the theologian. In other thirteenth-century theologians, such as Bonaventure, the role of Christ in fostering theological work can be quite pronounced and obvious. In talking about Christ as a teacher who invites some to enter into his teaching activity, certain basic christological convictions come to the fore. First, the Christology is insistently incarnational; the second person of God has become human, and thus the reality of Jesus must be read as that of the Word of God as truly human. Next, there is a pronounced preference for viewing the second person of God as, precisely, the wisdom and truth of God; the essential attribute of God is here appropriated to the second person, to do justice to the proper character of this divine person. Thus, it is wisdom itself that becomes incarnate, and Jesus is the incarnate wisdom of God. Finally, there is a proclamation of the special ***fittingness*** of the Word as wisdom becoming incarnate, one that highlights the link between creating and saving. All has been made by God in accordance with the wisdom of God; it is thus fitting that it is that divine person who becomes incarnate, in order to remake fallen humans and restore them to the correct path to God as end. In this rendering, ontological considerations have a certain pride of place: The person of Jesus is the Word as wisdom; the Word expresses perfectly both natures, the divine and the human. Yet there is also a considerable moral dimension: Jesus as wisdom incarnate is the perfect human, who discloses fully what God has intended in bringing humans into existence so that they might come, through their correct moral activity, to God as their end. In becoming disciples of this Jesus, Christians aspire to become like him, morally, as they continue their movement toward God. Discipleship and emulation can take many forms. In this particular case, by working as they do, teachers of theology have entered into Christ's own teaching activity.

The Christology that underlies this account of theological work as imitation of Christ is not peculiar to Bonaventure. It is Aquinas's own Christology as well, including in the preference for the designation of the person of Christ in sapiential terms. This is the case throughout Aquinas's career, from the remarkable prologue to the *Scriptum on the Sentences* (in which Aquinas imagines that the four books of the *Sentences* each have to do with facets of Christ as the wisdom of God), through the lengthy passages on Christ as wisdom in the fourth book of the *ScG*, to the repeated reflections on wisdom in the Tertia Pars of the ST. Thus, it is not surprising that in these texts, Christ as wisdom in fact also makes an appearance. Hence, in the Inaugural Lecture, in the midst of the reflections on the teachers of theology as "mountains" and therefore the need for them to be "high," Aquinas explicitly points to Christ, "the teachers' teacher," who himself shows what this should mean. Likewise, Aquinas's sapiential Christology figures in his account of the wise man in the opening of the *ScG*. In the course of his account of the proper subject matter of the Christian wise man, Aquinas observes (I.1.2), right after stating that the wise man aims principally at truth, "So it is that, according to His own statement [in John 18:37], divine Wisdom testifies that He has assumed flesh and come into the world in order to make the truth known." In the *ScG*, it is in fact the divine wisdom who directs the wise man in his twofold task. At the head of the entire work, Aquinas has put a quote from Proverbs (8:7), to describe what falls under the office of the wise man, and thus to characterize what will follow in the *ScG*: "My mouth will utter truth; wickedness is an abomination to my lips." As Aquinas explicitly notes at the end of the same chapter, these are the words of the divine wisdom itself, the Wisdom who became incarnate as Jesus. Thus, in taking up the office of the wise man, Aquinas is answering the call of Christ.

Tugwell (1988), pp. 355–60 (for the Inaugural Lecture); Marshall (2005); Torrell (1996b); Bazan (1985).

Theological Virtues   Virtues are good habits. Habit disposes its possessor to actions of a sort. Good habits are stable dispositions to good acts, to acts that are in fact perfective of the individual. As his discussion of the *virtues* shows, Aquinas knows of virtues that perfect the human's natural powers, rendering possible the attainment of natural good (that is, the good that is proportioned to one's capacities as human). He also knows of other virtues, which order the person to the supernatural end that is God. These extend the capacities of the person, elevating the person to a new form and possibility of life, one that can bring one to God as end. These are the theological virtues of faith, hope, and charity.

In his initial introduction in the ST of the theological virtues (I-II.62ff.), Aquinas gives three criteria for terming a virtue "theological" (I-II.62.1c). First, such a virtue orients the person to God as to one's supernatural end. The theological virtues give the capacity for acts that have God as their end. By *faith*, one assents to the truths about God that are necessary for salvation, not least that the triune God is the end of human existence. By *hope*, one aspires to God as future good, and has the confidence that one will reach that end by the help of God. By *charity*, one is directed to God as end and in a sense is united to God, even in this life, in that the beloved is in the lover by love.

Second, a virtue is theological because it is infused by God. The contrast here is with the virtues that perfect the natural powers of the person with regard to the natural good. Such are acquired by actions of that sort, so that by acting in a certain way, one obtains the habit, the stable disposition, subsequently to act in that way as occasion requires. Repeated courageous acts, for example, lead to a habit of courage out of which its possessor will subsequently perform. The theological virtues cannot be acquired in that way. Rather, they are, radically, a gift, given by God to those whom God chooses, in accordance with God's predestining will. One cannot of one's own initiative come to have habitual grace or the theological virtues that flow from that grace; any preparation in the person will itself be worked by God (see *Facienti quod in se est*). God infuses the theological virtues, and so puts the individual into a new relationship with God. God's love for the person is creative, transformational; habitual grace and the theological virtues are the product of that love, and through that love, new powers and capabilities are granted to the person. The person now can believe in God, hope for God, and love God as God wills for those called to God as their supernatural end. However, once received, the theological virtues are subject to the same manner of augmentation as are the acquired virtues: These habits too are increased through acts of the virtues; by acts of faith, hope, charity, one grows in these virtues.

Finally, virtue is theological when the virtue is known only on the basis of scriptural testimony. *Scripture* conveys the revelation of God, and in Scripture, as in 1 Corinthians 13, God has revealed these virtues and their importance for the movement to God as end. That text, incidentally, is also the basis for Aquinas's discussion of the duration of these virtues (I-II.67.6 sed contra; see also aa.4–5). These virtues characterize the journey of the person to God in this life (see *viator*). There is a difference between being on the journey and being at the end of the journey. The end comes only in the next life, in the immediate presence of God. In the present life, by faith one assents to what is unseen; by hope one aspires to the God who is future; by charity one is ordered in one's willing to God as to the beloved. In the next life, one will come face to face with God. And so faith will pass away, giving way to vision (I-II.67.5); hope too will end (a.4), for one does not hope for what one possesses, as will be the case in the *beatific vision*. Only charity will remain, although in its fullest, heightened form. The union that characterizes charity now will be succeeded by the full unity that is possible in the face-to-face encounter that characterizes the end of the journey.

In introducing the theological virtues, Aquinas can contemplate their standing vis-à-vis each other. Which takes the precedence? If one is asking about the order of generation, then faith is before hope, which is before charity (I-II.62.4c). To hope for something, one must know of that and how to get to that end, which knowledge is provided in faith; being confident of reaching that end by the help of God in turn inspires love for God. However, if one asks which of these virtues is the greatest, then it is charity that takes the precedence. In the other two virtues, there is, as it were, a distance between God as object of the virtues in this life, and God as God will be encountered in the next (I-II.66.6c). Recall in this vein the difference between faith and vision, between aspiring and attainment. But charity unites the lover with God even in this life. More fundamentally, charity is the greatest of all the virtues because it is the root and form of the virtues (I-II.62.4c)—not in the sense that the other virtues take their origin in charity (they do not; the other theological virtues, for example, are infused simultaneously with, not after, charity), but in the sense that the virtue of charity shapes all of the others and the acts that can arise from these virtues. Charity is the form of the virtues because it orders, as an efficient cause, the graced person, and her virtues and their acts, to God as the ultimate end of human existence (see also II-II.23.8c).

In ST II-II, Aquinas subjects the virtues to closer, individual scrutiny, building on what he has provided in the introductory overview of I-II.62ff. In treating each of the theological virtues in turn, he discusses the virtue and its acts, its object, the gift (or gifts, in the case of faith) of the Holy Spirit that perfects the virtue, pertinent precepts, and the vices opposed to the virtue. He opens ST II-II with a consideration of faith (1–16), and then turns to hope (17–22) and charity (23–46), before continuing on to the cardinal virtues and those minor virtues associated with them (47–170).

Porter (1990, 1998); O'Meara (1997).

Theology   In the opening question of the ST, designed through the consideration of *sacred doctrine* to provide an orientation to the work as a whole, Aquinas uses the word *theologia* in only two articles. In the sed contra of the seventh article, whose topic is whether God is the subject matter of this science that is sacred doctrine, he states that God is, for this science is called *theologia*. Here, *theologia*, speech about God, can be seen as synonymous with "sacred doctrine," the body of truths that are necessary for salvation, in which God definitively reveals God and is known as the beginning and end of all things (see I.1.3 ad 1).

The other use of *theologia* comes in the first article, in which Aquinas asks whether in addition to the philosophical disciplines another doctrine is needed. In the second objection in this article, Aquinas observes that a part of philosophy is in fact called *theologia*—metaphysics or first philosophy—and so there is no need, says the objection, for another doctrine. Everything that can be covered in a discipline is already covered in the different parts of philosophy. In the response to that objection, Aquinas makes clear the difference between the

theologia that is part of philosophy and the *theologia* that, as he says here, pertains to sacred doctrine. Sacred doctrine differs profoundly from the philosophical disciplines, which are built up through reason, through argument based on observation of the world. Philosophy in its highest parts aims at demonstration. The truths of sacred doctrine are, however, revealed, and the major truths in sacred doctrine, the *articles of faith,* lie beyond reason's scope to demonstrate. They must be revealed; otherwise we would have no inkling of such truths as God's triune character, God as the supernatural end of human beings (the example given in ST I.1.1c), Jesus Christ as the way to this end. The theology that belongs to sacred doctrine thus differs in kind from that that is part of philosophy. As is clear in this other usage of *theologia*, theology is not strictly synonymous with sacred doctrine, but is part of it.

As part of it, what holds of sacred doctrine, as disclosed in ST I.1, can be taken as extending to *theologia*, the *theologia* that will be pursued in the rest of the work (a *summa* of *theology*). The question on sacred doctrine falls into three sets of articles. The first article, on the necessity of sacred doctrine because it provides the truths necessary for salvation, stands by itself. The next set, aa.2–7, covers the scientific character of sacred doctrine. And the final set, aa.8–10, covers the ways of proceeding in sacred doctrine: its employment of argument (a.8), not to prove its principles (which are revealed) but to explore the articles of faith, show their meaning and plausibility, and defend them from attack; and its use, in Scripture, of figurative language (a.9) to convey God's saving truth, and God's establishment in Scripture of many levels of meaning (a.10). Although the focus in sacred doctrine remains on God and what God as principal teacher does in this doctrine, these articles in their own way shed light on the theological task, that is, the work of one who does the theology that pertains to sacred Scripture. The theology will itself be scientific, sharing in the scientific status of sacred doctrine; the point is explicitly made much later in the ST, in II-II.1.5 ad 2. And, as indicated by aa.8–10, theology will be very much concerned with an *intellectus fidei*—a reading of Scripture that aims at the ever more adequate recovery of God's saving truth and that is attentive to the different levels of meaning that the divine author has placed in Scripture, a thinking about the faith in order to show more perfectly the wisdom of what God has done for human salvation, and a restatement of the main ideas of the faith in terms that will be accessible to the modern age, including a defense of these truths as they undergo misunderstanding, even attack.

––––––––––

Torrell (1996b); Marshall (2005).

Transfiguration   In ST III.45, Aquinas reflects on the transfiguration. The question on transfiguration is noteworthy for several reasons. For one thing, three of the four articles in the question ask about *fittingness*; we meet particularly fine examples in this question of the pursuit of fittingness. Taking for granted an acquaintance in the reader with the transfiguration as rendered in the Gospel account (Luke 9; Matt. 17), Aquinas asks about the fittingness of specific elements of that account, that is, why it made sense for the transfiguration to have occurred and as reported in Scripture. Hence, he asks whether it was fitting for Christ to be transfigured (a.1), changed in his appearance momentarily; whether the choice of witnesses was fitting (a.3), that is, why these particular witnesses were selected; and whether the words from heaven, "This is my beloved Son," were fittingly uttered by the Father (a.4). The starting point of the inquiry after fittingness is the Gospel witness—in the sed contra of the first article, Aquinas quotes Matthew 17 that there was a transfiguration; in the sed contra of each of the third and fourth articles, he simply invokes "the authority of the Gospel"—and he

endeavors to show why Jesus acted wisely in this change of appearance in the presence of these others. Why, for example, was the choice of witnesses wise (a.3)? In terms of the apostles to whom he was revealed in this changed form, Aquinas points to the discipleship that leads to the end of the human journey that is God (see below). In terms of Moses and Elijah, Aquinas underscores the unity of the testaments and notes that the Old Testament figures who were saved, were saved on the basis of their faith in the Savior to come. Thus, they too make fitting witnesses to Jesus.

The discussion is of interest, secondly, because of the way that Aquinas puts such fittingness, as well as explains, in the second article, what was involved in the transfiguration, in this momentary change in appearance. Here, elements of Aquinas's *eschatology*, as well as specifically christological convictions, figure prominently. Human beings are on a journey to God as their end. Reaching this end occurs only in the next life, when the whole person is ushered into the immediate presence of God. The direct encounter with God brings the human soul to its perfection as a knower and lover. But the human body, involved as it has been in the movement in the present life to God as end, also comes to benefit from the direct encounter with God. There is a participation of body in beatification, which Aquinas terms an overflow from the soul as it enjoys God. In this regard he enumerates specific endowments granted to the body by God via the soul that mark the perfection of the body as resting in the term of the journey in God. Among these is a clarity of body, a transformation of the body to a new, spiritual quality of existence, as well as incorruptibility. Again, for humans the reaching of perfection, whether of body or soul, comes only in the next life. The present life should be a preparation for that end, through the exercise of *grace* and the *theological virtues* that bring one to the end that is God. Once God is reached, grace gives way to glory, and two of the theological virtues, *faith* and *hope*, give way to direct vision and comprehension of the end to which the person in this life has tended. Only *charity* remains, and in its complete, most intense form.

For Aquinas, however, Christ is an exception. From the first moment of his conception, he enjoyed in his soul as the gift of God the *beatific vision* (see *knowledge, Christ's*). Throughout his earthly existence, he was, therefore, when it came to his soul, at the end to which the rest of us aspire. For Aquinas, this gift is an appropriate prerogative of the one who is Savior, who makes possible the reaching of the end that is God. In himself, by virtue of the beatific vision, he shows the end to which we aspire through him. However, as in the discussion of the coassumed perfections and defects (see *Jesus Christ*), it was not fitting that the body of Christ enjoy the endowments that come to the body in beatification, in the next life. Rather, by divine dispensation, the overflow from soul was stayed. Hence, Jesus' body was passible. In discussing the coassumed perfections and defects, Aquinas's basic rule is to determine whether a given perfection or defect would help or hinder Christ's salvific work. Was Jesus' body impassible? If it participated in beatitude in this life, as did the soul, the answer would be yes, but that would hinder the salvific work of Christ on the cross. Jesus did suffer and die, as Scripture insists. Thus, the particular perfection of impassibility was not assumed, as neither were the other endowments of the beatified body. Jesus' body would receive those endowments only at the end of his earthly mission, when he was raised from the dead and into new life.

The transfiguration is thus interpreted by Aquinas eschatologically. In being transfigured, Christ's body momentarily experienced the gift of clarity that will permanently mark the body in the next life. In this momentary transformation in appearance, Christ thus shows the disciples the end to which they are heading

(a.1). But the path to that end is one of discipleship to Christ, and Christ's own movement to that end will be through his suffering and death. So too the disciples will be called to take up his cross, to pass through suffering in order to reach the end that is God. Thus, in being transfigured, Christ shows the end and gives his disciples the confidence and strength to continue on their journey. Just as his death will not be the final word on his existence, neither will be theirs. Through suffering and death they will attain God, and the attainment will transform them, body as well as soul.

The final article of this question makes these same points, but from a different angle. Was it fitting for the Father to say, during the transfiguration, that "this is my beloved Son" (III.45.4)? One can also put eternal life in more explicitly trinitarian terms. To be called to enter into God's own life of knowing and loving is to receive from God what belongs to God, to enter into an inheritance that is proper to the Son and that the Son eternally enjoys in relation to the Father and the Holy Spirit. What the second person of God has naturally, that is, as the natural Son of the Father, is offered to humans, through adoption, and they will come into their inheritance, body and soul, in the next life. Thus, in the transfiguration, the glimpse as it were of the future state, it was most apt for God to identify this one—this one to whom people are to be conformed in order to reach God—as the natural Son of God.

The question on transfiguration is noteworthy, finally, because of its placement. Aquinas divides the second main part of the treatise on Christ (see *Jesus Christ*) into four subsections. After treating the entry into the world (ST III.27–39), he looks at Jesus' life in the world (qq.40–45), his passing from the world (qq.46–52), and, finally, his exaltation, including his resurrection and ascension (qq.53–59). The question on transfiguration is the final on Jesus' life in the world. After looking at Jesus' manner of life (q.40), his *temptation* (q.41), and his doctrine (q.42), Aquinas devotes three questions to Christ's miracles. He asks in turn about these miracles in general (q.43), about the principal categories of miracles (q.44), and about the miracle that is the transfiguration (q.45). A miracle involves a change in something that is wrought by God. Jesus' miracles were performed in different sorts of things: in spiritual substances (III.44.1), in heavenly bodies (a.2), in man (a.3), in irrational creatures (a.4), and, finally in himself, in the transfiguration (q.45). There are two main, related reasons for miracles (q.43.1c). The first is to confirm doctrine; since the truths of the faith transcend the power of reason to demonstrate (see *articles of faith*), their truth can be confirmed by God's acting on things. The second is to show the connection between the one through whom God works the miracle and God; they stand in a special, close relation. Was it fitting that Christ work miracles? In Christ we meet the definitive revelation of God as triune and as the end of human beings, and we meet in Christ the way to that end. Thus, to confirm Christ's doctrine (see also q.42, on the doctrine of Christ), Christ works miracles. His miracles also show his special relation to God. Miracles are done by divine power. Christ is fully God, fully human. Christ did his miracles as, precisely, God, employing his human nature as the instrument (see *instrumental causality*) of his divine miracle working (q.43.2c).

But by virtue of his arguments for fittingness in q.45 and eschatological explanation of the clarity that Jesus' body momentarily experienced, Aquinas's placement of the question in its present location provides nice evidence of his pedagogical and organizational skill. The question does nicely round out the account of Jesus in the world. But it prepares as well for what is to follow, in the third and fourth subsections of the second main part of the treatise on Christ, on the passion and the resurrection, respectively. In the transfiguration, we are provided a foretaste of what at the end awaits those who are faithful to Christ, a faithfulness that will not bypass but will rather be through his cross, taken up as one's own.

————

Torrell (1999), vol. 1, ch. VI.

Transubstantiation   Aquinas's fullest discussion of transubstantiation comes in ST III.75.2–8. In the following question (q.76), Aquinas proceeds to examine in detail the mode of Christ's eucharistic presence. But already in 75.1—that is, before the in-depth treatment of transubstantiation—he insists on Christ's substantial presence in the sacrament. By starting q.75 as he does, Aquinas nicely underscores the crucial point. The affirmation of transubstantiation is subject to and in the service of the affirmation of Christ's substantial eucharistic presence. It is not as if for Aquinas, transubstantiation is a teaching independent of *real presence* or a belief that is held on its own or for its own sake. In asserting transubstantiation, he is stating how it is that the eucharistic presence comes about: By God's power, the substance of bread is changed into the substance of Christ's body, and the substance of the wine is changed into Christ's blood. Christ becomes present in truth by virtue of this change of substance into substance.

That transubstantiation is affirmed in connection with and support of the affirmation of true eucharistic presence is suggested nicely by Aquinas's reference to the words of institution in the first three articles of q.75. In the first article, concerned with affirming a true presence and not a merely symbolic one, Aquinas cites the words "This is my body." Here Christ has made a promise, to be present, which he keeps when the Eucharist is correctly celebrated. In the next two articles, Aquinas shifts to a consideration of views of the change that occurs in the Eucharist, views that he rejects but that he contemplates in order to shed light on transubstantiation. Can one account for the presence in terms of what was called at that time "consubstantiation," or the juxtaposition of substances (q.75.2)? In such a view, the substance of the bread remains after the consecration, but to that a second substance, that of Christ's body, is joined. Yet, Aquinas responds, that would seem to be a forced reading of "This is my body." Wouldn't we read in Scripture, rather, "Here is my body," in the sense that to this thing here—bread—something else—Christ's bodily substance—has been added? Likewise, when considering yet another way to account for real presence, one stating that the original substance, bread, is annihilated by God and then replaced by God with Christ's substance (q.75.3), Aquinas again points to the words of institution. These affirm an identity ("This is my body"), but they do not seem to be suggesting any destructive activity of God (the eradication of the first substance) to ground this identity; indeed, as the sed contra of that article, citing Augustine, reminds us, God causes being and the good, not the non-being of anything. While the juxtaposition and annihilation theories in Aquinas's telling fail to do justice to the words of institution, transubstantiation would seem to do a more adequate job. As Aquinas reminds us in 75.7 ad 3, the meaning of the words of the consecratory formula function as a complete unit; the change is wrought, by the divine power on the occasion of the saying of these words by Christ's due representative, when the entire statement is uttered. Yet the words do more than accomplish the change (that is, are more than performative); as a complete semantic unit they are also descriptive of what is the case at the end of the utterance. "This" at the end of the statement is the body of Christ; what the "this" was when the priest uttered the word has become, by divine power, the body of Christ. There is no addition of substance to perduring substance, or destruction of the prior substance and replacement by

another introduced by God; rather, the first substance is transformed into another, and this by the power of God.

In treating transubstantiation in q.75, Aquinas's approach is insistently comparative. He advances the analysis of transubstantiation by bringing in other events—or putative events—and asking how transubstantiation is like such events but also unlike them, to offer as adequate a telling of this miracle that is possible this side of the eschaton. In terms of these competing accounts of eucharistic change, just as they do, so transubstantiation too invokes divine power and links the exercise of that power to the coming to be present of Christ. But the exercise of the divine power is construed differently in the three cases. In consubstantiation, God acts by adding a substance while leaving the earlier substance of bread as is. In annihilation, God wipes out the substance of bread and introduces that of Christ. In transubstantiation, however, God's power to create is invoked, and a parallel is drawn with God's very creation of things *ex nihilo* (a.4). Just as God brings being from nonbeing by the divine power, so in the Eucharist, God makes one substance to become another, such that Christ is truly present.

In presenting transubstantiation, Aquinas also invokes natural change. The decision to so compare is apt; the language of substance here employed to render the eucharistic change has been taken over from Aristotle. As originally employed, "substance" has two related meanings: It indicates an individual, but it also can be taken as synonymous with the nature that makes the individual the sort of thing it is. To substance as individual pertains existence per se, and corporeal substances are modified by accidents. These accidents do not exist in themselves but in the substance that they modify and express. Do substances change? Change can occur in different ways. A bodily substance can be of a certain height, shape, smell, and can be perceptible; all of this is due to the accidents that exist in the substance as in their subject and that announce, as it were, that substance. A bodily substance, by its accidents, can grow or diminish, change color, take on a different odor, and the like. In such a case, there is a change with regard to accident, and unless the change is extreme—as would occur if the change in odor indicated a rotting of the substance itself, such that it was becoming something other than it is—the substance would remain throughout the change, although modified differently by its accidents. But sometimes there is a more complete change, one that touches substance. When a piece of paper is set on fire, it eventually becomes something else—ashes. Here there is a substantial change, in that what was paper has become ashes. Similarly, a seed can grow into a plant; what was a seed, now is a plant. Again, this is substantial change. But in both accidental change and such substantial change, there is a common subject, which links the extremes (the beginning and the end of the change). The substance as modified by its accidents stands in potential to the change, to the term of the change. Thus, a white body that has become brown stood in potential to that result; the accident has been modified, in that what is white has become brown. The paper stands in potential to becoming ashes, and when set afire, that is what it becomes. Transubstantiation conforms to neither manner of change, as described by Aristotle. There is, obviously, not a change of accident here. But the change of substance that occurs in transubstantiation goes beyond, is more radical, than normal substantial change. Bread does not stand in potential to the body of Christ. Bread is not the common subject of the change. Rather, what was bread, in terms of its actuality and its potential, has become something else, and totally; by the power of God, now this is the substance of the body of Christ.

While dependent on the divine power evident in the very creating of things, eucharistic change differs from creation in two important respects. Creation is *ex nihilo*; there is no existing substance or even matter (sheer potentiality) on which God might work in bringing things to be. In the Eucharist, however, there is an existing substance on which God exercises God's power, namely, the bread. God makes the bread into something else: the substance of the body of Christ. To complete the point, eucharistic change differs from creation with respect to the term of the change. In creating, God brings something into existence for the first time. But in the Eucharist, the end term of the conversion does already exist prior to the eucharistic conversion. Christ already exists, and exists, as risen, in heaven. In the Eucharist, God changes the bread in terms of its substance, such that the substance of the body of Christ comes to be. This occurs in such a way that Christ's body as it exists in heaven continues to be in heaven, related to that place by its bodily accidents. As a result of the eucharistic change, Christ's body is present, but not as mediated by its bodily accidents. As he insists in terms of *concomitance*, his bodily accidents are "present" as well, but not as they are present, as related to place, in heaven, but concomitantly, and in the mode of substance. At any rate, at the term of the conversion, what was bread really is Christ, rendered present by the power of God.

Brock (2001); Wawrykow (1993); Wéber (1993).

Trinity Aquinas's teaching about the Trinity has been subjected to severe criticism of different sorts. Might it not be too rationalistic, inattentive to the mystery of God, reducing God to the categories of reason? Has the Trinity been sufficiently integrated into Thomistic theology, or does Aquinas proceed, for all intents and purposes, as if his God were one-personed? Does Aquinas overplay the immanent Trinity—that is, the inner life of God—at the expense of the economic Trinity, which has to do with

God's dealings with the world? Such criticisms, however, seem misguided. While undoubtedly challenging, as befits the difficulty of the subject matter and the need to be precise and attentive to nuance, the Trinity in fact is crucial for Aquinas, and he approaches the topic with a keen sense of its importance for a genuinely Christian theology. He is also keenly aware of the mystery, of the inability of human beings to grasp the triune God. Thus, while he knows how important it is for the *theologian* to contemplate the triune God, to proclaim the teaching intelligently, and to defend it from misuse and misapprehension, he is never under the illusion that theological reflection will be able to explode the mystery. As is the case with other significant theological topics, his discussion of the Trinity in his various writings—the systematic writings that are the *Scriptum on the Sentences*, the *Summa contra Gentiles*, and the *Summa theologiae*, as well as his biblical commentaries (especially that on John) and the disputed questions *De potentia* (see qq.8, 9, 10; 2)— nicely typifies the traditional "faith seeking understanding." Aquinas begins in faith; the treatment allows him and his readers to grow in understanding of what they believe of God, but the end point in this life remains faith. Only in the next life, in the immediate presence of God, will faith give way to knowledge, when the triune God will be seen as God is.

The proper starting point for understanding Aquinas's teaching is his insistence that God is triune is an *article of faith*. Three points need to be stressed in this regard. First, that God is triune is revealed by God. This cannot be demonstrated by rational argument; this is a truth that lies beyond the argumentative capacities of the philosophers. The truth of God as triune must be held by faith; only in the light of faith, of God's revelation of God as triune, would one then detect in created reality vestiges or marks of the triune God. Revelation is the interpretative key, and the reading of

created reality will be in the light of what God has told us of God. Second, as an article that falls under *sacred doctrine*, the Trinity is necessary for salvation. Sacred doctrine is the body of truths necessary for salvation, and the triune God is eminently so needed. Faith acknowledges that it is the triune God who has brought things into existence and has ordered rational creatures to God as their end. This means that God has promised to these rational creatures the life that is proper to God, of knowing God perfectly and so loving God perfectly. That is the goal of human existence, a goal that is, radically, a gift. Without God's free promise, made in love, and without God making available the resources (see *grace*; *theological virtues*; *Jesus Christ*) needed to attain God as end, human beings would not reach that end. But given the divine initiative and offer, they can; the triune God is, thus, the content of human salvation.

As article of faith, the triune God reveals God's self in Scripture. *Scripture* is the locus of God's revelation, and all that is necessary for salvation, including the depiction of God as triune, is found in Scripture. In this regard, the discussion of the Trinity in the *ScG* can be taken as exemplary (IV.2–26). In the discussion of the second divine person (chs. 2–14), Scripture shapes the analysis. The analysis opens with a rehearsal of what Scripture proclaims: that there is generation, paternity, and sonship in the divinity (ch. 2), and that the Son of God is God (ch. 3). In the next block of chapters (chs. 4–9), Aquinas clarifies the scriptural witness to the second person, who is fully God, by recounting various heretical misreadings of Scripture. He looks in turn at Photinus (chs. 4/9), who seems not to affirm an incarnation, and of one who is a distinct person in God; at Sabellius (chs. 5/9), who is unaware of distinctions in the Godhead that would constitute persons, thinking that the names employed in Scripture—Father, Son, Holy Spirit—are simply different names for the same entity; and at Arius (chs. 6/8), who posits distinctions but does so absolutely, thinking that the Son differs in being and nature from the Father who is the Son's source. The value of this interrogation of heresy is that it makes clearer that Scripture proclaims distinctions in God while affirming the full divinity of what is distinct in God. The Father and the Son are not the same; they differ in person. But the Father and the Son are one and the same God. Having specified the link between dogmatic formulation and scriptural testimony in the remaining chapters on the Son, Aquinas strives to shed light on the mystery of the Son as proceeding from the Father that is proclaimed in Scripture (chs. 10–14). In particular, he reflects (ch. 11) on generation in divinity, on the appropriate model for construing the Son proceeding from the Father in such a way that the Son is not the Father but is one in being and nature with the Father from whom the Son arises, in an eternal act of generation. Again, Scripture guides the inquiry, in particular the opening of the Gospel of John, on the Word who was with God (that is, the Father) and who is God (that is, one in being with the Father, one and the same God as the Father). So too in the discussion of the Holy Spirit that follows (chs. 15–26): That the Holy Spirit is God and a subsistent person in God is the clear teaching of Scripture; heretics have been confused in their reading of Scripture, positing absolute distinctions between the Father (and the Son) and the Spirit, such that the Spirit is only a creature in their telling. As are Father and Son, the Holy Spirit is a fully divine person, one in being with the Father and the Son.

The teaching of the ST on the Trinity stands, materially, in profound continuity with that offered in the *ScG*. However, there is a different cast to the analysis, to the way that the Trinity is taught in the ST. In the ST, the role of Scripture is less obvious, although real; that God is triune is, after all, an article of faith, and Christians are dependent on the revelation in Scripture. But in the ST,

Aquinas is less concerned to show in detail how dogmatic formulation is rooted in Scripture. Rather, he employs a wide array of technical terms (e.g., procession, generation, spiration, person, relation, notional act, appropriation) to organize his presentation of the Trinity. Not all of these are scriptural, in the sense of "used in scripture," and the non-Christian origin of some of these terms, first deployed by philosophers, may be the reason that some have suspected that Aquinas's teaching is overly rational and so overly dependent on philosophy. Yet in using such terms, Aquinas in fact would seem to be keeping nicely to the hierarchy of *authority* in his theology sketched out in ST I.1.8 ad 2. There is no "synthesis" here of faith and reason, as if in his theology, faith provided some truths, reason and philosophy others. Rather, this theology, including its discussion of the Trinity, proceeds on the basis of God's revelation as apprehended in faith and makes use of all resources in order to clarify what is and is not involved in the faith. On the basis of his keen sense of the faith, Aquinas turns even to the philosophers in clarifying Christian matters. But as had his great predecessors, he modifies what he has appropriated, to suit Christian needs, as in the case of *person* in speaking of the Christian God.

The ST's treatise on *God* is lengthy (I.2–43), falling into two related parts. In the first part, the focus is put on the unity of the divine essence (qq.2–26); in the second, the focus is put on the Trinity of persons (qq.27–43). In both parts, it is the same God—the Christian God, proclaimed in Scripture—that is discussed, a God who is both one and three. In the first part of the treatise on God, Aquinas stresses what the three persons share in common, as one and the same God. In the second part of the treatise, he stresses the distinction of the persons, on what pertains to the divine person as person (q.29, prepared for by qq.27–28), and what pertains to the persons in themselves (qq.29–38), in relation to each other, and in comparison to the divine essence (qq.39–43). A healthy portion of the second part is given to each of the persons in turn: q.33 is on the Father; qq.34–35 are on the second divine person who is Son, Word, and image; and qq.36–38 are on the third person, the Holy Spirit, who is personal love (q.37) and gift (q.38).

While some have questioned the order of the treatise on God—might it not have been better to begin with the persons?—the ordering does make sense. It does *not* mean that first there is a nature, which is then actualized by the persons. The persons are eternally, and there is no potential in God that might be actualized (see *esse*). The divine essence and the divine persons eternally are, and are identical. There is a certain economy in this order of procedure, going from the common to the proper. And the first part of the treatise on God, so concerned with articulating the divine transcendence and so removing from God what is inappropriate while emphasizing the eminence of the perfections that are ascribed to God (see *epistemology, theological*; *negative theology*), prepares well for the second part of the treatise. In employing the technical terminology that suits the presentation of the Trinity, those who have worked through the earlier part should be disabused of the notion that they are here grasping, comprehending, the Trinity. They can talk less inadequately about the Trinity under Aquinas's guidance, but the mystery always remains.

By the time he reaches the second part of the treatise on God, Aquinas will have treated the perfections of knowing and willing that pertain to God as God. God knows God, and God knows all perfectly, including what proceeds from God as cause (see *knowledge, God's*). God also wills God perfectly, perfectly loving God. Such perfections are affirmed of the three divine persons equally; they are equally God, one and the same God. In the second part of the

treatise on God, Aquinas turns to what is proper to the divine persons, what distinguishes the persons from each other. It pertains to the Father to be the principle without a principle; the Father does not proceed from another, but is innascible. It pertains to the Son to proceed from the Father, whose Son the second person is. And it pertains to the Holy Spirit to proceed from the Father and from the Son as from a single source; Aquinas, in other words, affirms the *filioque*. In exploring Trinitarian relations, Aquinas is indeed guided by Scripture. In the relation of the Son to the Father, the opening lines of John provide the key, with its talk of *Word*. In knowing something, one forms an impression or inner word of what is known. In applying this notion to divinity, Aquinas speaks of an intellectual generation, one by which the second person receives from the first. It pertains to the Father to beget. In knowing God, the Father forms an inner word, which is the perfect grasping of God. This Word is distinct from the Father who speaks the Word, but the Word that is formed, eternally, in the Father's perfect grasping of God, is itself God. There are no accidents in God; what is in God is perfectly God. Thus, in speaking the Word in the eternal act of intellection of God, the Word receives from the Father, who is the Word's origin, what pertains to being God, the divine nature. The Father and the Word, distinct by this relation of origin, are one and the same God. In discussing what is proper to the Holy Spirit, Aquinas follows a similar model, building on the presentation of the Word. In loving, too, there is an impression that is formed of the beloved. What is known perfectly is loved perfectly. And so from the Father speaking the Word there is the eternal procession, spiration, of the Holy Spirit, the personal love in God.

An especially useful article in the discussion of the Trinity is I.32.1. For one thing, Aquinas explicitly stresses in the corpus that it is impossible to attain to knowledge of the Trinity by natural reason. That point will be developed at length in the consideration of the articles of faith, as in II-II.1. But it is the response to the third objection (I.32.1 ad 3) that is deserving of close consideration. Aquinas explains here why humans need knowledge of the Trinity, in the process anchoring the theological explorations that follow in the rest of the ST in Trinitarian discourse. There are, he says, two reasons why the knowledge of the Trinity was necessary for us:

> It was necessary for the right idea of creation. The fact of saying that God made all things by His Word excludes the error of those who say that God produced things by necessity. When we say that in Him there is a procession of love, we show that God produced creatures not because He needed them, nor because of any other extrinsic reason, but on account of the love of His own goodness. . . . In another way, and chiefly, that we may think rightly concerning the salvation of the human race, accomplished by the Incarnate Son, and by the gift of the Holy Spirit.

Aquinas returns to this second point in the question that completes the treatise on the Trinity (q.43), in which he deals with **mission**, of the Son as incarnate and of the Spirit as sanctifying those who strive to follow the Son incarnate on the way to God as end. In a word, the present passage grants to the whole of Aquinas's theology a profound Trinitarian cast. What is created—treated in the rest of the First Part—is created by the triune God, and creating mirrors the inner life of the triune God. In the subsequent parts, on the movement of the rational creature to God as end (I-II; II-II) through Jesus Christ (III), salvation too is construed in Trinitarian terms. Through the triune God, who has freely brought them into existence and called them to God's own life, humans are able to attain to God, to enter into the inheritance of children of God by their moral and affective conformity to the natural Son of God

(see **grace**), who has become human for their salvation.

Emery (1995, 1996b, 1998, 2003, 2004); Rikhof (2005).

Viator   Literally, "one on the way." Aquinas conceives of human life as a journey. The end of this journey comes only in the next life, when the successful traveler enters into the immediate presence of God and comes to share in God's own life (see **beatific vision**). Life in this world is viewed as preparation for this end, as the path that should lead one to beatitude. As had Augustine (e.g., *De doctrina Christiana*, book 1) and others before him, Aquinas perceives this journey as one especially of the affections. One reaches this end when one has believed, hoped, and loved correctly (see **theological virtues**) and has lived out of these affections through actions pleasing to God (see **grace**; **merit**). One who does not so believe, hope, and love, and who acts accordingly—by sinning—will fail to reach this end.

In his depiction of human life as a journey to God as end, Aquinas stresses the divine contribution. The human journey is possible only because of what God does, and it is fair to say that the story of humans takes its meaning from God's planning and work. The divine contribution to the human journey takes many forms; the human journey is placed in its correct setting only when one attends to God's creative and redemptive work. God's creative activity is intentional; God makes different sorts of beings, with their distinctive natures, and provides for creatures their appropriate ends. In terms of human beings, God has endowed them with rational capacities in addition to those that they share with other animals, and by these rational capacities, humans can know and will. By their will, they have control over their own actions; they can voluntarily come to the end set for them by God. In bringing rational creatures into being, God has intended for some the special end that is God. Such lies beyond the natural capacities of humans, but to those who are called to that fulfillment, God provides them with the grace that elevates them and extends their powers, so that graced humans can do what God seeks and reach God as end. In living out the journey, humans depend on God for the beginning and the end and the support and guidance that leads from this life to fulfillment in the next. Without God's contribution in these different forms, there would be no journey—certainly no successful journey.

Human life as journey figures in many of the discrete theological discussions that occur throughout the ST. Four can be mentioned here. The journey plays a prominent role in the consideration of grace. This life and the next are clearly distinguished and set in their proper order. This life is not the end to which we should aspire, but rather is the way to the end that is life with God in heaven. Grace pertains to the present life, and its principal value is as ordering the *viator* to God as end, to glory. Life in this world can be distinguished further into two parts or states: pre-grace and in grace. To qualify for eternal life, one must end one's earthly life in grace. Yet after the fall, people are not born into grace. There is need for a move by the individual, from the state of nongrace into the state of grace; there is need for conversion. In his account of conversion, Aquinas plays up the decisive role of God in bringing about the move from the state of nongrace to that of grace (see **Facienti quod in se est**).

Life as journey also helps to structure the account of the **sacraments**. The spiritual life that is fostered by the sacraments is akin to physical life. A human is born, grows, is nourished, and needs help when he falters and in the dire circumstances that are associated with dying. The same process pertains to the spiritual life and is employed by Aquinas to account for five of the seven sacraments. By baptism, one dies, with Christ, to sin and rises, with Christ, to new life; one grows in that new life through confirmation and receives in the Eucharist the sustenance that will keep one on the path to God as end (Eucharist as *viaticum*; ST III.73.4). Penance helps those who have gone off track to get back on track to God, while extreme unction provides the physical and spiritual solace for those about to leave this world and come before God.

The journey motif has a double function in Aquinas's Christology (see **Jesus Christ**). First, with regard to Christ himself, Aquinas puts the distinctiveness of Jesus in terms of his being—and alone being—both *comprehensor* and *viator* in his earthly existence. From the moment of his conception, Christ enjoyed the beatific vision. Hence, he was a *comprehensor*, enjoying the fulfillment of soul that others will attain only in the next life. Accordingly, Christ is not a *viator* in the same way that others are; what he does in this life will not bring him closer to his personal end, that is, life with God in heaven. In this life, he already possessed this end. But for Aquinas, it still makes sense to speak of Christ as *viator*, inasmuch through his action he nonetheless merits rewards—not for himself, but for others. By his morally and supernaturally good actions, he moves us closer to God, brings those who are united to him by faith and charity into position to reach God as their reward.

More significantly, Christ is in fact the *via*, the way that others must take in order to come to God as end. To return to the theme of the divine contribution: God establishes God's self as the end of the journey. God provides humans the wherewithal to reach that end, their natural capacities healed of sin and elevated to God's order, by grace. In Christ, God provides the way to God as end, through the example that Christ sets and in his actions, especially in his death and resurrection (see **cross**; **resurrection of Christ**), by which those who come to belong to Christ (see **church**) are enabled to reach God. Aquinas works this out in exquisite detail in the ST's Third Part. But he has already alerted the reader to the signal importance of Christ near the very beginning of the ST. In the prologue to ST I.2, where he outlines the three main parts of the ST, he states that in the Third Part he will be looking at Christ who inasmuch as he is man (*homo*) is the *via* to God. The statement itself is pregnant christologically, and in the Third Part he makes clear that far from stressing the humanness of Jesus in an exclusive way, it plays up the divine identity of Jesus, the Jesus who is both God and human. The Word of God, who eternally is a distinct person in God and one and the same God as the Father and the Holy Spirit (and, so, fully God), without loss to itself as fully divine Word, has taken up human nature and come to express that as well. The Word was made flesh; the Word became human, and as human is the way to the God who has established God's self as the end of human life.

Finally, the journey motif is present even earlier in the ST, in the consideration of *sacred doctrine*. Is there need for a doctrine, in addition to the philosophical disciplines built up by human reason (ST I.1.1)? Yes, says Aquinas in the corpus, because people are called to an end—God—that exceeds the grasp of reason. To come to an end, one must know of the end. And thus sacred doctrine is needed in order to reveal to humans where they are to go through their earthly activity. In this passage, Aquinas quotes in support Isaiah 64:4: "The eye hath not seen, O God, besides Thee, what things Thou has prepared for them that wait for Thee." As Aquinas's original readers would have recognized, this verse is quoted by Paul in 1 Corinthians 2:9, in the course of his discussion of the wisdom of God that the world finds so foolish, that is, the Christ who was put to death on the cross. By virtue of that quoting of Isaiah in his own reference to the text, Aquinas is thus able at the outset of the ST to indicate

not only the end to which humans are called but the very way to that end, through Christ.

————

Carbone (2000); Wawrykow (1998).

Vice   *see* **Sin**

Virtue   A considerable portion of the *moral theology* developed in the Second Part of the ST (I-II; II-II) is given over to the habits, identified by Aquinas (ST I-II.49, prologue) as the second of the intrinsic principles of human acts (the contrast is with God as extrinsic principle; see *law; grace*). The first of the intrinsic principles is the powers of the soul; since those have already been discussed in the ST's First Part (qq.77ff.), Aquinas can in I-II.49ff. turn directly to the habits. That Aquinas sees the importance of habit follows on his assessment of the powers of the soul. The powers are not determined to one act, and so can be exercised in different ways. Habits, for their part, stabilize a power of the soul, whether appetitive or intellective. A habit is a stable disposition to act in a certain way. It inclines the power, but does not necessitate it, to act in a certain way. The will, which elicits or commands all human acts (see ST I-II.8; 17), can contravene the habit. Yet by the habits there is an inclination to certain action, out of which the human may act. Acting will typically follow on the disposition provided by the habit.

Habits can be bad. They can dispose the person to acts that are not in fact fulfilling to the person, given the nature that the person has and the end to which the person has been set. Habits that establish a disposition to act in a way that is not fulfilling are vices. Habits that dispose the person to act in a way that is in fact fulfilling and does bring the person to the due end are virtues.

One way of distinguishing the virtues is according to the powers of the soul that they may perfect, and so by their proper objects. In this assessment, virtues will be deemed intellectual when they perfect the intellectual powers of the human; examples of such would be wisdom, science, and understanding, which perfect the speculative intellect (ST I-II.57.2), and prudence, which perfects the practical intellect (a.4). Virtues that perfect the appetite, whether rational or sensitive, are moral virtues (I-II.59–60). Following the tradition, Aquinas is aware that some of the virtues that perfect the natural powers of the soul are more important than others. Such are called the "cardinal virtues" (I-II.61), of which one, prudence, is perfective of the practical intellect, which is ordered to action. The other cardinal virtues are moral virtues. Justice, perfective of the rational will, has to do with rectitude in external relations among people. The other two cardinal virtues have to do with the passions of the soul, to render them subject to the rule of the reason. Temperance, perfective of the concupiscible faculty, provides moderation and curbs the passions from inciting to something against reason. Fortitude, perfective of the irascible faculty, has to do with preventing the passions from withdrawing a person from following the dictate of reason, through, for example, the fear of danger or toil; this virtue strengthens the human for that which reason dictates (I-II.61.2). In ST I-II, Aquinas provides a first introduction to the cardinal virtues. In ST II-II, he looks at them in much closer detail, discussing as well other virtues that may be associated with a given cardinal virtue. Thus, in II-II.47–56, he discusses prudence; in II-II.57–122, he discusses justice and such associated virtues as religion (qq.81–100) and piety (q.101). In II-II.123–40, he examines fortitude; finally, in II-II.141–69, he brings the treatment of the cardinal virtues and their related virtues to a close with a reflection on temperance.

Especially important for Aquinas's account of the virtues is the description of how different kinds of virtues are obtained. Here the principal division is between acquired and infused virtues. The virtues that are perfective of the powers of the soul and orient the person to the good that is natural to the person are the acquired virtues. One becomes virtuous, that is, obtains the given virtue, by performing actions of that sort, which habituate the person to act subsequently in that way. Practice, in other words, leads to such habit, which in turn disposes to like practice. The infused virtues are the **theological virtues** of **faith, hope**, and **charity**. These are not acquired through the correct use of one's natural powers. Rather, the theological virtues are, radically, the gift of God, infused by God in those whom God wills to give these virtues. The theological virtues raise the human person to the supernatural order and incline the person to the acts of believing, hoping, and loving that bring the person closer to God as end. Without the theological virtues, such acts are not possible for the person. By these virtues they are, for they perfect the person and so extend the powers of the person to a new plane of activity.

In discussing the acquired virtues, it would seem clear that Aquinas grants to the nongraced person a certain moral capacity, to do what is appropriate to the person as human and so gain a virtue that is perfective of the person at the natural level. Alongside this relatively optimistic account of moral capacity, one needs to set down what Aquinas says, in close proximity in ST I-II, about **original sin** and its consequences, and about the need for **grace**. There Aquinas makes absolutely plain that the morally good acts of the person, which may bring about the acquisition of moral virtue, do not suffice for salvation. It is not simply that salvation requires actions on the supernatural level, which presuppose habitual grace and the theological virtues. After the fall, human beings are fundamentally flawed, in a disordered state, and so even in terms of their natural good, their moral success rate will be slight. Aquinas nicely indicates his basic assessment in a comment in the treatise on grace. Can people who lack grace do anything that is morally good

(I-II.109.8c)? Yes, Aquinas notes, for it is not necessary that such persons always be sinning, or work out of the sinful inclinations that characterize the post-fall state. They can devote enough conscious effort and produce an act of will that can overcome their bad habits, at least for the moment, and so do what is good and appropriate.

Aquinas knows of an additional category of virtue alongside the acquired and the infused. He also affirms (in I-II.63.3–4) the infused moral virtues, given along with the theological virtues in the infusion of habitual grace. The affirmation of infused moral virtues was controversial in Aquinas's time and afterward. For those who preferred to keep the natural and the supernatural orders nicely segregated, and whose theological anthropology was considerably more optimistic than Aquinas's, there would seem to be no need for infused moral virtues. Moral virtues could be acquired by individual effort, and the person could work well enough out of them for the natural good. All the person would need at the supernatural level would be the theological virtues, which provide the elevation to allow one to reach God as end. For Aquinas, however, the acquisition of the moral virtues is no easy task, and after the fall could not be total for any person operating under the consequences of sin. Thus, just as grace heals as well as elevates, so in the infusing of the theological virtues there will be an infusion of the moral virtues, per-

mitting a more successful attainment of good even in terms of the natural capacities and goods of the human person as human.

In constructing his account of the virtues, Aquinas is indebted to a variety of sources. It is customary in the scholarship to stress the pagan contribution, and Aquinas has surely learned much from the *Nichomachean Ethics*. Yet the Christian contribution is profound. The setting of the treatise is a journey of the person to the transcendent end that is the Christian God. Aquinas discusses virtues that were unknown to Aristotle or Cicero and that for him as a Christian are decisive for the successful journey to God. The profound Christian sensibility of the treatise on the virtues is perhaps best illustrated by what is the preferred definition of virtue, taken not from Aristotle but from Peter Lombard's *Sentences*, and woven from the words of Augustine. Virtue is "a good quality of the mind, by which we live righteously, of which no one can make bad use, which God works in us, without us" (quoted at I-II.55.4 ob. 1) From this, it would appear that virtue in its fullest form is what we meet in, precisely, the theological virtues, and by the simple removal of the final phrase about God as efficient cause, we have a definition that comprises perfectly "the whole essential notion of virtue," whether infused or acquired (4c).

O'Meara (1997); Kent (2002); Houser (2002); Keenan (2002); Porter (2002).

Latin Terms

For the benefit of readers of Aquinas in Latin, here is a list of Latin terms that are common in his writings, keyed to particular *Handbook* articles.

aeternitas mundi	Eternity of the World (see Philosophy)
amor dei	Charity
an deus sit	Existence of God (see Preambles of Faith)
analogia	Analogy (see Epistemology, Theological)
angelus, angeli	Angels
articuli fidei	Articles of Faith
auctoritas	Authority
auxilium	Grace
baptismus	Baptism
beata virgo	Mary
beatitudo	Beatific Vision
caritas	Charity
causa	Causes
character	Character, Sacramental
Christus	Jesus Christ
co-assumpta	Coassumed (see Jesus Christ)
concomitantia	Concomitance
confessio	Penance
confirmatio	Confirmation (see Sacrament; Character, Sacramental)
convenientia	Fittingness
corpus Christi	Eucharist (see Concomitance; Real Presence; Sacrifice, Eucharistic; Transubstantiation)
creatio	Creation
creatura pure rationalis	Angels
credere	Faith
crux	Cross
culpa	Evil
deus	God
diabolus	Devil
dilectio dei	Charity
Dominus	Jesus Christ
doni spiritus sancti	Gifts of the Holy Spirit

duratio mundi	Eternity of the World (see Philosophy)
ecclesia	Church
eucharistia	Eucharist (see Concomitance; Real Presence; Sacrifice, Eucharistic; Transubstantiation)
fides	Faith
gratia	Grace
gratia gratis data	Gratuitous Graces
gratia gratum faciens	Grace
imago dei	Image of God
instrumentum	Instrumental Causality
iustitia originalis	Original Justice
lex	Law
lumen propheticum	Prophecy
malum	Evil
Mater dei	Mary
matrimonium	Matrimony (see Sacrament)
meritum	Merit
miraculum	Miracle (see Transfiguration)
missiones divinarum personarum	Missions
mors	Death
mors eterna	Eschatology
natura humana, homo	Anthropology
naturalis	Natural, Supernatural (see Grace)
oratio	Prayer
papa	Pope
pars moralis	Moral Theology
passio Christi	Cross
patria	Eschatology
peccatum	Sin
peccatum originale	Original Sin
persona	Person
philosophia	Philosophy
Philosophus	Aristotle (see Philosophy)
poenitentia	Penance
praeambula fidei	Preambles of Faith
preceptum	Law
predestinatio	Predestination
principium	Causes
privatio boni	Evil
productio rerum	Creation
prophetia	Prophecy
providentia	Providence (see Predestination)
resurrectio	Resurrection of Christ
revelatio	Revelation (see Scripture; Sacred Doctrine; Prophecy)
sacra doctrina	Sacred Doctrine; Theology
sacra scriptura	Scripture
sacramentum	Sacrament
sacramentum ordinis	Holy Orders (see Sacrament; Character, Sacramental)
sacrificium	Sacrifice, Eucharistic
salus humana	Salvation (see Cross; Sacred Doctrine; Prophecy; Beatific Vision; Eschatology; Grace)
sancti doctores	Doctors of the Church

sanguis Christi	Eucharist (see Concomitance; Real Presence; Sacrifice, Eucharistic; Transubstantiation)
Sapientia	Theologian
Satana	Devil
scientia, cognitio	Epistemology, Theological
scientia Christi	Knowledge, Christ's
scientia dei	Knowledge, God's
scientia moralis	Moral Theology
spes	Hope
subalternatio	Subalternation
substantia rationalis	Nature (see Person)
substantia separata	Angels
supernaturalis	Supernatural (see Grace; Nature and Grace)
supplicatio	Prayer
symbolum	Creed (see Articles of Faith; (Pseudo-)Athanasian Creed)
Symbolum Athanasii	(Pseudo-)Athanasian Creed
tentatio	Temptation
theologia	Sacred Doctrine; Theology
theologus	Theologian
transfiguratio	Transfiguration
transubstantiatio	Transubstantiation
trinitas personarum	Trinity
ultimus finis humanae vitae	Beatific Vision
unio in persona	Hypostatic Union
vestigium dei	Image of God
via remotionis	Negative Theology
virtus	Virtue
virtutes theologicae	Theological Virtues
visio dei per essentiam	Beatific Vision
vita aeterna	Eschatology
vitium	Vice (see Sin)

A Note on the Literature

For newcomers to Aquinas, it makes good sense to become familiar at an early stage with the range of his writings as well as with the major stages of his career. There are a number of fine introductions to the life and work of Aquinas, such as Weisheipl (1983) and Tugwell (1988), 201–67 and 291–344. Especially good is Torrell (1996c). Torrell, who has been a member of the Leonine Commission charged with editing Aquinas's writings, is an astute theologian and historian of theology. The value of his volume is enhanced by the inclusion of the "Brief Catalogue of the Works of Saint Thomas Aquinas" (330–61), prepared by Gilles Emery. This catalogue distributes the writings according to the principal categories, notes the best editions, and observes when specific writings are available in translation.

For most of the twentieth century, students of Aquinas were well served by yearly reviews of the literature, which identified the secondary scholarship and often provided brief evaluations of books and articles on Aquinas: *Bulletin Thomiste* (Soisy-sur Seine, 1924–1965) and *Rassegna di letteratura tomistica* (Naples, 1966–1993). Handy one-volume surveys (without evaluation) of the scholarship are found in Vernon J. Bourke, *Thomistic Bibliography, 1920–1940* (St. Louis, 1945); Terry L. Miethe and Vernon J. Bourke, *Thomistic Bibliography, 1940–1978* (Westport, CT, 1980); and Richard Ingardia, *Thomas Aquinas: International Bibliography, 1997–1990* (Bowling Green, OH, 1993).

With the end of publication of the *Rassegna*, keeping pace with the scholarship has become more difficult. The important journals in the field—in the USA, *The Thomist*, and in Europe, the *Revue Thomiste*—should be consulted.

The World Wide Web is an increasingly important resource. An outstanding site is the Corpus Thomisticum (http://www.corpusthomisticum.org/). Among other things, it provides access to the Latin texts used by Busa in preparing the *Index Thomsticus*, the computerized Thomas; it also lists, alphabetically, articles and books on Aquinas, with a separate enumeration of new publications.

Primary Bibliography

The following provides information about the writings of Aquinas to which reference is made in this *Handbook*. I list the Latin edition, and note when there is an English translation (ET) of the work. In the "Articles," I have quoted from these English translations. In references to the ST, my preference is for the translation prepared by the Fathers of the English Dominican Province. "Leon." indicates when the Latin text appears in the critical edition of the writings of Aquinas being prepared by the Leonine Commission (Rome and Paris, 1882–). For the complete list of Aquinas's writings, see Emery (1996a). I have used the categories employed by Emery in his catalogue in structuring this bibliography. Works in each category are listed in rough chronological order.

THEOLOGICAL SYNTHESES

Scriptum super libros sententiarum magistri Petri Lombardi Episcopi Parisiensis. 4 vols. Vols. 1–2 edited by P. Mandonnet, vols. 3–4 edited by M. F. Moos. Paris, 1929–1947.
For a translation of the prologue, see McInerny (1998), 51–54 (listed in the secondary bibliography).
S. Thomae Aquinatis Doctoris Angelici Liber de veritate Catholicae fidei contra errores infidelium, qui dicitur Summa contra gentiles. Edited by P. Marc with the help of C. Pera and P. Caramello. 3 vols. Turin, 1961.
ET: *Summa contra Gentiles*. Translated by A. C. Pegis (book I), J. F. Anderson (book II), V. J. Bourke (book III), C. J. O'Neill (book IV). Notre Dame, 1975.
S. Thomae de Aquino Ordinis Praedicatorum Summa Theologiae cura et studio Instituti Studiorum Medievalium Ottaviensis. 5 vols. Ottawa, 1941.

ET: *Summa Theologica*. Complete English ed. in 5 vols. Translated by the Fathers of the English Dominican Province. Westminster, MD, 1981.
Summa Theologiae. 60 vols. Latin text and English translation. Various translators. Includes introduction, notes, appendices, and glossaries. London and New York, 1964–. Blackfriars edition.
See below, under "Treatises": *Compendium theologiae ad fratrem Raynoldum*.

DISPUTED QUESTIONS

Quaestiones disputatae De veritate. Leon. 22. 3 vols. Edited by A. Dondaine. 1970–1976.
ET: *The Disputed Questions on Truth*. 3 vols. Translated by R. W. Milligan et al. Chicago, 1952–1954.
Quaestiones disputatae De potentia. In *Quaestiones disputatae*, vol. 2, edited by P. Bazzi et al. 7–276. Turin, 1949.

ET: *On the Power of God*. Translated by English Dominicans. Westminster, MD, 1952.

Quaestio disputata De anima. Leon. 24/1. Edited by B. -C. Bazan. 1996.

ET: *Questions on the Soul*. Translated by J. H. Robb. Milwaukee, 1984.

Quastiones disputatae De malo. Leon. 23. Edited by P. -M. J. Gils. 1982.

ET: *On Evil*. Translated by Jean Oesterle. Notre Dame, 1995.

The De malo *of Thomas Aquinas* (with facing-page translation). Translated by Richard Regan. New York, 2001.

Quaestiones disputatae De virtutibus. In *Quaestiones disputatae*, vol. 2, edited by P. Bazzi et al., 707–828. Turin, 1949.

ET: *On the Virtues, in General*. Translated by J. P. Reid. Providence, 1951.

On Charity. Translated by L. H. Kendzierski. Milwaukee, 1960.

Quaestio disputata De unione verbi incarnati. In *Quaestiones disputatae*, vol. 2, edited by P. Bazzi et al., 421–35. Turin, 1949.

ET: A translation of the first four articles, by J. L. A. West, has been posted on the World Wide Web at The Aquinas Translation Project (http://www.niagara.edu/aquinas/)

Quaestiones de quodlibet I–XII. Leon. 25. Edited by R. -A. Gauthier. 1996.

ET: *Saint Thomas Aquinas: Quodlibetal Questions 1 and 2*. Translated by S. Edwards. Toronto, 1983.

BIBLICAL COMMENTARIES

Expositio super Isaiam ad litteram. Leon. 28. Edited by H. -F. Dondaine and L. Reid. 1974.

Expositio super Job ad litteram. Leon. 26. Edited by A. Dondaine. 1965.

ET: *The Literal Exposition on Job: A Scriptural Commentary concerning Providence*. Translated by A. Damico. Atlanta, 1989.

Catena Aurea in quatuor Evangelia. Edited by A. Guarienti. Turin, 1953.

ET: *Saint Thomas Aquinas, Catena Aurea, Commentary on the Four Gospels*. 4 vols. Translated by M. Pattison et al. Oxford, 1841–1845.

Lectura super Matthaeum. Edited by R. Cai. Turin, 1951.

Lectura super Ioannem. Edited by R. Cai. Turin, 1952.

ET: *Commentary on the Gospel of St. John*, Part I (chapters 1–7). Translated by J. A. Weisheipl and F. R. Larcher. Albany, NY, 1980.

Part II. Translated by J. A. Weisheipl and F. R. Larcher. Petersham, MA, 1999.

Expositio et Lectura super Epistolas · Pauli Apostoli. 2 vols. Edited by R. Cai. Turin, 1953.

ET: *Galatians*. Translated by F. R. Larcher. Albany, NY, 1966.

Ephesians. Translated by M. L. Lamb. Albany, NY, 1966.

1 Thessalonians and Philippians. Translated by F. R. Larcher and M. Duffy. Albany, NY, 1969.

In addition, unpublished translations by Larcher on Hebrews, 1 Corinthians, 2 Corinthians, Colossians, and Ephesians have been posted at the following World Wide Web site: http://www.aquinas.avemaria.edu/Commentaries.asp The site is maintained by the Aquinas Center for Theological Renewal, Ave Maria University.

For the inaugural lectures, see McInerny (1998), 5–17, and Tugwell (1988), 355–60 (listed in the secondary bibliography).

COMMENTARIES ON ARISTOTLE

Sentencia Libri De Anima. Leon. 45/1. Edited by R. -A. Gauthier. 1984.

ET: *Aristotle's* De Anima *with the Commentary of St. Thomas Aquinas*. Translated by K. Foster and S. Humphries. New Haven, 1951.

Sententia Libri Ethicorum. Leon. 47. 2 vols. Edited by R. -A Gauthier. 1969.

ET: *Saint Thomas Aquinas: Commentary on the Nichomachean Ethics*. 2 vols. Translated by C. I. Litzinger.

Chicago, 1964. Reprint, 1993 by Dumb Ox Books, Notre Dame, IN.

Sententia super Metaphysicam. Edited by M. -R. Cathala and R. Spiazzi. Turin, 1952.
ET: *Commentary on the Metaphysics of Aristotle.* 2 vols. Translated by J. P. Rowan. Chicago, 1961. Reprint, 1995 by Dumb Ox Books, Notre Dame, IN.

OTHER COMMENTARIES

Super Boetium De Trinitate. Leon. 50. Edited by P. -M. J. Gils. Pages 75–171 (preface at 1–67). 1992.
ET: *Saint Thomas Aquinas, Faith, Reason, and Theology. Questions I–IV of His Commentary on the* De Trinitate *of Boethius.* Translated by A. Maurer. Toronto, 1987.
Saint Thomas Aquinas, The Division and Methods of the Sciences, Questions V and VI of His Commentary on the De Trinitate *of Boethius.* Translated by A. Maurer. Toronto, 1986.

Expositio libri Boetii De ebdomadibus. Leon. 50. Edited by P. -M. J. Gils. Pages 267–82 (preface at 235–64). 1992.

Super librum Dionysii De divinibus nominibus. Edited by C. Pera. Turin, 1950.

Super librum De causis. Edited by C. Pera. Turin, 1955.
ET: *Commentary on the Book of Causes.* Translated by V. Guagliardo et al. Washington, DC, 1996.

POLEMICAL WRITINGS

In defense of the mendicants

Contra impugnantes Dei cultum et religionem. Leon. 41A. Edited by H. -F. Dondaine. 1970.
ET: In *An Apology for the Religious Orders,* translated by J. Procter. Westminster, MD, 1950.
De perfectione spiritualis vitae. Leon. 41B. Edited by H. -F. Dondaine. 1970.
ET: *The Religious State, the Episcopate, and the Priestly Office.* Translated by J. Procter. St. Louis, 1903.

Contra doctrinam retrahentium a religione. Leon. 41C. Edited by H. -F. Dondaine. 1970.
ET: In *An Apology for the Religious Orders,* translated by J. Procter. Westminster, MD, 1950.

On the doctrine of creation, and what can and cannot be proved by argument

De aeternitate mundi. Leon. 43. 85–89. 1976.
ET: In *St. Thomas Aquinas, Siger of Brabant, St. Bonaventure: "On the Eternity of the World,"* translated by C. Vollert, et al., 19–25. Milwaukee, 1964.

TREATISES

De ente et essentia. Leon. 43. 369–81. 1976.
ET: *On Being and Essence.* 2nd ed. Translated by A. Maurer. Toronto, 1968.
Compendium theologiae ad fratrem Raynaldum. Leon. 42. Edited by G. de Grandpré. Pages 83–205 (preface at 5–73). 1979.
ET: *Compendium of Theology.* Translated by C. Vollert. St. Louis, 1947.

LETTERS AND REQUESTS FOR EXPERT OPINIONS

De articulis fidei et ecclesiae sacramentis ad archiepiscopum Panormitanum. Leon. 42. Edited by H. -F. Dondaine. Pages 245–57 (preface at 209–41). 1979.
ET: In *Catechetical Instructions of St. Thomas Aquinas,* translated by J. B. Collins, 119–31. New York, 1939 (of the section on the sacraments).
See also (for Latin and French) Emery (1999), listed under the secondary bibliography.

LITURGICAL WORKS, SERMONS, PRAYERS

Collationes super Credo in Deum.
See Ayo (1988), listed in the secondary bibliography, for the Latin text (Leonine) and English translation.

Secondary Bibliography

Aertsen, J. A. 1988. *Nature and Creature: Thomas Aquinas's Way of Thought.* Translated by H. D. Morton. Leiden.

Aillet, M., 1993. *Lire la Bible avec S. Thomas. Le passage de la littera à la res dans la Somme théologique.* Fribourg.

Arfeuil, J. -P. 1974. "Le dessein sauveur de Dieu: La doctrine de la prédestination selon Saint Thomas d'Aquin." *Revue Thomiste* 74:591–641.

Arias Reyero, M. 1971. *Thomas von Aquin als Exeget: Die Prinzipien seiner Schriftdeutung und seine Lehre von den Schriftsinnen.* Einsiedeln.

Aumann, J. 1978. "Thomistic Evaluation of Love and Charity." *Angelicum* 55:534–56.

Ayo, N. 1988. *The Sermon Conferences of St. Thomas Aquinas on the Apostles' Creed.* Translation from the Leonine edition, with introduction. Notre Dame.

Backes, I. 1931. *Die Christologie des hl. Thomas von Aquin und die griechischen Kirchenväter.* Forschungen zur christlichen Literatur- und Dogmengeschichte, XVII/3–4. Paderborn.

Bataillon, L. -J. 1993. "Saint Thomas et les Pères: de la *Catena* à la *Tertia Pars.*" In *Ordo sapientiae et amoris,* edited by C. -J. Pinto de Oliveira, 15–36. Fribourg.

Bazan, B. C. 1985. "Les questions disputées, principalement dans les facultés de théologie." In *Les questions disputées et les questions quodlibétiques dans les facultés de théologie, de droit et de médecine,* edited by B. C. Bazan et al., 13–149. Typologie des sources 44–45. Turnhout.

Berchtold, C. 2000. *Manifestatio Veritatis: Zum Offenbarungsbegriff bei Thomas von Aquin.* Münster.

Bernard, C. -A. 1961. *Théologie de l'espérance selon Saint Thomas d'Aquin.* Paris.

Bernath, K. 1969. *Anima forma corporis.* Bonn.

Biffi, I. 2001. "Il commento di S. Tommaso alle *Sentenze* di Pietro Lombardo." *Sacra Doctrina* 6:11–122.

Blanchette, O. 1992. *The Perfection of the Universe according to Aquinas: A Teleological Cosmology.* University Park, PA.

Blankenhorn, B. T. 2002. "The Good as Self-Diffusive in Thomas Aquinas." *Angelicum* 79:803–37.

Boadt, L. 1985. "St. Thomas and the Biblical Wisdom Tradition." *Thomist* 49:575–611.

Bonansea, B. M. 1974. "The Question of an Eternal World in the Teaching of St. Bonaventure." *Franciscan Studies* 34:7–33.

Bonino, S. -T. 1986. "La place du pape dans l'église selon saint Thomas d'Aquin." *Revue Thomiste* 86:392–422.

———. 1993. "Influence du Pseudo-Denys sur la conception thomiste de l'esse." *Bulletin de littérature ecclésiastique* 114:269–74.

182   Secondary Bibliography

———. 2002. "Charisms, Forms, and States of Life (IIa IIae, qq. 171–189)." In *The Ethics of Aquinas*, edited by S. Pope, 340–52. Washington, DC.

Booth, E. 1983. *Aristotelian Aporetic Ontology in Islamic and Christian Thinkers.* Cambridge.

Borresen, K. E. 1968. *Subordination et Équivalence: Nature et rôle de la femme d'après Augustin et Thomas d'Aquin.* Oslo.

Bouillard, H. 1944. *Conversion et grâce chez S. Thomas d'Aquin.* Paris.

Bourgeois, D. 1974. "'Inchoatio vitae eternae.' La dimension eschatologique de la vertu théologale de foi chez saint Thomas d'Aquin." *Sapienza* 27:272–314.

Boyle, J. F. 1996a. "St. Thomas Aquinas and Sacred Scripture." *Pro Ecclesia* 4:92–104.

———. 1996b. "The Twofold Division of St. Thomas's Christology in the *Tertia Pars.*" *Thomist* 60:439–47.

Boyle, L. 1982. "The Setting of the *Summa theologiae* of Saint Thomas." Etienne Gilson Series 5. Toronto.

———. 1983. "Alia lectura fratris Thomae." *Mediaeval Studies* 45:418–29.

Bracken, J. 1985. "Thomas' and Anselm's Satisfaction Theory." *Angelicum* 62: 501–30.

Brock, S. L. 2001. "St. Thomas and the Eucharistic Conversion." *Thomist* 65:529–66.

Brown, O. J. 1981. *Natural Rectitude and Divine Law: An Approach to an Integral Interpretation of the Thomistic Doctrine of Law.* Toronto.

Brown, S. F. 1998. "Thomas Aquinas and His Contemporaries on the Unique Existence in Christ." In *Christ among the Medieval Dominicans*, edited by K. Emery and J. Wawrykow, 220–37. Notre Dame.

———. 2002. "The Theological Virtue of Faith: An Invitation to an Ecclesial Life of Truth (IIa IIae, qq. 1–16)." In *The Ethics of Aquinas*, edited by S. Pope, 221–31. Washington, DC.

Burrell, D. 1979. *Aquinas, God, and Action.* Notre Dame.

———. 1986. *Knowing the Unknowable God.* Notre Dame.

———. 1993. *Freedom and Creation in Three Traditions.* Notre Dame.

G. Carbone. 2000. "*Homo viator et peregrinus* dans les oeuvres de s. Thomas d'Aquin." *Nova et Vetera* (Swiss edition) 75:63–77.

Catao, B. 1965. *Salut et rédemption chez S. Thomas d'Aquin: L'acte sauveur du Christ.* Paris.

Cates, D. F. 2002. "The Virtue of Temperance (IIa IIae, qq. 141–170)." In *The Ethics of Aquinas*, edited by S. Pope, 321–39. Washington, DC.

Cessario, R. 1982. *Christian Satisfaction in Aquinas: Towards a Personalist Understanding.* Washington, DC.

Chardonnens, D. 1997. *L'homme sous de la Providence: Providence de Dieu et condition humaine selon l'Exposition littérale sur le Livre de Job de Thomas d'Aquin.* Paris.

———. 1999. "Éternité du sacerdoce du Christ et effet eschatologique de l'Eucharistie: La contribution de saint Thomas d'Aquin à un thème de théologie sacramentaire." *Revue Thomiste* 99:159–80.

Chenu, M. -D. 1957. *La théologie comme science au XIIIe siècle.* 3rd ed. Paris.

———. 1964. *Toward Understanding St. Thomas.* Translated by A. M. Landry and D. Hughes. Chicago.

Congar, Y. M. -J. 1939. "The Idea of the Church in St. Thomas Aquinas." *Thomist* 1:331–59.

———. 1960. "Tradition und Sacra Doctrina bei Thomas von Aquin." In *Kirche und Überlieferung* (Festgabe J. R. Geiselmann), edited by J. Betz and H. Fries, 170–210. Vienna.

———. 1974a. "'Ecclesia' et 'populus (fidelis)' dans l'ecclésiologie de saint Thomas." In *St Thomas Aquinas 1274–1974 Commemorative Studies*, edited by A. Maurer et al., 1:159–74. Toronto.

———. 1974b. "Saint Thomas Aquinas and the Infallibility of the Papal Magisterium." *Thomist* 38:81–105.

Conlon, G. M. 1947. "The Certitude of Hope." *Thomist* 10:76–119, 226–52.

Corbin, M. 1978. "La Parole devenue chair: lecture de la première question de la Tertia Pars de la *Somme Théologique*." *Revue des Sciences Philosophiques et Théologiques* 62:5–40.

Cross, R. 2002. *The Metaphysics of the Incarnation: Thomas Aquinas to Duns Scotus*. Oxford.

Crotty, N. 1962. "The Redemptive Role of Christ's Resurrection." *Thomist* 25:54–106.

Crowley, P. 1991. "*Instrumentum Divinitatis* in Thomas Aquinas: Recovering the Divinity of Christ." *Theological Studies* 52:451–75.

Dauphinais, M. 1999. "Loving the Lord Your God: The *imago Dei* in Saint Thomas Aquinas." *Thomist* 63:241–67.

Davies, B. 1992. *The Thought of Thomas Aquinas*. Oxford.

De Broglie, G. 1953. "La Vraie notion thomiste des 'Preambula fidei.'" *Gregorianum* 34:341–89.

De Couesnongle, V. 1974. "Le 'Dieu de l'espérance' de saint Thomas Aquinas." *Studia Theologica Varsaviensis* 12:103–20.

Dewan, L. 1991. "St. Thomas, Aristotle, and Creation." *Dionysius* 15:81–90.

Dod, B. G. 1982. "Aristoteles latinus." In *The Cambridge History of Later Medieval Philosophy*, edited by N. Kretzmann et al., 45–79. Cambridge.

Dodds, M. J. 1986. *The Unchanging God of Love: A Study of the Teaching of St. Thomas Aquinas on Divine Immutability in View of Certain Contemporary Criticism of the Doctrine*. Fribourg.

———. 1993. "Ultimacy and Intimacy: Aquinas on the Relation between God and the World." In *Ordo Sapientiae et Amoris*, edited by C. -J. Pinto de Oliveira, 211–27. Fribourg.

Dubois, J. -M. 1983. "Transmission et rémission du péché originale. Genèse de la réflection théologique de saint Thomas d'Aquin." *Revue des Études augustiniennes* 29:283–311.

Elders, L., ed. 1990a. *La doctrine de la révélation divine de saint Thomas d'Aquin*. Vatican City.

———. 1990b. "Aquinas on Holy Scripture as the Medium of Divine Revelation." In *La doctrine de la révélation divine de saint Thomas d'Aquin*, 132–52. Vatican City.

———. 1997. "Thomas Aquinas and the Fathers of the Church." In *The Reception of the Church Fathers in the West*, edited by I. Backes. Leiden.

Emery, G. 1995. *La Trinité créatrice. Trinité et création dans les commentaires aux Sentences de Thomas d'Aquin et de ses précurseurs Albert le Grand et Bonaventure*. Paris.

———. 1996a. "Brief Catalogue of the Works of Saint Thomas Aquinas." In *Saint Thomas Aquinas*, vol. 1, *The Person and His Work*, by J. Torrell, translated by R. Royal, 330–61. Washington, DC.

———. 1996b. "Le traité de saint Thomas sur la Trinité dans la *Somme contre les Gentils*." *Revue Thomiste* 96:5–40.

———. 1997. "Le Fruit ecclesial de l'Eucharistie chez S. Thomas d'Aquin." *Nova et Vetera* 72:25–40.

———. 1998. "Essentialisme ou personalisme dans le traité de Dieu chez saint Thomas d'Aquin?" *Revue Thomiste* 98:5–38.

———. 1999. *Thomas d'Aquin: Les raisons de la foi; Les articles de la foi et Les sacrements de l'église*. Translated from the Latin, with introduction and annotation. Paris.

———. 2003. *Trinity in Aquinas*. Ypsilanti, MI.

———. 2004. "The Doctrine of the Trinity in St. Thomas Aquinas." In *Aquinas on Doctrine: A Critical Introduction*, edited by T. Weinandy et al., 45–67. London.

Emery, K., and J. Wawrykow, eds. 1998. *Christ among the Medieval Dominicans*. Notre Dame.

Fabro, C. 1961. *Participation et causalité selon S. Thomas d'Aquin*. Paris.

Falanga, A. J. 1948. *Charity: The Form of the Virtues according to Saint Thomas*. Washington, DC.

Foster, K. 1967. Introduction, appendix 1, and appendix 2. In *St. Thomas Aquinas. Summa Theologiae* I.50–64, Blackfriars ed., Vol. 9, *Angels*, translated by K. Foster. London.

Gallagher, J. F. 1965. Significando Causant: *A Study of Sacramental Causality*. Fribourg.

Gauthier, R. 1993. *Somme contre les Gentils: Introduction*. Paris.

Geenen, G. 1946. "Thomas d'Aquin VII: Saint Thomas et les Pères." In *Dictionnaire de Théologie Catholique* XV/1, 738–61. Paris.

———. 1952. "En marge du Concile de Chalcédoine. Les texts du Quatriéme Concile dans les oeuvres de Saint Thomas." *Angelicum* 29:43–59.

Geiger, L. B. 1974. 'L'homme, image de Dieu: À propos *Summa Theologiae*, Ia, 93, 4." *Rivista Filosofia Neo-Scolastica* 60:511–32.

Gillon, L. -B. 1959. "L'imitation du Christ et la morale de s. Thomas." *Angelicum* 36:263–86.

Gilson, E. 1968. "L'*esse* du Verbe Incarné selon Saint Thomas d'Aquin." *Archives d'Histoire Doctrinale et Littéraire du Moyen Age* 35:23–37.

Gondreau, P. 2002. *The Passions of Christ's Soul in the Theology of St. Thomas Aquinas*. Münster.

———. 2005. "The Humanity of Christ, the Incarnate Word." In *The Theology of Thomas Aquinas*, edited by R. Van Nieuwenhove and J. Wawrykow, 252–76. Notre Dame.

Goris, H. L. M. J. 1996. *Free Creatures of an Eternal God: Thomas Aquinas on God's Infallible Foreknowledge and Irresistible Will*. Publications of the Thomas Instituut te Utrecht, New Series 4. Leuven.

———. 2003. "The Angelic Doctor and Angelic Speech: The Development of Thomas Aquinas' Thought on How Angels Communicate." *Medieval Philosophy and Theology* 11:87–105.

Gorman, M. 2000a. "Christ as Composite according to Aquinas." *Traditio* 55:143–57.

———. 2000b. "Uses of the Person-Nature Distinction in Thomas' Christology." *Recherches de Théologie et Philosophie Médiévale* 67:58–70.

Gradl, S. 2004. *Deus beatitudo hominis: Eine evangelische Annäherung an die Glückslehre des Thomas von Aquin*. Leuven.

Hall, P. 1994. *Narrative and the Natural Law: An Interpretation of Thomistic Ethics*. Notre Dame, IN.

———. 2002. "The Old Law and the New Law (Ia IIae, qq. 98–108)." In *The Ethics of Aquinas*, edited by S. Pope, 194–206. Washington, DC.

Hankey, W. J. 1987. *God in Himself: Aquinas's Doctrine of God as Expounded in the Summa theologiae*. Oxford.

———. 1997. "Aquinas, Pseudo-Dionysius, Proclus and Isaiah VI.6." AHDLMA [Archives d'histoire doctrinale et littéraire du moyen âge] 64:59–93.

———. 2002. "Aquinas and the Platonists." In *The Platonic Tradition in the Middle Ages*, edited by S. Gersh and M. J. F. M. Hoenen, 279–324. Berlin.

Heintzmann, R. 1986. "'Anima unica forma corporis.' Thomas von Aquin als Überwinder des platonisch-neuplatonischen Dualismus." *Philosophisches Jahrbuch der Görres Gesellschaft* 93:236–59.

Hibbs, T. 1991. "*Imitatio Christi* and the Foundation of Aquinas's Ethics." *Communio* 18:556–73.

———. 1995. *Dialectic and Narrative in Aquinas: An Interpretation of the Summa contra Gentiles*. Notre Dame.

———. 1998. "Kretzmann's Theism vs. Aquinas's Theism: Interpreting Summa contra Gentiles I." *Thomist* 62: 603–22.

Hipp, S. 2001. *Person in Christian Tradition and the Conception of Saint Albert the Great: A Systematic Study of Its Concept as Illuminated by the Mysteries of the Trinity and of the Incarnation*. Münster.

Holtz, F. 1951. "La valeur sotériologique de la résurrection du Christ selon saint Thomas." *Ephemerides Theologicae Lovanienses* 29:609–45.

Hood, J. Y. B. 1995. *Aquinas and the Jews*. Philadelphia.

Hoogland, M. -R. 2003. *God, Passion, and Power: Thomas Aquinas on Christ Crucified and the Almightiness of God.* Leuven.

Hoonhout, M. A. 2002. "Grounding Providence in the Theology of the Creation: The Exemplarity of Thomas Aquinas." *Heythrop Journal* 43:1–19.

Horst, U. 2001. *Die Gaben des Heiligen Geistes nach Thomas von Aquin.* Berlin.

Houser, R. E. 2002. "The Virtue of Courage (IIa IIae, qq. 123–140)." In *The Ethics of Aquinas*, edited by S. Pope, 304–20. Washington, DC.

Hoye, W. J. 1975. *Actualitas omnium actuum: Man's Beatific Vision of God as Apprehended by Thomas Aquinas.* Meishenheim.

Hughes, L. 1975. "Charity as Friendship in the Theology of Saint Thomas." *Angelicum* 52:164–78.

Humbrecht, T. -D. 1993–1994. "La Théologie négative chez saint Thomas d'Aquin." *Revue Thomiste* 93:535–56, 94:71–99.

———. 1998. "L'eucharistie, 'representation' du sacrifice du Christ, selon saint Thomas." *Revue Thomiste* 98:355–86.

Jenkins, J. 1996. "Expositions of the Text: Aquinas's Aristotelian Commentaries." *Medieval Philosophy and Theology* 5:36–52.

———. 1997. *Knowledge and Faith in Thomas Aquinas.* Cambridge.

Johnson, M. 1989. "Did St. Thomas Attribute a Doctrine of Creation to Aristotle?" *New Scholasticism* 63:129–55.

———. 1992. "Aquinas's Changing Evaluation of Plato on Creation." *American Catholic Philosophical Quarterly* 66:81–88.

———. 1998. "Apophatic Theology's Cataphatic Dependencies." *Thomist* 62:519–31.

Johnstone, B. 2002. "The Debate on the Structure of the *Summa Theologiae* of St. Thomas Aquinas: from Chenu (1939) to Metz (1998)." In *Aquinas as Authority*, edited by P. Van Geest et al., 187–200. Leuven.

Jordan, M. 1986a. *Ordering Wisdom: The Hierarchy of Philosophical Discourses in Aquinas.* Notre Dame, IN.

———. 1986b. "The Protreptic Structure of the *Summa contra Gentiles.*" *Thomist* 50:173–209.

———. 1992. *The Alleged Aristotelianism of Thomas Aquinas.* Etienne Gilson Series 15. Toronto.

———. 1993. "Theology and Philosophy." In *The Cambridge Companion to Aquinas*, edited by N. Kretzmann and E. Stump, 232–51. Cambridge.

———. 1994. "The Competition of Authoritative Languages and Aquinas's Theological Rhetoric." *Medieval Philosophy and Theology* 4:71–90.

Keenan, J. F. 2002. "The Virtue of Prudence." In *The Ethics of Aquinas*, edited by S. Pope, 259–71. Washington, DC.

Kent, B. 2002. "Habits and Virtues (Ia IIae, qq. 49–70)." In *The Ethics of Aquinas*, edited by S. Pope, 131–50. Washington, DC.

Kerr, F. 2002. *After Aquinas: Versions of Thomism.* Oxford.

King, R. 1967. "The Origin and Evolution of a Sacramental Formula: *Sacramentum Tantum, Res et Sacramentum, Res Tantum.*" *Thomist* 31:21–82.

Kors, J. -B. 1922. *La Justice Primitive et le Péché Originel d'après S. Thomas.* Le Saulchoir.

Kossel, G. C. 2002. "Natural Law and Human Law (Ia IIae, qq. 90–97)." In *The Ethics of Aquinas*, edited by S. Pope, 169–93. Washington, DC.

Kretzmann, N. 1997. *The Metaphysics of Theism: Aquinas's Natural Theology in Summa contra Gentiles I.* Oxford.

Kretzmann, N., and E. Stump, eds. 1993. *The Cambridge Companion to Aquinas.* Cambridge.

Kühn, U. 1965. *Via Caritatis.* Göttingen.

Labourdette, M. -M. 1985. "Aux origines du péché de l'homme d'après saint Thomas d'Aquin. Dans le courant de la tradition." *Revue Thomiste* 85:357–98.

Laporte, J. -M. 1973. *Les structures dynamiques de la grâce: grâce médicinale et grâce élevante selon Thomas d'Aquin.* Montreal.

————. 2003. "Christ in Aquinas's *Summa Theologiae*: Peripheral or Pervasive?" *Thomist* 67:221–48.

Leget, C. 1997. *Living with God: Thomas Aquinas on the Relation between Life on Earth and 'Life' after Death*. Leuven.

Lohaus, G. 1985. *Die Geheimnisse des Lebens Jesu in der Summa Theologiae des heiligen Thomas von Aquin*. Freiburger theologische Studien 131. Freiburg.

Lohr, C. 1980. *St Thomas Aquinas. Scriptum super Sententiis: An Index of Authorities Cited*. Avebury.

Lonergan, B. 1971. *Grace and Freedom: Operative Grace in the Thought of St. Thomas Aquinas*, edited by J. Patout Burns. London.

Lynn, W. D. 1962. *Christ's Redemptive Merit: The Nature of Its Causality according to St. Thomas*. Rome.

Maidl, L. 1994. *Desiderii Interpres: Genese und Grundstruktur der Gebetstheologie des Thomas von Aquin*. Paderborn.

Mansini, G. 1995a. "Duplex Amor and the Structure of Love in Aquinas." In *Thomistica*, Recherches de théologie ancienne et médiévale. Supplement 1, edited by E. Manning, 137–96. Leuven.

————. 1995b. "Similitudo, Communicatio, and the Friendship of Charity in Aquinas." In *Thomistica*, 1–26. Leuven.

————. 1995c. "Understanding St. Thomas on Christ's Immediate Knowledge of God." *Thomist* 59:91–124.

————. 1998. "Representation and Agency in the Eucharist." *Thomist* 62:499–517.

Margerie, B. de. 1983. "Mort sacrificielle du Christ et peine de mort chez saint Thomas d'Aquin, commentateur de saint Paul." *Revue Thomiste* 83:394–417.

Marshall, B. 2005. "*Quod Scit Una Vetula*: Aquinas on the Nature of Theology." In *The Theology of Thomas Aquinas*, edited by R. Van Nieuwenhove and J. Wawrykow, 1–35. Notre Dame, IN.

McGinn, B. 1975. "The Development of the Thought of Thomas Aquinas on the Reconciliation of Divine Providence and Contingent Action." *Thomist* 39:741–52.

McInerny, R. 1996. *Aquinas and Analogy*. Washington.

————, ed. and trans. 1998. *Thomas Aquinas: Selected Writings*. London.

Megivern, J. J. 1963. *Concomitance and Communion: A Study in Eucharistic Doctrine and Practice*. Fribourg.

Merriell, D. J. 1990. *To the Image of the Trinity: A Study of the Development of Aquinas' Teaching*. Toronto.

Morard, M. 1995. "L'eucharistie, clé de voûte de l'organisme sacramentel chez saint Thomas d'Aquin." *Revue Thomiste* 95:217–50.

————. 1997. "Une source de saint Thomas d'Aquin: le deuxième concile de Constantinople (553)." Revue des sciences philosophiques et théologiques 81:21–56.

Morris, T. V. 1982. "St. Thomas on the Identity and Unity of the Person of Christ: A Problem of Reference in Christological Discourse." *Scottish Journal of Theology* 35:419–30.

Mostert, W. 1978. *Menschwerdung: Eine historische und dogmatische Untersuchung über das Motiv der Inkarnation des Gottessohnes bei Thomas von Aquin*. Tübingen.

Mulchahey, M. 1998. *"First the Bow Is Bent in Study": Dominican Education before 1350*. Toronto.

Mullaney, T. A. 1954. "Mary Immaculate in the Writings of St. Thomas." *Thomist* 17:433–68.

Narcisse, G. 1993. "Les enjeux épistémologiques de l'argument de convenance selon saint Thomas d'Aquin." In *Ordo sapientiae et amoris*, edited by C. -J. Pinto de Oliveira, 143–67. Fribourg.

Nicholas, M. -J. 1992. "Les Dons du Saint-Esprit." *Revue Thomiste* 92:141–53.

Nichols, A. 2003. *Discovering Aquinas: An Introduction to His Life, Work, and Influence*. Grand Rapids.

————. 2004. "The Mariology of St. Thomas." In *Aquinas on Doctrine: A Critical Introduction*, edited by T. Weinandy et al., 241–60. London.

Ols, D. 1991. "La bienheureuse Vierge Marie selon saint Thomas." In *Littera, Sensus, Sententia*, 435–53. Milan.

O'Meara, T. 1997. "Virtues in the Theology of Thomas Aquinas." *Theological Studies* 58:256–87.

O'Neill, C. 1963. "St. Thomas on the Membership of the Church." *Thomist* 27:88–140.

———. 1974. "L'homme ouvert à Dieu (*Capax Dei*)." In *L'anthropologie de saint Thomas*, edited by N. A. Luyten, 54–74. Fribourg.

O'Rourke, F. 1992. *Pseudo-Dionysius and the Metaphysics of Aquinas*. Leiden.

Owens, J. 1993. "Aristotle and Aquinas." In *The Cambridge Companion to Aquinas*, edited by N. Kretzmann and E. Stump, 38–59. Cambridge.

Paluch, M. 2004. *La Profondeur de l'amour divin: Evolution de la doctrine de la prédestination dans l'oeuvre de Thomas d'Aquin*. Paris.

Passau, R. 2002. *The Treatise on Human Nature: Summa theologiae 1a 75–89*. Translated, with introduction and commentary. Indianapolis.

Patfoort, A. 1964. *L'Unité d'être dans le Christ d'après s.Thomas*. Tournai.

———. 1993. "La vraie visage de la satisfaction du Christ selon S. Thomas. Une Étude de la Somme théologique." In *Ordo sapientiae et amoris*, edited by C. -J. Pinto de Oliveira, 247–65. Fribourg.

Pegis, A. 1934. *St. Thomas and the Problem of the Soul in the Thirteenth Century*. Toronto.

Pelikan, J. 1978. "*Imago Dei*: An Explication of *Summa theologiae*, Part 1, Question 93." In *Calgary Aquinas Studies*, edited by A. Parel, 29–48. Toronto.

Persson, P. E. 1970. *Sacra Doctrina: Reason and Revelation in Aquinas*. Translated by R. Mackenzie. Philadelphia.

Pesch, O. H. 1967. *Die Theologie der Rechtfertigung bei Martin Luther und Thomas von Aquin*. Mainz.

———. 1974. "Paul as Professor of Theology: The Image of the Apostle in St. Thomas' Thought." *Thomist* 38:584–605.

Pfürtner, S. 1964. *Luther and Aquinas on Salvation*. Translated by E. Quinn. New York.

Pinckaers, S. -T. 2002. "The Sources of the Ethics of St. Thomas Aquinas." Translated by M. T. Noble. In *The Ethics of Aquinas*, edited by S. Pope, 17–29. Washington, DC.

Pope, S., ed. 2002a. *The Ethics of Aquinas*. Washington, DC.

———. 2002b. "Overview of the Ethics of Thomas Aquinas." In *The Ethics of Aquinas*, edited by S. Pope, 30–53. Washington, DC.

Porter, J. 1990. *The Recovery of Virtue: The Relevance of Aquinas for Christian Ethics*. Louisville, KY.

———. 1998. "Recent Studies in Aquinas's Virtue Ethics: A Review Essay." *Journal of Religious Ethics* 26:191–215.

———. 1999. *Natural and Divine Law: Reclaiming the Tradition for Christian Ethics*. Grand Rapids.

———. 2002. "The Virtue of Justice (IIa IIae, qq. 58–122)." In *The Ethics of Aquinas*, edited by S. Pope, 272–86. Washington, DC.

Potvin, T. R. 1973. *The Theology of the Primacy of Christ according to St. Thomas and Its Scriptural Foundations*. Studia Friburgensia N.S. 50. Fribourg.

Power, D. 1993. *The Eucharistic Mystery: Revitalizing the Tradition*. New York.

Principe, W. H. 1974. "St. Thomas on the *Habitus*-Theory of the Incarnation." In *St. Thomas Aquinas (1274–1974) Commemorative Studies*, edited by A. Maurer, 1:381–418. Toronto.

———. 1976. "Thomas Aquinas' Principles for Interpretation of Patristic Texts." *Studies in Medieval Culture* 8–9: 111–21.

Prügl, T. 2004. "Patristische Fundamente der Ekklesiologie des Thomas von Aquin." In *Väter der Kirche*, edited by J. Arnold, 745–69. Paderborn.

———. 2005. "Thomas Aquinas as Interpreter of Scripture." In *The Theology of Thomas Aquinas*, edited by R. Van Nieuwenhove and J. Wawrykow, 386–415. Notre Dame.

Reynolds, P. L. 2003. "Philosophy as the Handmaid of Theology: Aquinas on Christ's Causality." In *Contemplating*

Aquinas: On Varieties of Interpretation, edited by F. Kerr, 217–45. London.

———. 2004. "Efficient Causality and Instrumentality in Thomas Aquinas's Theology of the Sacraments." In *Essays in Medieval Theology and Philosophy in Memory of Walter H. Principe: Fortresses and Launching Pads*, edited by J. Ginther and C. Still, 67–84. Aldershot-Burlington.

Rikhof, H. 1976. "*Corpus Christi Mysticum*: An Inquiry into Thomas Aquinas' Use of a Term." *Bijdragen* 37:149–71.

———. 2005. "Trinity." In *The Theology of Thomas Aquinas*, edited by R. Van Nieuwenhove and J. Wawrykow, 36–57. Notre Dame, IN.

Rocca, G. P. 2004. *Speaking the Incomprehensible God: Thomas Aquinas on the Interplay of Positive and Negative Theology*. Washington, DC.

Rorem, P. 1992. "'Procession and Return' in Thomas Aquinas and His Predecessors." *Princeton Seminary Review* 13: 147–63.

Ruello, F. 1987. *La christologie de Thomas d'Aquin*. Théologie historique, 76. Paris.

Ryan, C. 1989. "The Theology of Papal Primacy in Thomas Aquinas." In *The Religious Roles of the Papacy: Ideals and Realities, 1150–1300*, edited by C. Ryan, 193–225. Toronto.

Ryan, T. 2000. *Thomas Aquinas as Reader of the Psalms*. Notre Dame, IN.

Sabra, G. 1987. *Thomas Aquinas' Vision of the Church: Fundamentals of an Ecumenical Ecclesiology*. Mainz.

Scheffczyk, L. 1986. "Die Stellung des Thomas von Aquin in der Entwicklung der Lehre von den Mysteria Vitae Christi." In *Renovatio et Reformatio wider das Bild vom "finisteren" Mittelalter*, edited by M. Gerwing and G. Ruppert, 44–70. Münster.

Schenk, R. 1990. "*Omnis Christi actio nostra est instructio*: The Deeds and Sayings of Jesus as Redeemer in the View of Thomas Aquinas." In *La doctrine de la révélation divine de saint Thomas d'Aquin*, edited by L. Elders, 103–31. Vatican City.

Schneider, T. 1972. *Die Einheit des Menschen: Die anthropologische Formel 'anima forma corporis' im sogenannten Korrektorienstreit und bei Petrus Johannis Olivi*. Münster.

Schockenhoff, E. 1987. *Bonum Hominis: Die anthropologischen und theologischen Grundlagen der Tugendethik des Thomas v. Aquin*. Mainz.

———. 2002. "The Theological Virtue of Charity (IIa IIae, qq. 23–46)." Translated by G. Kaplan and F. G. Lawrence. In *The Ethics of Aquinas*, edited by S. Pope, 244–58. Washington, DC.

Schoot, H. 1993. *Christ, the "Name" of God: Thomas Aquinas on Naming Christ*. Publications of the Thomas Instituut te Utrecht, New Series 1. Leuven.

Seidl, H. 1987. "The Concept of Person in St. Thomas Aquinas: A Contribution to Recent Discussion." *Thomist* 51:435–60.

Shanley, B. 2002. *The Thomist Tradition*. Dordrecht.

Sherwin, M. S. 2004. *By Knowledge and by Love: Charity and Knowledge in the Moral Theology of St. Thomas Aquinas*. Washington, DC.

Sokolowski, R. 1982. *The God of Faith and Reason: Foundations of Christian Theology*. Notre Dame, IN.

Somme, L. 1997. *Fils adoptifs de Dieu par Jésus Christ: La filiation divine par adoption dans la théologie de saint Thomas d'Aquin*. Paris.

Staley, K. 1989. "Happiness: The Natural End of Man?" *Thomist* 53:215–34.

Stoeckle, B. 1962. *Gratia supponit naturam: Geschichte und Analyse eines theologischen Axioms*. Rome.

Stump, E. 2002. "Aquinas' Metaphysics of the Incarnation." In *The Incarnation*, edited by S. Davis et al., 197–218. Oxford.

Sweeney, E. 2002. "Vice and Sin." In *The Ethics of Aquinas*, edited by S. Pope, 151–68. Washington, DC.

Swierzawski, H. 1984. "The Mystery of Christ in the Ministry of St.

Thomas Aquinas." *Collectanea Theologica* 54:41–58.

Synan, E. 1974. "Brother Thomas, the Master, and the Masters." In *1274–1974: Commemorative Studies*, edited by A. Maurer et al. 2:219–42. Toronto.

Tanner, K. 1988. *God and Creation in Christian Theology. Tyranny or Empowerment?* Oxford.

Te Velde, R. 1995. *Participation and Substantiality in Thomas Aquinas*. Leiden.

———. 2005. "Original Sin." In *The Theology of Thomas Aquinas*, edited by R. Van Nieuwenhove and J. Wawrykow, 143–66. Notre Dame.

Tonneau, J. 1970. "The Teaching of the Thomist Tract on Law." *Thomist* 34:13–83.

Torrance, T. F. 1962. "Scientific Hermeneutics according to St. Thomas Aquinas." *Journal of Theological Studies* 13:259–89.

Torrell, J. P. 1991. "'Imiter Dieu comme des enfants bien-aimés,' La conformité à Dieu et au Christ dans l'oeuvre de saint Thomas." In *Novitas et veritas vitae*, edited by C. J. Pinto de Oliveira, 53–65. Fribourg. Reprinted in *Recherches thomasiennes*, 325–35.

———. 1994. "Saint Thomas d'Aquin et la science du Christ: une relecture des Questions 9–12 de la *Tertia Pars* de la 'Somme de théologie.'" In *Saint Thomas au XXe siècle*, edited by S. -T. Bonino, 394–409. Paris. Reprinted in *Recherches thomasiennes*, 198–213.

———. 1996a. "La causalité salvifique de la résurrection." *Revue Thomiste* 96:179–208. Reprinted in *Recherches thomasiennes*, 214–41.

———. 1996b. "Le savoir théologique chez saint Thomas." *Revue Thomiste* 96:335–96. Reprinted in *Recherches thomasiennes*, 121–57.

———. 1996c. *Saint Thomas Aquinas*. Vol. 1, *The Person and His Work*. Translated by R. Royal. Washington, DC.

———. 1997. "La vision de Dieu 'per essentiam' selon saint Thomas d'Aquin." *Micrologue* 5:43–68. Reprinted in *Recherches thomasiennes*, 177–97.

———. 1999. *Le Christ en ses mystères: la vie et l'oeuvre de Jésus selon saint Thomas d'Aquin*. 2 vols. Paris.

———. 2000. *Recherches thomasiennes: Études revues et augmentées*. Paris.

———. 2003. *Saint Thomas Aquinas*. Vol. 2, *Spiritual Master*. Translated by R. Royal. Washington, DC.

———. 2004. "L'interpète du désir: La prière chez saint Thomas d'Aquin." *La Vie Spirituelle* 84:213–23.

Tschipke, T. 2003. *L'humanité du Christ comme instrument de salut de la divinité*. Translated by P. Secretan. Fribourg.

Tugwell, S., ed. and trans. 1982. *Early Dominicans: Selected Writings*. New York.

———. 1988. *Albert and Thomas: Selected Writings*. New York.

Valkenberg, Wilhelmus G. B. M. 1996. "'By the Power of the Passion of Christ': The Place of Christ in Aquinas' Theology of Penance." In *Tibi soli peccavi—Thomas Aquinas on Guilt and Forgiveness*, edited by H. Schoot, 151–74. Leuven.

———. 2000. *Words of the Living God: Place and Function of Holy Scripture in the Theology of St. Thomas Aquinas*. Leuven.

Van Ackeren, G. F. 1952. *Sacra Doctrina: The Subject of the First Question of the Summa Theologica of St. Thomas Aquinas*. Rome.

Van der Ploeg, J. 1947. "The Place of Holy Scripture in the Theology of St. Thomas." *Thomist* 10:398–422.

Van Nieuwenhove, R., and J. Wawrykow, eds. 2005. *The Theology of Thomas Aquinas*. Notre Dame, IN.

Wadell, P. 1991. *Friends of God: Gifts and Virtues in Aquinas*. New York.

———. 1992. *The Primacy of Love: An Introduction to the Ethics of Thomas Aquinas*. New York.

Walsh, L. 1993. "The Divine and the Human in St. Thomas's Theology of Sacraments." In *Ordo Sapientiae et Amoris*, edited by C. -J. Pinto de Oliveira, 321–52. Fribourg.

———. 2005. "Sacraments." In *The Theology of Thomas Aquinas*, edited by R. Van Nieuwenhove and J. Wawrykow, 326–54. Notre Dame.

Wawrykow, J. 1991. "'Perseverance' in 13th-Century Theology: The Augustinian Contribution." *Augustinian Studies* 22:125–40.

———. 1993. "Luther and the Spirituality of Thomas Aquinas." *Consensus* 19:77–107.

———. 1995. *God's Grace and Human Action: "Merit" in the Theology of Thomas Aquinas*. Notre Dame, IN.

———. 1998. "Wisdom in the Christology of Thomas Aquinas." In *Christ among the Medieval Dominicans*, edited by K. Emery and J. Wawrykow, 175–96. Notre Dame, IN.

———. 2001. "New Directions in Thomas-Research." *Religious Studies Review* 27:34–41.

———. 2005a. "Grace." In *The Theology of Thomas Aquinas*, edited by R. Van Nieuwenhove and J. Wawrykow, 192–221. Notre Dame, IN.

———. 2005b. "Hypostatic Union." In *The Theology of Thomas Aquinas*, edited by R. Van Nieuwenhove and J. Wawrykow, 222–51. Notre Dame, IN.

Wéber, E. -H. 1988. *Le Christ Selon Saint Thomas d'Aquin*. Paris.

———. 1993. "L'Incidence du traité de l'eucharistie sur la métaphysique de S. Thomas d'Aquin." *Revue des Sciences Philosophiques et Théologiques* 77:195–218.

Weinandy, T. 2004. "Aquinas: God IS Man: The Marvel of the Incarnation." In *Aquinas on Doctrine*, 67–89.

Weinandy, T., et al., eds. 2004. *Aquinas on Doctrine: A Critical Introduction*. London.

Weisheipl, J. 1974. "The Meaning of Sacra Doctrina in *Summa Theologiae* I, q.1." *Thomist* 38:49–80.

———. 1983. *Friar Thomas d'Aquino: His Life, Thought, and Work*. Washington, DC.

West, J. L. A. 2002. "Aquinas and the Metaphysics of *Esse* in Christ." *Thomist* 66:231–50.

Wieland, G. 2002. "Happiness (Ia IIae, qq. 1–5)." Translated by G. Kaplan. In *The Ethics of Aquinas*, edited by S. Pope, 57–68. Washington, DC.

Williams, A. N. 1999. *The Ground of Union: Deification in Thomas Aquinas and Gregory Palamas*. Oxford.

Wippel, J. 2000. *The Metaphysical Thought of Thomas Aquinas: From Finite Being to Uncreated Being*. Washington, DC.

Wissink, J. B. M. 1994. "Aquinas: The Theologian of Negative Theology. A Reading of ST I, qq. 14–26." In *Jaarboek 1993 Thomas Instituut te Utrecht*, 15–83. Utrecht.

———. 1996. "Satisfaction as Part of Penance, according to Thomas Aquinas." In *Tibi soli peccavi—Thomas Aquinas on Guilt and Forgiveness*, edited by H. Schoot, 75–95. Leuven.

Wright, J. H. 1957. *The Order of the Universe in the Theology of St. Thomas Aquinas*. Rome.

Yocum, J. 2004. "Sacraments in Aquinas." In *Aquinas on Doctrine: A Critical Introduction*, edited by T. Weinandy et al., 159–81. London.

Zimmermann, A. 1992. "Natur und Tod gemäss Thomas von Aquin." In *Mensch und Natur im Mittelalter*, Miscellanea Mediaevalia 21, 2:767–78. Berlin.